TOWN AND COUNTRY

The contrasts and conflicts between country and town are an abiding theme of English life, literature and politics. Population and housing, our food and education, cars and trains, species and the environment, our heritage and happiness are at stake. Despite all the differences between them, urban, rural and suburban areas alike will share the consequences of market pressure and government policy.

Not only does the relationship between city and country respond to every social, economic and demographic change, it does so in intangible ways. It is integral to the nation's self-image. It raises deep questions about the past, present and future of our country.

Since 1995 The Town and Country Forum has discussed these questions in the belief that they demanded open-minded, non-partisan exploration and debate. This book is the product of its contributions and exchanges. It is edited by Roger Scruton, one of the foremost philosophers of conservatism, and Anthony Barnett, the moving spirit behind Charter 88, whose constitutional radicalism has influenced New Labour.

TOWN AND COUNTRY

EDITED BY
Anthony Barnett
and Roger Scruton

𝒱

VINTAGE

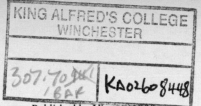
Published by Vintage 1999

2 4 6 8 10 9 7 5 3 1

Collection copyright © Anthony Barnett and Roger Scruton 1998
Individual essays copyright © each author

First published in Great Britain in 1998 by Jonathan Cape

Vintage
Random House, 20 Vauxhall Bridge Road,
London SW1V 2SA

Random House Australia (Pty) Limited
20 Alfred Street, Milsons Point, Sydney
New South Wales 2061, Australia

Random House New Zealand Limited
18 Poland Road, Glenfield,
Auckland 10, New Zealand

Random House South Africa (Pty) Limited
Endulini, 5A Jubilee Road, Parktown 2193,
South Africa

Random House UK Limited Reg. No. 954009

A CIP catalogue record for this book
is available from the British Library

ISBN 0 09 927698 4

Papers used by Random House UK Ltd are natural,
recyclable products made from wood grown in sustainable forests. The manufacturing processes conform to the
environmental regulations of the country of origin

Printed and bound in Great Britain by
Cox & Wyman Limited, Reading, Berkshire

Contents

Preface
Ian McEwan

I have been told by a Dutch friend that one of the inspirations for Piet Mondrian's famous neoplastic paintings was the experience of looking down from an aeroplane at the meticulous, regular landscape outside Amsterdam. Certainly, if you travel across Northern Europe, from Gatwick, say, to Berlin, you will see below you hundreds of miles of treeless geometry, neatly interlocking squares and rectangles, a colossal inhuman abstraction formed by the monoculture of agro-chemical farming. Is this the future British landscape? Returning to Gatwick, flying low over the Sussex Weald, you will be reminded that we still have much to be grateful for, and much to defend – the small irregular fields of medieval as well as eighteenth-century enclosures, thick hedgerows interspersed with mature trees – a huge, lush garden continuously maintained for centuries where food production and wildlife have flourished together.

In our long pre-history of hunting and gathering, agriculture and the settled way of life were late inventions. The cities, where most of us live, are even more new-fangled. It is hardly surprising that most of us are seized at some time by an unthinking restlessness. At weekends and on holidays we pour out of the cities towards the countryside and the beaches. We hardly need to question why. Those left behind gravitate towards the municipal parks. Many of us dream of settling down in some leafy place. Our biological past predisposes us to a fascination with animals and plants, and our cultural inheritance, reflecting this, teaches us the beauty of nature. For city-dwellers, the countryside is a repository of longing and illusion; it is a place of nourishment, innocence and ancient wisdom; it is the garden from which we have been expelled; it is more wholesome, more 'real' than buildings and streets. It is where the seasons still hold sway, where mythical childhoods are enacted and where we might go to find ourselves. We are nearly all descended from people who, only a few generations back, worked on the land. The countryside is our final link with them, and with a past which seems from here to have been more ordered and possessed of deeper certainties.

At the same time we know that the countryside is an artefact, as man-made as a suburban garden. What has been made can be re-made to suit us. With our longings and illusions comes a rapacity which threatens a large-scale tragedy of the commons. We want a tranquil, uninhabited Eden, but we want to penetrate it easily at the weekend by motorway; or we want to commute from there, or retire there, or find a place in the fresh air for a factory or a golf course or a hypermarket with convenient parking. We want the cheap food that only the most ruthlessly efficient farming can deliver. We want the old ways displayed for us at handy heritage centres by people in 'traditional' costume. We want hens to peck about the yard and sheep to safely graze, but we don't want the blood of foxes spilled.

It can seem as though we are set to destroy the things we love. And beyond the flurry of our own contradictory desires and mythologies lies the tragedy of farming policy. Since the Second World War we have lost nearly all our remaining woodlands, meadows, marshes and heaths, most of them unnecessarily put under plough. Despite the outcry over many years, the 'mondrianisation' of the English countryside continues. The Sussex Weald might not be safe for long. In Oxfordshire, near where I live, great stretches of land have been made bleakly unrecognisable by agro-chemical farming: giant cereal fields one mile across, no trees, hedgerows, grasses or flowers, no birds, no insects, no animals – wild or domesticated. There are no footpaths because no one would want to walk here. The causes of the tragedy are various and complex: the topsy turvy logic of EU and government subsidies, the arrogance and ignorance of the Ministry of Agriculture, Food and Fisheries in cahoots with the National Farmers' Union, the greed and 'philistinism' of some, but not all, farmers, the profit-lust of the chemicals industry and of City investors who have no connection with the land they acquire.

But the lacerating pleasures of pessimism and lament should be resisted. If the countryside is an artefact, then what has been destroyed can be partially restored – in time. It is right to be sceptical about the heritage industry, or about re-creating an idealised past; the eighteenth-century enclosures that set their characteristically delightful mark on English lowland agriculture entailed a degree of human misery and environmental disaster. But we should be careful about going too far in the other direction and ignoring methods patiently evolved over centuries. In the interests of a richer environment, we might just choose to be minimally less efficient. Mixed farming and four-crop rotation allow a more sensitive and sophisticated means of treating the land than the regular dustings with nitrates and phosphates that poison the water courses. And quite by accident, a system of smallish fields enclosed by hedges and trees has bequeathed us a treasure of farm-adapted biodiversity. I sometimes think that part of the appeal of the kind of English countryside we idealise has to do with its correspondence to the open spaces and occasional tree cover of the East African savannah where human kind evolved. As the biologist E.O. Wilson and others have suggested, it may be in our natures to be drawn to landscapes in which shelter and general visibility coincide.

On the other hand, such speculation may be one more aspect of the mythologising that the countryside, as well as the wilderness, attracts. In a sense, the source of our love of green, open spaces hardly matters: we are the stewards of our environments now, whether they are built, cultivated or wild. Their fates depend on the totality of our decisions, or lack of them. And these fates are tightly intertwined: if our urban areas fail us, then people will seek satisfaction elsewhere and the pressures on the countryside will intensify. It is this sense of interdependency that animated the Town and Country Forum in our lunchtime meetings over sandwiches and wine. We were drawn not only to various ideals of a thriving countryside, but also to the diversity, richness and paradoxical freedoms of the city at its best – the city, where all the decisions about the countryside are taken, and in whose art galleries, one hopes, the spirit of Mondrian's abstract purity may be safely confined.

Introduction
Anthony Barnett and Roger Scruton

If we set aside the great questions of international politics we find that many, even most, of the issues at the centre of current concern bring relations between town and country to the fore. From the food we eat to our vision of the nation, from the most basic needs to the most intangible, the future of the countryside affects our overwhelmingly urban society. Our attitudes to the environment, to transport, to the place where we live and want to live, to childhood, health, retirement and work — all pass through the matrix of urban and rural distribution. Consider only some of the issues that arose during the first year of the present Labour government: transport and road-building; mayors and the new regional development agencies; the projected need for 4.4 million new houses; pesticides; the BSE crisis and its aftermath; hunting; milk production and quotas; the policy on agricultural subsidies; the Dome and the millennium village; culture and heritage; the right to roam — each touches on the relation between town and country and each is surrounded, as a result, by a cloud of emotion.

In November 1995 a group of five people met in part of the Georgian terrace in London's Gower Street that belongs to Birkbeck College: Roger Scruton, Paul Hirst (respectively Professors of Philosophy and Social Theory at the College), Anthony Barnett, Bob Grant and Sophie Jeffreys. Roger Scruton had asked for the meeting. Three connected issues had aroused his concern: the rapid extension of chemically driven agribusiness; the plans for 4.4 million new houses, many of them in the countryside; and mounting hostility to hunting. All three, he felt, were in their different ways evidence of thoughtless destruction of an already weakened rural way of life. While expert work was being done in different areas, he wondered if it would be possible to conduct exchanges of a non-partisan kind between people from different political traditions, to deepen understanding of the issues.

The discussion that followed focused on two matters of principle. First, the countryside needs to be seen as an artefact: it is not intrinsically natural, organic or authentic in the sense of being more real or less 'made' than the urban environment. Even those parts of the country that remain apparently untouched are protected by policy and exist thanks to human agency. (A version of this argument can be found at the start of Anthony O'Hear's contribution.) Second, it is wrong to consider issues such as housing and food in terms of the dangers to the country posed by the city – as if one side is pure and innocent and the other restless and threatening. Rather, such issues need to be viewed in the context of the interrelationships and mutual dependencies of town and country.

Three great questions emerged: What future for the towns? What future for the country? And what future for the relations between them? It was agreed that a group – The Town and Country Forum – should be convened to explore these questions. That so many individuals with widely – even wildly – differing views felt drawn to attend the Forum, and that their contributions should so swiftly emerge as a book, is testimony to the energy and interest that the questions inspire and sustain.

The gathering that we established came together monthly. People were invited not for their beliefs or political credentials, but for their expertise and their willingness to address the issues. We, the editors of this volume, come from different ends of the political spectrum, but we share a concern for the long-term perspective and a desire for negotiated rather than dictated solutions. Moreover, we believe that the issues touched on in this book are so deep and important that they should not be surrendered to the short-term view of party politics.

We decided to invite the members of the Forum to contribute chapters, each addressing some matter that we have discussed at our meetings. For our greatest need is to think and to share our thinking – so as to reach, if possible, an agreed conceptualisation of the issues and an understanding of how they connect. Questions of transport, building, agricultural development, animal welfare, architectural style, open spaces, shopping, education and food production are treated, by both politicians and the experts and civil servants who advise them, as though they were independent. And on the surface they might appear to be. But only on the surface. As soon as we examine the consequences and the motives behind policy in any of these areas, we find ourselves pre-empting policy in the others. You cannot decide that new houses should be confined to 'brown-field' sites without asking about architectural style, shopping facilities, open space, schools and entertainment. You cannot place a moratorium on road-building without jeopardising aspects of the rural economy, and exacerbating the decay of rural towns subjected to heavy traffic through their fragile centres. You cannot ban hunting and expect farmers to care for habitats or to remain content with the traditional and comparatively unprofitable ways of farming that hunting encourages. You cannot build new housing estates in the countryside and prevent the out-of-town shopping malls on which their residents depend. You cannot allow suburban people to move to the country with all their comforts – including street lighting and cars – and expect wildlife to remain unaffected. You cannot ban beef on the bone or unpasteurised milk and at the same time hope for the small producers to stay in business. You cannot fight against agribusiness while subsidising food production, so pushing the price of land beyond the reach of the traditional farmer. You cannot expect urban spaces to attract care and commitment if they are maintained by contracted-out services which descend like vandals.

Nor can any of these problems be approached by considering either the town or the country alone. The changes to our countryside result from forces which are changing our cities in equal measure, and these forces lie deep in the modern condition. The first is expanding mobility, whether geographical, social, economic or sexual. The second is the exponential increase in the power to manufacture, transport, concentrate, communicate and sell both globally and nationally. The third is the cultural shift from socially imposed to freely chosen lifestyles – a shift which has fragmented and atomised inherited communities, but which may also lead to new voluntary associations of purpose. These forces are connected, and together generate the questions which this book attempts to address.

Whatever this combination of forces has done to our countryside, it has done to our towns and cities too. Consider only one question by way of illustration – that of road transport, studiously neglected by the Conservatives during their long period of office, and now, in consequence, at the top of the political agenda. Many who live in the country lament the motorways that plough through their pastures, bringing lorries and cars to places that will be diminished, and may even be destroyed, by their passage. But most country residents are entirely dependent on private transport; indeed people are moving to the country precisely because cars make the move so easy. Moreover the deleterious effects of motor transport are felt as much in the city as in the countryside. The motorways which pollute the fields also disgorge their burden into the towns, and force upon the residents the painful choice of trunk roads that atomise the townscape or congested streets poisoned by exhaust fumes.

The argument against expanded car ownership is well summarised in the chapter by John Adams. To put the matter simply: the constant expansion of the means of communication may well extinguish the purpose. Ruskin made the point a century and a half ago: it is all very well to find the quickest passage to your destination, but far more important to be content with what you find there. He was thinking of the railways. In retrospect, however (as David Wiggins and Mayer Hillman show), they were a genuine addition to our social ecology, expanding the settlement pattern, but in a close-knit and relatively undestructive way, while doing little irreparable damage to either town or country. It is doubtful that additional motorway construction will have so benign an outcome.

If we are to consider the consequences of policies in terms of their impact on connected ways of life, then the argument can be powerfully made that the motor car has brought unprecedented freedom, not to the wealthy and the powerful, who always enjoyed it, but to the poor and those of modest means for whom it is often an indispensable aspect of their dignity and freedom. Against this, however, it may be said that the real costs of motorisation are borne by the very same people: it is they who have to live in the blighted zones of cities ringed by motorways and bypasses; it is they who must guard their children from streets made dangerous, noisy and polluted by speeding traffic; it is they who, in their attempts to escape from the effects of a motorised economy, find themselves trapped for hours on motorways, on their way to resorts made noisy and ugly by cars.

The traffic jam, it has been suggested, is thus the system's answer to the over-use of cars, an unplanned consequence that provides the necessary counterbalance to exponential growth. With this happy thought, it is often said that the car has become the cornerstone of the modern economy. It is the thing most coveted by most people. It brings employment, exports and kudos of a kind that no government can ignore. And around the motor industry has grown a culture which has a real meaning to the many for whom the car offers a way to amplify their power and make an impact on the universe. People find their identity through their cars, are proud of them, and rehearse through them an experience of membership which they do not find elsewhere. Such feelings must be respected. If the public is to be persuaded of a new approach, therefore, it must be through example and experiment. It is possible to ban leaded petrol, but not to ban the motor car.

Because of the motorways there are no longer clearly defined areas of settlement; people can live in one place, work in another, have friends and family in a third to which they remain attached. A new town, suburb or housing development can be built in any place, as a pure speculation, by people who have never had and will never have any regard for the locality. Such developments are not new. They can be traced back more than a hundred years – to the time when the conservation movement also began. To what extent such changes are to be accepted or resisted is one of the questions that divides the contributors to this book. What is certain is that we cannot form a coherent transport policy without considering the consequences on settlement, building types and shopping facilities, on the urban and rural economies, and on the sentiments of community and locality which help people to co-operate with their neighbours. To say that traffic jams are the answer to too many cars is like saying that a plague is the answer to overcrowding.

Nor is it only individuals who are geographically mobile in the modern world. Enterprises also find it easier to move. In the last century factories and offices sucked the population from the countryside. They are now moving in the opposite direction. Industrialised farming has been, if anything, even more destructive of the traditional landscape and rural life than the motorways. (See the considerations presented by Robin Page and Julian Rose.) This is especially true of the recent rise of contract farming, in which an external investor acquires a substantial acreage and hires a management company to run it. This company in turn uses occasional contract labour to plant a standardised crop, administer sprays and then harvest the result, entirely on piece rates. The earth becomes a commodity. Indeed, it may be deprived of even this lowly status. It is an ultimate irony of the free market that there may soon be many thousands of acres of rich, fertile soil and no one at all, no leaseholder, manager or even distant lord, who has any residence upon them and who can say 'this land is mine'.

A drastic reduction in the agricultural workforce is one consequence. At the same time, however, the move of the professional classes to the cottages has made them available for managerial and administrative tasks which used to be performed only in towns and cities. This is a positive result for the countryside, since it imports the human capital that could, in the right circumstances, serve to revitalise the rural economy. (See the discussion by Paul Hirst.) It also poses obvious threats: the increase in house and land prices may force out those who work for local wages, while rural industry could, if improperly planned and insensitively located, destroy the environment as rapidly as urban sprawl.

As important as geographical mobility is 'moral mobility', as it might be called: the ability of people to break loose from their traditional codes of conduct, and experiment in the lifestyles that were once the privilege of the rich and the glamorous. The rural society described by Crabbe, George Eliot or Hardy is no longer with us; not merely because its economy has been transcended, but because the modern ideal of self-realisation, reinforced by the contemporary media, attracts to itself a cosmopolitan glamour. Traditional values lose their status and are seen as obstacles to fulfilment in a world of opportunity. This moral mobility has shaken rural society, since it has removed its self-image: as the repository of changeless values in a world of change. Rural people can no longer attract their children home from the cities with a promise of old-fashioned decencies and good homely sentiment. Those who love the pattern and rhythm of rural society must accept the paradox that it is now only by a conscious effort that a sense of rootedness can be revived. While we applaud efforts to conserve and maintain landscape and townscape, it is important, we believe, to acknowledge that the old beliefs in locality, and the traditional, historically defined attachments to communities, cannot be revived in their original forms. The authors of the chapters that follow are engaged in a common task, which is to show how town and country can grow and flourish, and supply the needs of each for the other, despite the loss of once inherited experiences of settlement and fate.

The connections between the many topics that are touched on in this book are often apparent at the political level. That is to say, we can see how decisions in one area affect decisions in another. But sometimes the connections are less easy to perceive – that between natural beauty and the structure of local government, for example (explored here by Tony Curzon Price); that between the vitality of a city and the provisions for its ghosts (invoked by Ken Worpole); that between the family farm and global mobility, both of which (Hugh Brody argues) are intrinsic to the neolithic origins of our society. There are factors of the greatest relevance to the quality of life in Britain, and to the maintenance of a healthy dialogue between rural and urban styles of living, which have yet to be properly considered, either by policy-makers or by the many experts who contend for a voice in the decision-making process. One such is light pollution, discussed here by Libby Purves, the effects of which – psychic, physical, cultural and even religious – are almost never mentioned by planners or their political masters. Another is the heritage industry – described by Bob Grant – which is busily packaging our landscapes and townscapes as varnished replicas of themselves, and perhaps impeding a more healthy relationship to the past.

Some of our writers are concerned to expose the simplifications and distortions of conservationists. Thus Paul Barker, in his defence of 'Edge City', and Tim Mars, in his carefully modulated paean to the suburbs, are concerned to puncture romantic illusions to which many of us are liable. If they are right, then the divide between town and country no longer has the same place, either economically or spiritually, as it may once have had in the lives of the British people. Other contributors point to neglected aspects of modern life – visiting, like Colin Ward, those fertile margins where the writ of planning does not run, or exploring, as does Julian Rose, the world of the organic farmer. Some of the issues that are touched on in these pages are vast and amorphous. How, for example, are we to educate young people to take the environment seriously, and to value the long-term perspective on which our future depends? This question is raised by Francis Gilbert, in a report from the front line of city life. What are the underlying aims and constraints that should be met by planning policy? What purpose is served and what interests advanced by obeying it? These are questions raised by Sophie Jeffreys, in a report from another front line in another city.

Other contributions bear directly on current debates. John Gummer explores the social and political background to the housing question, as we now confront it. Jeff Rooker describes his experience on joining the Ministry of Agriculture, Food and Fisheries as it manoeuvres to meet its many and conflicting obligations. Both give an insight into the pressures on government policy. Hugh Raven, an adviser rather than a politician, considers the importance of food to those who eat it and the consequences of the extraordinary lengths food now travels to get to our plates. George Monbiot defends the right to roam, suggesting that the intelligent commitment of the rambler is now a substitute for the eyes and ears of a vanished rural populace. Jane Ridley addresses the vexed question of animal welfare in the countryside – the issue which has dominated rural politics for a decade, with veal crates, BSE and fox-hunting all leading to legislative proposals. Many of these proposals, Ridley argues, fail to understand the kinds of relation between humans and animals that can serve the interests of both. Indeed, if David Coffey is right, our entire approach to other species is founded on an anthropocentric disregard for their well-being.

While we have tried to cover most topics that are pertinent to our common questions, we are conscious of several important omissions, from the social economy of gardens and gardening, to fishing villages, the seaside and the destruction of the species of the seas. Nor have we sought a systematic consideration of different regions which, properly undertaken, would take a full book. Instead, David Hayes's meditation on the northernmost marches of England, and the contrast he draws between them and the white cliffs of Dover, stands as our acknowledgement of the fact that our countryside is not one but many. This is not to speak of England's neighbours in the United Kingdom – nor do we pretend to speak *for* them. The problem that we have inherited in making the connections between town and country is a particularly English one. Without making a fuss about it, it is predominantly the English tradition we are debating, and the international perspective has yet to be brought into the Forum's discussions. Furthermore, the history of national heritage could provide material for another equally lengthy book, as Patrick Wright shows, evoking the contrasting traditions of indigenous rural myths and movements.

The historical experience that is most obviously missing from these pages is religion. The division between town and country has been partly shaped by religious institutions, and in particular by the Anglican Church and its nonconformist offshoots. The imagery and wisdom of the Bible are usually pastoral, and the Anglican Church is a rural institution, with its principal see in Canterbury, and its cathedrals located in old market towns. It internalised the social structures that prevailed in rural areas, with the landed estate and its village defining the nature and scope of its mission. Unlike the Roman Catholic Church across the Channel, the Anglican Church lost out when the population shifted to the industrial towns. At the same time, the nonconformist churches made use of the King James Bible, along with traditional hymns and prayers, so importing into the heart of urban worship the imagery of country life, and defining the predicaments of their congregations in terms taken from sheep-farming and vine-growing.

The King James Bible was a cornerstone of the national culture, and one of the instruments through which people could conceptualise the life of the countryside and come to see why it matters. Children brought up in the practice of the British churches became familiar with the Bible's long-term view and acquired a knowledge of the country way of seeing things. Those within the Church of England, in particular, became familiar with a monarchical institution that reinforced a belief in our country as a society shaped by the contest and collaboration of parliament and crown. The decline of this tutelary presence may be welcomed by those who see it as a bastion of class distinctions and a source of illusions. Nevertheless, we need to know what to put in its place if we are to arrive at the understanding necessary for a sustainable society.

Looking back, certain shared themes emerge from the wide variety of contributions, despite the differences. One is the need for the lively reproduction of social capital, rather than a mummifying conservatism of debris, as the best response to the past. David Matthews describes such a living tradition in his account of pastoral music; he also contributes to it as a composer. Another common theme is the need for the renewal of social life to be undertaken by people living where it matters. In a pathbreaking reconsideration of the greening of cities, Liz Greenhalgh shows that keepers are more important than views, and that a city needs to be a guarded rather than an open space. In their opposition to thoughtless development, both Sophie Jeffreys and Robin Page show the potential for active caretaking: the first in the town, the second in the country; while George Monbiot reinforces this with his idea of a roving citizenship. Across the board there seems to be agreement that people must trust themselves and not the central administration to protect town and country. Far from this being a call to facile populism it means hard and steady work, a claim of living that means both residence and care.

Our contributors were chosen for the relevance of their arguments, and not for their conclusions. Their interests and expertise range as widely as their political opinions: anthropology, historiography, politics, economics, literature, music, geography, philosophy, architectural history, planning, journalism, teaching, farming and veterinary surgery are each represented, and represented, we believe, to good effect. From the fertile disagreement of our meetings we have all learned much. It is our hope that the readers of this volume also will learn from it, however much or however little they may agree with the conclusions reached by any of its contributors. Our aim is to stimulate a wide-ranging public debate, about matters which concern the future of all of us, and which we ignore at our peril.

London and Malmesbury, Easter 1998

I

Reconceiving the Relationship

1. *Nomads and Settlers*
Hugh Brody

A family is busy in the countryside. Mother is making bread, churning butter, attending to hens and ducks that live in the yard and pens beside the house, preparing food for everyone. Father is in the fields, ploughing the soil, cutting wood, fixing walls, providing sustenance. Children explore and play and help and sit at the family table. Grandma or Grandpa sits in a chair by the fire. Every day is long and filled with the activities of this family. And the activities are contained, given purpose and comfort, by a piece of countryside at the centre of which is home.

This is a family with intense privacy, somehow separate from the rest of the world, sufficient unto itself, knowing and meeting everyone's needs. Loyalties are as deep and sure as the ground beneath them. There is loyalty, also, to the tasks and expertise and duties that each member of the family undertakes. Children have the job of being happy to help, and then happier yet to mature into their adulthood, gender and place in either this or another farm family.

So many children's books, and much adult literature, celebrate this farm family. Most of us have grown up in the vicarious glow of its warmth; have shared, at varying distances, in its peace and comfort; and have tasted, if only in our imaginations, fresh-baked bread and home-cured ham and apple pies that are spread, each afternoon, on the family farmhouse table. And these delicious images work a complicated magic on our adult selves: does my family or your family achieve this stability, plenitude, warmth and happiness? The difference between what we have and this half-known, almost remembered family life makes a poignant contribution to much sense of failure. These images of the farm family come close to defining what family is, and what so many of us, or our families, are not; it continues to offer a powerful sense of the past, a bittersweet ideal and sharp judgements upon ourselves.

The farm establishes the corresponding shape of the land and its buildings. The beautiful nest within which the perfect family thrives. The pattern of fields, with their walls and hedges and old gateposts and gates. The mixture of crops and copses, vegetables and wild flowers, domestic animals and the creatures of the wild wood, pigs and cows and sheep and horses as well as a few foxes and badgers and stoats and weasels, the gentlest of material culture and the prettiest, most controllable of nature. The farm may be grand, an estate perhaps, a park even; but its ideal is modest: large enough to provide abundance of foods and countryside to own and work, small enough for the family to know every corner of their place. This thing, this array of shaped land and buildings, is an image of an ideal and eternal home. The family in its farm is the family where it belongs. A place of integration, where work, play, childhood and age all share a safe and secure space.

There is a timeless, unchanging, stable unity to what we understand from the two words: family farm. An Eden. The people of the countryside, be they the poorest of landholders, share a profound conservatism: they sense that change is never going to be of help to them. They insist, and those who write about country people and celebrate their ways of life insist alongside them, that innovations are for outsiders, rival claimants to the soil, advocates of an antagonistic mode of life.

Yet the family farm is not without its fierce energy and local restlessness. Farmers have moulded the landscape, and insist that they must continue to do so. On a small scale, within reason. There are fields to be reshaped, walls to be remade, hedges to be laid, woodlands to be coppiced, a line of saplings to be planted, barns to add, sheds to take down. Also, there is buying and selling – of a field here, or even a whole farm in the neighbourhood. Imagine this persistent but gentle process, and you may be able to see in your mind's eye the making of the ancient English landscape. The cumulative actions of the family farm have created the countryside, the culture on which English nature depends.

These images of the family farm, along with the corresponding image of how it has shaped the land, invite a particular version of the town/country dichotomy. By comparison with the family farm of the countryside, the town family enjoys very uncertain peace and prosperity. Lacking the quiet solitudes, the conditions for family privacy and productive daily work that is also subsistence, having nothing natural on hand, without even views of calming landscapes to ease the soul, the town family is vulnerable to cacophonous intrusions of other people, discontent, poverty and restlessness. Living in a place of no natural merit and hence without intrinsic worth, the urban dweller has both a freedom and a compulsion to change and relocate. Consider the difference between moving house and moving farm – the one sounding quite ordinary, part of an urban routine; the other creating a sort of puzzle: is this possible? Surely it must refer to an individual rather than a family.

The farm family somehow sets the terms of what a family is or should be. And there is a profound acceptance of this ideal within the town, for the struggle there to have and to hold family is made to seem like a more or less doomed endeavour to have a real family – real in that the image of the farm family sets the conditions, and doomed because these conditions of family, which is to say the peaceful enjoyment of unquestioned division and unending experience of labour, are challenged by every kind of urban uncertainty.

This account of town/country difference may be anachronistic as well as fanciful, a prisoner of old ideas and spurious idealisations. It may appear to be literary, or no more than a sketch of quaint notions found at holiday teatime for Enid Blyton's Famous Five, or the domestic background to Arthur Ransome's Swallows and Amazons, or the norm inspiring the Swiss Family Robinson. But what of the farm and family that so draw the hero of D.H. Lawrence's *Sons and Lovers*, or the life that George Eliot's Dorothea longs for in her depths, or the rather grand version in much of Jane Austen? And what does Defoe's Robinson Crusoe emulate? The literature that works with these notions is vast and includes the most powerful of English writing. And when modern politicians express their commitment to family values, or seek to shift social conditions to ensure more stable home lives for us all, their image of the ideal family may well be that of the farmhouse of children's books and the guiding assumptions of the England of many of its literary classics. There is not only an idealisation of the countryside; there is also a profound acceptance of, or faith in, the farm and farm family.

There is indeed a way in which the family farm is at the heart of a human and social condition, not so much as an ideal but as the cause of its most dynamic element: a readiness to migrate, our nomadism. These terms need some refinement. The human condition at issue in this essay is the underlying force at the heart of farming, agriculture and town as these have developed in the last few thousand years. The nomadism is that of people who are attached to a socio-economic system, a mode of production, rather than to a particular geography. This is to paint with a broad brush, but I suspect that there is an argument here that explains many of the details of both town and country, and goes to some of the inner workings of our society and ourselves.

Return to that family and its farm. Not in the gentle settlements of well-established England, but to its fiercer and more archetypal form. Parents and children work to sustain a transformation – there could be a broad and tough version of the joke about the garden and God: 'You should have seen it when He had it.' Farmland in God's sole care is forest and savannah. The family farm is a determined and persistent struggle to make sure that God does not get the place to himself: the trees are felled, their roots hauled from the ground, stones are picked from the earth, invading wild plants and shrubs are rooted out again and again. There is no end to this labour: the soil will grow grass and vegetables and grains only if a great deal else is excluded or destroyed. Not only rival plant life, but also wild creatures that will harm seeds, seedlings, buds, fruits or, indeed, eat the domestic animals that are also part of the farm family. Weeds and vermin. These are the agents of wild nature that have to be walled out, scared off and killed. Otherwise the earth will not yield – more, it will not even exist.

The conditions of this archetypal farm are harsh. This is not Eden, but the curse of exile: by the sweat of the brow does the man provide food for the family. Not only the man, of course: the woman, too, must work all and every day. And the children: these are the labourers who will ease the burden of the curse – hence the double force of that other curse of Eden: 'in sorrow thou shalt bring forth children.'

And the woman is urged to have as many children as possible. The farm family, island of work and production, is also a world-historical centre for reproduction, that other kind of labour. Agriculturalists want large families. An original source for this may be a deep, as it were instinctive, desire for large families. The function of this family is clear to all: the children will be the workers, and as they grow and marry they will take over the running of the farm, securing for their parents the peace of body and mind that depend upon the continuity of their home and holdings through their old age and to the next generations. This may, in the long run, be the privilege and duty of one son; but the others can make alliances among neighbours and relatives (ah, the merit of the cross-cousin marriage!); and those who neither inherit nor marry well nearby may go far away and be able to take advantage of whatever opportunities come from not being tied to this one corner of the world. The division of role among children is thus, for farm families, a spread of economic measures. Labour, consolidation, inheritance and migration comprise a set of filial duties. Between them, the children must keep the family farm in its full and rightful place.

The arithmetic of this set of duties is, however, revealing. Agricultural life is nothing if not fecund: many nations' farmers and pastoralists have succeeded in raising very large families. The average for European rural families has varied from four to eight. Many households have had ten and more children live to adulthood. Even high levels of mortality, and periodic catastrophes, have not prevented the farm families of the world from producing astonishing population growth. Unless subdivision of land is acceptable to the family or system or agricultural era, only one of these children can inherit the family farm. And if subdivision does make it possible to keep many children at home, in the neighbourhood, as was the case in Ireland in the fifty years before the 1846 famine, this process itself will result in eventual catastrophic causes of emigration (as in Ireland 1846–1900), or a delay followed by a flood of human movement.* When the total number of family farms becomes constant, then one other child can expect to marry into a farm. Others may become farm labourers; and many must go elsewhere. In this way the settled countryside, in which the total number of farm families is more or less stable, and available marginal lands either in the ownership of large estates or in use to pastoralists or both, exports people.

Relatively modern history has included great displacements of country people by the concerted efforts and interests of other agriculturalists. The enclosures and Highland clearances are two notorious examples from British history. These drastic processes gave rise to some of the most anguished laments about movement from country to town or from one nation to another, and have made vivid contributions to the myth of the farm family. These systematic and internecine struggles within the countryside, expressive of class conflict rather than the nature of farming, may have underlying links with the settlement/restlessness tension within agricultural culture, but reveal different kinds of process. The emigrants this essay seeks to identify are those intrinsic to agricultural life, one of its continuous and inevitable long-term consequences.

Emigrants go, of course, to towns as labour or to new colonial lands as would-be settlers – part of the great farm family diaspora. And some of

* K. H. Connell's *The Population of Ireland, 1750–1845* (Oxford, 1950) is full of relevant insight. I have looked at the continuation and some corollaries of this change in rural Ireland in *Inishkillane, Change and Decline in the West of Ireland* (London, 1973).

those who do go to towns retain or develop a longing for a life on the land, as an idealised alternative to the hardships and tyrannies of urban or industrial labour. The Australian, American, Canadian and southern African frontiers have given the farm opportunity to many millions of European men and women. The settlement of Europeans in the Canadian west during the late 1800s, for example, is among the largest and most rapid movements of human beings in history. Throughout the history of agriculture, all over the world, on new-found lands, in the *terra nullius* of colonial frontiers, with the help of systematic clearing of indigenous occupants, migrants make their family farms. There they have many children, who also have many children. These children, in their turn, move on, pushing the frontier outwards until it reaches its limits. And thus there is another wave of movement from the frontiers to new towns, or to even wilder regions.

Willingness to go to unknown and harsh places, in defiance of Aboriginal resentment, taking part in the necessary colonial wars of conquest and 'pacification', accepting the curse of exile that is the relentless need to remake, with herculean efforts, a land of forest or rocks or sands into a patchwork of pasture and fields, knowing little comfort and no respite, ensuring that every hour of every day is aimed at securing an Eden within the exile, forcing sons and daughters into routine acceptance of their roles and destinies, setting pleasure and civilisation at the far end, the distant terminus, of a journey of hardship that is itself a religious attainment – these are the circumstances of the family farm that have secured its success in almost every kind of climate and landscape. These are the forces that have given order and landscape, society and productive environment, to what Europeans (and many other expansionist agricultural cultures) see as the signs and successes of civilisation.

This success is inseparable from a fascinating interplay between a passion to settle and a fierce restlessness; a need to find and have and hold an Eden, and a preparedness to go out and roam the world; an attachment to all that is meant by home, and a dominant commitment to a socio-economic system, to some form of profit, above all else. The inner life of the family farm holds these two opposite characteristics. Yet they are inseparable; the agricultural system is a form of settlement that depends upon, and gives rise to, the most pervasive form of nomadism. The urge to settle and a readiness to move on are not antagonists in the sociology of our era; they are the two characteristics that combine to give the era its geographical and cultural character.

No doubt we all are aware, in our own psyches, of both these conditions of agriculture. When viewed from this angle, on this macro-historical level, the town and the country are not such different systems. In both settings a love of place is secondary to the importance of prosperity. Loyalty to home or lands is recent, romantic and incomplete. Given the right price, everything is for sale. Attachment to home is no more and no less than the consequences of several generations of labour and a fear of the insecurity that comes with any loss of family lands. But if the exchange is between small farm and large, or between marginal lands and prime lands, then the farm family can move and feel that all is well. Just as a city dweller is ready to change jobs or city or even country if a new offer is good enough. In both country and town, if attachment to a better place can be trusted, then preparedness to move will prevail. Indeed, the measure of success in this town and country system of settlement and migration, conservatism and restlessness, is economic power – the ability to control a pool of resources in the interests of the family.

Behind all versions of the farm family system, a tough-minded economic sense dictates who does and doesn't stay, and whether or not to trade in the farm itself. By similar tokens of economic rationality, farmers are reluctant to trust to change – for they have something to lose. But if the deal is good enough, then they will. The threat that the kulaks appeared to pose to Stalinist ideals of Soviet authority came from their particular independence and security; the absurdity of collectivisation in the interests of the peasants comes from its being a plan that can only reduce the power and productivity, and therefore the security, of the farm family. But even successful peasants will exchange poor land for good, a marginal farm for a productive one. Clinging to a family farm in defiance of the need or chance to move can be poignant. Reluctance to move can speak to every kind of attachment to home and heritage. But overall patterns of movement, like most individual decisions to move or not to move, have a sense that is ultimately economic.

We can see many forms of the readiness to move, each of which cuts across town and country. Counter-cultural movements – from hippies to New Age shamanism – reject the conventions of the farm family, and display much enthusiasm for freedom that comes with reduced attachment to farms or houses with their bourgeois economic imperatives. They celebrate movement – on the streets, in imagination, away from homes and farms of many kinds. Yet these same movements are rich with enthusiasm for subsistence vegetable-growing, self-reliant communes, and a deep longing for their particular version of settlement in some new kind of place. With the same tension, which is as creative as it is contradictory, emigrants celebrate in song and poetry the opportunities of new frontiers and mourn the separation from all that is caught in the telling cliché, the old country. 'Oh give me a home where the buffalo roam . . .' But: '. . . for all these great powers he's wishful, like me, / To be back where dark Mourne sweeps down to the sea'. The farm family, along with the urban family, makes a home that most have to leave. Nostalgia and a sense of loss sit alongside dreams of foreign riches and adventure as twins of the agrarian imagination.

The move of country people to another countryside and to town, like the move of town people to every kind of other place, is intrinsic to the overall system. Newcomers to the countryside, be they agricultural entrepreneurs or people eager to get away from cities, are part of a continuing flow of life that includes the coming and going of farm families. The city-born family that has lived in the countryside for twenty years has deep attachments to the landscape, the home, the gardens, the land where it has made a life. This is not different from the attachments that 'traditional' rural people have to their homes and farms, except in so far as the garden may have little to do with actual prosperity. These are people living and making their decisions within the same cultural and economic tradition: they move, they settle, they make an Eden, they find – or their children or their children's children find – that they must move on. Exile is the deep condition; the longing to be settled, the defensive holding of our ground, and continuing endemic nomadism – I suspect that we share them all.

Who is this 'we'? The argument here pays no attention to class or even nation. The suggestion is that 'we', or some vigorous part of ourselves, is contradictory at some higher or deeper level of generality. We are conditioned by one of a number of human cultural or economic forms: we are the agriculturalists, the peoples who live by remodelling the land. We are the peoples whose story is some version of Genesis: we are outside any garden that can meet our needs, so we must roam the face of the earth looking to create or recreate some place, not in the image of the ideal, but as a more or less adequate source of what we need to eat. And we are doomed to defend this place, against enemies of all kinds: we know that just as we have conquered, others can displace us. This mixture of farming and warfare is the system within which our farms and towns and nation states and colonial expansion all have an inner and shared coherence. The world-view and daily preoccupations of the pre-capitalist farmer and the late twentieth-century executive have much in common. The one is able to dominate, exploit and thrive far more than the other. But their intellectual devices, categories of thought and underlying interests may well be the same. They speak one another's language, as it were; for all the inequalities between them, they can do business together.

The propositions that town and country share a profound contradiction, and that they are unified by restlessness and colonial energies, become less tendentious, more real, when we look at our world, our systems of life and thought, through the eyes of another way of being in, using and knowing the world. Imagine how the nomadism of our agricultural/urban system appears to hunter-gatherers. They do not make any intensive efforts to remake the environment, but rely, instead, on knowing how to find and use that which is already there. Their task is to make sure that it stays there – either through systems of harvesting or spiritual interventions. They speak again and again of 'respect' for the animals or the fish or the plants. To respect is to avoid taking too much, or wasting, or making fun of, or failing to acknowledge that to hunt an animal is to ask that it agree to be hunted. This web of rules about how to do things and shamanic ideas about why things can or cannot be done is the hunter-gatherer system. But this is a system that can work if and only if the people who live it are on intimate terms with a particular place. There has to be a territory that is known in extreme detail. This knowledge is what makes it possible to find the roots, track the animals, trap the fish. The technology for these activities is, for the most part, quite simple. The success of the technology, however, depends on great depths of specific knowledge. This means that there must be a territory; and if people have to leave this territory, then their knowledge – of place, creature and spirits – will probably fail them. To migrate is to risk death.

In this sense hunter-gatherers are not nomads. Like all human beings, they have at some point moved into their territories.* But once they are

---

* The times at which specific hunter-gatherer peoples first occupied their territories is a much disputed matter. The people themselves insist that they have always been there. Thus the indigenous people of the Americas give no credence to the Bering Strait land bridge theory of migration from Asia to the Americas. Similarly, the San of southern Africa and the Aborigine groups of Australia see

there, they establish this territory as the only possible place to live. They hold to an area – albeit a large one, with many sectors of use, and with a seasonal round, a pattern of movement within the territory to make sure that the match between knowledge and place is taking advantage of changing times of year. But no one leaves this total region, this people's land, except in extreme crisis or on rare journeys of adventure. All children are expected to stay within the territory. For generation after generation, movement is contained within a territory and its resources, deepening understanding of its animal movements, fishing sites, berry patches and plants. As Sahlins and others have pointed out so well, the hunter-gatherer population is accommodated within the place, in part by keeping needs low and in part by keeping population growth to a minimum.* These are peoples who do not hope to have large numbers of children; and their families are often ready to share out babies, making sure that no family is too large while no woman who wants to care for a baby is without. Everything about the hunter-gatherer system is founded on the conviction that home is indeed Eden, and exile must be avoided for all. Hence there is an underlying tendency to share harvests rather than store them or sell them to others.

The farmers appear to be settled, and the hunters to be wanderers. Yet if we look at how ways of life take shape across a number of generations, we can see that the agriculturalists, with their commitment to specific farms and large numbers of children, are forced to keep moving, resettling, colonising new lands. On the other hand, the hunter-gatherers, with their reliance on continuity in a single area, are profoundly settled. As a system, over time, the farmers generate 'nomadism', not the hunters.

In 1976 Simon Anaviapik spent two weeks in England. He had been my Inuktitut (Eskimo language) teacher, the person who, more than any other, had attempted to explain the Inuit world to me. Anaviapik (his Christian name existed only in administrative papers) had spent his life in the North Baffin region of the high Arctic. He had been born in his

themselves as the first humans of their territories. Creation stories for many hunter-gatherer peoples identify the human birthplace as in or adjacent to their existing lands. Archaeology, however, appears to be able to demonstrate that the peoples of the Americas first moved there between 25,000 and 10,000 BP. The Inuit of Arctic Canada and Greenland seem to have moved into their present-day territories relatively recently – somewhere around 1,000 BP. Whatever the theory or actual dates of these movements, however, these are all peoples who insist both with what they say and by the nature of their socio-economic systems that the only possible territory is the one they have 'always' occupied.
* The seminal essay on this subject is Marshall Sahlins, 'The Original Affluent Society', in his *Stone Age Economics* (London, 1974).

parents' sod and whalebone *karmak*, at a favourite spring and autumn fishing place, in about 1915. He had lived in various seasonal and semi-permanent campsites until moving to Pond Inlet in the 1970s. Although this move meant a permanent, all-year address in a Canadian government designed prefabricated house, Pond Inlet itself was developed on a site that had been used by Anaviapik's ancestors for many hundreds of years.

Anaviapik had always hunted, fished and trapped. This was a mixed economic life: since the late nineteenth century, families in the region had traded skins and ivory for European goods. The Hudson's Bay Company first set up a post at Pond Inlet in the 1920s. And by 1970, Christian missionaries had been effective for at least a generation. But Anaviapik and his family were hunters. He delighted in explaining that this land was perfect, and could never be replaced. The everyday rhythms of his life were shaped by the weather, movements of animals and fish, and what his family needed to eat. He knew nothing of the routines or priorities of agricultural life, although he was always curious to hear about how it differed from his own.

Anaviapik had never been away from the far north. His trip to London came as a result of his being chosen by his community to oversee the final cut of the Granada 'Disappearing World' film *The People's Land*. I had invited him to stay with me in central London, but feared that he would find his visit bewildering and unpleasant. Full of worry, I went to meet him at Heathrow. I wanted to go to the point where Anaviapik would step off the plane, and be with him to help in the encounter with passport control, baggage pick-up, etc. I explained that this was a man coming from the high Arctic, who had never been anywhere crowded before, and who spoke only Eskimo. Surely I could be given permission, under whatever guidance or guards they wished, to meet him as he stepped from the plane into the bewildering puzzle of this huge airport. The woman I was dealing with was quite scornful of the proposal – a scorn she expressed in part by showing no interest in the circumstances. I had hoped to be able to capture her sympathies if not her imagination by referring to the Arctic, sketching the vast distance that Anaviapik would have to travel, telling something of the extreme difference between his world and this one. But she paid little attention, and was unmoved. 'You've no need to worry,' she said. 'We've had Aborigines from Australia arriving here. No harm ever came to any one of them.' This left me no argument, no room for appeal, and I stood in high anxiety by the international arrivals gate – that boundary between close individual scrutiny and the anonymous mayhem of Heathrow.

Anaviapik arrived, escorted by a British Airways stewardess. He was wearing sealskin boots, brown trousers tucked into their patterned tops, just below the knees, and a dark jacket. Over his arm he carried a parka, complete with cross-fox trim round its hood. Eccentric clothing for a warm autumn day in London. But his face was alive with smiles. Not a flicker of worry or discomfort. We greeted each other with all those wonderful Inuktitut sounds and words of delight. Then we walked to my car in the multi-storey short-term car park, and drove towards London along the M4.

The traffic was dense and moving fast. I had to concentrate hard on the driving. Anaviapik sat beside me. As we were coming through Hammersmith, he broke a longish silence, saying: 'Now I understand why the southerners come to our land to get the oil.' These were not the words of the intimidated hunter-gatherer from the savage wilds. Nor was his comment the next day when we walked for the first time around the streets of Bayswater: 'How amazing that southerners live in cliffs. I would never be able to find my way here without you.' Over the next two weeks we often played a look-how-lost-I-am-game. Anaviapik would see if he could guide us from Bayswater tube stop to my flat – a distance of about half a block, with one left turn and a crossing of the road to the building's door on to the street. He never succeeded, expressed his mock dismay at being lost, and yet enjoyed reminding me that since we lived in cliffs, of course our houses were not easy to tell one from the other.

To get some relief from homogenised urban crowds, we took a trip to the Norfolk countryside. I hoped to give Anaviapik some sense of an England that is not all cliffs and cliff dwellers. So we set off, driving east, across Cambridgeshire, and through the Suffolk countryside. I chose a route that was as rural as could be. He looked out at the green and pleasant landscapes and said: 'It's all built.' He did not see the difference between town and country except as a matter of degree: the one had more people and more houses side by side, and the other had more fields and hedgerows. But all of this, hedgerows as much as houses, was made by people; none of it was nature – not, that is to say, a form of nature that he would recognise as such.

Anaviapik insisted on quizzing everyone he met. He stopped strangers in the street whose appearance intrigued him, and persuaded me to translate to them his questions. When we were in a shop, he would have us hold long conversations with anybody we bought things from. In cafés and restaurants, he persuaded me to draw people at adjacent tables into conversation. Where are you from? Where do you live? Do you have children? Where do they live? Do they have children? Are your parents alive? Do you have brothers and sisters? Where are they? These were the invariable start-up questions. And if the surprised stranger was able to overcome surprise – and most did – a long exchange of personal and family stories would follow. In this way Anaviapik conducted a thorough if not systematic interrogation of English life.

As time went on, he came to a sense of us as scattered and shiftless. Everyone was on the move. Families dispersed. Children far away, out of touch. Dreams of moving to some other country. Many, of course, said how much they wished they could live in Canada. No, not the Arctic. But Canada. They had relatives or friends there. They would go there too if they could. In London, in the countryside, he met the nomads, or the parents of nomads. He did not make judgements. He was full of admiration for everyone and everything he encountered. But he spoke more and more of the movement from place to place that he sensed and heard about. Not with a sense of dismay or disdain. If any emotion coloured his comments on what he learned, it was apprehension: might this remaking of environment and shiftlessness of people spread to his lands? Already he knew, and had spoken often to me about, the southerner's readiness to come and live even in the far north. All this posed a deep threat. Nomads have no real homes, so they cannot be relied upon to stay away from other people's.

The ironies of this cannot be left unstated. Moral supporters of the colonial process have cited the apparent 'nomadism' of native populations to justify advances of the settlement frontier. They have made much of the fact that hunter-gatherers lack year-round permanent settlements; they insist that these are peoples without the institutional life of the village; they equate a relative indifference to possessions with a low level of human evolution; and they claim that a primitive state is demonstrated by their roaming, poor and indigent, from place to place. Colonial occupation of tribal lands has also relied on a broad theory of manifest destiny, which claims that the occupation of 'nomad' peoples' lands by civilised farmers is ordained by fate or God. This doctrine of manifest destiny, developed in eighteenth-century American jurisprudence, deems the Indians to be 'as beasts of the field', for they roam around as if they were without any form of society.*

Both British and American courts have at times made the existence of organised society a test of Aboriginal claims to ownership of their lands. Hunter-gatherers have duly been failed, on the grounds that they lack the minimally necessary social institutions. 'Nomadism' has, of course, been a repeated if rather general term used by colonists to categorise those who have failed to achieve their self-styled levels of social organisation. Setting aside the grotesque charge implicit in the organised society test to the effect that these are peoples who lack what it means to be human, the proposition that supposed nomadism is evidence of lack of rights to land is a great and terrible paradox of the agriculturalists' judgement upon others. Great because it speaks to the entire range of frontiers that displace and expropriate peoples whose territories are wanted for new farms; terrible because this process gives rise to, and then relies upon, a frontier racism that is relentless and purposive. Perhaps this is a vast and self-serving projection: when it comes to seeking new lands, agriculturalists view hunter-gatherers as what they are themselves – lawless nomads.

The neolithic transformation of human history begins with the invention and development of agriculture – with its brilliant domestication of crops and animals, and the remaking of the landscape, the creation of countryside. Where agriculture has no place, beyond the farmers' frontier, there is no such thing as countryside. Instead, there is the wild: raw nature, a wilderness. Agriculturalists have much difficulty in imagining a human socio-economic system, as opposed to a few inchoate animal-like wanderers, living in this wild beyond. This gives farmers a self-styled moral freedom to enter the wild, tame it, farm it, and make it into countryside. And there they can reproduce, and give rise to that surplus of sons and daughters who move on. Thus agriculture creates the most extreme nomads, the true wanderers. In farms and towns this is the case, for both evidence the success of neolithic genius, both nurturing and benefiting from the neolithic's intrinsic restlessness.

---

* A secondary irony lies in the etymology of 'nomad', which comes from *nomadikos* and *nomades*, the Greek and Latin for pastoralists – the people who have lived by moving herds of animals between widely separated pastures. Bedouin with their sheep and camels; Masai with their cattle. In the history of neolithic transformation, pastoralism has been closely allied to agriculture. Archaeology suggests, in fact, that farming developed much sooner than pastoralism. All pastoralists know how to farm, and can do so if need arises. Also, pastoralists tend to share with farmers a deep hostility to hunter-gatherers, seeing hunter-gatherers as inferior, primitive, lacking real society or culture.

In this way the system that depends on the linkage between agriculture and city, country and town, contains intrinsic colonial energy and impetus. Its nomadism is a source of its power – to transform the world at hand and the world far away. We who have grown up within the neolithic – and that would include the vast majority of present-day peoples – know this within our minds and bodies. We experience the lure of opportunity, keep an eye open for where we might better be able to do what we do, and juggle, as we make decisions about where to live, deep in our selves, the pull of both town and country. Each kind of place seems right and wrong at the same time. Staying at home, having roots – these are important sources of comfort and satisfaction and many kinds of success. Moving on, making progress, asking ourselves if all might prosper there rather than here – these are necessary conditions not only for many kinds of individual success but for the collective achievement of our social order. Thus we experience our exile from Eden, our nomadism.

We experience the profound dichotomy that has shaped our era in a new, acute form. The achievements of neolithic genius are reaching startling levels. More than ever before, this genius seems to depend on restlessness, and urges that readiness to move be welcomed more fully, more quickly. The process is speeding up. But its successes – if this is what they are – rely on the same nomadic potential as ever. We are the new nomads, but we are not newly nomadic. As we move back and forth between town and country, or from one country to another, relocating as need and opportunity push and pull, we participate with a modern vigour in the neolithic system. To this extent, at this great depth, town and country are part of a unified, restless way of life.

The author wishes to thank the Connaught Fund and Ted Chamberlin of the University of Toronto.

2. *An Encroachment too Far*

Patrick Wright

In recent years, the cause of 'local distinctiveness' has commanded immediate loyalty up and down the land, and it has had the peculiar attraction of doing so without demanding that people settle their more intractable social and political differences. Under this flag the Yorkshire miner can apparently come to terms with the Surrey stockbroker, the Cornish fisherman with the Shropshire squire. In the name of local distinctiveness, we may even imagine the English stepping out from under the cover of the unitary British state to hold their own smaller patch of ground alongside the increasingly differentiated Welsh and Scots.

But if it is one thing to raise the standard for this most timely of causes, it is quite another to determine exactly what 'local distinctiveness' amounts to as a cause at the end of the twentieth century. We might say that it is about the unique quality of places and their particular cultures. We might describe it as the opposite of a shopping mall, a McDonald's and a National Trust shop too. Yet a teasing vagueness still clings to the term: indeed, as we attempt to define this much-praised virtue more closely, we find ourselves wandering through an exotic anthology of almost lost causes. For some, local distinctiveness is about the varied flora and fauna of the landscape, while for others it seems to emanate from lamp-posts, trolley buses and allotments. While it is much concerned with vernacular buildings, it also has to do with pre-modern cheeses, gas-holders, barred gates, kippers and increasingly scarce dialect words. In some places it may be about local stone, pargeting and thatch, but elsewhere it is a matter of corrugated iron, baling twine, and perhaps even abandoned US Airforce bases too.

A French critic once said of EuroDisney that the difference between a proper city and a theme park is that a city has ghosts. There can be little doubt where local distinctiveness stands in that contest: it takes the side of ghosts against anybody's themed experience or crafty manipulation of appearances, and it feels decidedly ambivalent about the kind of self-consciousness that tourism and other leisure-related development strategies bring to the identity of places.

If 'local distinctiveness' has become a cause and rallying cry in recent years, this has largely been the work of Common Ground, an environmentalist organisation, which adapted the idea from Michael Hough, a landscape architect whose book, *Out of Place*, is subtitled 'Restoring Identity to the Regional Landscape'.* Common Ground launched its campaign in May 1992, with the help of a graphically rendered Alphabet in which Mosques and Gasometers are accommodated alongside more rural residues, like Devonshire Cream Teas, Thomas Hardy, the Marshfield Mummers and the Mendlesham Chair.

The people at Common Ground were careful to include some urban and immigrant qualities in their Alphabet of Local Distinctiveness. Yet in its generalised sense of emergency ('Richness and diversity in our daily lives are being plundered'), and in the prominence it gave to endangered rural traditions, their campaign articulated many of the same anxieties that have more recently been expressed by the Countryside rally and march organised by the landowning and field sports organisations grouped behind the front of the Countryside Alliance. Here too an apparently common cause is built up from a diverse cluster of beleaguered experiences. A core group of hunters and landowners have galvanised a much wider and internally far from consistent amalgam of rural grievances, one that is held together by a distrust of strongly demonised urban values – epitomised by encroaching ramblers, interfering bureaucrats, tourists, sentimental animal lovers and, if some of the Countryside Alliance's wilder statements are believed, anyone who lives in the country but doesn't worship with sufficient ardour at the shrine of the pheasant and horse. It has been said that using field sports to rally the modern countryside is no more plausible than defending urban life by campaigning for town criers, yet there were plainly more serious issues at stake. The march may have been something of a Trojan Horse operation for some hunting organisations, but it was of wider significance for demonstrating how few channels there are through which rural interests can be expressed.

Partly as a consequence of this, we are still predisposed to think of the countryside as an organic whole, a way of life that is both sanctioned by tradition and grounded in nature, but which is also rudely penetrated by

* Michael Hough, *Out of Place: Restoring Identity to the Regional Landscape* (New Haven and London, 1990).

the ever more ruinous forces of the modern world. This imagery of encroachment may be justified by much that has happened to the rural areas in the twentieth century, but it is also significantly out of kilter with the practical reality of the countryside as it is today. The urban invasion has taken place. It is an accomplished fact not just a dire threat; and it is not always for the worse either. The rural areas are funded and subsidised by their own enemy, and their future is quite inseparable from that of the towns and cities. In this circumstance, it is surely worth asking why we are so predisposed to view the relationship between town and country through a lens that still seems to show urban 'encroachment' as all.

Two Sides of a Village Street

As a recent incomer to a village that is now poised to be absorbed into Cambridge, I only have to step out of the door to be reminded that the cause of the countryside has actually been highly contested: indeed, that it has been a battleground through more or less the entire length of the twentieth century.

The Fruit Shop is run by a local greengrocer called Richard Wombwell, a resilient and independent-minded man who favours English produce and is well liked for his contrary outlook. Never well served by any school, Wombwell has a prodigious knowledge of local flora and fauna, and also of archaeology, the latter derived with the help of a metal detector as well as through books. He also remembers a lost world of altogether more recent time. His grandfather used to run a pub in the village, a place that was noted for conversations in which tenant or council farmers and agricultural labourers took on the world together with left-wing intellectuals associated with Cambridge University. Some villagers remember standing at the roadside during the depths of the Cold War and watching as cars with unfamiliar East European number plates came and went through the village. And there was much knowing head-shaking in the pub whenever Chapman Pincher or some other Fleet Street spycatcher tried to unmask another retired member of the pre-war Cambridge circle that had produced traitors like Philby, Maclean, Burgess and Blunt.

The academic who stands at the centre of these local memories is Maurice Dobb, a well-known Marxist economist, who wrote many books expounding the achievements of the Soviet economy under Lenin and Stalin, and who lived in a large and well-appointed house in Fulbourn, at that time owned by his college.

Locally, Dobb is remembered as a man of principled eccentricity, who wouldn't travel in private cars (he is said to have insisted on using public transport, even in awkward circumstances), and who had his own forthright ideas on the improvement of the English countryside. In the late 1930s Dobb had been among the regular contributors to the *Country Standard*, a more or less Communist journal aimed at agricultural workers and initially published from East Anglia. The *Country Standard* delighted in crude stereotypes of the rural class struggle. On one page it would provide a rhyming denunciation of filthy-rich farmers who lounge in bed or eat vast meals off silver plates while their oppressed workers toil endlessly in the fields. On another, it conducted high-minded surveys of the amount of overtime that those same stinkers were 'filching' from British farm workers in defiance of statutory agreements.

The future envisaged by the *Country Standard* was to be achieved by breaking through the pseudo-organic idylls of class power. Contemptuous of field sports, its writers wanted to see the rural grandees dispossessed and, as war approached, urged that their mansions should be turned into hostels for the evacuated children of the urban working classes. Inspired by the progressive red tractors of the Soviet Union, the *Country Standard* was all in favour of mechanisation. Far from being replaced by machinery, however, the agricultural workers should have machines designed around their existing skills so that their labour would be amplified and augmented rather than displaced.

Disfigured by Stalinist assumptions, the *Country Standard* struggled through the Second World War and survived long enough afterwards to argue that disused wartime aerodromes should be turned into co-operative and collective farms. Dobb and his wife may be remembered affectionately in Fulbourn's Fruit Shop as people who really got involved in village life, and left money to various needy individuals when they died. But their Communist scenario for a revitalised countryside seems as remote as Cromwell or the Tolpuddle Martyrs.

The butcher on the opposite side of the road is at one with the greengrocer in the struggle to keep the high street going, and in his opposition to the threats of big capitalism, represented for both these local shopkeepers by the huge Tesco superstore that recently opened nearby. Michael Beaumont does his bit for the village on festive occasions and takes great pride in being the winner of various regional awards. He keeps his replica olde-worlde van parked on the road – an advertisement, but also a sign of old-fashioned community. Our butcher represents a Conservative outlook which finds its own traditional values – prominent among which is an idea of the organic village community – endangered by the 'free market' and ever more demanding state regulation. His judgement of EU bureaucracy is such that he must have had at least some sympathy for the Referendum Party in the 1997 general election.

In over-the-counter discussions, the problems of village life quickly become emblematic of our national condition. And our butcher doesn't waste an opportunity to get out the Union Jacks and bunting. The fiftieth anniversary of VE Day was a big event – one could hardly get into his shop for commemorative mugs and flags, and the bunting above his traditionally lettered doorway stayed there for the best part of a year, crinkled and as sun-dried as a Sainsbury tomato, but still rattling in every gust of wind. The butcher is a punctilious and tidy man, but he was evidently reluctant to relinquish a patriotic ritual that would never again be observed with the same respect and devotion.

More recently, Michael Beaumont's shop has been full of mental Spitfires, scrambled over the different front line represented by British beef. Improvised notices remark that, if the government raised tax revenue from meat – as they do from far more dangerous substances like tobacco and alcohol – then it certainly wouldn't be making such an ass of the law by banning the Englishman's T-bone steak. For several years, his shop has also been full of speculative theories about the origins of BSE – including, in the early stages of the crisis, one that attributed the contaminating prion to another well-known 'enemy within', namely Arthur Scargill. In this ingenious fable, which has since failed the test of time, the disaster occurred not because of deregulatory dogma applied by Margaret Thatcher's government, but as a result of the miners' strike of the early 1980s, said to have created such an energy shortage that some animal feed manufacturers had no option but to stop heating ground-up carcasses as effectively as they had done before.

Despite their obvious differences, these are both patriotic outlooks, in which the condition of the village is emblematic of our condition as a nation. The Communist scenario for the redemption of the British countryside is utterly derelict, a broken eccentricity fit for display only in the museum of time-expired pastoral utopias. The organic ideal of country life has lasted rather better, although we may still wonder how we got into this habit of thinking of country life as an already achieved historical identity – a national totem that has ceaselessly to be defended against a threatening modern world.

It is not just patriotic butchers who have been reaching out for explanations as the ground disappears beneath their feet. Indeed, anyone who followed the press on St George's Day in April 1996 might reasonably have concluded that this activity has become a characteristically English habit. *The Times* took the pulse of England, and pronounced it stone dead. The tabloids, meanwhile, clamoured for resuscitation. Lamenting England's reluctance to celebrate its patron saint, the *Daily Express* recruited Saint George, sharpened his lance and shoved him into the front line of its 'crusade' against the Eurodragon. Meanwhile Richard Littlejohn, the uninhibited columnist who had just moved from the *Sun* to the *Daily Mail*, tried to brace his readers with an invigorating history lesson: 'Any objective reading of history would conclude that the English ran the most benevolent and benign empire in history'; and yet here the English people were reduced to being the one ethnic minority in Britain without rights. Charging against the Commission for Racial Equality, he thundered that 'To be English in England today is almost a criminal offence'. Littlejohn wasn't afraid to declare English reserve and self-effacement far superior to 'the maudlin swaggering of the Scots, the drunken sentimentalism of the Irish, or the blazered bravado of the Welsh'. According to this crusader, the English are now 'a race in denial' – no less than 'the nationality that dare not speak its name'.

We've Been Here Before

Defenders of local distinctiveness have been conscious of battling against overwhelming and vividly imagined odds for many decades. We might remember Ian Nairn, a fighting architectural conservationist of the 1950s and 1960s. In 1955 he organised a special issue of the *Architectural Review*, a magazine with which John Betjeman was also associated. The issue, which was called 'Outrage', contained a comprehensive attack on the diverse forces that were burying the English landscape in a mediocre uniformity. 'Subtopia', so Nairn wrote in that issue, is 'the annihilation of the site, the steamrollering of all individuality of place to one uniform and mediocre pattern'. Nairn worried that 'if what is called development is allowed to multiply at the present rate, then by the end of the century Great Britain will consist of isolated oases of preserved monuments in a desert of wire, concrete roads, cosy plots and bungalows'. He feared that there would be 'no real distinction between town and country', for both would consist of 'a limbo of shacks, bogus rusticities, wire and aerodromes, set in some fir-poled field'. Drawn up only a few years after the Second World War, his list of Subtopia's agents includes arterial roads, ribbon development, wire, dumping grounds and military installations.

Ten or fifteen years previously, a spirited defence of local quality was mounted by those pioneers of organic farming who eventually came together as founding members of the Soil Association in 1946. These people were far-sighted in many ways. They worried about soil erosion and the woeful inadequacy of the industrialised urban diet, and they wanted to see many more people living on the land. They argued, with an early 'preventative' emphasis, that the orientation of the new National Health Service should be shifted from sickness to health, and that agriculture should be counted as 'one of the health services'.* They were critical of the way mechanisation was being used to concentrate profits and reduce agricultural employment; and also of the new agricultural marketing boards, which the state seemed to be using only to increase the distance between local producers and consumers, while lining the pockets of powerful distributors. As one veteran remembers, the heart of the organic movement of that time was committed to a 'defence of locality' – based on the 'hypothesis that health would be built up on the local'.† They wanted fewer imports and a greater commitment to home agriculture, an increase in livestock, the decentralisation of industry and the reopening of local mills and slaughterhouses.

As with Ian Nairn's attack on Subtopia, the Soil Association's attempt to resurrect the local was mounted in the face of opposition that seemed hugely powerful and overwhelming. This can be sensed in the insistence by Lady Eve Balfour (the Association's founder) that the health of the nation was more important than the profits and share dividends of any large combine, that the 'new world order' of the post-war planners must be extended to take proper account of the soil, and that the prevailing idea of 'the conquest of nature' was of the same order as 'the Nazi conquest of Europe'. The pesticide and herbicide revolution had yet to take off, but even before that was added to her troubles, Lady Eve was in no doubt that the soil would die unless 'the false idols of comfort and money' were

---

* Quoted from Lady Eve Balfour, *The Living Soil* (London, 1944).
† I quote from Mary Langman, who was secretary to the doctors at the organic Pioneer Health Centre in Peckham before the war, and has been involved with the Soil Association since the early days.

dethroned. She concluded, with a characteristic mixture of desperation and determined upper-class pluck, that the restoration of locality could only really come with the restoration of Christian society, and that this meant avoiding the Nazi ideology of 'deifying the state'.

We can follow the beleaguered cause of local distinctiveness further back into the 1930s. This was a decade in which doughty English villagers opposed the Post Office's imposition of red telephone boxes on their communities, condemning these amenities – which are now defended as vital features of the landscape and, indeed, the very emblems of traditional British character – as a monstrously uniform 'intervention of red' into the locally diverse national scene. The 1930s also produced the artists who were commissioned in the early years of the war to paint pictures for the 'Recording Britain' scheme. Employed to portray the cherished Britain that was threatened by the Nazis, they travelled through the counties and, following the advice of local branches of the Council for the Preservation of Rural England, came up with a singular contribution to the war effort – a collection of images of a country that had apparently already gone to war with all that was best in itself: villages threatened by ribbon development, valleys threatened by municipal reservoirs, houses threatened by insensitive local authority regulations about what was fit for human habitation, a few mansions sunk into military and 'institutional' use.

That was also a time when the diverse charms of the traditional British forest were being vigorously defended against the improving endeavours of the state. The Forestry Commission, which had been set up shortly after the First World War and charged with ensuring that Britain never again suffered the kind of timber shortage that had come with the German submarine blockade, was under especially vehement criticism. The idea had been to plant a 'strategic reserve' of timber which would, so the original Commission hoped, enable the country to be self-sufficient in timber for three years. Within a few years the Commission was under attack for imposing an abstract geometry of coniferous monoculture on the traditionally deciduous national landscape.

Much of this criticism was fully justified, as will be obvious to anyone who has visited the Commission's Sitka plantations in the Scottish uplands, or counted up the acres of ancient woodland that were poisoned and converted into conifer plantations, or looked at Forestry Commission journals from that period and noticed their enthusiastic advocacy of ploughing up what are now protected as rare heaths. However, it also flared into a curious demonisation. The Commission's conifers became an army of invasion, marching in rows across the native British landscape. The symbolism used by the critics of the pre-war Forestry Commission could be excessive and detached from reality. The conifers themselves may have come from Scandinavia and the north-western Pacific, but the fact that the Commission adopted methods of plantation forestry from the German tradition of silviculture gave its critics licence to revile this new statutory body as a planter of Huns. The historian G. M. Trevelyan led the National Trust into a battle for the Lake District, claiming, reasonably enough, that the introduction of the conifer was 'a crime against Nature's local bye-laws', but then protesting, altogether more emotively, that the English fell should not be converted into 'German pine forest'.* H. J. Massingham, a major defender of the countryside in that inter-war period, also took a frantic line on this subject, condemning the Commission for taking a place like the Breckland in south-west Norfolk (now one of the Forestry Commission's conservation showcases) and turning it into 'a parade ground for conifers, equidistant, each the spit of its brother and all of them set out in standardized rows as though the voice of Nature had just bawled "Attention!"'†

Whose Jackboots?

Towards the end of 1995 I received a leaflet in the mail, from a group calling itself 'The Movement for Middle England'. Headed 'Middle England Awake' and displaying a quotation from G. K. Chesterton, 'For we are the People of England that have never spoken yet', it announced a conference to be held in Oxford, and invited people to 'work for a society you'll be proud to live in'. The Movement for Middle England was in favour of devolution and autonomous English regions. Spurning party politics, it favoured belonging – 'taking root in your region and helping to run it'. It wanted to 'encourage local moots of around 50 householders', and to establish them as 'the basic building block of future democracy'. It was in favour of ecological sustainability and described itself as 'a dynamic English not British campaign to disengage the English identity from the Norman English chauvinism that has so devastated other peoples and

---

* Quoted from David Cannadine, *G. M. Trevelyan: a Life in History* (London, 1992), p. 156.
† See the article entitled 'England Laid Waste', in H. J. Massingham's *The Heritage of Man* (London, 1929), p. 301.

cultures – most especially our celtic neighbours'. In her statement the organiser, Catherine Perry, regretted that we had lost our ability to sing songs, and admitted to being rendered wistful by the vibrant Afro-Caribbean, Irish and Asian cultures in Britain – 'I would like to know what my culture is too, so that I can contribute to the multi-cultural scene'.

I must admit to feeling disconcerted by the idea of Middle England rising up to assert itself as another oppressed ethnic minority. Was this the beginning of a genuine resistance movement, I wondered, a grass-roots resurgence in which bamboozled and browbeaten Anglo-Saxons would finally throw off the yoke of the centralised and, as the leaflet put it, Norman British state? Was it a harmless fantasy addressed to the retired colonels and morris dancers of the deep English shires? Or was it a primitive historical cult convened more in the spirit of Goose Green? Picking up the phone, I discovered that the Movement for Middle England had been founded in Leicester in 1988, some years before John Major fell on the idea of Middle England and tried vainly to improve his flagging electoral fortunes with it.

The Movement for Middle England was formed by grass-roots activists – co-operators, Quakerish peace campaigners, bottom-up democrats. And I discovered that these Chestertonian campaigners were familiar with being misunderstood. Their existence has been noted with a certain unfounded suspicion in the green press and they have to argue their way through similar reservations when they take their stall out into towns and festivals. Their flag shows a cross of St George, adorned with a burgeoning English oak and discreetly dismembered to signify regional devolution – and it has led some people to suspect that they must be a front for the British National Party. It appears, as Catherine Perry told me, that the very word 'English' has been captured by Fascists.

Meanwhile, when the people at *Horse and Hound*, the field sports magazine, sat down to create a striking slogan for use on the Countryside Alliance's London march of March 1998, they came up with SAY NO TO THE URBAN JACKBOOT. And in their statements, the spokesmen for the Alliance left no doubt of their belief that the 'urban jackboot' is worn not just by hunt saboteurs, ramblers and proscribers of the T-bone steak, but by everyone who would turn the countryside into a leisure resource or a picturesque theme park for ignorant urban visitors.

Here too, the historical record is informative. Over the years, distrust of the urban onlooker's merely 'scenic' view of the countryside has led many to try to disentangle a deeper, more authentic countryside from the pretty touristic image. H. J. Massingham was a prodigious writer of books on the English countryside. Now only dimly remembered for his nostalgic celebrations of rural craft and custom, this erstwhile guild socialist was a great hater of 'scenic' definitions of the countryside. He described the picturesque as 'a giant worm' that had 'trailed its slime' all over the counties of England.[*] Noting that there had been no such thing as 'sightseeing' of the countryside until the late eighteenth century, he deplored the picturesque as an aesthetic born of land enclosure. This traumatic development drove many people from the land. But it also had the effect of breaking utility from beauty, thus creating 'a profound split in the national consciousness'. Utility followed the dispossessed peasantry into the booming industrial towns. Beauty suffered a comparable degeneration — 'for the picturesque means beauty divorced from the service of men's needs' and falsely attached to an idea of 'nature gone wild'. The country became a mere 'antidote' to the miseries of urban life.

The decadence of the picturesque was further emphasised, in those inter-war years, by the extent to which it thrived alongside an agriculturally 'derelict' countryside. People nowadays may mutter about theme parks and heritage shops, but Massingham was at it fifty years ago. Dismayed to see the countryside dying while its image was served up as the dreamy 'antidote' to industrial squalor, he railed against 'The suburban villa, with Tudoresque half-timbering nailed on, ye olde hostelrie, the hobby of antiquarianism . . . the exploitation of the beauty spot . . .' The rise of this merely 'scenic' idea threatened to kill the countryside in its own name, but it also brought a new division into national life, setting those who came to look against the few impoverished figures who remained there as little more than quaint objects to be gawped at — human curios stuck in aspic.

Massingham was by no means alone in his attitudes. Not long after the First World War, John Robertson Scott founded *The Countryman* magazine with the aim of cutting through the 'pleasant seeming' in order to expose the 'haggard reality' of country life as it really was.[†] This disillusioning cause was joined at both edges of the political spectrum. The Communist *Country Standard* (one of whose writers, Sylvia Townsend Warner, had been much influenced by Robertson Scott), desired a local vitality that was

---

[*] H. J. Massingham, *Remembrance: an Autobiography* (London, 1942), pp. 20–1.

[†] J. W. Robertson Scott, *The Dying Peasant and the Future of his Sons* (London, 1926), p. 3.

certainly not just scenic 'distinctiveness' of the kind admired by weekend-ers. Incoming middle-class preservationists were among its class enemies: people like the 'Save the Sussex Downs' campaigners who were 'appalled' by the sight of new bungalows but indifferent to the poverty of the exploited country workers.

But there were also anti-scenic rural activists whose politics were anti-collectivist and pointed in the opposite direction. Rolf Gardiner was one of the more ambitious rural revivers of the 1930s. A youth-leader with strong connections in Germany, he dedicated his Springhead estate in north Dorset to the reintegration of beauty and utility, and to reviving rural England's rural way of life 'from the herb to the hymn'.* The project entailed organic farming and forestry, morris dancing, communal singing and the recovery of seasonal rituals like beating the bounds, and it was premised on a strongly anti-urban attitude.

Gardiner deplored the conversion of the countryside into a town-centred image. When the Youth Hostels Association was formed in 1929, Gardiner proposed an alternative self-managed network based on working farms that would offer more than just a 'scenic' resource for urban hikers. A little later, when the National Trust was beginning to acquire its first country houses, he and his fellow rural revivers were eyeing the country estates with a very different prospect in mind. Far from seeking to preserve the landscaped grounds in their Georgian emptiness, they wanted to resettle them with new yeomen farmers trained from unemployed industrial workers. Gardiner thought the Crown should be able to dispossess landowners who were not prepared to set up co-operative rural industries for their impoverished villagers; and he loathed the pheasant as a 'foreign intruder' which exemplified the decadence of an aristocracy too corrupted by money and leisure to assume the responsibility of social leadership.

Gardiner was a rural fascist of sorts, albeit one who was more inclined to temporise about the Nazis than his acquaintance Captain George Pitt-Rivers. A major Dorset landowner, Pitt-Rivers was so convinced that the main parliamentary parties were in the pocket of the urban majority (to say nothing of the plutocratic usurers who had, in his view, suborned the State), that he fought the 1935 election as the candidate of his own Wessex Agricultural Defence Association – a fact that might interest the wing of the Countryside Alliance who are now considering the same manoeuvre. He

* For an account of Rolf Gardiner, Pitt-Rivers and the English Array, see my *The Village that Died for England* (London, 1995), pp. 150–202.

campaigned against tithes, which were still being levied on agricultural land by 'parasitical' clergy and Oxford colleges. But this 'agricultural defender' was also an unrestrained anti-Semite, who saw a Jewish conspiracy behind every turn of twentieth-century history. Former servants remember swastikas in his manor house, and also the relief they felt when this eccentric squire was eventually interned as a Nazi sympathiser.

Viscount Lymington's English Array was no less alarming. Grouped in deliberately undemocratic 'musters' scattered around the country, the members of this curious Masonic body tried to 'revive the English type', with the help of wholemeal flour, compost heaps, slogans like ENGLISH FOOD IN ENGLISH BODIES, and a patriotic interest in 'native stocks' that was not confined to trees. Their theorists wrote vile things about the urban working class – perceived as hideously fecund, hybrid and degenerate in every way – and were plainly of the view that the Nazis could have been a lot worse. Their anti-Semitism was apparently to prove too much for H. J. Massingham, whose widow once told me how she and her husband had walked out of a weekend conference at Lymington's Hampshire home in the early years of the Second World War.

Some of the arguments made in England by Lymington, Pitt-Rivers and others found more consequential expression in Europe – in the 'Blood and Soil' ideas of the Third Reich, to be sure, but also in France, where, long before Le Pen started rallying the countryside, the peasant activist Henri Dorgères ran a movement of Greenshirts, who went around breaking left-wing strikes and organising boycotts and direct action by market gardeners which, on several occasions in 1936, actually closed Les Halles, the main vegetable market in Paris.*

These ideas were contested in their own time, and at least one of the organisations that grew from them has since undergone thoroughgoing transformation. Lady Eve Balfour formed the Soil Association on the inspiration of Lord Lymington's alarmist tract *Famine in England*, but she laundered his organic vision of its most alarming cultural aspects – its anti-Semitism and its sheer hatred of the city – and confined its dreams of purity to the soil and the wholefood shop. The Soil Association may have started out taking the side of the local 'organic' community against the regulating state, but it now works *as* the regulating state: promoting and also

---

* See Robert O. Paxton, *French Peasant Fascism, Henri Dorgères's Greenshirts and the Crises of French Agriculture, 1929–1939* (New York and Oxford, 1997), p. 117.

regulating organic food production as an agency of the European Community.

Other products of this history, however, are less transformed. Anyone who doubts this should drop in on W. H. Smith's and pick up a copy of *This England*. This popular heritage quarterly is precisely concerned with the local distinctiveness of the English scene: the historical quality of towns and counties; the traditional arts and crafts of the countryside; and an endless fantasia about thatching, steam engines, and the charisma of undiminished royalty which has been running since the late 1960s. Much of this magazine is inoffensive, yet it has a decidedly unpleasant undercurrent. This sometimes spills out in the editorials, but it is also displayed on the letters page where expats and other affronted patriots leave no doubt at all that the distinctiveness of *This England* is that it offers no quarter to coloured immigrants, long-haired students, trade union barons and homosexuals. In some issues of the 1990s, the 'Forever England' column has been written by one Stuart Millson, a former member of the British National Party who made it quite clear what he meant when he raised the fallen flag of St George. There is enough here to explain, if not justify, the suspicions that fell upon the hapless Movement for Middle England. And also to suggest that the field sports lobby might sensibly think twice before going on about the 'urban jackboot'.

Nature Moves to the City

I do not point to this disconcerting strand of English ruralism in order to discredit those who defend the countryside now. It is true that what Ian Nairn described as the place-annulling forces of uniformity (to say nothing of the government's plans for house-building) are as rampant as they've ever been; but that is all the more reason why we should avoid trying to focus on them through the polarising lens of 'encroachment' alone.

The commentators and activists who used such a perspective in the past have identified their cause with the defence of a traditional way of life that fewer and fewer people are really prepared to live any more, and they have been inclined to take a highly simplified view of the forces constellating the society in which they have lived. At their worst, they have linked the defence of the countryside with an atavistic outlook, and they have proved that if you reject the state, commerce, industrialisation, and every other modern energy in sight you are left to build your patriotic house with very strange materials indeed.

One cannot review the history of this troubled relationship between the town and the country without realising that there is symbolic misrepresentation on both sides. According to Germaine Greer, who apparently takes a very dim view of her fellows' intelligence, urban people persist, even in the age of agribusiness, in seeing the countryside as 'nature in the raw'.* But rural Britons play this game too and are adept at projecting their own worst qualities – greed, indifference, philistinism, bossiness, etc. – on to the city they like to imagine as a pullulating violation of 'nature'. Greer's parody of urban perceptions is easily matched with another in which countryfolk view the city as the nightmare domain of a mongrel population that should be confined at all costs, stacked up in tower blocks and further walled in, if at all possible, by the green belt.

To take up the cause of the countryside now must also be to grasp it as it really stands: i.e., not against urban life but in defining relation with it. This will certainly mean making the most of the fact that the State and government, far from always being an encroaching monster, can be an instrument of rural conservation and development rather than just its enemy.

It also means that if we are going to campaign for 'local distinctiveness' we should conceive it not as a fully achieved historical identity, but as a contemporary quality, historically formed but also open to the present and future. Without that we will have little more than relics on the one hand, and self-conscious whimsy of the sort associated with bad public art on the other: quirky indulgences which, in the absence of any serious cultural ground, will seem arbitrary and self-indulgent.

Some of those old veterans I have been discussing knew this very well. It was surely in this spirit that Ian Nairn once remarked that 'To re-use a palace as the town's post office is better than turning it into a museum'.† A similar point was made by Wilfrid Hiley, a forest economist, later employed at Dartington Hall, who was among those who defended the Forestry Commission in the early 1930s. As he wrote, 'The danger of "preservation" is that in killing the disease it will also kill the patient and that the relics of the countryside, duly and reverentially embalmed will be preserved as a mummy for the admiration of future tourists'.‡ He added, 'In contrast to the mummification of the country is the intensification of its vitality,

---

* Germaine Greer, 'Natural Born Killers', *Observer*, 1 March 1998, p. 25.

† Ian Nairn, 'Counter-Attack', *Architectural Review*, December 1956.

‡ W. E. Hiley, *Improvement of Woodlands* (London, 1931).

which comes from the vigorous pursuit of rural industries.' Hiley may now seem to have been over-enthusiastic about industry as well as pine trees, but he was surely right to insist that mummification is not the answer to the problems of the countryside. The revitalisation that is possible in our time is also more tolerant of tourism. Indeed, it recognises that the countryside is defined by diverse perspectives, some being more indigenous or agricultural, and others – equally legitimate – reflecting the urban interest.

And what of nature? Rather than viewing the city as an aberration against nature, we might consider a point once made by Stephen Jay Gould. For this evolutionary biologist, nature is about variety above all, and it finds its correlative more in the hubbub and mix of the city than in the intensively farmed countryside. Generations of romantic pastoralists may have condemned the city as a great wen, but Gould is full of enthusiasm for those densely populated urban areas where worlds intersect on the street corner, where nothing can with absolute certainty be fixed to a single meaning, and where discontinuity rather than ancient settlement is the norm. As a resident of a large, more or less suburban village in East Anglia I see daily evidence that even the wildlife – the birds as well as the foxes – are learning to find this urbanised form of nature more congenial. 'Biodiversity' seems to be moving into the villages and towns, leaving the fields to the monocultural subsidy farmers. Fortunately not all farmers are like that, even in East Anglia, a fact that brings me back to our local greengrocer. He has just bought 12.5 acres of arable land from the council farm on which he was brought up and he assures me, without any reference at all to Maurice Dobb, that he is going to re-establish it as a proper English wood.

3. *Heritage, Tradition and Modernity*
Robert Grant

About fifteen years ago, as paying members of the public, my family and I visited a much-altered, somewhat decrepit country house built in a ramshackle and not particularly tasteful medley of historical periods. It did not belong to the National Trust, but was evidently still in the full possession of the family who had owned it for a couple of centuries, and possibly (I forget) even from its William and Mary beginnings. The grounds were pleasant enough, with some handsome oaks and cedars, but inside the paint was flaking, the panelling was worm-eaten and the plasterwork and gilt were everywhere falling off.

Presided over by the elderly chatelaine, who was dishing out admission tickets from a small table, the large entrance hall looked exactly as if a jumble sale were in progress, though in fact it was a (presumably) permanent exhibition of family heirlooms, loose dog-eared photographs, domestic junk and even superannuated kitchen equipment. All was mixed up indiscriminately and displayed on trestle tables, with rough handwritten slips safety-pinned to the exhibits to the effect that (for example) this was the Hon. Mary X's christening robe in 19— when the Prince of Y stood godfather to her, and that was her brother Lord Z's bassinet, etc. The stairs up to the former servants' quarters were lined with yellowing prints. Some had gone missing, leaving pale rectangles where they had hung. A notice accused the visiting public of having stolen them, and threatened to close the back stairs if the thefts continued.

All this had a crazy, defiant, even heroic charm, with a strong imprint of personality upon it, but it was also not unlike a beggar (albeit an exceedingly proud one) displaying his sores. And indeed it was plain that the whole performance was only being put on, and reluctantly, for money.*
Unlike a typical National Trust property, the house undeniably recorded

---

* I do not mean, of course, for profit, but simply to defray some of the enormous expense of owning such a place.

an existing way of life (and also contained some haphazard evidence of an earlier and superior one), but not (I should say) one greatly worth preserving, nor, on reflection, very dignified. 'Come and see the aristocracy on its last legs' is not an appealing slogan.

What are people seeking when they pay to view such, or indeed other and dissimilar, relics of a past that is usually not (so to speak) 'theirs', sometimes not even real (e.g. 'Arthurian' Tintagel), and at other times not even truly past? What, if anything, links the spectacle just described with (take a deep breath) the Tower of London, Strawberry Hill, Saltaire, Cornish teas, the *Cutty Sark*, Laura Ashley, Blenheim Palace, Georgette Heyer, the Chamber of Horrors, New Lanark, Past Times (the knick-knacks company), the Victoria & Albert Museum, Mackintosh's Quality Street, the British Museum, Stephenson's *Rocket*, Mr Kipling's Exceedingly Good Cakes, Spielberg's *Amistad*, Strachey's *Eminent Victorians*, reproduction furniture, the family album, Durham Cathedral, *Brideshead Revisited*, the Campaign for Real Ale? And how precisely, apart from those things all having some connection with or allusion to the past – straight, ironical or opportunist as may be – are we to distinguish them from (say) Habitat, the Pompidou Centre, this year's holiday snaps, *EastEnders*, Jennifer's Diary, Graceland, the London Planetarium, the rest of Madame Tussaud's (including a wax Sir Elton John), the Royal Academy's *Sensation* exhibition, Washington's NASA museum, a David Attenborough wildlife TV series, New York's MOMA, *Hello!* magazine, Channel 4's *Eurotrash*? Does it make any difference whether we take our moral and existential bearings from, or in relation to, a real or imagined past, as opposed to a real or imagined present? And in either case, in what way do we do so? Sentimentally, cynically, or in some more realistic, creatively engaged fashion?*

Two or three centuries ago people were not greatly preoccupied with the past. They simply took it for granted. Nor were they with the present, except in a rough-and-ready way, born of the recognition that it was here and ineluctable. Even as recently as the Arts and Crafts period well-heeled, educated people would throw out or give to the servants their everyday

---

* An exceptionally complex and witty attitude to the past, at once ironic and genuinely affectionate, is displayed in Grant Wood's famous 1930 painting *American Gothic* (in the Art Institute of Chicago). Irony predominates in his later *tour de force* of 1939, *Parson Weems' Fable* (Amon Carter Museum, Fort Worth), which both illustrates George Washington's biographer Mason Locke Weems's story of the cherry tree and represents it as invention. The infant Washington, outrageously, wears the head of the elderly statesman as seen on dollar bills.

Chippendale or Hepplewhite, and replace it with something new and often (to modern eyes) grotesquely inferior. Beautiful Georgian buildings were pulled down without a thought or a qualm, and equally jerry-built but ugly Victorian substitutes run up in their stead. What has happened, that today even comparatively ill-heeled and uneducated people care about these things, to judge at least by their appetite for viewing whatever survives from before they were born?

We might ask first why people want to view anything at all. At the lowest level there are prurience, compulsive scopophilia and even (since nature abhors a vacuum) sheer intellectual vacancy. (The emergency services could not reach the scene of the 1972 Staines air disaster because of traffic jams caused by sightseeing motorists.) Then there are curiosity and wonder. A glimpse of other worlds produces a sensation, and sometimes the reality, of mental enlargement. For various reasons people enjoy contemplating lives different from their own, including animals'. The most important are the desire to identify oneself, or at least empathise, with other lives; and its near-antithesis, the desire to define oneself by contrast with them.* The only appeal of the Chamber of Horrors for normal people is the reflection that we, thank God, no longer do such things, and our lively revulsion ensures that we continue not to do so.

In proportion as the self has (as we shall see) historically waxed in importance, so too have the things out of which, and upon which, it is constructed. For the most part those belong to the past, since what one is, and thinks of oneself as being, extends well beyond the present moment; whereas the future, though it also does so, bears no stamp of reality until it too is past.

Our collective past matters to us even more than our individual. For what I am individually depends upon what I am and have been for others, and vice versa. Each of us is literally an idiosyncrasy, a unique synthesis of many overlapping social relationships, all of which are in debt to a past, either having developed gradually from nothing or having some definite, agreed starting point. And this is true even of people of revolutionary epochs, for whom the past that is repudiated (*their* Chamber of Horrors) is every bit as important to their self-conception as their envisaged future. The question in all cases, however, is 'Which past?' The past which 'really

---

* Both desires were satisfied simultaneously by that admirable bygone spectacle, the chimpanzees' tea party.

happened'? The documented past? The remembered past? The reputed or mythical past? Which of these pasts is centrally constitutive of our identity?

There is a sense in which, for the historian, the past does not and indeed *must* not matter. Other than in his disinterested concern for truth and his self-respect in maintaining it, his self-conception is not involved, nor ought it to be. But the past that really matters to us, just because it matters, cannot be an object of disinterested judgement. Some of it may not be historical at all, but fabulous, mythical or supposititious. However much or little of it 'really happened', this past exists purely to serve present purposes. It no more needs to be 'true' than the Trojan War, though it will not serve its purpose properly, perhaps, unless it is believed, or at least half believed, to be authentic. It is a practical, ideological, consolatory and solidarity-inducing past: an anthology of moral and political *exempla* (some doubtless genuinely useful), a storehouse of warnings, injunctions, exhortations and reassurances, a summons to action, pride or lethargy as may be. In short, it is a reservoir of motivation. It gives us, all of us, a reason why we exist and a reason to continue in existence.

Particularly when embodied in buildings, landscapes, museum collections and the like, this practical past is often called 'heritage'. Heritage is now the subject, not only of a government department (lately renamed 'Culture'), but also of a major industry whose output ranges from the scholarly and refined (preservation societies and their publications, a good many traditional galleries and museums) to the vulgar, meretricious and emptily nostalgic (costume drama for its own sake, almost any Hollywood film set more than about half a century earlier than its manufacture, almost anything to do with Disney, advertising's idea of 'tradition',* any past whose marketability depends on its being sentimentalised or turned into a version of the present).†

At the highbrow end of this spectrum we are evidently dealing with something like genuine historical interest, where the past is cultivated, and things preserved, for their own or (the same thing) curiosity's sake. One might see an interest in aesthetic quality as part of this general impulse, were it not that many such things – bygone kitsch, 1960s council tower

* At Safeway, the label 'Heritage' denotes a superior grade of meat; at B&Q, a simulated mahogany shelving system.

† No past, or indeed present, is more easily sentimentalised than the rural, or less easily forgiven for turning out to be different, as the confrontation between the government and the Countryside Alliance shows. As for 'history made present', TV's *Blackadder* was a kind of anarchic spoof on 'heritage' in this sense, albeit with a hefty dose of *1066 and All That* thrown in.

blocks, instruments of torture, the South Bank – have *only* historical interest; unless (as I have already suggested concerning instruments of torture) we also preserve them as examples of what we now wish to dissociate ourselves from. And indeed the heritage industry can trace the respectable side of its pedigree back beyond even the Society of Antiquaries (founded 1707) to seventeenth-century antiquarians' concern for ecclesiastical buildings threatened by the Civil War.* The idea that the past is interesting and valuable in itself, rather than aesthetically, or for any particular bearing it may have on our immediate business, has obvious affinities with another activity which emerged in something like its modern form about the same time, namely science.

The popular craze for heritage is more than a century and a half old.† Thanks to steam power, the early Victorian period saw a vastly increased supply of 'heritage', via cheap books and pamphlets (for information), and cheap, rapid travel (for sightseeing). We cannot know whether there was a latent popular demand for 'heritage' before this time. It seems possible that there was, however, if only because something like it (the Grand Tour, eighteenth-century Gothick) already existed and had found expression at more exalted socio-economic levels. At all events, the heritage craze evidently satisfies a quasi-perennial need. Its comparative newness, and its huge scale in the present century, suggest not so much that the need for identity which it appears to supply was wholly novel, but that its growth has been proportionate to the declining ability of something else to supply that same need.

Heritage, let us hazard, is a response, in all probability a justified, even necessary, response, to modernity. Further, if modernity's central features, secularisation and rationalisation, seem regularly to provoke it and similar responses, heritage as a concept may actually be *characteristic* of modernity. The modern age is marked by the gradual and increasing dissolution of historic certainties and of a sustaining, overarching, authoritative framework of belief. To be sure it has its own beliefs and certainties, but they tend to be physical rather than moral and spiritual, which is the kind of certainty that people most need and seek. Along with the fading of collective certainties goes that of the collective dimension generally, and an increasing individualism, fragmentation and social atomisation.

* See David Lowenthal, *The Heritage Crusade and the Spoils of History* (New York and London, 1996), p. 24.
† See Peter Mandler, *The Fall and Rise of the Stately Home* (New Haven and London, 1997), ch. 1 ('The Victorian Idea of Heritage').

There is no reversing these tendencies, so it is idle to deplore them. In any case they are not all deplorable. (They are the consequence, or obverse side, of a freedom we have mostly come to value.) But we should note what they point to, which is the loss, not so much of a past, but of a confident, unselfconscious, tradition-saturated *present*. What has disappeared in three centuries of modernisation, and especially in the last, is the sense that meaning simply lies to hand, a fund of cultural capital on which all may draw freely. We are speaking here really of a kind of practical knowledge that is neither amenable to rationalisation nor reducible to mere technique. (It involves a knowledge, not merely of means, but of ends too. Those may be hard to specify, though Aristotle made a convincing attempt in his account of *phronêsis* or 'practical wisdom'.) Faced with the ceaseless and almost meaningless multiplication of 'options', we no longer know quasi-instinctively what to think, how to behave, what to feel, how to paint, compose or build. What passes for 'style' nowadays, in fact, in art as in conduct, is rootless improvisation, or the lack of any true style. (The last 'genuine' architectural and decorative style, it seems to me, was so-called Art Deco.)*

In consequence we no longer know who we are, and are driven to rediscover (or reinvent) ourselves by reference to the (or a) past. Where once the past was mostly tacit, embodied unconsciously in a current way of life (that is, in the then present), it now has self-consciously to be reconstituted. (Religious fundamentalism, founded on an outright rejection of modernity, is a parallel.) And in its reconstituted form, preserved in aspic, it is forbidden ever to change, as it was not when alive. Heritage is frozen tradition. In fact, the whole point about heritage – or at least the past with which the popular heritage industry concerns itself – is not that it is 'threatened', but that it is already effectively dead, and thus beyond any possibility of the change which might have enabled it to survive.

This mummifying of things classified as 'heritage' denies them any new or continued life, at least on the old terms. If I own and inhabit an historic building, I cannot alter it, as I once could, to suit my and my family's needs.

---

* Art Deco had its own vocabulary, order and discipline, so that, unlike (e.g.) Art Nouveau at its tasteless worst, it contained intrinsic canons of 'rightness' and 'wrongness'. Further, though it was new, drawing heavily on comparatively exotic styles (Aztec, Egyptian, Assyrian, etc.), it bore a perceptible relationship to existing styles. Finally, it showed ample possibilities of further development and transformation. It is not clear what killed it off, though the opulent lifestyles, such as the world of ocean liners, which it embellished at its grandest (though it also influenced cinemas and suburban interiors) disappeared with the Second World War.

(For that reason, 'listing' is among the surest of ways to convert a house from a home into a museum.) Of course it is right that I should not be able (unlike Margot Beste-Chetwynde in *Decline and Fall*) simply to raze it to the ground or completely transform it, especially if it is of any aesthetic merit, since we all acquire some kind of interest in a house in virtue of its being a public, visual object. It contributes to the shared landscape or townscape, to our common mental furniture, and to that of future generations. But even the things we preserve in aspic bear the marks of their own previous, practical and changeful history, so long as they are allowed to do so and are not deliberately 'done up' into some notionally pristine state. (There is perhaps an analogy with the now rather dated fashion for 'authentic' musical performance.) The object of such refurbishments may often partly be to erase all 'impure' accretions and with them the evidence that what is now 'heritage' was once a self-supporting, ongoing form of life.

A feature of heritage, at least in Britain, is that the past it seeks to preserve or (more accurately) commemorate is very largely aristocratic: great houses, art collections and the like. This is perhaps not so surprising: the aristocracy, after all, were best placed to afford and commission beautiful things, whose brilliance also served, perhaps not unreasonably, to legitimise their position. It is true, and important, that we also have stone circles, morris dance societies, folk museums, listed industrial buildings and even the odd listed post-war prefab; but, strangely, most of what the popular mind esteems as heritage is exactly what, while the aristocratic order which created and sustained it retained its political authority, emergent popular democracy most resented and did its highly successful best, through death duties and the like, to destroy.[*]

I suggested earlier that whatever qualifies as 'heritage' is not so much 'threatened' as already dead; but one might add that a major threat to any institution, artefact or way of life, indeed its likely death sentence *as a going concern*, is precisely a preservation order. We have already seen this in the case of listed buildings. Officially to designate anything as 'heritage' is indirectly to expropriate its owner, since ownership consists of nothing else than rights of disposition and use, which listing, preservation orders, the need for export licences and the rest restrict. It may be that one's literal inheritance is threatened by nothing so much as the heritage industry.

But a problem arises here, namely, of whose inheritance, or heritage, are

[*] See Mandler, *Fall and Rise*, pp. 160 ff. ('Radicalism against Heritage, 1885–1905').

we speaking? Who is this 'one'? How and why are the citizens of a modern democracy entitled to consider the property of merely some among their number (in this case, their former rulers), and more particularly its aesthetic qualities. and historical significance, as somehow belonging to and embodying the values of all? In what sense is it 'ours' as well as (or possibly rather than) 'theirs'? The answer, I take it, must involve saying, or at least asking, just what makes a society more than a random, arbitrary collocation of individuals or classes.

In a society which is no more than that, individuals or classes will very likely be nakedly antagonistic. The wealth of the haves will be taken from them just so soon as the have-nots have acquired sufficient power, even though the said wealth may amount to virtually nothing when redistributed (or be wasted if nationalised). But what is not so easy to see is why, in our rather different society, the erstwhile have-nots and their more affluent descendants should have wished to conserve the splendour which that wealth once supported, not in order to trick themselves or their leaders out with it and so (like the rebel Jack Cade, in Shakespeare's hilarious account) to glorify their own newly acquired power, but for something very like its own sake.

Perhaps we can come at an answer by considering the restoration of public buildings, or (even if the buildings in them were private) public spaces, destroyed by war or violence. The old Gothic town square in Brussels was levelled by Louis XIV as a punishment for some delinquency or other on his neighbours' part, and promptly, as an act of defiance, rebuilt by them exactly as it was (and now is). A similar case is Warsaw Old Town, razed to the ground by the Nazis. Mercers' Hall was destroyed by the Luftwaffe but meticulously reconstructed after the war. And after some witless post-modernist suggestions that, like the Windsor Castle fire, the Bishopsgate bomb was a heaven-sent (or rather IRA-sent) opportunity, it has finally been decided that St Ethelburga's should be rebuilt.

Generally, where the destruction has been deliberate and hostile, the decision to restore things exactly has been uncontroversial. It has been seen not merely as understandable, but also as a positive point of pride. It is, in fact, a political act, and a reaffirmation of communal identity. This would obviously make less psychological sense in the case of accidental destruction, for example by fire, though both Windsor Castle and the National Trust's Uppark have in fact been reconstructed.*

---

* Another curiosity: the Windsor Castle post-modernisers were evidently moved in part by the idea

Something similar lay behind the cult of antiques, and antique lifestyles, in the Communist bloc. Just as they frequently maintained their parents' and grandparents' religion, people surrounded themselves with pre-Communist furniture and knick-knacks, either inherited, or purchased at considerable expense, in order to keep alive, in private, the culture and its attendant values which Communism had banished from the public sphere. One Czech dissident I know of wore ninetenth-century aesthete's garb at home; while according to a newspaper report there were in the 1980s young Russians who collected portraits of Nicholas II, worshipped in Orthodox churches, and, with superb pathos, decked themselves out in Tsarist officers' uniforms.

Such cases may seem to resemble 'heritage', but, in their spontaneity and unorganised, unofficial character, they bore witness to an inheritance which was still very much alive and functioning, and kept so by a determined act of will. (It also has to be said that under Communism, the forces inimical to culture were much more obvious, and in a sense easier to oppose despite the penalties, than they are in modern liberal democracies.) It may be, as I have suggested, that our own 'heritage' is by comparison effectively dead (i.e. is literally a museum piece), but it is still not impossible to take a broadly positive view of it, or at any rate of some of the motives behind it.

Apart from the general reflections offered earlier concerning everyone's need for a past, there are two main reasons, I think, why the heritage industry, for all its faults, flourishes among us. As already suggested, one is that the public at large regards the former ruling class's aesthetic legacy as being in some sense its own property too. That is to say, the popular view of the matter repeats the one traditionally offered by the rich and grand in defence of their privilege, that they were in effect trustees of a national inheritance. The National Trust and the like, on this view, took them at their word as far as national inheritance went, while offering to relieve them of the trusteeship, which had often, independently of tax, and except for the very rich, become a genuine burden.* The process has an almost

---

that, as the monarch's residence, the Castle is in some sense a showcase for national culture. If, as in the past, Uppark had been in private hands and burnt, it might very likely have been rebuilt in a more modern style without anyone's minding. But since it was already a museum, whose object was to display a given past style, all that it made any sense to do was reconstruct it exactly.

* For example, the change in women's opportunities in consequence of the First World War, together with increasing industrial employment for both sexes, resulted in vastly higher wages for domestic servants (a pattern repeated after the Second World War). At the same time (until the introduction of subsidies) agriculture continued its long decline, which had begun with the repeal of the Corn Laws and got worse after 1874. According to Mandler the income on many estates fell by more

exact parallel in the democratisation of politics. And the second reason is that many owners of these 'national' treasures seemed to have failed in their trusteeship. Every obituary I saw of the late (and middle-class) James Lees-Milne retailed his famous story of how he came to divert the National Trust's attention from landscapes and coastlines (its original remit) to country houses, as a result of seeing his drunken host at Rousham vandalising his own pictures and statues for his guests' amusement.[*] Matthew Arnold, albeit amiably enough, referred to the English upper class as the Barbarians.

We all have our favourite National Trust horror stories: houses stripped of the random but vital clutter of generations and done up in 'authentic' Germolene pink; the tourist-tat shops selling not local but Ye Olde honey mass produced at the opposite end of the British Isles; the Trust's meanness to other heritage organisations and its extortionate prices for lending transparencies or items for temporary exhibitions; the ridiculous and prohibitive conservation requirements often attached to such loans; and so on. Such tales can often be outdone by municipal heritage ventures. Here, so far from encouraging nostalgia, 'heritage' may be used to thrust politically correct history down visiting schoolchildren's throats, so that, for example, the dairy, kitchen or laundry of a once-great house will sport notices descanting in patronising baby-talk on the iniquities of past domestic service, the latter often being represented by life-size papier-mâché mannequins engaged *in situ* upon some supposedly degrading task.

Having said all that, though, one has to ask what the alternative was and is. In the late nineteenth century the new Radical contingent in politics, and the tax measures Liberal governments had to introduce in order to retain its support, did a very great deal to make the 'great house' unviable. But that kind of militant, unapologetic egalitarianism, together with straightforwardly confiscatory tax regimes, has been on the wane for a couple of decades now. It seems likely, moreover, that, even without estate duty and the rest, the rise of manufacturing the decline of agriculture and the drift to the cities would have doomed, not this or that individual establishment, but the country house as (what it was at its best, barbarians notwithstanding) a culture and a serious way of life. The latter is surely beyond resurrection. One reason among many is that the high culture

---

than half in the last quarter of the nineteenth century (*Fall and Rise*, p. 118).

[*] James Lees-Milne, *Another Self*, pp. 93–5; quoted in Lowenthal, *Heritage Crusade*, p. 25, and Mandler, *Fall and Rise*, p. 302.

which the country house underpinned owed its seriousness partly to the fact that those who had it also ruled and understood the responsibilities of rule. So far as high culture exists at all now, it is politically marginal, like the class which once supported it, while prime ministers play host to loutish pop musicians and deservedly get insulted by them in return.

Those owners who did not want simply to sell up and quit could either make their property over to the National Trust whilst continuing to live in it out of sight, either as custodians or not, or themselves turn it over to a tourist attraction, in a manner which has become familiar since the 1950s, with or without zoos, safari parks, funfairs and the rest. The latter are obviously no contribution to 'heritage', but the revenue from them certainly supports it. And even without them, it is amazing what the public will pay to see, as the example with which I began this essay shows.

We seem to be stuck with 'heritage' *faute de mieux*. Ben Jonson's Penshurst and Marvell's Appleton House were largely poetic fictions, though none the worse for that. They have gone, and so has the more plausible and better documented world of the Victorian country (and town) house. In his brilliant elegy, 'Ancestral Houses', even that staunch supporter of aristocracy W. B. Yeats doubts whether the great house was ever more than an idyll ('Mere dreams! Mere dreams!'). On the other hand, he says, the imaginative ideal it stood for was real, for

> . . . Homer had not sung
> Had he not found it certain beyond dreams
> That out of life's own self-delight had sprung
> The abounding, glittering jet; though now it seems
> As if some marvellous empty sea-shell flung
> Out of the obscure dark of the rich streams,
> And not a fountain, were the symbol which
> Shadows the inherited glory of the rich.

In a sea-shell one hears as something external, the sea, what is only the amplified whisper of one's own blood. Maybe 'heritage' is an analogous phenomenon. Some of it, doubtless, is phoney, debilitating and exploitative. But there is no reason why, any more than anything else, 'heritage' should be entirely of a piece. So far as the rest and the best of it answers to a real need, it should engage our sympathy. It shows great generosity in the modern democratic public that, so far from resenting as monuments to oppression the beauty and high culture of a past aristocratic age (as many contemporary authorities would have them do), they still (and rightly) attribute to those things a universal, class-independent value. (Just as the bygone aristocracy would and did attribute such a value to classics of popular culture such as Bunyan, Dickens and Verdi.) In this respect, from its prehistory in Carlyle, Ruskin, Morris and the Mechanics' Institutes to the post-war Attlee government, Old Labour's cultural thinking, to the effect that 'nothing's too good for the workers', was humane, enlightened and right.

Our current masters, however, seem to think that, from Oasis to the Millennium 'Experience' (sc. Dome) and *powerhouse::uk*,* nothing can be too banal, or ephemeral, for any of us. And it is important to see that, whether intentionally or not, and although ostensibly backward-looking, the vulgar, ersatz, chocolate-box side of the heritage industry (i.e. commercialised 'heritage' in all its forms) could well work in exactly the same way and to the same end, by effectively crowding out our real, live traditions. Without traditions we lack the power to make our own lives and to resist those who, by 'rebranding the nation', would rather impose theirs. Furthermore, political propagandists and media manipulators can easily use the manifest fraudulence and tastelessness of fake heritage to discredit as 'outmoded' our genuine inheritance, as if all were indeed of a piece. Among much else that is under threat, that means precisely those real, live traditions of law and government, on which our freedom, together with our sanity and self-respect, depends, and the ceremonial forms in which they are rationally and authentically embodied.

* The double colon, we are told, represents a nation 'fizzing with ideas'.

4. *Ozymandias on the Solway*

David Hayes

This too is the last of England. The Solway estuary west of Carlisle is a desolate place of salt marshes, migratory birds, industrial relics and imperial ambitions. The Roman wall reached its limit at Maia (Bowness today), part of a defensive system that stretched forty miles down the coast. African legionnaires were here a millennium before the Normans. The Brythonic (Welsh) kingdoms of Rheged and Strathclyde straddled both sides of this narrow firth. Norse settlers from Ireland and the Isle of Man spread through the region. The expansion of Northumbria led to new forms of cultural synthesis, as the Anglo-Scandinavian stone crosses at Gosforth and Dearham indicate. The Scots held sway when the Domesday Book was being compiled elsewhere, and contested the area for two centuries after the arrival of the Normans. In the nineteenth century, a canal and railway built by Irish labour attempted to link Carlisle with the sea. The past of this 'corner of a corner of England', to adapt Hilaire Belloc, 'is infinite and can never be exhausted'.[*]

It is also part of the oldest political frontier in Europe. This is the only terrain where the lines of demarcation of second-century empire and medieval statehood coincide. There is much of the contingent and disjunctive in this. The northern campaigns of Agricola included a famous victory at Mons Graupius (AD 81), and Antonine's earth wall (AD 143) sought security at the Forth–Clyde isthmus. But the Tyne–Solway line 'was to prove the best location for a frontier that could be found'.[†] A shared recognition of Cumbria as part of Scotland broke down in the twelfth century, amid conflicts over a much wider region. The contours of different zones of authority were not preordained, but established by power and accommodation. England was forged in history here.

The process of formation occurred over centuries among the variety of

---

[*] Cf. Patrick Wright, *The Village That Died for England* (London, 1996), pp. xv and 240.
[†] P. Salway, *The Oxford Illustrated History of Roman Britain* (Oxford, 1993), p. 121.

peoples who inhabited this territory, and in relation to those who would develop an alternative self-definition. It was also driven by the imperatives of war and resistance. The crucial landmarks of the first millennium – including battles from Catraeth (600) and Nechtansmere (685) to Brunan-burh (937) and Carham (1018) – helped to shape collective identities as well as reordering territory. The conflicts of the second millennium formed the connection between physical environment and nationhood. Borders developed not only on the land but in people's minds.

The Solway (from *sulwath* or 'muddy ford' in Norse) is now part of England's far north, remote from and unconsidered by what are significantly called its 'home counties'. The basic components of the landscape – water, farming plain, village settlement, the view of higher ground – are hardly unique. This is very much countryside, even if it would not normally be considered as 'the' countryside. In this, the Solway may be emblematic of those diverse components of England – some (Cornwall,* East Anglia, the North-East) quite sharply defined, others (the West Country, the North-West) perhaps less so, yet which all themselves subsume numerous odd corners seeming to escape easy categorisation. For the regional status of the Solway is ambiguous – a northern extension of the Lake District, a western promontory of the Borders, an eastern territory of the Irish Sea, yet not quite belonging to any. This too is the work of history. Many ambitions of power lie buried here. The Roman wall has been recycled into churches and farms, the anchorage at Skinburness (from which a large English fleet sailed north in 1296) was reclaimed by the sea, the ruined harbour at Port Carlisle is lonely evidence of industrial failure, the massive toxic weapons dump at Beaufort's Dyke is a sunken monument to military vanity.

It is another monument I have come to see today, walking around the wide expanse of Morecambe Bay, past the disused airfield at Anthorn, and on to the narrow firth that bridges two nations. Waders on the sandbanks are observed by a few twitchers with huge lenses propped up on their car windows. Some isolated farms, a lavishly friendly collie, a fresh wind in a grey sky. The seventh-century missionary St Cuthbert called this 'a land of vast solitudes'. It is indeed a bleak landscape, but on this October day not a hostile one.

The dark outline of Criffel, highest of the 'Scotch mountains' of

---

* This designation would be disputed by some Cornish nationalists.

Wordsworth's 1810 tour, is just visible over to the west. The other coastline is astonishingly close, a vivid reminder of historical intimacy. An embrace of settlement, trade and plunder across these shores is the work of centuries. The vulnerability of this land is apparent in the churches at Newton Arlosh and Burgh by Sands, which have fortified towers with walls seven feet thick. Narrow slits, turret access, space for cattle, avoidance of wood – these are sites of last-ditch survival as much as worship.

In this, the Solway unequivocally becomes borderland. To visit Appleby, Lanercost, or Hexham (whose abbey, says a panel, was 'five times sacked by the Scots, yet is still in full use for Christian worship') is to realise the relentless force of northern depredations. Many of the incursions came from waths thrown across the Solway at low tide. It is a commonplace that England's historic enemies are continental, and that the country has not been invaded since 1066. Here, the sense of the past is otherwise. In the borders, people have often had to look even further north, by necessity alert to the intentions of their neighbours. Endurance and adaptation matter here.

The raiding was never only one way, of course. The classic invasion routes to the north were along the east coast or through the Cheviots, giving access to the rich pastures of Lothian. Galloway, and the high valleys of Eskdale and Liddesdale, were always more wild and troublesome for any intruder. The northern kingdom had developed by an analogous process of conquest and coalescence among several peoples – Picts, Scots, Welsh, Angles, Norse, French. Between the ninth and the thirteenth centuries, a federative, conservative society acquired 'regnal solidarity' across a variable terrain, containing forces able to contemplate both expansion and defence of its core territory.

Dynastic uncertainty and royal ambition turned crisis into war in the 1290s, as the subjugation of Scotland became a strategic aim for England's king. Wales had been conquered with the defeat of Llwelyn ap Gruffydd in 1282, but a prolonged conflict saw Edward I's claims to overlordship in the north defied by Wallace (executed in 1305) and now Bruce. The western 'march' (border zone) was the king's line of approach in 1307, the ninth army sent to subdue the Scots in his last dozen years of power. Moving west from Carlisle with agonised slowness, Edward's army camped at Sandsfield where, weakened by dysentery, the 68-year-old king died on 7 July.

It is striking to see, just past Cardurnock, a tall flagpole with an English flag billowing. Waverley House's affirmation, or defiance, seems appropriate when the Dumfriesshire coast commands the horizon. But in Port Carlisle, an old cottage with pink roses around the door is named Scotia. The appropriation of an adversary's mystique to defuse its threat is an ancient reflex, yet this feels a long way from (kilted) Balmorality. The intertwinings of a borderland are often unexpected.

It is hard pounding through Glasson and Drumburgh along the line of the wall. A turn north at Burgh, along a rough track until, from a distance, the destination is in view.

This is the loneliest monument in England. On the very edge of the marsh, in the middle of a field of cows, a sandstone pillar of thirty feet surrounded by a fence and topped with a cross. Erected in 1685, it was rebuilt in 1803 after flooding, and restored in 1876 when subterranean peat workings had caused it to list. In this mournful setting, with the carved tribute ('Edwardi primi famam optimi Angliae regis . . .') fading and the hills beyond still indomitable, it is impossible not to think of Ozymandias.

What D. H. Lawrence called 'the spirit of place' is an idea both dangerous and (sometimes) irresistible. It is palpable that this is a monument to failure. The monarch who handed over the great seal of Scotland with the words 'A man does good business when he rids himself of a turd',* now has a memorial ringed by cowpats. It is tilting again; this is shifting ground. Iron will and sovereign power do not rest easy here.

Edward's death in the field, 'quo finit marchia regni' (says a contemporary account) imparts a dramatic character to this forlorn place. But if – beyond the contingencies of a particular encounter – any meaning does indeed inhere in this combination of stone, metal, sky and soggy grass, it surely can be discovered only by reclaiming the debatable lands of a multilayered history. English ground contains a myriad stories as real and arguable. Here again, the Solway is only one of many of the country's landscapes which tell of thwarted achievement, of contingency and possibility.

The king's body was carried to Burgh church, where a stained-glass window now depicts him in regal pose, the cross of St George resplendent on his cloak. He looks down today on the harvest festival fruits and flowers. The most common word in the visitors' book is 'peaceful'. It is a long way from Westminster Abbey.

* G. W. S. Barrow, *Robert Bruce and the Community of the Realm of Scotland*, 3rd edn (Edinburgh, 1988), p. 61. This work of humane scholarship is indispensable for the entire period.

Edward's instruction that his bones be boiled down and carried into battle until the Scots were crushed was not obeyed. The famous appellation 'hammer of the Scots' was only fixed on his Westminster tomb in the Tudor era. Now, as the artefacts and enchantments of monarchy have been marketed for tourism, the first Plantagenet king is too troublesome to be incorporated in a harmonious national narrative. There are no biopics of this gargantuan figure. Perhaps it is significant that the greatest mythologist of English history, William Shakespeare, never wrote a line about him. The sceptred isle has many mansions, but the most ruthlessly ambitious of English rulers cannot be easily accommodated. The 'full Heritage' treatment of his monument which Jo Darke warned 'would as usual annul all romance and sense of personal discovery'* must be considered improbable.

Such treatment would in addition entail violation of world and self. A belief in the present as having somehow escaped from history animates the heritage cult and the fashionable celebration of modernity alike. It is one of the most profound illusions of a mediatised world. A true engagement with history, by contrast, seeks also to understand what is living and dead from the past in order to grasp the particularity of the present. One reward of understanding is the chance of meaningful action; one difficulty in the way is that the past is not singular – it can be burden or resource, and its meanings are not static. The past also, it might be said, lives within history. Thus, for example, Edward's monument was raised on land bought from the Duke of Norfolk by the Lowther family, who as earls of Lonsdale came to wield enormous power in Cumbria for generations. (A 1777 history noted the remorseless increase of the Lonsdale estates, 'from age to age purchasing, and never selling again').† The understandings it could generate in the time of James II and Victoria, or during the Napoleonic wars, have their own integrity. An aura of royal or strategic failure may not be the most immediate. But a return to this refractory terrain in the late 1990s suggests a distinct freight of meaning from Edward's day. It is in the protean nature of history and of modern Britain that it is unlikely to be the only one.

The idea of the unification of Britain under southern leadership has deep roots. The tenth-century ruler Athelstan, as later kings of Wessex, claimed authority also over 'all the nations round about'. The Anglocentric vision,

---

* Jo Darke, *The Monument Guide to England and Wales* (London, 1991), pp. 235–6.

† Quoted in Nigel Everett, *The Tory View of Landscape* (New Haven and London, 1994), p. 168.

evolving 'an ideology of uniformity, unity and conquest'* in the twelfth
century, achieved its flowering during Edward's long reign. His vigorous
centralisation, wars of conquest, and pride in the native realm over the
fetish for Europe, brought this prospect closer. The many propagandists of
the era 'enshrined English nationalism in a confident doctrine', writes
Geoffrey Elton. 'This nationalism rested on a powerful streak of chauvinism
– of hatred for all foreigners who, it was repeatedly asserted, were battening
on the wealth and welfare of the English.'[†] The drive to unity foundered,
however. Wales and Ireland never lost their sense of difference, while
invasions of Scotland generated over time the coherence among disparate
forces necessary for successful resistance. The eventual integration of the
island had to be accomplished under another banner, and was provisional
even then.

The imposition from the south 'of an alien political authority of an
interventionist and exacting sort';[‡] a powerful leader driven 'by ambition
and circumstance to attempt too much in too many places',[§] but whose
ineffectual successor faced far greater humiliation; the cult of sovereignty,
renascent xenophobia, an expanding state, Celtic disaffection, the 'sneer of
cold command' – all these figures descended from the late thirteenth
century are deeply familiar. Their toxic efficacy in the present, however,
only emphasises how problematic the political conscription of the national
past has become.

'Of our conceptions of the past, we make a future,' wrote Thomas
Hobbes. The image of England has been often recycled to suit
contemporary needs. The confident liberalism of the mid-nineteenth
century, for which the constitutional settlement of 1688 was a touchstone,
gave way to the age of Empire and a rediscovery of Tudor autocracy and
expansion: Englishness was pushed back a century.[¶] The modern problems
of state in Britain also have a national dimension, and the historical self-
understanding of the English is again at issue. The multiple meanings of
both past and territory remain contested on the eve of the third
millennium.

* R. R. Davies, *Domination and Conquest, the Experience of Ireland, Scotland and Wales 1100–1300*
(Cambridge, 1990), p. 128.

† Geoffrey Elton, *The English* (Oxford, 1992), p. 70.

‡ Robin Frame, *The Political Development of the British Isles 1100–1400* (Oxford, 1990), p. 167.

§ B. Wilkinson, *The Later Middle Ages in England 1216–1485* (London, 1969), p. 98.

¶ Cf. Robert Colls, 'Englishness and the Political Culture', in R. Colls and P. Dodd (eds) *Englishness,
Politics and Culture 1880–1920* (London, 1987), pp. 29–61 (p. 44).

An England seeking a renewed sense of itself within, or out of, a loosening Britain cannot simply disown the periods of its largest reach. But just as British history did not begin in 1707, so that of England did not end. No nation lives outside of its own (and now world) history; to engage with this history means also to situate oneself in the present. The official ideologues who seek to promote what Kipling revealingly called a 'peptonized patriotism'* know this well. The intoxicating triumphalism of the 1980s Right was fuelled by such a narrowly instrumentalised version of the national (English-to-British) past. A timeless greatness and exceptionalism are its potent assumptions; for it, feminism or trade unionism or republicanism (and by extension their modern proponents) can only be deviations from, not integral parts of, the 'national story'. Margaret Thatcher's 1982 Cheltenham speech is the fountainhead of this vision: 'The lesson of the Falklands is that Britain has not changed.' History is frozen in the self-image of the powerful.

The exigencies of self-understanding thrown up by political transformation are also territorial. England ends at the Solway, yet this 'bow-shaped headland' (indeed the entire Borders region) has little place in the imaginative geography of the nation. The white cliffs of Dover at the opposite corner of England carry an iconographic charge – as island fortress, beacon of home, site of nostalgic longing – independent of geology and history. The core symbols of nationhood – Stonehenge, Windsor, Stratford, the Cotswolds – are not only real places but cultural artefacts, keynotes in the composition of an intellectually satisfying and lucrative narrative of national identity. Charles Townshend remarks that the dominant view of rural England 'rediscovered' in the century of industrialisation was 'largely southern in its topographical connotations' – the heart of this 'supercharged national identity' located by Kipling and Belloc even more precisely in Sussex.† 'Deep England', in Patrick Wright's pregnant phrase, is a country of the mind – evocative of the village green and thatched cottage yet not confined to any individual location – somehow more truly representative of an always-elusive essence even than (say) its fishing towns or hill farms, far less its urban streets. A nexus of interests, including tourism, reinforces an emotionally coherent symbolic

---

* Peter Keating, *Kipling, the Poet* (London, 1994), p. 174.
† Charles Townshend, *Making the Peace: Public Order and Public Security in Modern Britain* (Oxford, 1993), p. 20. Cf. also Alun Howkins, 'The Discovery of Rural England', in Colls and Dodd, *Englishness*, pp. 62–88.

ordering that is exclusive and ahistorical but also comes to acquire myriad powers of self-validation.

This league-tabling of Englishness according to layers of authenticity draws on rich resources of historical and cultural experience, but its appearance of naturalness is the work of ideology. A particular part of the nation is first mythologised, then made to stand – repeatedly, and in a multitude of contexts and associations – for the whole. The central domestic metaphor of 'home counties' and 'regions' is balanced internationally by a vision of superiority, where (in Peter Taylor's words) 'Upper England' transmutes into 'Greater England'. 'Other countries have "homelands" or "fatherlands" that encompass their whole territory. For the Anglo-British "Home" denotes only a few counties in one corner of the country.'* Between these ideational pincers the richly various landscapes and histories of the actual nation are rendered invisible or passive.

The quiet integrity of Far England, where this very particular country slides away into the Tweed or the fluctuating Burgh Marsh, has been hard won. From the perspective of the Borders, the 'lack of territorial emphasis in English sensibility'† is as significant as the reduction of its history to a few tendentious symbolic tableaux. A calm, prideful recognition of the resourcefulness of their compatriots in this austere northern landscape over many centuries, might be expected as one register of national self-awareness. It is astounding how little this note is struck. The patriotism of 'Great Englishness'‡ sees the frontiers of its own land as if from the military jets which thunder across them: in a blur. Yet the whole of England can be authentically 'englobed' through this territory as much as through its routine southern typifications. The lineaments of this englobing might include nuances of experience, memory and outlook unavailable elsewhere.§ England looks more textured from here: an area that is part of the wider borderland which encompasses its Scots neighbours, of a diffuse 'north' (for there are several 'norths' as indeed there are several 'midlands' and 'souths'), as of a broader national community. The reflex of absolute sovereignty, organicist metaphor, or sentimental rhetoric about 'the countryside' (a term invented – like so much else in Britain – in the

---

* Quoted in Richard Muir, *Political Geography* (London, 1997), p. 14.

† John Osmond, *Divided Kingdom* (London, 1988), p. 168.

‡ Cf. Anthony Barnett, *This Time: Our Constitutional Revolution* (London, 1997), ch. 9.

§ The use of this idea is borrowed from Edwin Ardener. Cf. 'The Problem Revisited', in S. Ardener (ed.) *Perceiving Women* (London, 1975), pp. 19–27.

nineteenth century), do not flourish in this often hard and conflictual environment.

The need for a more comprehensive view of England is a matter not only of scholarly accuracy or ideological preference, but a consequence of the distinctive political moment of the late twentieth century. Convulsive global changes are impacting profoundly on Britain – loss of Empire, end of Cold War, European integration, casino capitalism. One kind of response (devolutionist and regionalist pressures, Scottish and Welsh nationalism, environmentalism, constitutional reform campaigns) can be understood as a search for newly effective and legitimate forms of political community which can mediate and manage these changes. Another (unionism, constitutional conservatism, Euroscepticism) responds by seeking to revivify the central institutions and ideas which have guaranteed British state power for three centuries. The debate is inevitably concerned with the meanings of past and nation that can be an imaginative support for different political strategies. And as the challenges to the centre have gathered pace, it is understandable that the 'core nation' of Britain should itself become a contested site. For in England especially, rapid social change renders problematic inherited assumptions long experienced as natural. Beyond the passions surrounding the political mobilisation of 'the countryside' lie concerns (about farming, hunting, transport, rural economy) which enjoin a rethinking of the city/country divide. The questioning of ingrained definitions may be the fruitful precondition for real intellectual and social advance.

It is harder for the English to disentangle their national past from Britishness and to rework it creatively to meet present needs (as the Scots, Welsh and Irish have begun to do). A past that is so lengthy, prolific and versatile is also rich in possibility. But the temptation to reprise visions of closure – grandeur and elite reform, peaceful social integration, cosy rural harmony – is especially strong in periods of wrenching transformation. An English history that culminates (poetically) with *Little Gidding* or (televisually) with *Dad's Army* may also be a retreat into the imaginary safety of the past, rather than a living dialogue with it.* This form of thought will do well to incorporate 1997. The year of the anti-Tory landslide, of the Diana days, of the referenda, suggests that this old country is still moulding its

---

* Cf. Kenneth Baker, *English History in Verse* (London, 1987), p. 432; Jeffrey Richards, *Films and British National Identity* (Manchester, 1997), pp. 362–6. The argument of course is not with the rich creative works cited here but with their placing in a narrative of Englishness.

history through a healthy exploration of its shared and competing identities. The revival of the 'English question' predates these impressive events yet is given renewed focus by them. The past has rarely seemed less resolved, more alive. The real English, and British, story is one of complexity, plurality and conflict; and an open, critical and radical standpoint may be the most truthful way to explore this 'heritage'. A monument to greatness, by contrast, is designed to intimidate and disarm; but it cannot endure on hollow foundations, still less by 'fencing off the obtrusive modern world'.*

The debate over England and its countrysides is, then, a necessary dimension of the historical moment. The diverse attempts to reimagine the nation can choose to focus on a range of referents – the constitution, the English language and its literature, rural life, the regions, the urban mix – each of which can be seen to embody dense layers of experience and symbolism. But the heart of their encounter must surely address (as the Conservative Party and the Campaign for a Northern Assembly are now in different ways doing) the evacuation of politics from this once deeply political nation. An identity centred on art, music or sport can disguise but never escape from the class, power and regional realities at England's core. A form of nationalism may be an unavoidable accompaniment to a revived discourse of the political nation; and the nationalism glimpsed through the murk of post-devolution, millennial England is often qualified, even by its putative adherents, with the words ugly, nasty or crude. No outcome is predetermined. But a deeper historical, and broader regional, awareness might question whether the multifarious and tolerant people of England will meekly file into the impoverishing cloisters so often assigned to them.

Out here on the Burgh Marsh, the living strands of the Cumbrian past seem so vividly clear. Perhaps this is only another illusion of the light. A totemic status in the national landscape might prove elusive, but that tangled and regenerative process, Englishness, evolves here too. Land and machine, sword and book, stone and stained glass, most of all an enriching mixture of peoples, have shaped this area. There is much to hate here, much to forgive. But standing on this debatable ground, it is hard to believe that the kind of nationalism memorialised here can long withstand the melancholy, quietly subversive tides of the Solway.

* Wright, *The Village That Died*, p. 41.

II

The Countryside:
Myths and Realities

5. *How Beauty Can Survive*
Tony Curzon Price

Natural beauty is under threat. The ordinary tools of public policy assessment cannot protect it, nor, usually, can private property rights. So are we condemned to the (dubious) pleasures of nostalgia? Alpine valleys have precociously felt the pressures that our own areas of natural beauty will soon feel. The cultural similarity and institutional diversity of these valleys provides the 'natural experiment' for a causal account – 'Why does natural beauty *sometimes* survive?' Political processes are important, and Swiss-style participative democracy appears to be a good protector. To preserve natural beauty (and not just its memory), we would be wise to heed the lessons from the Alps.

Why We Should (But Often Do Not) Take Natural Beauty Seriously

When questions of education, employment, health or pensions occupy our political thinking, a concern for natural beauty needs a serious justification. A golf village will create *n* rural jobs, a change of land-use category raise *x* million pounds of taxes and so provide more hospitals or schools.

Is it not today callous romanticism to worry about natural beauty? No. There are two main reasons why even the hard-headed should pay attention. The first reason is that our public policy-making methods and institutions are glaringly flawed when *irreversible* decisions over *irreplaceable* goods are made. Such decisions necessarily affect all future generations. Future generations have only a very quiet voice in our political process, and even when their voice is audible, the difficulty of determining what their interests will (or should) be can too easily drown in the noise of today's interests.

The second reason is that the institution of property, often adequate to the task of turning rarity into value through preference, cannot be counted on to preserve natural beauty. Natural beauty is usually depletable and non-excludable; *depletable* because most of the ways we enjoy beauty reduce beauty – driving to a beautiful location means building roads there; living with beauty close by may mean intrusive building; visiting as a tourist adds to the crowd; *non-excludable* because it is usually difficult to restrict access to it – a landscape in the Peaks will be visible from many places; many land or house owners will be able privately to profit from the demand for it. When a good is depletable and non-excludable, individuals may profit privately by promoting its consumption and yet not control the overall rate of its consumption.

The value of preserving natural beauty is diffuse across both people and generations, whilst the monetary benefits of exploiting it can be captured by individuals who do not bear the cost of its destruction. This typically leads to overexploitation, in a process whose dénouement is now called the *tragedy of the commons*.* Common lands (and common oceans, etc.) are typically depletable and non-excludable; if *I* overgraze or overfish, I will receive some of the benefit (fatter cows, a bigger catch), and *you* will bear some of the cost (poorer-quality grazing, smaller fish stocks). 'Rational fools' will always exploit such opportunities to benefit privately from the transfer of costs to others. In a community of rational fools, goods held in common will indeed be left in a tragic state.

Lessons from the Alps

That the tragedy as applied to natural beauty is spread over a large number of people and many generations does not mean we should ignore it: it means we should aggregate it. Whilst self-centred thinking often can be transformed into a concern for the desires of others through market processes, here it leads us only to behave as if a multitude of thinly spread benefits are not benefits at all. Our aim must be to find or devise an institution which efficiently constrains those who might fall for the allure of 'rational foolishness' in such potentially tragic circumstances. The Enlightenment philosopher David Hume recommends that we should design and judge institutions under the assumption that 'every man must be supposed a knave', even if this is overly pessimistic. I hope that the institutional evaluation that follows is true to Hume's maxim: the outcomes I describe do not depend on any spontaneous public spirit, but only on the judicious

* See Garrett Hardin, 'The Tragedy of the Commons', in G. Hardin and J. Baden (eds.), *Managing the Commons*, San Francisco, 1977.

channelling of interest, power, anger and resentment. If any arrangements should also foster community (I believe that the best do, as a side-effect), then that is an added bonus.

Several parts of the world have precociously had to face similar pressures to the ones that will soon burden our countryside. These are the natural starting point in the search for lessons and appropriate institutional forms. However, the difficulty in learning from these experiences is to distinguish all the possible confounding causal factors that have led to better or worse outcomes, to decide which are accidental and which are fundamental.

The half-dozen valleys around the Mont Dolent (where the borders of France, Italy and Switzerland meet at a point, and in which, on and off, I have lived most of my life) provide an almost controlled experiment. Their inhabitants share culture, religion and tradition; they intermarry and even share language. Up to fifty years ago, they would have been largely indistinguishable. Over the past fifty years, every one of these valleys has been profoundly transformed by the demands of tourism; the valleys have prospered, but each in very different ways. The French and the Italians have, almost without exception, carpeted their valley floors with villas, chalets, apartment blocks; they have built 'amusement cities' on high plateaux (Flaine, a purpose-built resort, advertises itself as 'La ville à la montagne'); municipalities have become indebted (and often gone bankrupt) in a rush to acquire the capacity to take x thousand people per hour up the mountain.

A drive up the valley of Abondance tells the story. Abondance itself is at the limit of the skiable, so this old monastery village has become bankrupt installing lifts that are too infrequently used. (The village is currently under direct control from Paris, and at the last local elections no one even stood for office.) Nevertheless, property prices here are cheaper than at higher altitudes, so holiday-makers and tour companies do buy and build. It is fifteen kilometres from Abondance to Châtel, at the head of the valley. The road has recently been widened to ease the avant-après-ski traffic jams. Like layers in a mille-feuille, chalets, villas and blocks line the southern slopes over those fifteen kilometres. The village of Châtel merges seamlessly with all villages down-valley.

At the head of the valley, on the Pas de Morgin, is the Swiss border. After passing the first village, there are few signs of the tourist trade until Champéry, in its situation almost a mirror image of Châtel. But Champéry remains compact; old outlying farms and chalet clusters have, of course, been converted for the new tourist trade; on the outskirts of the village there are a handful of *fin de siècle* hotels in whose art deco charm one can imagine a perfect retreat, at any time of year (or life). Several huge chalets have been built inside the village – the valley lives by tourism, and this must be served. They have been built around the centre of the old *bourg*. Champéry's cemetery, in an affront to profit maximisation, remains next to the church, on a flat(-tish) southerly plot that must surely excite holidaying real-estate agents.

This drive, of course, is just an anecdote. Are there not any number of reasons why two valleys should develop so differently, and serve different segments of the tourism market? Yes. But what *is* remarkable is that with great consistency, it is the Swiss villages and valleys that have conserved the beauty of their environment, whilst in France and Italy similar locations have developed into sprawling amusement parks. Nor are these amusement parks obviously more privately profitable than the Swiss alternative, where the premium on quality is still sufficient to make incomes there significantly higher than over the borders. The French and Italians never *decided* to cater for mass tourism, they simply discovered that this was all they could provide. Ask today's inhabitants of Châtel whether they would prefer to have managed the tourist boom as was done over the border; most would say yes.

Swiss villages, it seems, have resolved the tragedy of the commons, whereas in France and Italy it will soon be too late to reverse it. Can we usefully learn from these valleys how our rural beauty might be conserved? Given the similarities of culture, religion and history (up to 100 years ago, at least), why is it *borderlines* that divide these communities' responses to increased demands on their environments?

Nationally specific differences that do not depend on culture or tradition are needed for an explanation. Here are two candidate hypotheses: the general context of economic development in the three countries since 1945; and the differing political institutions of the three countries.

The first hypothesis has a superficial plausibility: Swiss tourism is largely an export, which must be bought by foreigners with traditionally expensive Swiss francs; so the Swiss villages are forced to provide a high-quality service to compensate for high prices. There are many things wrong with this argument, but the most relevant flaw in it is the following: if villages are indeed providing a high-quality service, then the temptation for a single individual to over-profit from this will be all the greater. (A real-estate developer, for example, could do this by providing a lower-quality service, at a lower price. This service nevertheless captures some of the non-excludable benefits of all others' provision of a high-quality service, such as beauty, environmental quality, 'cachet', and so on.) In other words, if true at all, it would only make it more remarkable that the Swiss have avoided the tragedy of the commons.

The hypothesis that political institutions play a determining role is much more plausible. In the following analysis, I borrow greatly from an unpublished study by Professor Ricq of the University of Geneva of the development and institutions of three municipalities – Champéry (Switzerland), Les Houches (France) and Saint Rhémy (Italy). Unfortunately, the Italian village is not entirely comparable to the other two in terms of its level of tourist development. My argument is that the Swiss institutions of participative democracy can be credited with avoiding the potential tragedy of the commons, and conversely, that the (poorly) representative system of local government in France has exacerbated the problem.

Here, schematically, are the formal workings of local government in Les Houches and Champéry:

Les Houches, France
- Every six years, a nineteen-member assembly is elected; this is the legislature.
- The legislature elects amongst its members a mayor and five deputies; this body is the executive.
- As has happened in all our representative democracies, the executive formulates policy, which is discussed (but usually rubber-stamped) by the legislature.
- Meetings of the legislature and executive are not open to the public.
- Since decentralisation (1984), higher levels of government have no power of oversight in the areas of local government competence, although municipalities are controlled in the types and amounts of tax they can levy, and (less successfully) the indebtedness they may contract.

Champéry, Switzerland
- The municipality itself has the responsibility to choose its political process (within guidelines set by the canton).
- Every four years, the citizens elect a seven-member municipal council

(amongst whom is the council president; only the president and a clerk are remunerated).

- The legislature, or primary assembly, is made up of every voting member of the population.
- The municipal council proposes policy, which the legislature (i.e. every citizen) must vote on before it is put into effect (rubber-stamping is clearly difficult here!).
- The bourgeoisie (i.e. those native to Champéry) constitute another assembly, the Commune Bourgeoisiale. This body elects a burghers' council (this council's relationship to its assembly is the same as for the municipal council), whose responsibilities are primarily to propose and execute public infrastructure projects (*tâches d'intérêt public*).
- Many aspects of municipal policy are subject to oversight at the cantonal level, but the federal level protects the principle of municipal autonomy – the competences of the various levels of government are governed by a strictly applied subsidiarity principle, which allows municipalities, among other things, a great deal of fiscal autonomy (for example, they can set local income tax and borrow money).

Even from this brief description one can start to feel the impact these institutional differences might make: local government in Champéry is very close to the citizens, whereas in Les Houches it is more distant; the executive in Les Houches thus has more autonomy from the electors, but may more easily alienate them – in Champéry, once elected, you are likely to be re-elected and stay in post for fifteen to thirty years; not since 1955 in Les Houches has a mayor completed two successive terms. Direct democracy will *allow* consensual decisions to emerge: projects are publicly discussed before being returned to the executive. In French local democracy, on the other hand, it is very likely that grievances will be overlooked by the municipal council, as long as sufficiently tailored special interest benefits are appended to policy. In Les Houches, a mayor will need to strike deals amongst a few councillors for policy to proceed; in Champéry, special pleading must be done in public. The Commune Bourgeoisiale is an institutional recognition that (even at the level of a village) it is important to recognise the different claims and responsibilities of different groups. The Commune Bourgeoisiale is composed of families who have lived in Champéry many years, and of 'newer', but non-transient residents. Public infrastructure is thus largely decided by those with a long-term commitment (both emotional and financial) to the village.

One of the most important decisions that a council makes, both in terms of the 'game' of local politics and for our particular concern with beauty, is to determine a land-use plan. The formal process in the two villages is as follows.

Les Houches, France
- Before developing a land-use plan, the municipality may use its powers to redistribute landholdings; it may also use its right of pre-emption on all property sales, and its own portfolio of property to influence who benefits from changes in the land-use plan.
- The mayor and his deputies prepare a land-use plan with the help of the regional government.
- The municipal council deliberates, and, after modification (if any), the plan is submitted to a public inquiry for a minimal period of one month.
- Affected parties can register complaints, which the municipal council debates and may take into account.
- Final approval is given by the municipal council.
- Individual building permits are granted by the mayor.

Champéry, Switzerland
- If the councillors wish to make any changes to the land-use plan, they inform the legislature (the citizens), who have sixty days to respond (in writing if they wish).
- After sixty days, the proposed change is passed up to the cantonal authorities, who check it for consistency with cantonal regulations (matters of public safety, for example).
- If approved, the modified plan is then put under public scrutiny for thirty days.
- The primary assembly (all citizens, in Champéry) votes on the project.
- Individual building permits are granted by the primary assembly.

Once again, even at the level of the formal process, it is easy to see the gulf between land-use planning in Les Houches and Champéry. In the Swiss village, individual citizens are called on three times to participate and approve policy on new building (four if one counts the building permits);

in Les Houches, a single (short, complicated and non-binding) consultation suffices. Moreover, the French municipality has an array of powers that make it a direct actor in the real-estate market.

That there is a land-use planning process at all is a recognition that decisions in this area impact on more than just the private parties to them, that there are non-excludable effects of policy (that there is a tragedy to be avoided). But what is it in these two processes that makes one of them suited to mitigating the tragedy of the commons but not the other? How do political institutions mediate and filter the conflicting interests at the heart of the tragedy?

Consider first the case in which there is no land-use plan at all, just property rights and a free-for-all. One landowner insensitively sells a plot, depletes the beauty and turns a private profit. Those without appropriate land, or whose livelihood depends on the beauty (hotels, restaurants . . .), may feel resentment, anger, indignation. But there is no process of recourse. Other landowners may also feel these sentiments, but as the resource depletes, the value of *all* landholdings falls (since part of their value, whether monetised or not, is dependent on the beauty). Therefore, there is an incentive to join the depleters early.

Now consider the case in which privately profiting from depletion requires the authorisation of nineteen people (in a total population of 2,000), as in Les Houches. The nineteen wield substantial power (indeed may have sought office for it), and can choose to grant authorisation for any number of reasons apart from the good management of the common resource: building political alliances, establishing quid pro quos, (even) privately profiting. Just as in the free-for-all, this breeds anger and resentment amongst those who do not have the right sort of hold over the nineteen. Of course, they can eventually vote them out of office (as happens with great regularity in Les Houches), but the damage is done. The new team of councillors will have their own (different) alliances to build, and so the damage typically spirals. Within a few political generations, there are several millionaires, an ugly agglomeration, and a village dedicated to mass tourism. The anger and resentment generated by 'free-riders' is translated into further free-riding.

Consider the case of Alain, who (unusually for his generation) has decided to work the land in his native village. The village is at low altitude, on a French mountainside close to the Swiss border – sites like this are a popular part-time residence for the (knowledge) workers of Geneva (only an hour away). Building land is at a monetary premium. The new mayor of the village embarked on a process of land redistribution combined with a new land-use plan. His (difficult) multiple objectives were to increase the amount of new building land, to secure the agreement of the municipal council, and to avoid 'sprawl'. Redistribution of land was therefore an essential policy tool: the municipal council would agree to changes of land use only if these benefited the right political coalition. But the land owned by members of this coalition could not be developed without sprawl, since it was land *in the wrong places*. With redistribution, the objectives were potentially reconcilable.

After the rather opaque consultation process, surveyors started to stake the new holdings. It was only then that Alain understood what had happened: some of his best fields (flat, sunny ones) were no longer his; others he could no longer reach with his tractor without destroying what would soon be manicured lawns. When Alain knocked on doors in the village with a petition to sign, his anger and indignation were clear. With the petition he hoped to enlist the support of the prefect (the representative of central government) to reopen the consultation process, but the mayor had done everything according to the rules – no administrative fault, no cause for reconsideration, despite the fact that the consultation process had been so opaque that few could perceive the consequences of the proposals.

Of course, the mayor's objectives were in a sense laudable: to avoid sprawl while recognising the pressures of exurbia. But the means will backfire. Alain's father had been mayor, and he has the credentials to mount a challenge to the incumbent. I think it almost certain that one day he will. Although his farm and fields will not be recoverable, he will be able to punish enemies and reward friends by tampering once again with the land-use plan.

The tragic cycle is this: a narrow group privately profits from depletion and creates resentment. Eventually, *after* some damage is done, the aggrieved gain power and use what tools they can to right the balance of justice. This usually involves the depletion of the common resource to the benefit of a *new* narrow group. And so it continues . . . It is not as if citizens commonly elect to deplete now and take the profit, it is that their institutions are very unlikely to lead to any other outcome.

What of the participative case? An individual (or coalition) attempting to profit from depletion must publicly convince a majority of citizens (the population of Champéry is 1,000). The resentment that any of us naturally feels in the face of harmful egoism will usually block a policy that greatly benefits the few *to the detriment* of the rest. And if the only way of profiting from common resources (beauty, slope, altitude) is to agree with a large number of people equally dependent on it for their livelihoods, and with whom one will need to settle this sort of issue again and again, one is much more likely to settle on policy dominated by common interest.

Conflicts continue to arise, of course. There are *real* trade-offs between preserving beauty and developing tourism (the huge chalets and ski-lifts in Champéry attest to these). There are also real conflicts that remain between generations – every child who needs to move down-valley for work is paying a price for conservation. But the institutions of representative local government in France *compound* the inherent difficulties of these trade-offs with the added, foolish logic of the commons.

The institutions of participative democracy, far from compounding these problems, may even help to solve them: care for the welfare of our children will be more likely to serve the concerns of future generations if we can be confident that *they* will not be faced with a commons tragedy; moreover, regular participation in the local public realm may foster the feelings of belonging and responsibility that are so easily destroyed by modern nomadism and 'hugeness'. The participative process is no guarantor of any particular outcome – citizens *may* freely choose the path of maximal short-term profit (although usually in Swiss villages they do not). But between an institution that permits good outcomes, and one that promotes foolish ones, the choice seems easy.

The hope of the democrat is that institutions can help to substitute 'we thinking' for 'I thinking' when appropriate. The lesson from the Alps is that the detailed nature of those institutions is important in determining the extent to which they succeed. A climate favourable to institutional experimentation is back; for the sake of natural beauty we must hope that the new designs will at the very least avoid precluding good outcomes.

6. *The Myth of Nature*
Anthony O'Hear

Many of us feel that there is something wrong with the world. More specifically we feel that there is something wrong with our relationship to the natural world, and that we are creating an environment unsuited either to life in general, or to human life in particular. Is the environment we are creating one to which – even as we create it – we can no longer adapt? Are we manifesting a fundamental impiety or at least a dangerous hubris as we delve deeper into nature's innermost recesses? I have some sympathy with the worries that underlie these questions; but as the storm clouds gather at the end of the twentieth century, I am reminded that Ruskin observed exactly similar phenomena at the end of the nineteenth. Nor do I think that the vexed and complex question of our relationship to the natural world is helpfully addressed by reliance on a naive sense of the natural as opposed to the human or the artificial. My aim in what follows is to show why this is so, as a preparation for a more sensitive and better-judged approach to questions which concern us all, environmentalists and non-environmentalists alike.

As we become more surrounded by artifice, ingenuity and invention, so grows a yearning for the simple, the unadulterated and what is called the natural. While people in the underdeveloped world can think of no fate more desirable than to enjoy the fruits of scientific, technological and economic development, we teach children in our schools that there is something immoral about 'the tearing of our mother's breast', as one environmentalist described the offer of a more effective plough to a third world tribe. Mining and road-building become rape, on this view, exemplified in road protesters addressing contractors as 'earth-raping scum'; and the physical earth our mother, in the hyper-charged rhetoric of environmental protest. As formal, dogmatic and man-focused religion declines, nature itself is accorded a religious aura, all the more potent for its protean diffuseness.

We patronise the Body Shop, with its natural oils, its decomposable packaging and its cosmetics latterly untested on animals. Reared on tales of thalidomide and Opren, we are suspicious of pharmaceuticals and have a prejudice in favour of herbal remedies and traditional cures. We talk a lot about energy, and deplore the need for coal-fired and nuclear power stations. We have mixed feelings about high-tech surgery, and are dubious about biotechnology. We are against the despoliation of the landscape by the building of houses or roads. The National Curriculum for Morality tells children to repair habitats devastated by human development, though not to cherish those enhanced and beautified by centuries of patient human effort. We may well admire campaigns against whaling and atomic testing by organisations such as Greenpeace, and even contribute to their funds. We will urge the merits of breast-feeding and natural childbirth against the suppliers of processed infant food and the advocates of medical intrusion.

It seems that the list could be extended without much difficulty, though this simply raises the question, what is it a list of? We feel we know, and if pressed most of us would probably respond by referring to nature and the natural. I believe this appeal to be an illusion and that nothing is clarified or justified by it. What is gained is a kind of emotive or even a religious charge, but while this, like theft, has the advantage over honest toil, it is an advantage which brings its possessor no credit that could be banked against a moment's analysis.

If the causes in whose service 'nature' is enlisted are valuable – and some of them are – this is because they have merits and arguments quite separate from their supposed naturalness. If, for example, there is something undesirable about a coal-fired power station, this is not because burning coal is less natural than setting a windmill up on a hill. Both are interventions by human agency, and both have advantages and disadvantages, which must be weighed up and compared on their merits and demerits (which in the case of high-tech windmills are obvious to those who live near them). And even where some procedure is, in a clear sense, more natural than another, as in the case of childbirth without drugs or surgery, this is not in itself any argument in its favour. For those whose lives have, like mine, been saved by surgery, there can be no general presumption that the unmodified technique is better than the modified. Nor is natural childbirth at home such a good thing if it turns out to be a breech birth or if the baby needs oxygen. Of course, medical interventions *can* be objectionable, particularly at the closing of a life, or where they fruitlessly prolong the torments of a severely handicapped baby. But this is because such interventions are assaults on human dignity or hubristic attempts to stave off the inevitability of death, not because they are 'unnatural'. Again each case must be judged on its merits in the light of the goals we are seeking, and the advantages and disadvantages of each possible route to our particular goal.

The invocation of the natural does evoke a powerful quasi-religious aura: we are dealing with a myth which for once really does need deconstruction.

Natural and Artificial

A fundamental distinction is that between the natural and the artificial, although what precisely the distinction amounts to will depend on the underlying notion of nature. In the standard terminology of 1998, 'artificial' refers to what is added or produced as a result of human activity, as in the usage 'no artificial colouring or preservative'. It is unclear why artificial additives are objectionable *per se*, particularly when we reflect that sometimes the very same ingredients can occur both naturally and artificially, as in the case of sugar which both is found in and can be added to fruit. There is, nevertheless, a strong predilection in favour of 'natural' and additive-free foods, a predilection advertisers have not been slow to exploit. They wax lyrical, for example, about organic bread, made by hand, 'baked in wood-fired brick ovens'. Such bread is, of course, historically more primitive than the cheaper and longer-lasting mass-produced bread favoured by the British housewife. It tastes better, as well, but that does not make organic bread any less artificial than a sliced white loaf, nor, despite all the propaganda, is there any solid evidence that it is superior from the point of view of nutrition or health. Handmade is still human-made and so are wood-fired brick ovens, which do not occur in the wild. And whether particular additives do good or harm is an entirely empirical matter, to be decided case by case (and in specific cases may well not admit of a conclusive answer).

We should be cautious of a presumption in favour of the natural here, a presumption unfortunately implicit in the regulations regarding drugs. Remedies and medicines based on herbs and plants are not subject to the same rigorous toxicological investigations and regulations as synthetically produced drugs, but this does not mean that they may not be poisonous. Many plants of course are. Two interesting examples are belladonna and fly agaric, interesting because both have been used for their special effects, belladonna by Renaissance women to dilate their pupils and fly agaric by Viking warriors before battle to produce a hallucinogenic state of self-belief and a manic grin which terrified the enemy. The naturally occurring toxins would eventually poison the warriors who took it and who survived long enough for the poison to work through. Analogous problems arise with more established herbal remedies.

Aristotelian Naturalism

There is a more philosophical notion of the natural, which stands in a somewhat different relation to the artificial as we understand things today, at least so long as the former is understood as that which occurs without any contribution from us. I refer to the Aristotelian cosmology, in which all things, including human beings, have some end or nature which they will fulfil should they develop properly. An acorn fulfils its nature by becoming an oak, and an oak should grow straight and full and massive. A lion fulfils his nature by commanding his females and catching his prey. From this point of view, there is no reason to suppose that a well-functioning animal or plant will necessarily serve our particular ends as individual human beings.

Moreover, when we come to the human, Aristotle does not draw the distinction between the natural and artificial where we in the twentieth century would be disposed to draw it. For Aristotle a certain type of social organisation, though clearly artificial in depending on human activity and construction, is natural in that only within such an organisation will human beings fulfil their nature. Thus, for Aristotle, man is by nature a political animal, meaning that only in a city or polis will certain activities, fundamental to human flowering, take place and this, of course, requires artifice.

Aristotelian thought has an important lesson for us. It is that Aristotle sees man as part of nature and hence our doings as part of nature. If it is man's nature to use his intelligence to change the way things are prior to his coming on the scene, what results is as much part of nature as the wildernesses we are exhorted by ecologists to leave untouched. Indeed, one could mount a case for saying that it is just as natural to have a humanly altered world as to have one we fastidiously refrain from interfering with, were such a thing possible at all. All creatures change their environment simply by existing and taking sustenance and shelter from it. That, if anything, is a law of nature, so why should it be more in accord with nature for human beings to act *unnaturally* in this respect? We could also reflect that many of the landscapes we cherish and seek to preserve – often for good aesthetic reasons, as in the case of Twyford Down – are the fruit of centuries of cultivation and of ruthless and systematic deforestation.

There is, though, a big difference between Aristotle and most twentieth-century thought. For Aristotle, the cosmos had an overall end or goal – that determined for it by divine intelligence – and so did the separate species and the individual members of those species. To live naturally was to fulfil that goal and to contribute both to one's own well-being and to that of the whole.

Evolutionary Theory

Those assumptions form no part of our current Darwinian understanding of nature. There is no overall goal for the cosmos, nor is there any assumption that it might have or has had some state of maximum perfection in which all is in harmony. Evolution inspires no thoughts of an ecological Golden Age. Species are not static, nor are their environments, nor is what conduces to the flourishing of some individual or species necessarily good for their coexistents or for the environment as constituted at any particular time. Everything – individuals, species and environment – is subject to change and development, and many of these changes are irreversible. Species die out when confronted with changed environments and superior competitors. It is indeed in the nature of species to die out, something we would do well to remember when confronted with statements about the daily death of one or other species of plant in the Amazonian jungle. Just as it is in the nature of things that moribund species should die off, so is it in the nature of things that new species should emerge to take advantage of new conditions. And all this leaves aside ticklish questions of how exactly we count species: do those who deplore the disappearance of old species ever put new growths into the equation? And might not the balance in nature we are exhorted to preserve alongside diversity actually, at times, *require* extinction?

We should, in any case, remember that something which works well in one environment may actually be disastrous when things change, as eventually they will. From an evolutionary perspective, while we may regard nature as constituting some sort of system, or collection of interconnected sub-systems, neither system nor sub-systems is ever stable, nor were they designed to operate as systems with clearly defined parts or functions. Like species they constantly alter and mutate, and stability is never more than a precarious moment between change. All this should make us wary of taking the present set of balances in nature as either ideal or permanent; nor can there be any presumption that the future alterations (which will come anyway) are likely to be dysfunctional. Indeed, given that they happen at all, they will happen precisely because they are functional: so, at least, is the prediction of the law of natural selection which underlies evolutionary theory. And given the amount of dysfunctionality there already is in nature, it is not hard to see how a change might well increase functionality and overall coherence, however much such a change might offend our aesthetic or moral sensibilities.

This is a point Darwin would surely have appreciated. For Darwin was well aware that evolutionary fitness is relative both to particular environments and to the actual competition. If having a less complex organisation or shedding faculties or organs produces a greater adaptation to one's environment, then evolution will favour it, as it has on occasion favoured blind cave-dwelling insects descended from sighted forebears, and birds who have lost the power of flight (in New Zealand). Further, natural selection never implies perfect co-ordination between individuals and their environment, but only better co-ordination than that of rivals. As Darwin wrote in *The Origin of Species*, we ought not

to marvel if all contrivances in nature be not, as far as we can judge absolutely perfect; and if some be abhorrent to our ideas of fitness. We need not marvel at the sting of the bee causing the bee's own death; at drones being produced in such vast numbers for one single act, and then being slaughtered by their sterile sisters; at the astonishing waste of pollen by our fir-trees; at the instinctive hatred of the queen bee for her own fertile daughters; at ichneumonidae feeding within the bodies of live caterpillars; and at other such cases. The wonder indeed is, on the theory of natural selection, that more cases of the want of absolute perfection have not been observed.*

The picture which biology paints of nature and the natural world is in stark contrast to the idea which captivates the popular mind – namely that what is natural is in some sense pure and normal, and that we should aspire to

* *The Origin of Species*, Penguin edition, Harmondsworth 1984, p. 445.

this condition. As the natural world is in a state of continuous evolution, it is arbitrary to fix on one moment as the 'pure' or 'normal' or 'natural' state. It is possible to prefer the sea before it is used to discharge oil tanks or a down before a motorway is driven through it. It is also possible to regard sites unvisited by human beings (such as Antarctica) as valuable for scientific research precisely because they are unaffected by the introduction of human beings. But we should not think of the earlier states of sea or down or Antarctica as in some absolute sense pure or normal or, in the case of the down at any rate, as not the product of centuries of human activity. Beauty is worth preserving, but it is covertly anti-human to seek to preserve something solely because it is untouched by human work and, in the case of most road projects in the British Isles, dishonest to boot. It is also worth remembering that the railways and canals, now regarded as environmentally friendly, were the nineteenth-century equivalent of today's motorways, cutting through tracts of scenic wilderness (and were condemned by Ruskin for doing so).

Human Intervention in Nature

Underlying the 'purity of nature' theme is a more pervasive, but even less persuasive feeling: the feeling that human activity necessarily messes things up. Oil slicks, chemically polluted rivers and forests devastated by acid rain come to mind. But for every oil slick there are a thousand examples of landscape gardening, for every polluted river many acres of reclaimed marshland, for every devastated forest many carefully tended plantations, all cases where human intervention has enhanced nature to great effect – to say nothing of the way the best architecture and town planning adds to an otherwise mute, meaningless and often dreary terrain. Imagine, for example, East Anglia without Ely and Norwich and Peterborough, or the Peloponnese without the temples and castles which render its savagery Arcadian.

No doubt environmentalism of the uncritical variety flourishes most easily among those who have least experience of nature and its cycles – those living in cities and knowing nature largely from TV documentaries. Hence, as we see in the National Curriculum for Morality, 'environmental education' is all about 'repairing' habitats 'destroyed by human development', but not about those triumphs of human work over nature, such as Venice and Edinburgh and Delft, or the countless olive groves and terraces in the classical world. In much environmental activism, there is a deep suspicion of our own kind, never more insidious than when it exploits the naivety and innocence of the young.

Nature is in fact a constantly changing scene, and we are part of it, like all other species contributing to its changes, and like all other species being affected by them. The fact of the matter is that we are different from other species precisely in the way in which we can intervene intentionally. We are not like beavers, say, who intervene unintentionally. They instinctively dam up rivers for shelter, thereby changing landscapes as a by-product of what they instinctively do. We can plan and intend to change the way things are. around us. But while our foresight and our intelligence are unique in nature, they are still part of our natural endowments. They themselves are products of nature, building on traits and dispositions that we share with other species.

People who contrast human intelligence and culture unfavourably with nature and instinct are, by implication at least, displaying a suspicion both of intelligence and of the effects of civilisation itself. But to defend this suspicion on the basis of an ontological distinction between nature and culture is to attempt to make evaluative bricks with analytical straw.

Human Population

Whatever we might feel is most 'natural' for us, we cannot live as close to nature as human beings were 15,000 years ago. Present population levels can be sustained only through the industrial and technological development which has been freeing peasant peoples from dependence on the land all over the world for the past 2–300 years. As early as 1795, an American historian was remarking how in his country 500 thinking beings were then prospering in an area where previously only a single savage could 'drag out a hungry existence' as a hunter. People who have the choice to leave the land for towns do so, whether this means living in the slums of Manchester in the 1830s or in the bidonvilles of Mexico City or Calcutta or Lagos today. If anything is natural, then that is, as is the slow-down in population growth once a reasonable level of prosperity is reached. Nor is there any empirical evidence to suppose that, except at the margins, populations in a given area will long outgrow the available resources to feed them – unless they are encouraged to do so by subsidies and grants from other parts of the world.

There are those who for one reason or another deplore development and population growth and their untidy and unaesthetic effects. The human population of the world took until the year 1800 to reach 1 billion. It is now around 5.5 billion and is estimated by the World Bank to reach around 9.6 billion by 2050. Whether or not this prediction is right, we should not forget that increases in population tend by further differentiation and division of labour to make more resources available. As Hayek used to argue, there is no reason to suppose that greater populations should not lead to advances in material and spiritual conditions – rather the contrary. At any rate, there is no reason to suppose that even an increase as big as predicted will in itself leave our children and grandchildren without the means of feeding and sheltering themselves.

The plain fact is that it is hard to know in advance just what levels of population are sustainable globally. People may have ideas and intuitions about what nature and the biosphere 'demand', but neither nature nor the biosphere demands anything. Talk of Gaia notwithstanding, they are not even in any predetermined sense systems, as opposed to collections of interacting individuals and forces, developing in ways both unpredictable and unplanned. People who evoke the demands of the biosphere often reveal not so much love of other kinds as suspicion of their own kind. They give little inkling of how existing and foreseeable human needs are to be met or how the levels of population they prefer are to be achieved, but sometimes more than a hint that they despise the ordinary hopes and fears of the millions now living, who depend on our continuing to exploit nature's resources to the best effect. Saying this in no way rules out taking care for the future of our children and grandchildren – but that will be possible only if we approach nature with the best of our knowledge and sensitivity. Unfortunately as things stand today, irrationality has got such a grip that it looks increasingly as if many in our country have replaced traditional Christianity with a diffuse and idolatrous form of nature worship.

Nature: A New Religion

The new religion encourages irrationalism (unjustified and unreasoning anti-scientific prejudice, which makes a reasoned criticism of scientific developments more difficult). It has its sins of doctrine and practice (speciesism and anthropocentrism). It has its Day of Judgment and apocalypse (the impending global cataclysm). It has its doctrinal disputes (as between animal rights and deep ecology, for example). It has its Sunday worshippers (who might go to the Body Shop and avoid furs and additives) and its enthusiasts (who might be vegans and commune dwellers). It has its martyrs and gurus such as Petra Kelly, Aldo Leopold, Rudolf Bahro and James Lovelock. It appeals to other often ill-understood religious or quasi-religious practices (meditation, Taoism, yoga). It has its Mammon (the industrial 'megamachine'). It also has its God, or more accurately, its Goddess.

Gaia is sometimes referred to as a hypothesis, but the notion functions far more like a personified dogma: the earth itself personalised as an organism whose cycles we have to respect and whose whims we have to placate. As already suggested, there is no warrant for the view that nature or the earth is one single thing, let alone one thing with organism-like properties, as opposed to one stage on which many different and conflicting things take place. It is true, trivially so, that things which happen in one place affect things in other places. It is also true that things which happen on earth (including things we humans do) can affect the conditions which make life on earth possible – just as the earth's life-sustaining atmosphere itself is a by-product of the blue-green algae which first appeared some 3 billion years ago, before oxygen had entered the atmosphere. It is also true that there is life all over the planet.

But none of this means that the earth itself is an organism, or that its parts can be seen as serving organic functions. We can identify the parts of a plant or an animal in terms of their functions. But that is because we can think of a plant or animal as having the aims of survival and reproduction. In the case of the earth there is no such aim, in terms of which the rest of its activities can be analysed. It is not a living thing, striving to exist. It is not striving to reproduce itself. And if billions of living things live on it, that is not what it is for, nor is it that in terms of which its elements (sea, atmosphere, mountains, inner core, etc.) demand to be analysed. To worship an inanimate and mindless object such as the earth is an idolatry as primitive as any that has been practised in the history of the human race. To endow it with characteristics of personality is to indulge in an anthropomorphism which will not bear a moment's scrutiny.

Conclusion

We are of course interested in the survival of our children and their children, and in the survival of the human race. Equally for aesthetic, utilitarian and moral reasons, biodiversity and conservation are important aims. But do not let us deceive ourselves or our children into thinking that there is anything 'natural' about these latter concerns, or that promoting them through conservation demands that we adopt a mystical or sentimental or unscientific attitude to 'nature', marked off in some Manichaean way from science and human intervention. In fact, rather to the contrary, the truth is that only an intelligent, informed and interventionist approach to nature will promote either conservation or the other goals we have.

Ruskin wrote that

> God has lent us the earth for our life. It is a great entail. It belongs as much to those who follow us as it does to us, and we have no right by anything we do, or neglect to do, to involve them in unnecessary penalties, or to deprive them of the benefit we have it in our power to bequeath.

It seems to me that we should ask ourselves what stewardship might entail, how we might seek a *via media* between the polarities of idolatrous nature worship and a barbaric short-sighted utilitarianism. Much of the argument amounts to little more than a stand-off: freeze nature just as it is, or despoil it completely, with 4 million new 'homes', or whatever is the current fashion. A steward improves, works and cultivates, but *with* the grain of nature, pious towards the past, and with a care for the long term. If in this essay I have been critical of uncritical environmentalism it is because uncritical environmentalism, in its inflexibility and dogmatism, leaves little room for intelligence or compromise, and thereby encourages and exacerbates the very philistinism it deplores.

At the close of the twentieth century, we know enough of the modern world and its dehumanising attitude to the past and to any sort of habitable environment. But in our reaction to modern impiety, we should not adopt a set of values which, if applied at the relevant time, would have prevented the founding of Rome or Venice or ancient Athens.

Bibliography

Aristotle, *Metaphysics* ed. and trans. W. D. Ross (Oxford, 1924).

Aristotle, *Physics,* ed. and trans. W. D. Ross (Oxford, 1936).

Attfield, R. and Belsey, A. (eds) *Philosophy and the Natural Environment* (Cambridge, 1994).

Darwin, C., *The Origin of Species* (1859), ed. J. W. Burrow (Harmondsworth, 1982).

Goldsmith, E., *The Way* (Dartington, 1996).

Hayek, F. A., *The Fatal Conceit* (London, 1988).

Leopold, A., *A Sand County Almanac* (Oxford, 1953).

Lovelock, J., *Gaia, A New Look at Life on Earth* (Oxford, 1979).

Ruskin, J., *Collected Works*, ed. E. T. Cook and A. Wedderburn, 39 vols (London, 1903–12). See especially *Modern Painters*, (1843–60), *The Queen of the Air* (1869), *The Storm Cloud of the Nineteenth Century* (1884), *Deucalion* (1875–83).

7. *The Music of English Pastoral*

David Matthews

The English landscape has been the inspiration of much of our greatest painting and poetry, and has also profoundly affected English composers since the end of the nineteenth century, when a pastoral school began which in many respects parallels the school of English landscape painters a century earlier.[*]

The association of music with landscape is essentially a Romantic phenomenon, a departure from the classical conception of music as an abstract language concerned in a general way with the expression of feeling but with no particular relation to the external world. At the end of the eighteenth century, Classicism, the art of the city, and of man as a political and social animal, decorously practising religion, ordering nature into formal gardens and parks, gave way to Romanticism, with its central image of the emancipated individual wandering alone through the world amidst the splendour and beauty of wild nature, finding God (if anywhere) in his sense of awe at nature's grandeur. The result, in early Romantic art, was the poetry of Goethe and Wordsworth, the paintings of Friedrich, Constable and Turner; and, in music, Beethoven's *Pastoral* Symphony, the 'Scène aux champs' from Berlioz's *Symphonie fantastique*, Weber's *Der Freischütz* and other pieces which began to explore the new, colouristic possibilities of the symphony orchestra (for landscape music is almost exclusively orchestral). On one of his several visits to this country, Mendelssohn visited Fingal's Cave on the Hebridean island of Staffa and out of this experience he wrote his overture *The Hebrides*; but this early example of a musical seascape did not inspire any work of similar quality from his English followers. They were more affected by *Elijah*, and the result was dozens of dreary oratorios. England did not produce a great Romantic composer until Elgar.

---

[*] I am using 'English' rather than 'British' throughout this essay simply because all the composers I deal with *are* English. A more comprehensive survey of music inspired by British landscape would include such Scottish composers as Hamish MacCunn, as well as other English figures such as Bax whose inspiration was entirely Celtic.

Elgar's music has two voices. One is energetic, extrovert, confident, urban: we associate it with Elgar's own time (what more appropriate music to accompany the images of Edwardian England could there be than the *Pomp and Circumstance* marches, or the opening of the First Symphony?) but it is grounded in the past too, in visions of medieval chivalry, and above all in the plays of Shakespeare, of which Elgar had a deep knowledge. Despite his swagger, Elgar was an uneasy Edwardian: even at his most confident, his music has a precarious stability. He is conscious that he stands at the end of an era, that what he celebrates will soon vanish. Hence his taking refuge in the past, though here he only finds confirmation of what he senses in the present. In what is perhaps his greatest work, the symphonic poem *Falstaff*, chivalric splendour fades into wistfulness, and finally into disillusion and death.

In *Falstaff* we also encounter Elgar's other voice. This is reflective, nostalgic, sometimes heartbreakingly poignant: it is a rural voice, the voice of his native landscape, the Severn valley near Worcester where he grew up. For most of his life Elgar chose to live close to this landscape – in Worcester, Hereford and Malvern – and his music drew strength from its being composed in proximity to the source of its inspiration. Since, however, the musical influences on Elgar's style were almost wholly German – Schumann, Brahms and Wagner – it might seem surprising that he sounds so English. There is no explicit influence of folksong, as in Vaughan Williams or Holst, yet his melodies have a naturalness which is like folk music. Elgar's characteristic melodic fingerprints may be traced back to his childhood: the tunes he invented when a boy are remarkably like those he wrote as an adult. Elgar in fact made his own folk music, and it is not too fanciful to suggest that it came out of the Worcestershire landscape, since this is what he himself said. In his sixties, he wrote to a friend: 'I am still at heart the dreamy child who used to be found in the reeds by Severn side with a sheet of paper trying to fix the sounds and longing for something very great.'* The special quality of Elgar's pastoral music was well expressed by Vaughan Williams when he wrote that it 'has that peculiar kind of beauty which gives us, his fellow countrymen, a sense of something familiar – the intimate and personal beauty of our own fields and lanes'.† Vaughan Williams emphasised that this quality was not found in

* Letter to Sidney Colvin, 13th December 1921, in Jerrold Northrop Moore ed., *Edward Elgar: Letters of a Lifetime*, Oxford 1990, p. 359.
† Ralph Vaughan Williams, 'What Have we Learnt from Elgar?' in *National Music and Other Essays*, 2nd edn., Oxford 1987, pp. 251–2.

Elgar's 'popular' style, 'but at those moments when he seems to have retired into the solitude of his own sanctuary'.

One difference between Elgar and his younger contemporary Delius is that Delius never left the solitude of his own sanctuary. Delius is a supreme Romantic individualist in that his music is exclusively about his own sensations and his relation to the natural world, which he looks at in a typically *fin de siècle* way: his Nietzschean life-worship is tempered with world-weariness, and his love of beauty with an acute consciousness of its evanescence. Delius frequently expresses feelings of nostalgia, in the true meaning of the word: the sense of loss and longing in his music is so painful as to be at times almost unbearable. Nostalgia is a peculiarly English affliction, and this may be one reason why Delius's music sounds English, for though he was born in England his ancestry was German, and his musical background – like Elgar's – was mostly Germanic too, but also included the influence of Grieg, and of the Negro spirituals he heard when he lived in Florida as a young man. Moreover, the landscapes in his mind when he wrote his music were mostly not English: some were Norwegian, from the summer holidays he spent walking among the Norwegian mountains; others French – and especially his own garden at Grez-sur-Loing, outside Paris, where he lived from the age of 35. Despite this cosmopolitanism, Delius's music has a persistently English voice (and incidentally is rarely appreciated outside this country), and he did write one of the crucial English pastoral pieces, the 'English Rhapsody' *Brigg Fair*, which is based on a folksong that the Australian composer Percy Grainger had collected in north Lincolnshire and presented to Delius in an arrangement for chorus, with chromatic harmonies similar to those Delius himself used. The poignancy of this chromatic harmony changes our perception of the beautiful, innocent tune; it tells us that the world it came from is dying, if indeed it ever existed except in the imagination. *Brigg Fair* was written in 1907 and can be heard now as an elegy for the mythical golden age of rural life that ended with the First World War.

Grainger was an assiduous collector of folksongs between 1905 and 1908, the heyday of the folksong revival headed by Cecil Sharp. Under Sharp's influence, Vaughan Williams too had begun collecting folksongs in 1902 and notated over 600 during the next ten years. This was part of a widespread investigation of our national musical heritage, for at the same time the treasure chest of English music from the Tudor and Jacobean periods was being unearthed, edited and published. Vaughan Williams was also editing *The English Hymnal* (published in 1906) to which he himself contributed several of the finest hymns in the collection, for example 'Come down, O Love divine', whose tune he called 'Down Ampney' after the village in Gloucestershire where he was born. Some twenty years later he was to edit the *Oxford Book of Carols*. Despite his own agnosticism, the Anglican Church and its music and traditions were a constantly important factor in Vaughan Williams's life: the Church provided an exemplar of quiet continuity and resistance to ephemeral fashion (at least it did in his day). Folksong, which for Vaughan Williams included hymns and carols, and the choral music of such Tudor composers as Tallis both became central to his musical world, and transformed his musical language. In a series of lectures given in 1932 and published under the title of *National Music*, Vaughan Williams argued that, in order to be truly universal, music should first be rooted in the composer's native country, and his own music is a vindication of these beliefs.

If I had to single out one piece to demonstrate what I think of as Englishness in music it would be Vaughan Williams's Fifth Symphony, and specifically the modal opening of the first movement whose soft horn calls over a flattened seventh in the bass seem to summon up an archetypal English landscape of summer pastures and distant hills. Others might choose the *Fantasia on a Theme of Thomas Tallis* or *The Lark Ascending*. In *The Lark Ascending*, the dialogue between the solitary listener and nature – the lark – becomes, at the end, a monologue for the lark, the solo violin, who leaves the orchestra behind to climb up alone into the clear air. The lark's pentatonic music is a distillation of folksong, and how much more affecting is this song than if Vaughan Williams had tried to imitate it more closely, as Messiaen was later to do. For the lark's song is made a human song and thus, as Wilfrid Mellers has written, 'by no other composer is the interdependence of man and Nature more movingly expressed'.

This nature music is never nostalgic, as Elgar's or Delius's is; it quietly celebrates the timeless moment – and one can draw comparisons with English mystical writers such as Traherne. But Vaughan Williams is by no means all pastoral idyll. In his Second Symphony, the *London*, Vaughan Williams paints a vivid and warm-hearted portrait of the city before the First World War, just as Elgar had done in *Cockaigne*. Both composers see London from their perspective as visitors from the country – there is a

certain wide-eyed innocence in their approach, as compared with the svelte
sophistication of a genuine city composer like Gershwin. (There is no
London equivalent to *Rhapsody in Blue*, Gershwin's great hymn to New
York.) The First World War, in which Vaughan Williams served as an
infantryman in the trenches, made it impossible to recapture this innocent,
benevolent vision of the city, and threatened the tranquillity of his pastoral
images. The Fourth Symphony of 1934 is a ferocious piece from which
pastoral serenity is all but excluded. It is regained in the Fifth Symphony,
but temporarily lost again in the terrifying Sixth, whose unremittingly bleak
conclusion some have seen as a prophecy of nuclear winter (it was written
just after the end of the Second World War). If the Fourth and Sixth
Symphonies are to be called urban – a better word would be anti-pastoral –
then Vaughan Williams takes from the modern city only inhuman images
of mechanisation and destruction. He is disturbed by these things, but his
refusal to ignore them is part of his greatness: his music never becomes one-
dimensional. His last works continue his quest for meaning in the modern
world, and unsurprisingly come up with no final answer, but the sense of
deep calm which was there from the start is never entirely lost.

The darker side of Vaughan Williams owes something to his close friend
Gustav Holst, whose music shares the influence of folksong, to which
Vaughan Williams had introduced him. Both Vaughan Williams and Holst
consciously changed their musical language: their attitude to tradition was
different from the previous generation who still drew on a natural
inheritance from the past, and is that of the typical twentieth-century
composer who makes his own tradition from what he finds most important
to him. Vaughan Williams's Englishness, as I have implied, was deliberately
cultivated, while Holst made great efforts to reject the nineteenth-century
German music on which he had been brought up in favour of a simpler,
purer style. It took Holst many years to refine his language so that he could
precisely capture the vision he sought: he finally achieved it in late works
such as *Egdon Heath*, an orchestral evocation of Hardy's Wessex landscape.
The score of *Egdon Heath* is prefaced by a quotation from *The Return of the
Native*: 'A place perfectly accordant with man's nature – neither ghastly,
hateful, nor ugly: neither commonplace, unmeaning, nor tame; but, like
man, slighted and enduring; and withal singularly colossal and mysterious in
its swarthy monotony.' The tone of Holst's music corresponds quite
uncannily to this description. During the composition of *Egdon Heath*,
Hardy invited Holst to lunch at his house near Dorchester and, typically,

Holst walked there from Bristol, a distance of some seventy-five miles. The intimate knowledge of the landscape that Holst acquired from his frequent long solitary walks helped produce the inscapes of *Egdon Heath* which are remote from any facile attempt at scene-painting.

The next generation of English composers had a more equivocal attitude towards folksong and Englishness. Walton was the inheritor of Elgar's popular urban style, and the edgy Romanticism of much of his best music – for instance the Viola Concerto or the First Symphony – is urban too. Walton lived the first part of his life like an eighteenth-century composer, supported by the aristocratic patronage of the Sitwells, and the second half, after his marriage, in Italy, which had always represented his own ideal landscape. His contemporary Michael Tippett, however, while never nationalistic in his outlook, asserted his Englishness when he continued the strain of Vaughan Williams's visionary pastoralism in such pieces as the Concerto for Double String Orchestra, the Ritual Dances from his opera *The Midsummer Marriage*, and the *Fantasia on a Theme of Corelli*. Tippett initially followed Vaughan Williams in deliberately using folksong as a basis for melody, and the strength and freshness of his renewed pastoralism is striking. Like most important English composers this century, Tippett chose to live and work in the country and developed a close relation with it, a relation whose fullest expression appears in *The Midsummer Marriage*, where the uniting of two young couples takes place against the background of a symbolic landscape on Midsummer Day. Tippett's music evokes the life of nature at its most fecund, and there are moments of ecstatic stillness which have no parallel in English music, even in Vaughan Williams at his most rapturous. The lyricism of *The Midsummer Marriage* persisted in Tippett's music right to the end of his life: in the wonderful slow movement of the Triple Concerto, or in the rarefied, singing lines of the Fifth String Quartet.

At the very time that Tippett was discovering folksong as a fresh way forward, the folksong movement was being amusingly satirised for its preciosity in *Music Ho!* by Constant Lambert, who claimed that it was a wholly artificial recreation of something that was already dead. Lambert noted that London bus conductors were not singing tunes from Vaughan Williams's folk opera *Hugh the Drover* but, if anything, the latest American popular hits (this was in 1934). He was wrong, however, in supposing folksong to be now exclusively the province of an effete middle class. He missed its survival in pockets of working-class culture, in town as well as country, where it awaited a second and more extensive revival in the 1950s, when its influence began to spread to current popular music: this continues today – but that is another story. Lambert also attacked 'self-conscious Englishry', as he called it, pointing out that 'the strength of the English tradition in art is that it has always been open to foreign influences, which have been grafted on to the native plant without causing it to wither away'. No one would disagree with that, of course, certainly not Tippett; nor did Vaughan Williams imply that a composer should be totally insular – he himself had studied with Ravel and taken in the productive influence of French musical Impressionism. Folksong simply provided Tippett, as it had provided Vaughan Williams and Holst, with a vernacular language that he could adapt in his own way, just as later he was to make use of the vernacular language of the blues.

Britten, who was 20 when *Music Ho!* was published, did reject self-conscious Englishry as represented by Vaughan Williams, but he remained loyal to his teacher Frank Bridge who, though his later music inclined towards modernism, had also been a wholehearted pastoralist in such pieces as his orchestral rhapsody *Enter Spring*. Bridge's tone poem *The Sea* was the first orchestral work Britten heard as a boy, and in his own words he was 'knocked sideways' by it. Britten went on to produce a series of definitive English seascapes in his opera *Peter Grimes*, inspired by the North Sea at Aldeburgh near which he lived for most of his life. Britten's intuitive understanding of the sea and its various moods in the *Four Sea Interludes* from the opera is as profound as Holst's had been of the landscape in *Egdon Heath*.

It can now be seen that Britten's rejection of Vaughan Williams and what he stood for was simply a necessary part of defining his own musical personality, and that in his own way Britten was as attracted to folk music as were his predecessors – he made, after all, over sixty arrangements, or rather recompositions, of folksongs (including French and American ones), and his highly original harmonisations move the songs out of their old-fashioned contexts, and make their sentiments modern. His ambivalence towards the English tradition was typical of him, the master composer of ambivalences. At the very end of his life Britten wrote what is his most explicit landscape music in his *Suite on English Folksongs, 'A time there was'* (the subtitle is from Hardy's poem 'Before Life and After', his evocation of lost paradise). The suite is dedicated to the memory of Percy Grainger, and the last movement, 'Lord Melbourne', is based on a folksong that Grainger collected and which is played in the piece by a solo cor anglais exactly as Grainger notated it. At the end, the cor anglais reaches its final phrase as the strings make a cadence into C major, its E flat sounding a bittersweet – and characteristically English – dissonance against the strings' E natural. The words of the folksong here are 'But now to death I must yield'. The phrase is repeated by the clarinet and, inconclusively, by the flute, while the strings prolong their C major chord, quietly fading into darkness. The effect is similar to the end of Mahler's *Das Lied von der Erde*: man lives and dies, but nature is eternal.

The mood of deep sadness that pervades 'Lord Melbourne' no doubt has much to do with Britten's thoughts on his own impending death, but its elegiac tone is also typical of the way we look at our landscape today. We are constantly reminded that so much of it is threatened in various ways, while at the same time nostalgic imagery from the lost Eden of pre-First World War England pervades our television screens and cinemas, usually accompanied by pastiche Delius or Vaughan Williams, which emphasises that these composers represent a vanished past. It is hard now to look at a beautiful landscape with an innocent eye: its imagery has been ruthlessly sentimentalised by the nostalgia industry, and appropriated by advertisers who use it to try to sell us cars or anything else they choose to thrust at us, indifferently corrupting our sensibilities. This is just one of many reasons why the English pastoral school, which was pre-modern, not to speak of pre-post-modern, cannot be sustained as it was. It belonged to a more innocent age that is gone for ever.

So when English composers today write landscape pieces, their perspective tends to be somewhat bleak. Almost all Peter Maxwell Davies's work of the past twenty-five years has been inspired by his chosen landscape of Orkney, and he has evoked its strange, barren beauty in such pieces as *Stone Litany*. His musical language, however, grew out of his early immersion in the Second Viennese School, so that his intended Sibelian objectivity has to compete with a tendency to Expressionist *angst*. It is certainly a deeply troubled music, even desolate. Harrison Birtwistle's music is also dark and tense, and pervaded by undercurrents of violence. We might associate its rough grittiness with the Pennine landscape where he grew up, but it is a dour landscape he gives us, devoid of any spirit of delight, though often with a weird beauty of its own (as for example his *Silbury Air*, whose starting point was the great prehistoric burial mound of Silbury Hill in Wiltshire). Both composers have an authentic vision to communicate, if a rather narrow one. Both Maxwell Davies and Birtwistle have had a big influence on younger generations of composers, who mostly share their underlying pessimism. For their music would seem generally expressive of an almost universally held feeling today that nature is fighting a losing battle with man, and that the world is headed for ruin. In the face of this profound melancholy about our future, how can we continue to rejoice? How can we not take refuge in the past? And if we try, in an old-fashioned way, to celebrate the beauty of nature, how can we avoid lapsing into sentimentality?

These may, at present, seem impossible questions to answer. And yet, despite our apprehensions, we should not entirely lose heart. We should not forget that the simple fact of the return of spring can still delight us afresh each year, as it always did, and we are not obliged to deconstruct our delight. Nature is not yet spent. And it is particularly appropriate for us now, with our keen awareness of the past, to look deeper into our landscape beyond the innocent eye. In his marvellous book *Landscape and Memory*, Simon Schama demonstrates how Western cultural history is intimately bound up with the landscape, whose contours everywhere reveal the influence of man. He writes about the 'veins of myth and memory' that lie beneath the surface of things, waiting to be rediscovered. We do not have to look to other cultures, Schama says, to find surviving nature myths, 'of the primitive forest, of the river of life, of the sacred mountain'; they 'are in fact alive and well and all about us if we know where to look for them'. To walk in a forest may summon up numerous associations for us, of sacred groves, royal hunts, bloody battles once fought there. Remembering all this, we gain a perspective far wider than our initial simple response to the picturesque.

This is a fruitful field for the composer. The response to nature that Schama describes is not one of nostalgia (though an element of nostalgia may be present) but a more complex feeling that brings the past into communion with the present, and which may be translated directly into music. For instance, towards the end of Holst's *Egdon Heath*, a grave folk-like tune is heard, like a procession of ghostly dancers drifting across the landscape, while at the very end a trumpet sounds out a lonely fanfare. By these devices, Holst reminds us of the presence of man, 'slighted and enduring', in Hardy's words, in the seemingly empty landscape, and thus adds another layer of meaning to the musical experience he provides for us. The use of the vernacular here, in the folk-like tune, is particularly telling, as it was in Britten's 'Lord Melbourne'. In order to invoke memory, music must surely make some use of the musical vernacular – that is, simple diatonic or modal melody – as the most appropriate musical metaphor; for the whole of Western music up to the advent of modernism was grounded in the vernacular. Modernism excluded it, but at great cost to musical language's comprehensiveness.

A pastoral music for the future, then, if there can be such a thing, will be comprehensive, in its musical language and in its content: it will reflect the complex way we now view our landscapes, their richness and their density. (Within such a complexity, beauty too will have a place.) Above all, it must be a genuine expression of feeling. To understand his Third Symphony, Mahler told a friend, 'you would yourself have to plunge with me into the very depths of Nature.'* Mahler sounds like Ruskin here, who advised the young artist to 'go to Nature in all singleness of heart . . . having no other thoughts but how best to penetrate her meaning'.† Singleness of heart, identification with the source of one's inspiration, and, I would add, a kind of intoxicated delight in one's material – this is the only way to produce anything of real value in music, or in any other art.

Bibliography

Bauer-Lechner, Natalie, *Recollections of Gustav Mahler* (London, 1980).

Fuller, Peter, *Theoria* (London, 1988).

Holst, Imogen, *Gustav Holst* (Oxford, 1938).

Holst, Imogen, *The Music of Gustav Holst*, 2 edn (Oxford, 1968).

Kemp, Ian, *Tippett: The Composer and his Music* (London, 1984).

Lambert, Constant, *Music Ho!* (London, 1934).

Matthews, David, *Michael Tippett, an Introductory Study* (London, 1980).

Matthews, David, *Landscape into Sound* (St Albans, 1992).

Mellers, Wilfrid, *Vaughan Williams and the Vision of Albion* (London, 1989).

Moore, Gerald Northrop, *Edward Elgar, A Creative Life* (Oxford, 1984).

Palmer, Christopher, *Delius, Portrait of a Cosmopolitan* (London, 1976).

Palmer, Christopher (ed.) *The Britten Companion* (London, 1984).

Schama, Simon, *Landscape and Memory* (London, 1995).

Vaughan Williams, Ralph, *National Music and Other Essays*, 2nd edn (Oxford, 1986).

* Bauer-Lechner, Natalie, *Recollections of Gustav Mahler*, London 1980, p. 62.

† Ruskin, in Cook, E. T., and Wedderburn, Alexander, eds., *The Library Edition of the Works of John Ruskin*, London, 1903–12, vol. IX, p. 293.

8. *Conservation by Rights*

George Monbiot

It wasn't easy for the townspeople who watched it go past to work out what the huge Countryside March in March 1998 was all about. The proposed ban on hunting with hounds was, of course, a major theme, but the organisers were at pains to explain that it was about more than just that, that the very existence of the countryside was at stake. The rally, organised by such bodies as the Country Landowners' Association and the Scottish Landowners' Federation, had been called, we were told, to defend the countryside from the town, whose tyrannical and uncomprehending governance of rural areas was leading to the collapse of rural employment and the smothering of farmland by new housing developments. Deferential as ever, we townies were careful not to display our ignorance of rural life by asking who had sacked the agricultural labourers whose demise the landowners so publicly lamented, or who had sold the land to the house-builders. If the rural environment has been destroyed, rural livelihoods lost and 'country values' dissipated, then, our urban leader writers all agreed, it must be the fault of the cities.

Our culpability is plain for all to see. We are impertinent enough to spend only £10 billion a year in agricultural subsidies and price support. Single mothers in Bradford and Gateshead are so stingy that they donate only 2.5 pence over and above the market price to the struggling landlords every time they buy a pint of milk. City people spent just £3 billion rescuing farmers from the BSE crisis which, of course, was entirely the fault of what the rally organisers so aptly described as 'the urban jackboot'.

Worse still, we are responsible for polluting the rustic purity of the countryside's most eminent representatives by trapping them in our dens of urban iniquity. The Duke of Westminster, the rally's main funder, who, as his title suggests, is a horny-handed son of rural toil, has been so thoroughly browbeaten by urban domination that he is forced to spend his weekdays suffering the indignity of working in London, where he has to manage his Mayfair and Belgravia estates and battle the undemocratic tendencies of the urban oppressor from the benches of the House of Lords. Happily, he has managed somehow to find one or two other country landowners in the Palace of Westminster. He can also, if necessary, take refuge with other cowering rural folk in the headquarters of the Country Landowners' Association, conveniently situated in Belgrave Square.

But, hesitant as we were to question the rural wisdom of our social superiors, some of us townies couldn't help wondering how representative of the concerns of rural people, or even of farming people, this rally really was. We couldn't help making unkind comparisons with the New Model Army, many of whose rank and file had joined up to fight enclosure, and whose officers included the nation's most rapacious enclosers.

For no one has suffered more from the depredations of maximised agribusiness than the conscientious farmer. Farmers who respect both their land and the rest of the community have been hammered repeatedly by both the lobbying power and the reputation of those who are unmoved by any consideration other than their profit margins. Subsidies, captured and colonised by rapacious agroindustrialists, systematically discriminate against prudent land use, small farming and robust rural employment. The BSE crisis, engendered by high-volume, low-care agribusiness and the manufacturing industry associated with it, has hit the small, specialist livestock farmer hardest. Though conscientious farmers number among Britain's most ardent country lovers, they have been tarnished by the ill-repute that deservedly accrues to the absentee robber barons who now dominate the industry. It is a source of enduring mystery to us ignorant townies that good farmers continue to allow themselves to be represented by the National Farmers' Union, the Country Landowners' Association and the Scottish Landowners' Federation, all of which are controlled by predatory men in suits.

The distinction between town and country promoted by the organisers of the Countryside Rally is an artificial one, nurtured by a city-based squirearchy seeking to deflect attention from its own exploitative practices. Its conflation of the concerns of big business with the concerns of all rural people amounts to straightforward misrepresentation. The countryside is not, as some of the march organisers sought, confusingly, to suggest, against landscape protection. The countryside is not opposed to a right to roam: indeed vox pops I conducted for a television programme found far more vociferous support among country people than among urban people. It is hard to understand how one can campaign against a ban on hunting and for a ban on roaming, from any position but the narrowest sectarian self-interest.

In truth there is a huge and growing gulf between what most British people, whether urban or rural, want to see happening in the countryside and what is taking place there. A tremendous public enthusiasm for landscape protection has failed to prevent the recent loss of most of our semi-natural farm landscapes. In the past sixty years, according to the Royal Society for the Protection of Birds, 82 per cent of the wet grassland in England and Wales has disappeared. We have lost 40 per cent of our heathland since 1950, and our native pinewoods have declined to just 1 per cent of their original area. The Department of Environment, Transport and the Regions calculates that 45 per cent of our Sites of Special Scientific Interest have been damaged in the last ten years. Perhaps most distressing are the injuries inflicted on our definitively non-renewable resource: archaeology. No firm figures have yet been published, though Bournemouth University's forthcoming Monuments at Risk Survey should help; nevertheless archaeologists hazard that something in the region of half the historical record has been erased since the Second World War. New farming methods are responsible for the majority of the recent losses of both habitats and archaeology.

It is becoming hard to see what large-scale intensive agriculture in Britain is for. Land-based rural employment is collapsing. A smaller proportion of the population is engaged in farming in Britain than in any other agricultural nation: the city state of Hong Kong has twice as many farm labourers per head of population. Yet, though large farmers' incomes are rising, we continue to shed farm labour at the rate of over 10,000 people a year. There is a massive and widening disparity of wealth between surviving rural labourers and those who live in the countryside but work somewhere else.

Farm animals are treated abominably by agribusiness. Researchers at Bristol University found that 90 per cent of the intensively reared broiler chickens they studied could not walk normally. Twenty-six per cent were believed to be in chronic pain and discomfort. The regulation battery cage is at no point wide enough for a hen to stretch its wings. One quarter of the dairy herd suffers from lameness; over 30 per cent of milking cows contract mastitis (a cripplingly painful inflammation of the udders) every year.

Pesticide residues in fruit and vegetables have shaken consumer confidence in British food. In the latest report from the Ministry of

Agriculture (MAFF) Working Party on Pesticide Residues, 13 per cent of UK winter lettuces were found to contain sufficient pesticide residues to indicate what MAFF calls 'pesticide misuse'. Forty-six per cent of the potatoes they sampled contained organophosphate residues. The prodigious use of farm chemicals, as well as changing patterns of cultivation and the destruction of marginal habitats, has led to an astonishing decline in the populations of farmland birds. According to the British Trust for Ornithology, woodcock and turtle doves have declined by 69 per cent in the last twenty-five years, spotted flycatchers by 79 per cent, grey partridges by 86 per cent and grasshopper warblers by 91 per cent. Skylarks, song thrushes, lapwings and tawny owls are also in danger of disappearance.

To portray these, as the rally's organisers sought to do, as exclusively urban concerns is to plumb the depths of absurdity. It is rural people who all too often have woken up to find the downlands, watermeadows, barrows or heaths which surrounded their homes ploughed out for seamless monocultures of rape and barley. Changes in the quality of their surroundings exert an enormous impact on the quality of their lives. This is, in truth, a conflict not between town and country, but between impunity and accountability, between the attitude of many landholders – that the land is theirs and they can do what they want to it – and that of many of the rest of us: that the fabric of the nation is our common inheritance, in which we all have an active interest.

Landscape protection in Britain is both inadequate in principle and ill-enforced in practice. Only the stupid or the ill-briefed farmer is prosecuted for destroying a Scheduled Ancient Monument (SAM) or a Site of Special Scientific Interest (SSSI). Thanks to numerous loopholes, procedures which seem designed to encourage the unscrupulous landlord, and the congenital ineffectiveness of both English Nature and English Heritage, the crafty and well-informed can destroy the nation's historical and ecological endowment without fear of prosecution. Farmers can even obtain express permission – called Class Consents – to continue ploughing out Scheduled Ancient Monuments.

Moreover, SAMs, SSSIs and national nature reserves comprise just a tiny proportion of the country's valuable archaeological remains and wildlife habitats. The great majority, though critical to our sense of place, have no legal protection whatsoever. Rapacious landlords can treat the rural landscape as if it were a factory floor. They often boast about doing just this.

Bizarrely, farming and forestry are not classified as development, so they are subject to no form of public accountability or control. The General Development Order even grants farmers exemptions from the building controls to which the rest of us have to adhere: as long as they are no bigger than 465 square metres in area and twelve metres high, clamps, silos and intensive pig units can be raised without so much as a note to the neighbours. As silos and concrete barns blot the most pristine horizons – National Park or Area of Outstanding Natural Beauty designations notwithstanding – the suspension of planning control for built agricultural development becomes ever more anomalous.

It is time to put the public back into the picture, to make farming reflect the wider public interest, rather than just that of the holder of the land. This necessitates the introduction of two things in which rural land management is peculiarly lacking: transparency and accountability.

No one who has witnessed the incremental loss of SSSIs and SAMs needs persuading that their protection procedures must be strengthened and simplified, but the more perplexing question is how to defend the remainder of our landscape features. Trying to legislate on the basis of farm activities would lead only to a bureaucratic cat's cradle. One could attempt, for example, to make the ploughing of all pastureland subject to some form of planning procedure. But, quite apart from adding to the farmer's burden of paperwork, and the taxpayer's burden of costs, this would hardly address the problem. Many pastures, being seeded with a single ryegrass cultivar, have already lost nearly all their biological and historical value. The diversity of the remainder is threatened as much by muckspreaders or changes in grazing routines as by ploughs. It is clear that, following this approach, you would soon need a planning committee for every farm in Britain.

Blanket planning prescriptions would be misguided not only when applied to activities but also when applied to habitat types. Laws against destroying all heaths, ponds or moorlands, for example, would swiftly run into the sands of definition, as conservationists and landlords fought over whether heath was scrub or old mine workings were ponds.

The only remaining option is the listing of individual features – the documentation of every round barrow, stone wall and watermeadow worthy of protection. The common response to this proposal is that the existing listed landscape features – such as SSSIs and SAMs – cannot be adequately protected, so what hope would there be of looking after many times that number? The task of mapping and defining them, moreover, would be monumental.

To answer the second point first, the bulk of the job has already been done. Most local authorities possess either field-by-field maps of their regions, recording all notable landscape features, or a list of locally important sites. Six hundred thousand archaeological sites have been mapped and documented. All that remains is to fill in the gaps and open negotiations to turn the informal maps into a definitive one, like the definitive map which has largely succeeded in maintaining our 120,000 miles of footpaths. Landholders wishing to alter the management of one of the listed features would then apply for the equivalent of the Diversion or Extinguishment Order they need when altering a footpath.

The major flaw in current protection mechanisms for SSSIs and SAMs is that they rely almost exclusively on an under-staffed bureaucracy, and make little use of the huge public enthusiasm for landscape protection. Footpath monitoring, on the other hand, while legally the concern of local authorities, largely relies upon ordinary people, who report illegal obstructions to their councils and, especially through the Ramblers' Association, ensure that they are removed. Not only does this work, it also allows ordinary people a role in the countryside – essential if we are to believe that the nation belongs to all of us, and all of us belong to the nation. But this mechanism cannot work for landscape protection without a right to roam.

Opponents of a right to roam claim that access would destroy the very resources that visitors value. The hidden beauties of the countryside, exposed to the unkempt and ignorant mass of humankind, would rapidly wither away. It is true that there are places, like Derwentwater and Dovedale, where the pressure of numbers does damage the land, and there are others where the fauna or flora is so vulnerable that it can tolerate no intrusion. But these conditions are rare and localised. They fail to justify our exclusion from uncultivated land in the rest of Britain. Indeed, looking at most of the places to which access is allowed, it is hard to escape the conclusion that public participation protects wildlife and archaeological sites, rather than destroying them. If damaging change takes place where people walk, there is a public outcry. But what no one sees, no one grieves – or not, at any rate, until it is too late.

When we are physically excluded from rural land, we are also excluded from participating in its development. It is pertinent, therefore, to look at the other reasons given for keeping us out. Landlords often claim that access to their land would represent an intrusion on their privacy. Gamekeepers will confront trespassers with this argument even when they catch them out of sight of the house, or on an estate owned by an absentee landlord. Why some people's privacy should extend across a substantial proportion of Britain, while most of us are content to let people walk past our front doors, is never adequately explained.

Visitors, it is claimed, do not understand the countryside, and will therefore cause chaos to farming, forestry and field sports. It is true that some visitors do, as landholders suggest, damage hedges or frighten livestock. But restricting these activities (and there are plenty of laws with which to do so) surely does not necessitate excluding the harmless majority, any more than stopping people from spraying graffiti or breaking shop windows means keeping everyone off the streets. In an empty countryside, vandals can set to work with little fear of detection. With a right to roam, they can never be sure that they are unobserved. If people are ignorant of the countryside it is surely because they have been so successfully kept out.

We are told that we have an adequate network of footpaths, from which there is no need to stray. Regrettably, many of the most charming and engaging corners of Britain are wholly inaccessible by public path. Perhaps more importantly, one visits the countryside to escape the constraints of dedicated space, the narrow regimentation imposed by the pavement, the office or ten square metres of garden. Keeping to the footpath does little to relieve our sense of confinement.

In truth, excluding people from the land is not, as landlords suggest, a duty, but a privilege. In buying a swathe of Britain you buy the right to exclude other people from it. The exclusive use of land is perhaps the most manifest of class barriers. With physical exclusion, one obtains a guarantee of social removal from the common herd. The rest of us are, quite literally, pushed to the margins of society. We must sneak around the countryside like fugitives, outlaws in our own nation.

We have, as a nation, forgotten one of the oldest principles of English law: that property and land are different things. Property is a bundle of rights pertaining to a piece of land, not the land itself. Indeed the only true land*owner* in the country is the Queen, which is why we describe land as real, or royal, estate. All the leaseholders or freeholders have is a licence allowing them to reap certain benefits from that land.

Until 2–300 years ago, there was scarcely a field in which only one person had property. Through enclosure of different kinds, both direct and indirect, the holders of the land have subtly appropriated more and more of those rights for themselves, until we, the rest of the population, are excluded from any stake in our inheritance. Landholders opposing a right to roam have argued that all the public wants is rights without responsibilities. In truth the landlords have successfully secured almost total rights, without any meaningful responsibility towards the public interest. Today's needs are, of course, very different from those of 300 years ago. But it seems to me imperative that the pre-enclosure principle is reasserted: that people's active interest in the land should be matched with rights. We need rights of access, of engagement, of participation in the land-use decisions which affect not only the holders of the land but also their neighbours and the wider community.

All over the world, the leaders of undemocratic states argue that good decision-making can take place only when the common mass of the population is excluded. With embarrassing regularity, the opposite proves to be the case. The same applies to land-use policies in Britain. The wider is public involvement in decision-making, the better and longer-lasting the emerging decisions are likely to be. Without a role in determining the future of our most fundamental resource, we will continue to suffer from the justifiable impression that full citizenship is the preserve of the fortunate few.

Bibliography

Fairlie, Simon, *Low Impact Development: Planning and People in a Sustainable Countryside* (Charlbury, Oxfordshire, 1996).
Harvey, Graham, *The Killing of the Countryside* (London, 1997).
Shoard, Marion, *This Land is Our Land* (London, 1997).

9. *Restoring the Countryside*
Robin Page

What has happened to our countryside? What has happened to our family farms? And what has happened to our traditional villages? My first memories of the land are clear and fresh; my parish contained six or seven farms and half the men in the village worked on them. The fields were a mixture of grass meadows and arable crops, including wheat, barley, oats, potatoes, kale and good old mangel-wurzels. All the farms had animals too; there was no need for the prefix 'free range' as there was no such thing as intensive beef or battery eggs. There was wildlife on and over the land – skylarks were forever singing their summer song, cowslips grew by the thousand in the spring, and at dusk, almost every dusk, the white owl (the barn owl) quartered the ancient watermeadows as it hunted for food.

It was a living countryside, producing good food sensibly and humanely, providing employment, while at the same time creating rich and varied habitats for wildlife in an attractive landscape. Those living in the village had a close link with the land, a link that went back many generations; it was a link that gave physical and spiritual security.

The village was a living community; with so many men, and sometimes women, working on the land, money circulated within the village through two thriving shops and two pubs. Travelling vans selling meat, groceries, bread and fish filled any gaps, and with a shoemaker living in the village too, there was hardly any reason to leave.

I still live in the village where I was born. In fact I write this just fifteen feet from the room next door where the midwife delivered me. Some may say that as a consequence my view of the world has a very limited horizon and that my lack of mobility has given me a romantic, nostalgic view of the land, one deeply rooted in the past.

I disagree. By remaining on the same farm, in the same village, I have witnessed change on a massive scale. I do not need a politician, an economist or a sociologist to explain the changes that have taken place in rural Britain, I have seen them and experienced them at first hand; very often it is the 'expert' that has missed the true reasons for change. Similarly I do not need an environmentalist or a Ph.D. researcher to tell me about the decline in farmland birds or inform me of the skylark's diminishing song – they have been obvious to me for years. Indeed nearly twenty-five years ago I wrote about the increasing pressures of change in my book *The Decline of an English Village*; then, with my friend Gordon Beningfield, the artist, we tried to warn of the losses, but our observations and fears were largely ignored. Evidently there is no problem unless a politician or a scientist sees it first.

Over the years the spring and summer mornings have quietened and I have seen wildlife disappear: the barn owl, the English partridge, the otter, the brown hare, the harvest mouse, the cowslip, the bee orchid, the marsh marigold and many more. Even the lapwing has ceased to breed and just visits us in winter. In addition, during my childhood there were usually fourteen pairs of breeding swallows on our small family farm; for the last three years we have been swallowless. This depletion represents more than statistics; to me they are real, personal losses and have diminished the quality of my life. What makes it worse is that they are losses that could easily have been avoided with a minimum of 'care', 'responsibility' and attention to 'sustainability'. Sadly these three words have almost disappeared from the farming vocabulary, to be replaced with a more sinister foursome: 'efficiency', 'productivity', 'profitability' and 'subsidy' – although how the brain-dead leaders of the farming and political establishments can marry the first three with the last, requires mental gymnastics of gold medal standard.

The truth is that over the years many of our farms have been turned into factories and the land has been transformed into featureless fields – the factory floor. Alas, the greed of production and the search for the third BMW has taken the 'culture' out of agriculture. Cheap food has been the aim of our urban-based leaders – surpluses and a dying countryside are the direct result.

Of course for an overpopulated island it is only sensible to have a farming policy that produces enough food to feed the country. At the end of the Second World War that was not the case. As a child in the years immediately after hostilities ended I well remember the rationing of cheese, bread, meat and chocolate. Clearly there was a case for increased production. But how did the politicians see that increase being achieved? Apparently by increasing the area of land in production; consequently attractive grants were offered for ripping out hedges, draining wetland and ploughing grassland. Even then the urbanisation of Parliament was producing politicians who did not understand the land and who did not understand farming. With more knowledge they would have understood that farming itself is in a constant state of change, development and improvement. Advances in animal and crop husbandry; breakthroughs in botany, biology, chemistry and technology have for years meant higher yields. Consequently just as more land was being brought into production, agricultural sciences were rapidly increasing yields and making self-sufficiency attainable in any case. As a result, by the time we joined Europe – to face quotas actually reducing our own, national self-sufficiency – we quickly drifted from a situation of food deficiency to one of food surplus. So, after millions of pounds had been paid to bring land into production with huge damage being done to our natural and semi-natural environments, even more money was then paid to take much of that same land out of production as 'set-aside'. What remarkable long-term planning; yet no politician or bureaucrat has taken the blame for this expensive madness. The most successful policy to date is to instal a system of non-accountability.

To assist bringing land into production thousands of lowland rivers and streams were assaulted by 'dredge and drain' maniacs, many of whom called themselves drainage engineers. With remarkable skill they turned some of our most valuable wetland ecosystems into nothing more than drainage ditches. Incredibly, as late as 1971, the madmen reached the brook on the southern edge of our farm; they lowered the brook bed by an astonishing five feet; wildlife was destroyed in a heartbreaking way – pike starved, kingfishers disappeared, the flowering rush and marsh marigolds became memories. This act of legalised hooliganism meant that the wet meadows and the flood plain meandering alongside the brook could be ploughed. Neighbours removed hedges to incorporate the newly dried out land into large cereal fields, and meadows that had produced hay, autumn grazing and wildlife became part of East Anglia's grain prairies.

In a natural drainage system water flows away during wet weather and is held back during drought. The newly drained brook, by contrast, became almost a flushing system – adding to the flooding problems in the Ouse Washes downstream, and allowing cultivation to take place right up to the brook bank. This in turn almost certainly led to nitrate leaching and pesticide drift, so helping to contaminate the river system. Incredibly too, it meant that the cereal land dried out so quickly that some farmers began to use irrigation systems to water their crops – compounding the long-term problem of water loss in the driest part of Britain. This madness, and more like it, took place throughout lowland Britain.

Even the scientific advances did not pass without problems. New systems and new chemicals were used with insufficient research; several of the DDT-based chemicals threatened to cause a wildlife catastrophe of their own. As herbicides and nitrates killed the wildflowers in the meadows, the poisons killed the barn owls, otters and sparrowhawks.

The industrialisation of farming did not end with this. What had once been seen as a way of life became a business. Agricultural colleges began to preach only 'efficiency' and 'profit' and even farm animals were seen not as cows and pigs, but as 'units' and 'products'. Farming, as an extension of nature using the rhythms of the seasons, became agribusiness, often working against nature and being driven solely by the economics of production. As the land worker was replaced by even bigger machines, so the 'farmer' became nothing more than a 'land manager'. The change in values and perceptions could be seen in the appearance of farms too; high-tech productivity was accompanied by an almost obsessive tidiness. Every odd corner of grass or farm track was mown or sprayed and hedges were trimmed every year for neatness's sake. The needs of nature – the hedgerow berries for wild bird food and tangles of branches and weedy corners for nesting places – were sacrificed on the altar of 'efficiency' and farming fashion.

Unfortunately Europe and the Common Agricultural Policy (CAP) did not check the process, but made it worse. Many environmentalists argue the case for the European Union, claiming that Europe-wide environmental directives clean up rivers and safeguard special areas. Their naivety and political correctness are touching; the fact is that the vast mass of land in Europe is farmed land and the CAP has overseen the destruction of wildlife and rural communities on a massive scale. Now, with bureaucratic indifference and environmental illiteracy, Brussels is threatening to take its wildlife destruction and social disruption into Eastern Europe with potentially even worse consequences than those caused by the old corrupt and inept Communist regimes.

The most absurd aspect of the CAP is that it rewards production with grants and subsidies, rather than subsidising the *means* of production.

Subsidies are used to control or promote production, and the environmental considerations of growing wheat, rape, linseed, beef or eggs are of little concern. At the present time in Britain about £3 billion annually is devoted to production subsidies, and about £100 million to environmental subsidies.

Nothing exposes the Mad Farming Disease pioneered by Europe more completely than the Integrated Administration and Control System (IACS). This annual handout, amounting to about £1.5 billion per year, was introduced in 1992. It assumed that CAP reform would lead to a 33 per cent drop in the price of grain. There was one slight problem: for the first four years the price did not drop and so farmers were paid compensation for a fall in prices that did not occur. The subsidy amounted to over £100 per acre for all wheat grown, over £200 for linseed, etc. It meant that all those who had removed hedges, ploughed old grassland and drained wetland were rewarded, while all those who had farmed responsibly and kept their woods and wet meadows received less.

The scheme was supposed to help the small farmer and the family farm; in Britain quite the reverse occurred: 80 per cent of the money annually went to 20 per cent of the largest landowners. With their good fortune, many of them have used their new-found wealth to devour their smaller and poorer neighbours. Last year there were at least eleven IACS millionaires and an estimated 5,000 farmers received IACS payments of over £50,000. Consequently, smaller farmers are being driven from the land, rural communities are suffering as a direct result and the situation will get worse. Between 1966 and 1994 the number of farm holdings of over 50 acres fell by 113,000 as many were absorbed by their neighbours, and in the past ten years over 88,000 jobs have been lost on British farms. This rate of loss is expected to accelerate.

With the 'global market-place' now featuring in the plans of the politicians, grain prices are tumbling and many farmers now need their support. With more worldwide free trade talks due, the situation will worsen and unless sanity returns a huge proportion of the rural population in both the first world and the third world will be destabilised on a scale never before seen. The only people to benefit will be the large producers and the large countries – for GATT (the General Agreement on Tariffs and Trade: now the World Trade Organisation) read Guarantees America Tripling Trade.

In Britain livestock farming has not escaped the process of industrialisation based on production, again promoted by the CAP. Since the introduction of the EU Sheepmeat Regime in 1980, the sheep population of Britain has risen by almost 40 per cent to 41.5 million. In the same period sheep subsidies have increased from £42 million to nearly £422 million. This has led to overstocking, overgrazing, and a greater use of chemicals for worm and fly control. Environmentally it has been a disaster, with our upland wildlife now coming under similar pressures to our lowland wildlife. Just as the skylark has plummeted by over 50 per cent in the last twenty-five years, the lapwing has fallen by a similar amount in just twenty years.

Those who doubt the damage and dangers of industrial farming should look no further than the disaster of BSE. It was a monster created by the drive for greater 'efficiency', faster production and higher profits. It was thought to be morally and economically acceptable to feed offal to cattle, turning herbivores into carnivores. Add the fact that the herbivores' nervous systems were already affected by organophosphate chemicals for the control of warble fly, and it is hardly surprising if a wholly new and devastating disease should result. BSE is a condition created by the system, and again the bureaucrats and politicians responsible for the regulations which allowed it to happen have not been held accountable. Interestingly too, the EU has played its part in the disaster. Although the full implications of BSE did not emerge until 1996, the European Commission knew of the consequences as early as 1990 and quite cynically tried to conceal them. As early as 12 October 1990, minutes of the European Commission's Consumer Policy Unit are revealing:

We must remain cool so as to avoid unfavourable reactions in the market-place. We must no longer mention BSE. And it should no longer appear in the agenda for forthcoming meetings . . . We are going to request officially that the United Kingdom ceases to publish any further results of their research . . . It is necessary to minimise the BSE affair by using disinformation. It would be advisable to state that the Press has a tendency to exaggerate.

If it had not been for the delving of the Referendum Party's research department, these sinister minutes would have gone unnoticed.

Once it became obvious that the full implications of BSE could not be contained, the European Commission went from one extreme to the other, imposing absurd restrictions on British beef, to the huge trading benefit of other European producers. Even after the threat of BSE had been successfully overcome the barriers were left in place, creating a financial crisis for thousands of British livestock farmers. Instead of coming to their aid, successive British governments, Tory and Labour, kowtowed to the Brussels Eurocrats imposing ridiculous bans and restrictions on British meat, of which Dr Cunningham's famous banning of beef on the bone was only one. The absurdity of the situation was aptly described by Senator Dan Glickman, American Secretary for Agriculture, at the 1998 Oxford Farming Conference. He said:

I was heartened recently to see British consumers recognise that things are getting out of hand. When the government banned bone-in beef, there was a rush to butcher shops to stock up before the ban went into effect. Consumers were on the news saying 'they've gone too far'. These kinds of actions leave a strong perception in the United States that here in the European Union legitimate public food safety concerns are being manipulated for political purposes.

The outlook for agriculture in the immediate future is not encouraging. Under the supervision of urban-orientated and environmentally illiterate politicians it seems that people are still destined to be driven from the land, to the detriment of our villages and the land itself. The further industrialisation of farming for the benefit of 'efficiency' and 'competitiveness' on the world market will increase the threats to our farmland wildlife and with the use of antibiotics, chemical cocktails and genetic engineering, food scares and health scares are likely to grow in number rather than fall.

But all is not lost. Many farmers have been most reluctant to follow the path of factory farming and there are signs that the rural community has had enough. On 1 March 1998, 285,000 country people marched in protest through London, myself included. Although organised by the hunting lobby, because of the threat to their cultural heritage, the march was also about BSE, the attacks on the family farm, the damage being done to rural communities, the outrages of the CAP, and many other grievances which politicians have chosen to ignore.

My own father failed to follow the absurdities of farming fashion and kept his hedges and grassland. Hugh Oliver-Bellasis, farming in Hampshire, has, with the Game Conservancy, pioneered ways of farming with wildlife, where hedgerows, beetle banks and a degree of untidiness allow nature to coexist with the best elements of modern farming. Similarly, in Norfolk Chris Knights farms on a large scale, very intensively, yet he also farms sympathetically – which means that as a wildlife film-maker he can actually make films about some endangered species living and thriving on his own productive farm. Others too are farming without chemicals, and in Shropshire Richard Mayall and his daughter Gini have been pioneers in organic farming. These and many more have shown, and are showing, that profitable farming can be carried out in a sustainable and responsible way – a way that the CAP should follow and encourage.

With a group of friends (including Chris Knights and Richard Mayall) I am trying to take the process further. After years of talking about the problems, and trying to get solutions accepted in high places, we decided to form the Countryside Restoration Trust (CRT). Our aim is to show that land devastated by over-intensive, industrialised farming could be brought back, and that profit could be obtained side by side with environmentally friendly farming.

The birth of the CRT was a long and unexpected process. After interviewing Sir Laurens van der Post for an article, we became friends and discussed at length what could and should be done to halt the steady slide of farming and the general countryside. I was also interviewed by Gordon Beningfield for a television programme and we too became firm friends. It was in 1980 that our concern took us to the then Director of the Royal Society for the Protection of Birds to discuss the problems of farming and the general countryside. But at that time he only seemed interested in 'nature reserves' and Sites of Special Scientific Interest and so our mission failed. Fortunately over recent years the RSPB has changed its stance and has added the clout of over 1 million members to the argument.

On our small farm changes were going on too. Following the disaster of the brook we finally persuaded the Environment Agency to stop cutting the banks each year, and gradually habitat returned. Then in 1990 we planted a small hay meadow, with traditional seeds – an idea developed and promoted by the remarkable Miriam Rothschild. With sponsorship from the Country Gentlemen's Association, the meadow quickly began returning to a recognisable old-type hay meadow, complete with cowslips. With both the brook and the meadow we could see that restoration was beginning to work. So, with no money, no members and no experience of running a charity, the Countryside Restoration Trust was formed, with Sir Laurens and Gordon Beningfield as founder trustees. Sir Laurens became the CRT's first Patron and he described its birth perfectly: 'I used to think that in conservation we want to train leaders; but it has gradually dawned on me that this concept is out of date. It is no good waiting for leaders, we have to lead ourselves.'

A landowner agreed to sell us 40 acres of land right next to the brook. It was exactly what we wanted: it was land that had been ploughed up after the brook had been 'drained' and it had been in continuous cereal production ever since. What followed was remarkable – otters suddenly returned to the river system of the upper Cam and showed a preference for the stretch of overgrown brook on the farm; the 40 acres would provide another length of potentially good otter habitat. A financial consultant warned us not to launch our Trust. 'You will only raise £2,000,' he said, and we needed £80,000. So, in July 1993 we launched. In the five years since we have raised nearly £1 million, we have bought almost 250 acres of land and we have a membership of 5,000. We have been astonished at the reaction and enthusiasm of ordinary people, and other conservation bodies are now following our concern for the general countryside.

Those first 40 acres have been transformed. The flood plain of the brook has been taken out of cereal production and a Miriam Rothschild hay meadow mixture planted. The arable has been separated from the hay meadow by a long hedge of fourteen species, planted by volunteers. We have grass margins and unsprayed headlands; a spinney has been planted, a pond dug and a meander has even been restored to the brook; as a direct consequence wildlife is flooding back and our tenant farmer is making a profit.

The return of wildlife has been astonishing, showing that if given a chance nature can restore itself, and that the process can take place surprisingly quickly. The otters are still in the area and appear to be thriving, English partridges are now breeding, as are yellow wagtails and reed buntings, and last year we had a pair of grasshopper warblers. Grass snakes have been seen, the brown argus butterfly has appeared and harvest mice have returned – all within four years.

The growth of the land has been just as remarkable and heartening. My elderly father sold the CRT 50 acres of the family farm adjoining the CRT land, for just £10,000, which the CRT will farm when my brother retires. Then out of the blue a block of 140 acres next to this came on the market in the autumn of 1997. The land had been in college ownership since 1352 and it would turn our experimental plot into a 'farm'. Laurens would have called such an unexpected sequence of events 'synchronicity'.

The land was perfect: 140 acres of wall-to-wall wheat – farming at its most industrialised – including another long length of cultivated flood plain. Again we needed money, but this time we were successful with a Heritage Lottery Fund bid, and after much tension and the manufacture of large amounts of adrenalin, the land was successfully acquired.

Now we will be able to put all our principles into practice. They are quite simple: we want to put the 'culture' back into agriculture; we want to create a living countryside, not a lifeless food factory; we want to stimulate the rural economy through our activities, and we aim to put people back in touch with their rural roots. We want to set new standards for sustainable farming and land use and we want production and conservation to go hand in hand with education and recreation. There will be numerous benefits as a direct result of our methods – less soil erosion; less water used; reduced pesticide use, nitrogen use and leaching; reduced threat of chemical drift; the creation of rural employment and attractive landscapes; the encouragement of more wildlife; the growing of high-quality food; high standards of animal welfare and, above all, hope for the future.

We are convinced that this is the way forward for farming and food production, not just in Britain, but worldwide. What we want is a network of demonstration farms owned and run by the CRT throughout Britain, and we are willing to take on gifts of land. We want to produce good-quality food and seasonal food, showing that the whole concept of 'cheap' food pushed by the politicians and the supermarkets is destructive socially, environmentally and spiritually.

We have chosen the skylark as our logo and we want to get the lark singing again over every field. The irony is of course that the politicians could achieve all this at a stroke if they had the will and the knowledge. All they would have to do is switch subsidies from production to the means of production. The British countryside could be transformed almost overnight – our wildlife would be restored, our rural communities invigorated and the CRT would be made redundant. How I long for that day.

Details of the CRT can be obtained from The Countryside Restoration Trust, Barton, Cambridgeshire CB3 7AG.

10. *Can Rutland Learn from Jutland?*
Paul Hirst

I f rural Britain is to remain *rural* it will need to find sources of local employment for local people. It can no longer be assumed that a significant proportion of such employment will be provided by conventional agriculture and services ancillary to it. If the distinctiveness of Britain's countryside is to be maintained then we shall also have to find ways of avoiding or containing the futures that seem to be in store for it: being converted into suburbs, landscape museums, or agribusiness prairies. These outcomes are already occurring to a greater or lesser degree. They seem to be the most likely possibilities for areas within car commuting distances of cities, of at least a minimum level of natural beauty, and that will allow big farming companies to compete on world markets in a post-subsidy trading regime. If these developments seem unattractive, think of what will happen elsewhere. None of these options will be available in much of Wales or northern England, nor in substantial pockets of the West Country. These remaining areas will probably become rural slums, with cast-off populations heavily dependent on the increasingly tattered remnants of the welfare safety net.

Agriculture may go the way of coal: an industry built up by public policy to sustain a perceived national need and then discarded when cheaper alternatives in the new regime of international trade present themselves. The run-down of coal has cast the miners aside. No sustained effort has been made to bring work to mining villages. Let us hope we can do better by the ordinary small farmer and farm labourer. I shall argue that small-scale manufacturing offers an alternative to both destructive development in the countryside and rural neglect. This cannot be achieved spontaneously, by the free working of market forces within the context of our existing institutions. Public and private institutions currently conspire against small-scale enterprise. The promotion of small-scale manufacturing and other enterprises in rural areas will require changes in institutions and public policy interventions, with the aim of making possible individual and community initiative. The policies in question are not statist and top-down regimes of intervention and subsidy, but serve to clear the way for local action.

We can learn some lessons from areas of Europe where rural manufacturing has grown and prospered as an alternative to or complement to agricultural work. Industrial employment used to be commonplace in the British countryside: peasants and farmers engaged in craft work during the winter; the putting-out system distributed industrial work to rural households, and artisans such as hand-loom weavers worked mainly in cottages and small villages. This was mostly swept away by the growth of mechanised industry in the towns, and the current separation of urban industry and rural agriculture is largely a product of the Industrial Revolution and the spatial specialisation and division of labour it introduced. In parts of Europe this division has never been so clear cut.

What is the Rural?

One might ask what is so special about the 'rural' that we should make exceptional efforts to preserve it, especially if the area concerned is not one of outstanding natural beauty? The rural is hard to define: sociologists and anthropologists have spilt lagoons of ink over it. Suffice to say that it is pointless to argue about what essentially distinguishes the rural, nor is it necessary to romanticise the countryside in order to wish to maintain it. Britons have used the land in hard-headed and utilitarian ways since at least the sixteenth century – economic rationalism is nothing new here* – and they have also gone romantically soppy over selected bits of it since at least the second half of the eighteenth century.

Let me simply contend that the rural is now defined in relation to its opposite, the urban. Rural areas have spatial patterns and social relationships that are not the same as those of the cities. A small, congested country needs to maintain areas that offer something *socially* distinct to the cities: options of living and not just national parks for the recreation of urban dwellers. What the rural can actually offer is complex and changing, but its enduring feature is that it is what the city is not. This does not involve the illusion that the countryside is the original authentic source of social life – cities being secondary and artificial. Modern rural areas have very little in common with those of fifty years ago, let alone five hundred. If anything,

---

* See Alan Macfarlane *The Origins of English Individualism* (Oxford, 1978).

modern social life is defined by urban features: by social and geographical mobility, by the dominance of mass communications, and by manufactured identities. The issue – the value of the rural – is not that the rural is more real, but that it is, in often subtle and minor ways, different. That remains the case if a substantial part of that difference is constructed both imaginatively and by the social engineering of public policy.

The advantage of reasoning in this way is not just that it avoids some of the traps of rural romanticism and defers to certain commonplaces of modern social theory, but that it provides a rationale for preserving the distinctiveness of places that are nothing special. It explains why we need workaday rural places, and not just historic sites or outstanding natural landscapes. Otherwise we face the options of deadening preservation or unbridled development or neglect. Trying to build up or maintain places that are not museums, dormitories or deserts requires a combination of public policy and individual initiative. The aim is to create appropriate local economic and social institutions. Central and local governments, financial institutions and big business are woefully ill adapted to the task. We need a radical departure in policy if we are to preserve the vitality of rural areas as sources of employment and output in an era of agricultural crisis.

Rural Manufacturing in Europe

To see how we might promote employment we have to reject the idea that the English countryside is unique and look at experiences elsewhere in Europe. A comparative perspective is essential on this issue. The key to understanding modern rural industry is that since the early 1980s social scientists have rediscovered the phenomenon of the industrial district. An industrial district may be defined as a population of small- and medium-sized firms in a particular branch of industry localised in a specific area and participating in a production system characterised by a division of labour between firms. Thus firms will engage in patterns of interchange that combine co-operation with competition. Industrial districts were first conceptualised by the English economist Alfred Marshall in his *Industry and Trade* of 1919.[*] Marshall drew attention to such British examples as the textile industry of south-east Lancashire, the Sheffield cutlery industry, and the large complex of small metalworking firms in Birmingham. Such districts were, of course, urban: by then the division of urban industry and rural agriculture was well established.

[*] London, 1919.

In the 1980s Italian economists like Giacomo Becattini and Sebastiano Brusco rediscovered this phenomenon in the Third Italy, a series of districts in north and central Italy with diverse industries, very different in character from the large firms of Milan and Turin and from the economically backward south.* Such districts were highly successful in the main, having experienced rapid growth and making key contributions to Italian export success in sectors like food products, textiles, machine tools and light engineering. Some districts were centred in industrial cities like Bologna, others around smaller towns like Prato, and some in rural areas like the Veneto. What the Italian experience showed, argued Charles Sabel and Michael Piore,† was that there was an alternative route to industrial efficiency to that based on large firms and the economies of scale of standardised mass production. Italy was very successful, at least north of Rome, in making high-class manufactured goods in small- and medium-sized firms, often in sectors like clothing and footwear that are written off by conventional economists as inevitably condemned to be replaced by low-cost imports from developing countries.

Many of these manufacturing centres were rural or based in small towns. Typically, the more organised districts had local sources of finance and institutions that provided collective services to industry, allowing them to enjoy both productive flexibility and some of the advantages conferred on larger firms by economies of scale. The industrial district was regulated by co-operation between local public bodies, trade associations, local industrial training schools and labour unions. Such districts are made up of local entrepreneurs, independent artisans and predominantly skilled workers, not by offshoots of big companies. As such they offered a regular passage from waged work to self-employment, as workers founded new firms in complementary products and were often helped to do so by their old bosses.

The discovery of the Third Italy led to a wave of studies of similar industrial districts in countries as diverse as France, Germany, Japan, Spain and the United States. For our purposes two countries are of particular interest, Denmark and Ireland, since they provide examples of industrial

---

* See, for example, Giacomo Becattini 'The Marshallian Industrial District as a Socio-economic notion', in F. Pyke et al (eds) *Industrial Districts and Inter-Firm Co-operation in Italy* (Geneva, 1990) and Sebastiano Brusco 'The Emilian Model: Productive Decentralisation and Social Integration', *Cambridge Journal of Economics* 6 (1982), pp. 167–84.

† *The Second Industrial Divide* (New York, 1984).

development in rural areas, and particularly because these developments have been most impressive during the 1980s and early 1990s, periods of generally slow growth and depression in Europe.

Denmark is well known for the capacity of its rural economy to respond in successive phases of development to international competitive pressures and changing industrial conditions. Danish farmers prospered in the mid-nineteenth century, but were threatened by low-cost grain imports to Europe from Russia and North America from the 1870s on. Danish farmers responded with a move of cultural renewal centred on the Folk High Schools movement and by switching to the production of milk and pork for butter and bacon exports. Peasant farmers combined to form co-operatives centred on common production facilities like dairies and slaughterhouses. It was by no means inevitable that the small farms/co-operatives route to modernisation would be followed. Attempts to dominate a variety of sectors by big business interests, imposing large-scale production, were partially successful. They were frustrated in the dairy and bacon industries because the co-operatives were able to establish product quality among large numbers of small farmers without centralised control and were able to give all members of the co-operative, irrespective of size, a say in policy.[*]

In the 1970s the previously decentralised, democratic and robust agricultural co-operatives were well and truly in disarray. Large dairies and slaughterhouses replaced the smaller ones, and imposed increasingly tough terms on farmers. Although nominally co-operative, the larger organisations like MD controlled the bulk of national milk production. Yet by the 1970s areas like West Jutland were becoming centres of local manufacturing production focused on small towns in sectors such as furniture and knitwear. Districts grew up around the railway towns, nodes in the old agricultural distribution network that had a history of small enterprises and craft production. As Peer Hull Kristensen points out, agricultural workers shifted from the stagnant food production sector to manufacturing industry.[†] Young people in the rural areas used the training system to obtain an apprentice education. He argues:

Their yeoman inheritance as independent, self-employed farmers or

---

[*] See Peer Hull Kristensen and Charles F. Sabel, 'The Smallholder Economy in Denmark', in Charles Sabel and Jonathan Zeitlin (eds) *World of Possibilities* (Cambridge, 1997).

[†] Peer Hull Kristensen 'Industrial Districts in West Zutland, Denmark', in F. Pyke and W. Sengenberger (eds) *Industrial Districts and Local Economic Regeneration* (Geneva, 1992).

craftsmen was a strong impetus towards the creation of their own businesses, now outside agriculture. Together entrepreneurship and educational transformation created a self-reinforcing mechanism, as new small craft-based enterprises have a high inclination to hire and educate apprentices who in these areas then will often create their own businesses.*

This is a dynamic one also sees in Italy. Its existence requires local self-governing institutions, responsive at neighbourhood or small-town level. In both Denmark and Italy local banks and other financial institutions, such as co-operatives, have provided the main sources of capital for this process of upgrading firms and entrepreneurial spin-offs of new firms by skilled workers. Furthermore, localised industrial training controlled by the district and providing skills appropriate to the local industries aided by specific inputs from firms is important in allowing the children of rural workers to switch occupation. As we still see, it is in these things that England is grossly deficient.

It should not be imagined that national economic and welfare policies in Copenhagen have always favoured such local economic strategies. During the post-1945 boom Danish policy was oriented toward promoting large-scale mass production. West Jutland developed in spite of rather than because of national policy. As a peripheral area its wages were lower than Copenhagen's, although they now compare favourably with those of most European countries. Moreover, firms moved from the localised production of the railway towns to competing in national and international markets. Jutland's experience can thus be judged a success in providing alternatives to conventional agricultural employment and one that grew up in a relatively backward area.

Ireland since the 1980s provides another example of the successful promotion of industry and alternatives to farm employment in rural areas. Until its entry into the EU in 1973, Ireland was an economic backwater and it then faced a period of crisis and macro-economic adjustment. Now it is nicknamed the 'Emerald Tiger', and has the highest rate of growth of GDP in Western Europe. Ireland has a superior record of inward investment to the UK (allowing for size). Contrary to fashionable beliefs in the UK, Ireland has achieved this with a system of corporatist negotiated

* Peer Hull Kristensen 'Industrial Districts in West Zutland, Denmark', in F. Pyke and W. Sengenberger (eds) *Industrial Districts and Local Economic Regeneration* (Geneva, 1992).

governance between industry, organised labour and the state, centred on the National Economic and Social Council. In particular it has continued to use negotiated national wage bargaining norms in order to control inflation.*

Ireland has an impressive record in recent years of local partnerships to promote industry and employment. The range of programmes is considerable and the results impressive, as documented by a recent OECD report.†
Indeed, so complex and numerous are these activities that the Report's main criticisms are that they raise problems of co-ordination and of disseminating the most successful practices. Until recently the Republic of Ireland was a highly centralised state, having inherited and reinforced a governmental pattern set during English rule. Ireland has benefited by decentralising late, and using partnership structures. It can thus use social co-operation and negotiated governance, rather than trying to use administrative machines to perform development strategies. Ireland, of course, has the real advantage of local community relationships that enable forms of policy experimentation to be pursued in a context of dialogue between actors who know one another well and show a fair degree of trust. Ireland has relatively high unemployment and the representatives of excluded groups still feel they are far from the centre of these partnerships. Nevertheless, the example shows that such local strategies can work in a country not markedly dissimilar to Britain, and one in which Dublin traditionally played much the same role as Westminster.

Why Is Britain Different?

These European examples show that manufacturing provides an alternative source of local employment to farming. Modern industry can exist in the countryside and in easily accessible small towns. Such manufacturing growth would stop local country people having to commute long distances to find jobs. It would also boost ordinary people's incomes and enable the less affluent country dwellers to afford housing. Small and medium-sized enterprises are well suited to farm, village and small-town sites. Moreover, agricultural and industrial renewal could work together. Linked to high-quality farming, local food processing by smaller firms may offer a challenge

---

* Patrick Commins and Michael J. Keane, 'Developing the Rural Economy', in *New Approaches to Rural Development* (Dublin, 1994).
† *Ireland – Local Partnerships and Social Innovation* (Paris, 1996).

to big food factories with their bland industrial products. Other industrial sections may well find the country highly suitable, and, given suitable encouragement, may extend the repertoire of employment beyond traditional crafts.

However, as things stand, current institutional arrangements make such developments extremely difficult, not merely for agricultural areas but for small manufacturing farms generally. There are virtually no industrial districts in the UK. The small and medium-sized enterprises sector is relatively weak in British manufacturing industry. The reasons for this state of affairs have been outlined by Jonathan Zeitlin in a provocatively titled paper 'Why Are There No Industrial Districts in the United Kingdom?'.* Even the urban areas Marshall wrote about have long been swept away.

Britain in the twentieth century has sacrificed its legacies of craft skill, diversified production and medium-sized family firms in pursuit of an ideal of industrial efficiency it has never managed to attain: the large American-style standardised mass-production firm. British industry has been decimated by a mixture of adverse macro-economic policies and by competitive pressures from more customised and flexible forms of production that developed elsewhere in the world in response to the volatile market conditions of the 1970s.†

Successive British governments promoted industrial concentration, from the rationalisation movement of the 1930s to the efforts of the Industrial Reorganisation Commission in the 1960s. In merger moves, encouraged by the stock market, big firms took over a larger and larger slice of both manufacturing and services. Most smaller manufacturing firms are subsidiaries of larger ones or tied into constraining relationships with bigger firms as subcontractors. British firms are isolated in purely commercial and competitive relations with one another, and the balance has shifted decisively against co-operation whether publicly orchestrated or informal.

Finance for smaller firms in the UK is extremely difficult, especially for start-ups. Banks are unwilling to advance loans without security, and equity financing is expensive. Britain lacks local banks – the major clearing banks long ago ceased to perform that role and have reduced the long-service branch bank manager to a figure from history. Britain also lacks alternative

* In Arnoldo Bagnasco and Charles Sabel (eds) *Ce que petit peut faire: les petites et moyennes entreprises en Europe* (Poitiers, 1994).
† Paul Hirst and Jonathan Zeitlin, 'Flexible Specialization and the Competitive Failure of UK Manufacturing, *Political Quarterly* 60 (1989), pp. 164–78.

co-operative financial institutions such as those of Denmark or Italy. Low-cost industrial finance for small firms is crucial for the development and maintenance of the sector.*

Local government in the UK is primarily directed toward service provision and operates bureaucratically; it lacks both the powers of general competence and the democratic entrepreneurial spirit needed for local development work. Moreover, English local authorities are the wrong size to perform economic development roles effectively: they are too small and too ill resourced to act like regional governments elsewhere in Europe in providing collective services to industry, and they are too big to be genuine neighbourhood organisations answerable to local people. Attempts by the Conservative governments in the 1980s and early 1990s to reform local government and to devolve services for business to bodies like Training and Enterprise Councils (TECs) and Urban Development Agencies (UDAs) have not greatly helped in this respect. In the interests of 'efficiency' services have been removed from local democratic control, but effective partnership organisations have not been built up.[†]

Technical colleges have become centrally funded, managerially controlled corporations. The TECs are not specifically concerned with the needs of rural areas and are too big to serve as the focus of localised industrial training of the kind one finds in these areas of Europe where small-scale and rural industry is relatively strong. By and large, local authorities act as obstacles to developing rural industry, imposing planning limitations and doing little to help. Rural people who might want to set up or work in small factories and workshops are often the last people to be listened to, after households and the heritage industry.

Can We Learn from Europe?

So much for the tale of woe. Can we do anything about it? In *Undermining the Central Line – Giving Government back to the People* Ruth Rendell and Colin Ward argue that Britain has delocalised government to an unhealthy degree and that other countries have far more effective local institutions.[‡] This is an irony, since eighteenth- and nineteenth-century England was

---

* Will Hutton, *The State We're In* (London, 1995).
† For a devastating critique of centralisation in Britain see Simon Jenkins, *Accountable to None – The Tory Nationalisation of Britain* (London, 1996).
‡ London, 1989.

seen by continentals as being much less centralised. The answer is hardly to be found in local government reorganisation, or creating local institutions by Acts of Parliament. Effective ways of building up rural industry, and much else besides, must bypass both big business and existing local government. The issue is not confined to rural areas: similar problems beset the rejuvenation of blighted inner-city districts. In both town and country we need to govern by partnerships between the relevant affected interests and by negotiation rather than by bureaucracy. We also need to promote effective action by voluntary associations, rather than by big firms or the state.

However, public policy and central government have to help here, clearing obstacles and providing access to finance. First, creating sources of low-cost finance is essential, through tax breaks, legal changes and grants. Local financial institutions – like industrial credit unions and mutual savings institutions oriented to industrial lending – have to exist before a significant population of local firms can establish itself. Second, local people have to be given access to training funds to use as they see fit, if necessary taking the money from the Further Education Council and the TECs. This will follow the development of a cluster of local firms, who should be encouraged by government incentives to offer apprenticeships and to develop a common scheme of local skills formation, if necessary by contracting local further education colleges or training firms to run suitable courses. In the end local firms must control syllabuses and hold the purse strings. Third, government should sponsor and provide funds for rural entrepreneurial agencies that provide expertise to build up local partnerships. Such partnerships form a public sphere for local industry, encouraging the dissemination of information, identifying problems, acting as advocates in relation to local and central government and as the focus for developing collective services. Collective services like training, research and design assistance, commercial intelligence and co-operative marketing are essential if small firms are to survive. They form the long-term foundation for partnership institutions.

State aid is wasted if it does not call forth efforts by society, promoting non-state action. We have been exceedingly bad at this in Britain, and only recently have we begun to get better. Rural areas do not have to be divided between the well-to-do commuters, the retired, telecottagers, wealthy farmers – and the rural workers, scraping by with intermittent and generally badly paid waged work. A society of yeomen – artisans, small entrepreneurs, skilled workers – could well return, if we work at it. This would provide not only alternative work, but alternative ways of living.

III

Food and Animals

11. *An Organic Connection*
Julian Rose

The philosophy which has sustained organic farming's rise from virtual obscurity to relative prominence is clearly a force to be reckoned with. Never easily assimilated by those seeking quick-fix solutions nor accessible as a tool for short-term gain, its appeal is nevertheless universal.

However, the 'holistic' approach which underscores organic farming is, in terms of general interpretation, still a fledgling force in society: one which hardly features even in the conference agendas of conservation organisations, let alone in boardrooms or government think-tanks. The omission is serious.

As we approach the millennium, it seems highly desirable that our attitudes towards energy, food and raw material production should converge, overlap and interrelate at the local level, so as to bring a new sense of social cohesion and regional identity. 'Sustainability' will only take on reality when this symbiotic process gets under way and is translated into policy decisions that replace the segregated, piecemeal, monocultural approach we have endured for too long. Agriculture's role purely as food provider is no longer tenable. We have witnessed the virtual destruction of our indigenous biodiversity during the past fifty years under the cloud of a rampant 'production ethic'. This ethic must be transformed if we are to set the next millennium on a sustainable course.

It was in 1946 that Lady Eve Balfour and one or two colleagues drew around them a small but influential group of scientists, farmers, doctors and those with a special interest in nutrition. These individuals were to become the founder members of the Soil Association. What they had in common was a deep concern: that the Brave New World of modern farming would turn out to be a costly, short-term expedient with potentially devastating long-term effects on soil fertility, biodiversity and human health. They had witnessed the scarcity of food during the Second World War and were aware of the need to overcome the poor agricultural yields associated with the Depression of the 1930s. The answer, they believed, lay not in the cheap new bag of synthetic nitrate fertiliser, but in the judicious recycling of composted animal manures, vegetable residues and fertility-building grass clover leys. The seeds of the 'ecological' versus 'agrochemical' debate were sown.

More than fifty years later the debate rages around the agricultural arena; but back in 1946 almost nobody concerned with 'progressive' farming methods paid a jot of attention to those early pioneers of organic farming. After all, these people were talking about retaining crop rotations to prevent disease and encouraging diversity of field and hedge, birds and insects, beetles and bugs. Surely they were just misguided romantics clinging to a bygone era?

Then, in the early 1960s, Rachel Carson wrote *Silent Spring*. Her investigations of the side-effects of the widespread application of the organochlorine pesticide DDT were to shock both citizens and the farming establishments of North America and Europe. Here was proof, on a large scale, that agrochemicals kill more than just the 'pests' of the arable fields. The cyclic, symbiotic principles of organic farming were vindicated. It became apparent that health depends on enhancing the cycle of life that passes from soil to plant to animal and to man, and back to soil. Interrupt this dynamic and a breakdown will eventually ensue in all areas. If the insect life, which forms a key element of the diet of birds, is destroyed by pesticides, then the birds die too. If the water that supports the living organisms essential to the diet of fish is polluted, then the fish also succumb. If the ability to grow a large volume of cheap food is dependent upon destroying those elements of nature that naturally cohabit with the agricultural crops, then what will the repercussions be for other creatures whose existence hangs on the availability of a wide diversity of plant and insect life? And what about man?

For a short while these momentous questions hung tantalisingly in the air. But the rapidly developing juggernaut of factory farming had only sustained a puncture, a brief setback, and was soon rolling on down its high-input, high-output pharmaceutical highway. The arsenal of pesticides, herbicides and fungicides became ever greater and ever more widely taken up by farmers determined to get maximum yields, and fearful of failing to keep up with the rapid technological changes that would make such yields possible. Nevertheless, some people never forgot the message of *Silent Spring*; most of these were not farmers, but ordinary citizens.

In the midst of these upheavals organic farming was gradually emerging.

First as an alternative and more recently as a general solution to the degradation suffered by food and land world wide. In the late 1950s the Soil Association pioneers had felt it necessary to demonstrate the viability and scientific credibility of organic methods on the ground. They did this by subjecting trial sites to different levels of synthetic and natural inputs. The area comprising a variety of livestock and entirely natural (organic) inputs eventually outperformed and outyielded those dependent on synthetic sprays and fertilisers. This was the Haughley Experiment, named after Haughley in Suffolk where it took place. The trials, which extended into the 1960s, established and qualified the essential message that a fertile, living soil is the foundation for the quality and nutritional value of the food it grows and, therefore, for the health of society. It also revealed that a chemical-based approach is inherently destabilising and ultimately destructive. No longer could it be justifiably proclaimed that only agrochemically inspired farming could feed the world.

Conventional scientists, however, greeted the trials with scepticism, claiming that the control methodology was not in line with classical models. They were already wedded to the high-input, high-output mono-cropping regimes and refused to entertain the idea that organic mixed farming methods might get better results. Government listened to the scientists.

By the time I joined the Soil Association Council in 1984 the environmental as well as animal welfare dimension of the agricultural debate was hotting up. We had started to convert Hardwick's land in 1975, when there were still very few exponents to turn to for help, and my background had been in experimental theatre! But by starting small and gradually working up a livestock and arable mixed farming enterprise, we discovered for ourselves that organic methods do eventually deliver, and that it is possible to produce adequate volumes of nutritious flavourful food without getting on the agrochemical treadmill.

In considering the origins of the market for the newly emerging organic produce, we need again to look back to the 1960s. As a first wave of reaction to the emerging mass food processing industry, 'wholefood' shops started to spring up in the towns and cities of North America and northern Europe. A new generation of 'health conscious' citizens frequented them, seeking out foods that had not been denatured and devitaminised. However, the supermarket chains, working in tandem with agribusiness, food processors and eventually governments, increasingly exerted their authority over the market-place throughout the 1970s and 1980s.

Their axiom 'pile it high and sell it cheap' soon expressed the ethos of the entire conventional food and farming industry. And as the more urban-based 'new consumers' steadily outnumbered those retaining some understanding of and connection with the countryside, so the power of the multiple chains expanded. Soon the wholefood products were subsumed by the giants and the little shops that had started the revolution were forced out of business. Today, in the UK, 80 per cent of all groceries are purchased from superstores, as well as most organic food. The average distance travelled by the produce that lines their groaning shelves is 3,000 kilometres.* By the 1980s the local supply and demand market was a dwindling phenomenon, with seasonability and regionality of food largely relegated to a scattering of farm shops and 'pick your own' enterprises. The food market had gone global.

If organic farming and growing is to maintain its momentum as a serious force for reform it will need to be at the forefront of efforts to change these patterns. This will involve revising its own contribution to food miles. The most likely way of achieving this is by recognising the potential in our own back yards, in the hamlets, villages and market towns. These provide the sadly diminished social base for most country people, but were once the centre of a bustling rural economy. Not so long ago farriers, carpenters, butchers, bakers, shopkeepers, millers, farming folk and poets all rubbed shoulders in the course of their daily work, and village life hummed with activity. As recently as 1965, when I was in my teens, the adjacent villages of Whitchurch-on-Thames and Pangbourne still sported two bakeries, three butchers, three or four general stores and post office combinations, a mill and a blacksmith. Our bread and meat was not only of superb flavour but was delivered to the door! Up and down the country the same story could be told: once-thriving communities, now just a shadow of their former selves. And that shadow, more often than not, is enshrined museum-like for the benefit of curious groups of tourists. Today, the purchase of knick-knacks and curios constitutes the main trading activity of many such a village.

This lamentable decline, from the heartbeat of a vital economy to the level of a museum exhibit, vividly illustrates the changes that have

* A Paxton, *Food Miles Report*, S.A.F.E. Alliance, London 1994

occurred in Britain since the war – changes that have left us almost totally dependent on the shifting global economy.

A 1997 report by the Rural Development Commission reveals that half of all rural UK food shops closed in the six years since 1991. Eighty-two per cent of rural parishes now have no food-only shop and seven out of ten are without a general store. But we should not view the future as an inevitable extension of the recent past. There are signs that a new rural economy – addressing the pressing issues of today and tomorrow – can rise from the ashes. Organic farming is well placed to be a pioneer in this area. It is, after all, a direct continuation of earlier time-honoured agricultural practices that were bypassed in the agrochemical rush for ever higher production levels. Most of the techniques, such as the utilisation of crop rotation and mixed husbandry, were the domain of virtually all farmers not so long ago. The modern organic movement is endeavouring to improve knowledge and expertise in the sustainable management of the farming cycle. The next step will be firmly to attach organic farming's rising fortunes to those areas most in need of a similar change of heart: our disenfranchised villages and market towns.

According to a Soil Association report, UK sales of organic food amounted to approximately £400 million in 1997. But 70 per cent of this came from imports. There is no reason why fresh, flavourful and wholesome food reflecting the regional variations of our countryside should not directly supply most of our market towns and villages. It could provide the staple dietary requirements of each region or county, and there would be no need to purchase from further afield. Any overproduction would be available for adjacent regions with a shortfall. Clearly certain types of food like citrus fruits, spices and other exotics would still have to be traded on the world market; but to import our basic dairy food requirements from California, Peru, Kenya and Australia is not only unnecessary but highly destructive socially, environmentally and economically.

Having absorbed the logic of this approach, it is a short step to realising that energy requirements should also be part of the same 'local and regional' distribution pattern. Insufficient research has been carried out in the UK to tell us exactly how much 'renewable' material is required to sustain our regional energy requirement. But there is little doubt that a combination of solar, wind, biomass (from trees) and other renewable sources of power would go a long way towards meeting our targets. This would also bring the relation between people and means of production into a proper human scale. Most building materials can also be produced locally, For example timber structures for light industrial units, based on local renewable forestry production, utilise a fraction of the energy and cause far less pollution than steel portal constructions, whose manufacture and transportation are the cause of considerable pollution.

At present there are few signs of financial incentives to develop local/ sustainable initiatives. Currently just 3 per cent of UK taxpayers' money used to support conventional agriculture goes towards social and environmental improvement schemes. This is a paltry contribution, given the degradation suffered over the past four to five decades. Erosion alone has contributed to an annual soil loss of between 5 to 8 tons per acre on many conventional arable farms that have long since abandoned returning farmyard manure to their starved land. The removal of pesticide residues from drinking water costs over £250 million annually and the mounting bill directly applicable to the BSE crisis is already over £4 billion. This last is a crisis that need not have happened if organic and extensive farming methods had been respected. Large-scale hedgerow, bird and wildflower losses have already been well documented.

Many farmers, particularly those on the small and medium-sized farms already struggling to compete in the subsidised European market-place, are going to find life impossibly tough in three or four years' time, as GATT world trade rules force European CAP subsidies to be tapered off. Already 10,000 UK farmers have gone out of business each year for the past decade, leaving less than 2 per cent of the national workforce still on the land. Only a radical change of emphasis in the production and distribution of food, energy and shelter requirements can turn this situation around. The newly emerging Regional Development Agencies would be the right vehicle with which to begin this process.

Already, under the general heading of 'Community Supported Agriculture', farmers and growers are taking their own initiatives. Boxes of seasonal, fresh organic fruit and vegetables supply some 20,000 UK families up and down the country, in some cases at prices lower than those in the supermarkets. One such 'box scheme' operates from my farm, under a share-farm agreement with the Tolhurst family who joined us in 1987. They manage a 10-acre field plus 2-acre walled market garden site and are now growing and distributing forty or more varieties of home-grown vegetables over a nine-month period.

The Hardwick box scheme supplies over 200 families in Reading and Oxford, both within twenty miles of the farm. Its success lies in its simplicity. For around £6.50 the customer gets a variety of seasonal organic vegetables (and fruit) harvested on the day of delivery and made up to a standard weight. No packaging, no processing. The boxes are then transported to an agent, who acts as the collection point for those living in his or her part of town. Agents get a free box for their role in distribution. Once or twice a year participants in the scheme come out to see the farm for themselves. Sometimes they also help out with weeding or harvesting. A certain symbiosis is respected. Town and country are drawn closer together and the popularity of the scheme has ensured the economic viability of an area of land unlikely to be profitable under any other management regime.

Half a mile away, up the hill, is the Old Dairy Farm Shop. This is the retail outlet for Hardwick's organic beef, lamb, milk and cream as well as market garden produce. Free-range eggs and table poultry are also raised on the farm and sold through the Old Dairy. Organic pig production is coming along. Elizabeth Rose has taken the enterprise from a 'farm gate' single-room operation doing freezer packs of organic meat in 1991, to its current status as a fully stocked farm shop, carrying a wide range of artisan and organically grown foods.

Elizabeth took on the job with no previous retailing experience, armed only with a degree in social anthropology gained the hard way as a mature student, simultaneously raising a young family. One thing we both agree about is that as a place to study people (and their purchasing habits) the Old Dairy is second to none.

Local production and consumption is catered for by both the farm shop and box scheme. Seventy miles due west, in Bath, the first UK farmers' market now attracts increasing numbers of both producers and buyers. The majority of its produce is also fresh, local and seasonal.

Forestry is equally ignored as a valuable resource base. Hardwick Estate's forestry enterprise consists of 450 acres of mature beech, oak and ash as well as softwoods like larch and Douglas fir. Firewood is produced from the tops of 150-year-old felled beech and sold locally, as are planks, cut on site utilising a mobile sawbench and seasoned for up to two years. By maximising our local resources we are also able to keep individuals employed who in other circumstances would have been laid off. Three times the number of people now earn a living at Hardwick as did twenty years ago. Eight estate cottages house them. But it is still tough. The small fields and hills of the Chilterns are more subsistence farming territory than profitable agricultural material.

Nevertheless, our small contribution to a more 'sustainable' society does offer a clue for other estate and farm owners. This clue connects with the last Rio Summit 'Agenda 21' proposals for moving societies away from their addiction to the high fossil fuel consumption and attendant toxic pollutants that aggravate global warming and accelerate the collapse of biodiversity.

These problems require a collective response. Some would advocate a Ministry of Rural Affairs: but whether this would amend the situation or exacerbate it by reinforcing the centralising trend is open to dispute. Better perhaps to establish regional bodies charged with encouraging the rural sector towards a genuinely integrated framework, embracing our rural communities, food and energy production as well as the implicit environmental and employment challenge, as one common concern. For at bottom that is what they really are. And only recognition of this will bring the right results.

These changes should not be viewed as solely the domain of the formal economy. Informal organic growers, for example, arguably greatly outnumber their professional counterparts. Allotment plots all over the country bear witness to eager green fingers sowing and reaping their own organic harvests. Vegetable gardens planted in back gardens and deserted plots are springing up in all our major cities. City farms also introduce farm animals. The Henry Doubleday Research Association has more than 25,000 members, eager to practise organic growing on whatever plot of land they can get their hands on. All over the countryside, people are reverting to bartering and sharing outside the strictures of the conventional economy. We have witnessed a partial return of the house cow along with the fully domestic pig and hen. Often these animals are kept in paddocks adjoining cottages and farmhouses long since vacated by those once employed in full-time agriculture. These are all 'people'-oriented, small-scale organic enterprises. Yet the social element of formal farming is lamentably ignored by policy-makers in England. A little economic realism would soon reveal that more people are needed on the land, not less.

If our 12-acre market garden enterprise can employ three workers and

supply 200 local families with their weekly fruit and vegetable requirements, then why does the MAFF think-tank insist that the only way for
farming to remain 'efficient' is for one man to run 1,000 acres of arable land
planted with genetically modified seed and harvested by a satellite-
instructed combine harvester costing £250,000?

If we employ woodmen to provide enough fuel from the offcuts of a
traditional mixed Chiltern forestry enterprise to keep the same 200 families
warm, why do we need to import nuclear electricity from France?

If our thirty-five Guernsey cows can provide those same 200 lucky locals
with their weekly fresh unpasteurised milk, why should they each drive a
twenty-mile round trip to the supermarket in order to pay the same price
for the tasteless, pasteurised look-alike, which has already travelled over 300
miles to get to the store?

The fact is that agribusiness, factory farming, feed merchants, supermarkets, governments and even agricultural colleges all fall into line in holding
on to the myth called 'efficient farming'. The BSE crisis bears powerful
testimony to the folly implicit in this dogged single-mindedness.

The culture which has brought supermarkets so much into prominence
has played a significant role in giving conventional agriculture the sterile
face that it has today. The farming methods required to satisfy the multiple
chains' desire for near perfect-looking, carefully packaged uniform
produce, involve monoculture on a grand scale and the full armoury of
agrochemical sprays. In stark contrast to organic systems, 90 per cent of the
pigs and poultry sold in supermarkets are raised in controlled environments,
never seeing the light of day and living on feed permanently laced with
antibiotics to ward off the inevitable diseases. As if this were not bad
enough, proponents of such excesses are now vigorously proclaiming the
wonders of genetic engineering whose sinister bag of tricks contains animal
cloning, and the production of genetically modified organisms in both
plants and livestock. This must be the ultimate betrayal of ethical
responsibility and human dignity. The deliberate and cynical distortion of
our inherited gene pool will almost certainly carry potentially irremediable
distortions into every avenue of life. So far, in the world of food and
farming, only organic organisations have refused to countenance this latest
and most abhorrent of technical fixes.

There are abundant challenges facing those who care about the plurality,
diversity and richness of life. Even as I write, the future of unpasteurised
milk is under threat, hot on the heels of beef on the bone. There is a real

danger that increasingly interventionist governments may attempt further to standardise our food supply. The result would be fewer and fewer immunological challenges. Sterile depleted foods such as heat-treated milk, pasteurised eggs, irradiated chickens, processed cheeses and genetically engineered soya and maize are a direct threat to the health of our reproductive and immune systems. Human welfare, animal welfare and environmental welfare are organically connected.

The alienation of the individual from his or her means of survival brings with it an alienation from fellow workers and therefore from society. Farmers and growers remain the essential workforce everywhere in the world, although (particularly in the West) this is often forgotten. Organic farmers and growers, although currently only numbering about 800 in the UK, should be at the forefront of a revival of agricultural practices that will bring about environmental, social and economic change. Nearly all other European countries have taken a significant lead in supporting organic farming. Austria now has 12 per cent of its farms running on organic methods. Much of the southern hemisphere, while suffering many other problems, is at least not yet wholly dependent upon expensive agrochemicals. British agricultural policy, until now unwilling to offer serious help to organic farming or related social concerns, needs to demonstrate its willingness to get off the agrochemical treadmill and take the sort of innovative leap of imagination that Tony Blair seems keen to promote. For at the grass-roots level a storm is brewing in the countryside and only by acting imaginatively can we turn nagging discontent into renewed hope and opportunity.

Town and country can no longer view their futures in isolation. We must revive the underlying historical links inherent in the design, layout and aesthetics of most of our market towns, villages and even cities: links that offer proof of our daily dependence on food, fuel and fabric. We must reconnect these fundamental needs to the place where they arise, rather than importing them from halfway round the globe. Couple this 'proximity principle' to the fast-growing development of green (sustainable) techniques and materials and the tougher lessons of the Industrial Revolution may at last have been learned.

12. *Food, Farm and Future*
Hugh Raven

Food symbolises the body of Christ. It is an aid to seduction. Eating some foods, like the *fugu* of Japanese cuisine, can be exquisite suicide, as its poison numbs the throat. Bad food makes us sick, and fatty foods thicken our blood. Anorexics die from fear of getting plump, while legions succumb to obesity. Policies for growing food waste £20 for every British household each week. Food causes conflict: from rivalries in the produce tent at village fêtes, to armed confrontation over access to famine relief. Bananas, tuna fish, hormone-laced milk and beef on the bone, transgenic soya and irradiated prawns: food looms large in trade disputes too.

There's a more gentle battle being played out in the UK's food supply, a dialectic between two visions of how we should feed ourselves. On the one hand there is the industrial food economy, big, brash and clever; and then there is the food artisan. Economically they are incomparable, but both tell us about our values and culture and the country we want to inhabit. For most of us – all but the very poor – food is freedom, a weekly, daily or hourly chance to express our twenty-first-century destiny as consumers. Food – fast or whole, grazed or feasted – is our most frequent expression of choice. Our options have expanded enormously – the great achievement of industrialisation. But at a cost.

The industrial food economy is characterised by scale, uniformity and ruthless competition. Its chain of command starts at the farm. The UK is an overcrowded country, yet we have the largest farms in the European Union, and they are getting larger still. Consequently fewer people work on the land – at 2 per cent and falling fast, a lower proportion of the workforce than any other country in the OECD bar one: metropolitan Singapore, with no farmland to speak of.

With larger farms come fewer enterprises: mixed farming is now a rarity, and production is divided like oil and vinegar between the arable east and the pastoral west. Monotony is found too in the things we produce, with a narrowing genetic pool and inbreeding. The top three varieties of spring wheat account for 86 per cent of plantings; oats 77 per cent, winter wheat 51 per cent and sugar beet 61 per cent. It is the same in our commercial flocks and herds, dominated by super-breeds: the dairy Holstein, the large white porker, the laying Warren and the Ross table chicken, with heavy thighs and bones often incapable of bearing its weight.

As farming abandons the four-course rotation which revolutionised eighteenth-century England, it relies more and more on external inputs. Where the livestock are gone, there is no call to maintain the hedges. Fields get larger, so bigger tractors are more economic – and burn more diesel. Energy input-to-output ratios decline – moving away from sustainability. As plant food in bags supplants farmyard manure, half the industrial arable farm's energy consumption comes in the form of glistening white granules – nitrogen fixed from the air, each pellet a speck of gelled power. A truncated rotation means more persistent weeds; and mile upon mile of uniform crop made lush with bag-N is the ideal nursery for pests and diseases – so we call for the sprayer, another outing for the tractor, more fossil fuels burned.

Increasingly our large farms are producing on contract. The market-place of the economist's dreams, with many buyers and sellers, has given way to oligopoly. A few large buyers, the retailers and processors, can dictate the terms. In this food economy, agricultural products have become industrial feedstock – undifferentiated milk, grain or slabs of meat, like the frozen pork bellies of Chicago trading-floor fame. Who would recognise a cube of protein soaked in scarlet sauce on a plastic tray as part of a chicken's anatomy – by sight, or even by taste? And when their tastes are disguised, ingredients are easily substituted. If the potatoes for starchy snacks get too pricey, new technologies allow wheat, maize, cassava or rice to be used instead.

As ingredients are substituted, so too are suppliers. The horticultural trade is particularly vulnerable: a perishable product gives more power to the buyer. With fresh vegetables, supermarkets stipulate the exact type of packaging and labelling to be used, on pain of rejection of produce. According to the trade magazine *The Grower*, 'multiples tend to specify equipment from different manufacturers, for example for computer generated labels. Labelling machinery has been a matter of constant change as supermarkets first switched to bar coding and then to endless variations on the theme.' There's no room in that supply chain for the small business.

It takes investment beyond the means of most farmers even to be eligible to sell produce to supermarkets.

This dominance comes from a highly concentrated market, with nearly three-quarters of sales through just five supermarket companies. In some areas – such as Sutton, in Surrey – one retailer can have nearly two-thirds of the sales. Since competition law defines a monopoly as 25 per cent or more of the market at a national level, this local dominance escapes the authorities' notice. Yet to the consumer it is what matters, as in spite of the growth of car use, food shopping is still a local activity. It is no consolation to the shopper in Plymouth that there may be more competition in Bristol, let alone in York.

Large stores are the urban expression of the industrial food economy, both a consequence and a cause. The larger they are, the wider their dominance – and the more traffic they generate. Of eight categories of new urban development in the traffic planners' trip-generation model, only restaurants cause more car journeys for a given space. It is widely believed that modern shopping patterns have reduced the number of shopping trips. In fact there are more of them, they are longer, and more are by car. The total number of shopping trips is up nearly a third over the last twenty-five years; the distance covered by drivers has more than doubled. The car is now totally dominant: in the mid-1980s less than two-thirds of people did their main food shopping by car; ten years later it was over three-quarters.*

If getting people to their food has changed, so too has getting food to the people. Take the Welsh hill farm I know with its annual field of carrots, sold through two shops in the local town. One distribution route is from soil to greengrocer direct in a sack, total distance travelled five miles. The other is via pack-house and regional distribution centre and back to the town's only supermarket: distance travelled twenty-five times further – and the carrots, on arrival, less fresh.

Ninety-eight per cent of the supplies to an average superstore come via such a distribution centre, and 'just-in-time' delivery has replaced storage on site – so most modern superstores have minimal warehousing space. The result is a huge increase in freight. As an industrial sector, food, drink and tobacco account for about one-tenth of GDP (with tobacco declining), but more than a third of the growth in road freight. Thankfully no other sector comes close to such an explosion in demand for lorries and

---

* Figures derived from the National Travel Surveys of 1975/6 and 1989/91, and from a report from the Policy Studies Institute to the authors of *Off Our Trolleys?* (see bibliography).

motorways. We eat the same amount as we did a quarter-century ago, but it travels over 50 per cent further within Britain. Air-freighted food tonnages have increased even more, doubling in the 1980s and now growing faster still.

The companies and trends characterised in this picture dominate the food economy. While it has delivered Britain's famed cheap food policy – we spend less each year on sustaining ourselves, and are arguably better fed and undoubtedly living longer than ever before – in many respects it offers a bleak prospect for the future. It delivers diversity on the shelf, but stifles it in the field. It also does damage to much that we value.

Yet look more closely and you see other things happening too, apparently contradictory movements. Small seedlings are sprouting like convolvulus in the monotonous landscape, taking root and spiralling to bind more people to the land.

Ironically, the artisan food economy has recently been enjoying a major renaissance, simultaneous with the tightening grip of industrialisation. But perhaps it is not ironic; perhaps it is the natural human tendency to seek or recreate colour amidst greyness, to build a stockade on the prairie and plant it with wallflowers. Though the number of independent bakers continues to decline, in some towns they are coming back. Certainly there are more cheese-makers. New and piquant chutneys and mustards are made, alongside more traditional preserves. Tamworth, Middle White and Gloucester Old Spot pork is available again – like the plump ham I had surreptitiously sent across the country in the Christmas post. Smoked or jellied eel is easily obtainable, and with a bit more effort, chewy hot-smoked venison, cured wild boar, even dormouse, grey squirrel from a Wealden butcher, and prize-winning Cornish salami. One food writer, Henrietta Green, makes a living from celebrating the new speciality food producers of Britain. Her publications get thicker each year.

If these are the glimmerings of a revived local food culture, organic production is the sun around which they revolve. Much nonsense is talked about organic farming, from thinly veiled hostility in the agricultural press to the sneering disdain of Britain's farming leaders. Even campaigning environment groups – including those dedicated to the countryside – have been arrogant and patronising. As a result, the UK's record in organic production is deplorable. We import 70 per cent of organic food consumed here, much of which could be grown in the UK; and we have the lowest level of payments for organic farmers – pitiful in comparison with mainstream subsidies – and consequently the lowest organic acreage of any EU country. Yet we have more reason to support it than most: Britain inflicted BSE on the world by ignoring the precepts of sound husbandry.

The distinctive features of the artisan food economy are the inverse of its industrial foe. It is small-scale and labour intensive, with organic farming shown to provide 10–50 per cent more employment per acre, and still more downstream off the farm. With no artificial fertilisers and strict limitations on sprays, energy use is lower. The benefits for landscape and wildlife are even clearer: crop diversity is obligatory on organic farms, hedges and other landscape features must be maintained, and birds, invertebrates, wildflowers and butterflies thrive as a result.

Artisan food producers are also finding new ways – or in some cases reviving old ways – of marketing their produce. Most feature direct trade between producer and consumer, ensuring freshness, reducing food miles, delivering good value for the buyer and the full retail price to the seller by cutting out middlemen and distribution costs. Despite tighter food hygiene rules, mail order is one well-tried route. Farm shops are springing up (like the prize-winning Old Dairy near Pangbourne – see Chapter 11 by Julian Rose) which, to succeed, must carry a variety of goods – so encouraging a wider range of enterprises on the farm. A handful of farmers' markets have appeared, where farmers come to town one or two days a week and sell direct: from small beginnings, there are now nearly 2,500 such working markets in the US, serving a million shoppers each week.

In the UK perhaps the best-developed model of direct marketing is the thriving network of box schemes, where the grower establishes a distribution round in a local town, delivering a box of mixed produce on a weekly basis for a fixed sum. Direct contact between consumer and producer leads to experimentation with new crops and varieties. Jan and Tim Deane's box scheme in Exeter, perhaps the best-known in the country, welcomed feedback from the customers – and the number of crops grown has increased from twelve to over forty as the Deanes got to know their customers' tastes.

New plots are being dug for food-growing in towns. The famous Guinness site in Wandsworth, south London, under occupation for a summer in 1996 by land-rights campaigners from The Land is Ours, sprouted vegetables, herbs and fruit trees. More enduring are some of London's community schemes, like the garden and orchard in Camberwell Green, and the vegetable plot in Hackney's Grazebrook Primary School.

The Battlebridge Centre in King's Cross uses raised beds to bring life to a contaminated site. 1998 has seen the first city harvest festival for London's produce, an effort to emphasise the potential of London's 2,500 acres of allotments, 4,000 acres of derelict land and 1.5 million household gardens, parks, rooftops and playgrounds. In Salford, Reading, Nottingham and Bradford, food is being produced on communal land. In Glasgow, surplus produce from Westthorn allotments is sold through the local food co-op, while the West Midlands' Sandwell co-op is starting new allotments to produce its own fruit and greens.

Of course this characterisation of opposing food economies is an oversimplification of a complex food system. Even the staunchest defender of local production will buy household detergents from the supermarket; and many artisan producers aspire to sell, or sell already, through the multiples (though many others will not). The industrial food economy is fast to react to any challenge to its hegemony, by co-opting the characteristics which mark out its counterpart. The high street bakery may have gone, but some of its features have reappeared in Sainsbury's; similarly with the fishmonger, butcher and greengrocer. Organic produce, long spurned by the big retailers, has now penetrated even Marks & Spencer. Home delivery – traditionally the preserve of the specialist, high-quality grocer – is newly available from superstores. There are even a few products – very few, but high profile, given what they signify – stocked only in the superstores closest to where they are produced. Five years ago the retailing leviathans said this was impossible, given centralised distribution. Today these products have become a totem of local commitment.

So the edges are blurred, but the distinction remains. Two systems compete. Does it matter which wins?

I think it does. It matters because industrialisation of the food system has such huge hidden costs. It matters because diet is so closely connected to health and well-being. And it matters because, with the homogenisation of food culture, we risk becoming stateless in the culinary world.

In Britain we demand cheap food. As a proportion of income we spend one-third as much as the Portuguese and Greeks, and half as much as the Italians. Within the EU, only the Irish spend less. Yet cheap food has exacted a heavy price, though not one denominated in cash.

We have paid with the loss of one mile of hedgerow for every hour of daylight in the last twenty years, with the disappearance of our horticultural smallholdings and of thousands of jobs on the land. Our street markets, auction marts and shopkeepers have gone; town centres are now studded with the same national chains. Our towns are clogged with traffic, the urban air choked with fumes. Lorries pound our roads and jets scar the sky; the orchards and hop fields of Kent now grow corn, their trees and bines long since grubbed. Public policy must share the blame for this loss, but no industry is more guilty than the one which brings our food. In the economist's jargon it has externalised its costs, and prospered at the expense of much we hold dear.

We are suffering too from the diseases of affluence. Of the twenty-three countries in Europe, Scotland tops the toll of deaths from ischaemic heart disease, followed in third place by Ireland and fourth by England and Wales. Cancer, some types of which have a strong dietary link, comes second as the cause of premature death. Our more sedentary lifestyle means that we should take more care; to prevent both diseases we must eat more fruit and vegetables. For most of us that means less processed food, much of which is high in fat and sugar. But processed foods are highly profitable for the food industry, and are therefore heavily promoted.

As consumers we are relinquishing control over the ingredients of what we eat: almost a third of our food is now consumed away from home, and a third of what is eaten at home comes pre-prepared. Cooking skills are in decline. Fewer than half of 7- to 15-year-olds know how to boil an egg or bake a potato, and cooking is now seldom taught in our schools. School meals are no longer subject to nutritional standards, victims of a food industry campaign against state interference. Plans for better nutrition labelling have gone the same way.

The third area of loss is our traditional food culture, the distinctiveness of the regional dish or local variety. Of course our culinary repertoire has grown, and we have daily access to a cornucopia that would amaze our forebears. But globalisation and convenience foods crush local flavour in the name of the brand. British railway food illustrates the point: sandwiches, burgers, fried noodles and chicken tikka – dishes from four culinary traditions, a menu from anywhere in the world. I don't decry choice, but fear the industrial muscle that makes the words 'coca' and 'cola' the second and third most widely understood in the world (the most widely understood word being 'OK' if it counts as a word). This way lies homogeneity, ultimately one global diet.

The food writer and broadcaster Derek Cooper, who has done more than most to promote good food in Britain, defines his ideal food economy as one in which you could travel across the British Isles and know where you were by the types of food on sale. It is an image of an artisan economy restored, and one that is gathering disciples. I suspect one such is Mary Ann Gilchrist, restaurateur in Wales, who describes her philosophy in the 1998 *Good Food Guide*. She says, in a section of the introduction entitled 'Go Local':

> It is my belief that modern British cooking needs to be rooted first and foremost in British ingredients. I am not suggesting that we ignore the most exotic items from abroad which we British use to such effect, but that we should look first at the marvellous array of seasonal local produce. English asparagus is only with us for six weeks; use it during its short season, then forget it till next year. British strawberries are superb, bursting with flavour and sometimes even available into October. And don't ignore the comforting root vegetables of winter. Deep-fried julienne of parsnip goes perfectly with the rich, gamey meats that Britain is justly famous for.

It is a mouthwatering homily to the artisan cause. At Tesco, parsnips are available in August from Fremantle, Australia.

There are many ways in which we can help a benign realignment of food growing and selling, and a rekindling of interest in our national food lore. As consumers and citizens we have complementary roles. We can return to the high street, buy fruit from the market and ask the superstore manager to stock local cheese. We can eat seasonal vegetables, plant a local variety of apple tree and petition the council to provide more allotments. We can use our homes for cooking, and restore the pleasure of eating to its rightful centrality to our social lives. We can provide for ourselves and our children a delicious, healthy and nutritious diet.

And we can demand better from those who govern us. Government – both national and local – has closed off many of our choices, conniving with centralised distribution and the concentration of retailing in fewer and fewer hands. Some local exceptions have stood out: Birmingham defends its street markets (it has the highest number in Britain) and several planning committees nobly opposed applications for out-of-town stores. Bath held the first farmers' market; Sheffield provides financial help and facilities for a Healthy Gardening Group.

Only central government can tackle excessive food transport, however, and say no to the road lobby's domineering food barons. Competition policy could tackle local monopolies, and prevent the predatory pricing which bankrupts small shops. New planning guidelines could restrict store developments to a maximum size, emphasising that food shopping is a local pastime.

Only government can change perverse farm subsidies, which drive industrialisation and reward agrochemical use. We must have more support for organic and small farmers, and a system of incentives to restore degraded landscapes and provide rural jobs. Only better, citizen-responsive government can reform health service provision, improve preventive health care and stress the connections between diet and health. But we can do it – and the resurgence of the artisan food economy suggests that we are succeeding.

Bibliography

Blythman, J, *The Food we Eat* (London, 1996).

Body, R, *Our Food, Our Land* (London, 1991).

de Selincourt, K, *Local Harvest* (London, 1997).

Garnett, T, *Growing Food in Cities* (London, 1996).

Raven, H and Lang, T, with Dumonteil, C, *Off our Trolleys? Food retailing and the hypermarket economy* (London, 1995).

SAFE Alliance, *The Food Miles Action Pack – a guide to thinking globally and eating locally* (London, 1996).

Tansey, G, and Worsley, T, *The Food System* (London, 1995).

13. *Animals in the Countryside*

Jane Ridley

Animals represent one of the chief points of friction between town and country. Townspeople are angered by beef farmers whose apparent greed and negligence have allowed lethal diseases to enter the human food chain. Conservationists are alarmed at the effects of pesticides on endangered species. And many urban people feel that field sports – and especially hunting with hounds – should be outlawed on grounds of cruelty. Until recently the countryside has remained silent. But the attempt by Mike Foster, MP to impose a ban on hunting provoked a backlash, leading to the remarkable Countryside March in March 1998. Evidently, the countryside dislikes being dictated to by the town. Nor does it believe that the town has any right to the moral high ground. Animals in towns – pets – are kept under artificial, confined and unnatural conditions. Marauding cats have contributed to the catastrophic decline in Britain's songbirds; yet many cat lovers would cheerfully argue for a hunting ban. The closer you look at the attitude of the British towards animals, the more confused and contradictory it appears. Animals are second only to families in causing quarrels, hypocrisy and raised blood pressure. As town and country pull apart on this issue, there is a real danger that the town will exploit its majority to impose legislation which, by importing urban expectations into the rural context, will damage the animals that it is designed to protect. The problem, I believe, is one of communication. Neither town nor country understands the other's position. Until they do so, the conflict will escalate.

We should begin by reminding ourselves that the relationship between people and animals has changed dramatically over the past century or so. Keith Thomas has delineated the history of that relationship in *Man and the Natural World*. In early modern England animals were everywhere. In 1500 three sheep existed for every person; by 1955 the ratio was the other way

Animals in the Countryside

around.* The towns thronged with horses, and pigs; cows and hens roamed freely in the streets. In Scotland and Wales country people cohabited with their animals: the typical country dwelling was the 'long house', a long, low dwelling, entered by a central door, the human beings living on one side, the cattle on the other. The mud floor of the cattle end sloped slightly, to allow for the seepage of manure and ammonia. Stone-built long houses in the Hebrides stand empty and bare of thatch today, many having been deserted only since the 1960s with the advent of prefabricated bungalows.

The relationship was very intimate. Animals were daily companions, almost members of the family. No wonder that in early modern times people believed that animals could think and reason, and spoke to animals in species-specific languages. Some of the oldest words in the English language are preserved as animal language. The age-old language of the horseman – 'Gee', 'Whoah', 'Heeck' – is essentially Celtic.† The pre-modern relationship was functional and unsentimental. Dogs were everywhere in early modern Britain, but they were working dogs – watchdogs, sheepdogs, turnspits; they were unceremoniously hanged or drowned when they had outlived their usefulness. Very rarely were animals given human names.

Flora Thompson was brought up in an Oxfordshire farming village in the 1880s, and she recalled how each cottage fattened a pig, which was kept in a lean-to at the back. The family pig was pampered, petted and fed, men called on Sundays to admire and scratch its back; but when it reached the required fatness it was invariably killed. A noisy bloody business it was too. The wounded, screaming pig was hoisted on to a rough bench to bleed, in order to preserve the quality of the meat. The scene, with its mud, blood and flaring lights, recalled the savagery of the African jungle: 'but the country people of that day had little sympathy for the suffering of animals'.‡ They were too poor; they needed meat too badly. Like French peasants, they wasted none of the pig, eating the entrails and making puddings of the blood.

By Flora Thompson's time, however, the relationship with animals was beginning to change, transformed by the agricultural revolution and the subsequent rise of large-scale capitalist farming. Now known as 'livestock',

* Keith Thomas, *Man and the Natural World* (London, 1983), p. 94; W. G. Hoskins, *The Making of the English Landscape* (Harmondsworth, 1988 edn), p. 137.
† Keith Thomas, *Man and the Natural World* (London, 1983), pp. 96–7.
‡ Flora Thompson, *Lark Rise to Candleford* (Harmondsworth, 1973 edn), pp. 24–6.

cows and sheep were a crop or product, living in purpose-built buildings, routinely reared, fattened, dispatched to market and killed by professional slaughtermen. Selective breeding made them bigger and fatter. Valued for their size and capacity to convert food into meat, these animals were advertised in prints of near-rectangular Bakewell sheep or pedigree cattle. They became specialised products in a way that the early peasant animals were not. No longer could the shepherd recognise each individual ewe in his flock by its face, as he could in medieval times. Farm animals today are members of a herd, rather than individuals, their status symbolised by the plastic ear-tag which bears their number.

In 1800 farm animals were banished from the streets of towns. Victorian railways increased the volume of traffic so much that the number of horses actually rose; but the advent of motorised transport made horses redundant. The less *necessary* animals were to the city economy, however, the more were they *needed* emotionally by city dwellers. Animals still lived in cities, but in a different relationship with man: as pets.

The rise of pet-keeping is one of the strangest and least noticed phenomena of city and suburban life. Yet the cats and dogs of the suburbs and inner cities have transformed attitudes to the animal world.

People have befriended and loved their animals since classical times, and the rich have always kept pets. The miniature lapdogs of fashionable Elizabethan women lived in their sleeves, slept in their beds, ate from their plates and licked their lips.* Then as now the royal family was irrationally devoted to small, non-functional, yapping dogs. Charles II is still remembered for his own-brand spaniels. But pet-keeping only really became widespread around 1800. As the fashion spread for keeping non-essential pet dogs, so their status rose. Dogs which were once excoriated as dirty curs – a lowly status still reflected in the word 'bitch' – were now praised as man's trusty servant and friend. They were given human names and shamelessly anthropomorphised – human qualities such as intelligence, loyalty, courage are all ascribed to dogs; and Landseer sentimentalised them in paint.

Cats enjoyed an even sharper change of fortune. Medieval people rarely kept domestic cats. Cats, they thought, should not be fed but starved in order to increase their efficiency as pest controllers. In the seventeenth century cats were hunted by hounds, and burned alive with papist effigies

* Thomas, *Man and the Natural World*, pp. 107–8.

so that their screams added to the effect.* Every witch kept a cat along with her broomstick; they were thought to be evil and therefore female. Only in the eighteenth century did the cat's reputation improve. With the vogue for domestic cleanliness the pet domestic cat came into its own. It too has been anthropomorphised. The cat artist Louis Wain painted cats with human expressions wearing human clothes, and in 1939 T. S. Eliot published the best-selling *Old Possum's Book of Practical Cats*. Like dogs, cats are given human names, most notoriously Humphrey the Downing Street cat, whose rumoured disappearance in 1997 provoked an outcry from outraged cat lovers.

'A dog is for life, not just for Christmas,' warns the Canine Defence League, and most pets are loved and cherished by their owners. They return affection, they learn behaviour. Who is not familiar with the vegetarian pet lover who feeds her (it is usually her) beloved cats or dogs on expensive cuts of meat she would never dream of buying and preparing for her meat-eating human friends? Greater love hath no man than the pet. The pet is given the status of an honorary person. No longer perceived as a member of the cat species, it is an individual: Tommy the cat, whose closest bond is to his owner family.

Parents give children a hamster or guinea pig in order to teach them how to care for a creature which depends upon them utterly for all its wants. I have a friend whose mother crushingly told her that she couldn't possibly look after a baby – she had never even looked after a pet. No doubt pets teach children to be responsible for another dependent creature. But it is an essentially artificial relationship. The pet does not choose to enter it; and when the child loses interest, the lonely rabbit crouches miserably in its hutch.

Pets pay a high price for their privileged relationship with man. Their animal nature is subordinated to their owners' needs. Like humans, many live sedentary, indoor lives; they are overweight and sterilised. And pets have impacted upon the balance of nature in ways that are only beginning to be recognised. Cats continue to massacre Britain's population of songbirds. Dog mess is a major urban hazard for which many dog owners still refuse to take responsibility, regardless of the health risks to small children in parks.

The pet is the only animal that many urban people ever really get to

* Ibid., p. 110.

know, and this must surely condition their attitude to other animals. They unthinkingly assume that *all* animals are individuals, rather than members of species, that all exist independent of their natural habitat and insulated from the biological imperatives of the Darwinian struggle. Wild animals in particular are 'petified' and perceived as honorary humans. There are deep-seated cultural and psychological reasons for this.

The tendency to individualise wild animals is implanted in us almost unconsciously in childhood. Children are naturally drawn to wild animals and to books about animals – a trait which may well be an evolutionary survival from our hunter-gatherer ancestors. Classical texts such as Aesop's *Fables* testify to children's enduring fascination with animals. But the narrative of the fairy tale has changed in recent times. The animals in Aesop's *Fables* are not individuals, but are defined by their species nature. As a result, they are far from nice. This was after all an era when wolves really did eat babies. Today the animal world is no longer a threat, and animals are companions rather than functional necessities. Children learn a very different story about wild animals. The forest is no longer a frightening place. On the contrary, it is a cosy, harmonious, vegetarian idyll, seen on *Blue Peter*. In a secular world, it has become our new fairy tale; our virtual Garden of Eden.

The sentimentalising of wild animals began with the Edwardians. Its cultural roots have not been properly explored, but I guess they lay in the rise of pets, coupled with the never-grow-old feyness which produced *Peter Pan* and the era's fascination with fairy painting. Beatrix Potter created a world of wild animals who behaved like domestic pets. She gave wild animals human names and human emotions – Peter Rabbit and Benjamin Bunny, Samuel Whiskers (a rat) and Mrs Tiggy-Winkle (hedgehog), Jeremy Fisher the frog, Tommy Brock the badger and Mr Tod the fox. 'Nobody could call Mr Tod "nice" ', she wrote; but by making him an individual she unwittingly allowed him to become the object of sympathy. Kenneth Grahame's *Wind in the Willows* created a lovable, fallible character in Mr Toad, but recognised the boundaries; the Wild Wood where the weasels live is frightening, dark and savage: a remnant of the ancient myth of the forest.

Victorian and Edwardian literature, by humanising animals, at least made it possible to be ambivalent about them. Toad and Rat are moral beings, capable of good and evil. It is perhaps Walt Disney who first exploited the pre-lapsarian innocence of the animals in order to raise them *above* the human sphere, both morally and aesthetically. In *Bambi* the human is the cruel and selfish predator, the deer his cute, innocent and harmless victim. In *Fox and Hound* the fox makes friends with the hounds and lives happily ever after. One of Roald Dahl's top-selling children's stories demonises shooters as bloated, grotesque brutes. *The Animals of Farthing Wood* is a perennially popular children's television cartoon tale about a troop of wild animals who band together against cruel hunters. Never mind that in the wild the weasel would kill the rabbit and the fox would gobble the mole. The moral message is clear. Man has a monopoly of cruelty. Wild animals left to themselves form a peaceful, harmonious, caring community. Far from seeing the innocence of animals as a sign of their moral incompetence, the sentimentalist elevates it – as once we elevated the innocence of children – into a kind of angelic purity.

Given the dominance of pets and the tendency to sentimentalise wild animals, it was only a matter of time before people began to argue that animals possessed rights. The seminal text was Peter Singer's *Animal Liberation* (1975). If women and blacks should be liberated, argued Singer, why not animals? After all, they are sentient; they can suffer. Singer's work fuelled the 'hard' animal rights movement of the 1980s. As Roger Scruton has shown, however, the argument addressed by Singer and his followers makes no contact with the real moral questions. Animals are not language-using self-conscious beings; having neither personality nor the concept of it, they are not moral beings. This is true even of pets. We have an obligation to the pet, but this does not mean that the pet has rights against us. 'It is part of the pathos of a pet, that it stands always on the edge of a moral dialogue, staring from beyond an impassable barrier at the life which is now everything to it, and which yet it cannot comprehend.'* It was Jeremy Bentham, the founder of utilitarianism and, incidentally, a cat lover, who wrote: 'the question is not can they *reason*? Nor, can they *talk*? But, can they *suffer*?' As Scruton shows, however, Bentham's utilitarianism – the greatest happiness principle – provides an entirely inadequate basis for morality. Moreover, by giving rights to animals we tie them to obligations they can neither fulfil nor comprehend, and this in itself is a form of cruelty. 'Only by refraining from personalising animals do we behave

* Roger Scruton, *Animal Rights and Wrongs* (London, 1996), p. 41.

towards them in ways that they can understand.'* The real moral questions concern animal welfare, not animal rights. If we allow rights to animals then inevitably the individual takes precedence over the species, and the welfare of the species is sacrificed to the local and fleeting concern of human beings.

It is a fallacy to assume that all animals deserve or require to be treated in the same way. This is a simple but fundamental point that has been persistently ignored. It seems to me to offer a way to resolve the emerging conflict between urban and rural attitudes to animal welfare. Not all animals can or should be equated to the urban pet. Quite the contrary, in some cases it is not only wrong-headed but positively harmful to do so. Animals exist in a variety of different relationships with man, and different standards apply in each case; we should distinguish three relationships with animals that are specific to the countryside.

First, animals reared for food. Rural attitudes towards factory and battery farming of meat and eggs have been condemned, and the crises and scares over listeria and BSE seem to vindicate this criticism. But before blaming farmers we should reflect that factory farming represents an attempt to respond to the urban demand for cheap meat. Battery farms exist because urban people want cut-price eggs, chickens and meat. One way to meet this demand is to cut production costs: to turn the farm into a factory, rearing animals in dark, overcrowded, stinking sheds, feeding them growth-inducing hormones and cheap foods. This is not a natural development from traditional husbandry. Many farmers refuse to go down this road and abhor the idea of rearing animals in this fashion. Only a minority of beef farmers have taken advantage of the cheap foods which caused BSE. As many as 84 per cent of beef suckler herds have never had a case of BSE. Nothing is more indicative of the confusion introduced by sentimentality than the indifference with which England viewed the mass slaughter of these unaffected herds – the very same urban England that had driven firms out of business for the sin of transporting calves to their fate.

Nevertheless, the result of BSE is that many urban consumers have lost confidence in British meat farming. It is little wonder that an increasing proportion of urban people are becoming vegetarian. But the consequences of this widespread vegetarianism are seldom envisaged. Without meat-eating, farm animals would not exist; and without animal husbandry, much

* Roger Scruton, *Animal Rights and Wrongs* (London, 1996) p. 67.

of the countryside would be permanent prairie relieved by neither woods nor pasture. Rather than abandon meat, we should demand better-quality, possibly organic meat and dairy products. The terms of the compact between town and country may need to be renegotiated; the premium is no longer on cheapness but on the quality of the food the country produces.

There are signs that this is beginning to happen. One encouraging development is the farm shop, selling local eggs, handmade sausages and meat supplied by named local producers. This kind of outlet allows the farmer a far closer relationship with the consumer than is ever possible in the supermarket. A farmyard egg, muck-stained, speckled and with down attached, is a thing of beauty which the country ought to share with the town.

The second type of animal specific to the country is the working animal. Horses and working dogs are trained to perform specific functions. They live on close terms with men. Sheepdogs live with their masters. Horses kept in stables require several hours of daily attention: mucking out, feeding and exercise. They respond with affection to their masters, and they are capable of complex 'learned' behaviour. They are not pets, however, but essentially functional. Of course, sentiment enters into these relationships. A working dog performs as well as it does because of the emotional bonds that tie it to its master; it is rewarded with affection. Tales told since classical times of dogs mourning their dead masters testify to the animals' loyalty. The relationship between man and horse is in a category of its own. Centaur-like, horses confer special powers. In feudal times the man on the horse was the symbol of authority.

Horses and working dogs excite little interest among urban people today. The banning of fox-hunting would cause an estimated 15–20,000 horses to be destroyed, but this leaves urban animal lovers dry eyed. Foxhounds too are immune from urban pity. Even more than the hunter, the hound is a specialised purpose-bred animal. Foxhounds could never be domestic pets, as anyone will tell you who has ever walked a hound puppy or had the house wrecked by it. A hunting ban would require the vast majority of Britain's 20,000 foxhounds to be destroyed. This matters less to urban people because they have little conception of a working relationship between man and animal. The urban relationship between man and animal is a *playing* relationship – and that is how many people envisage the future of horses and hounds, should they think of it at all.

Wild animals form the third category of animal in the countryside. City dwellers believe they have a right to legislate for wild animals in order to 'protect' them: wild animals have joined the ever-widening class of 'victims'. The problem is that there are unresolved conflicts as to what 'protection' amounts to.

Take the case of conservation. This seems on the face of it a simple – and now urgent – matter of preserving rare or endangered species. Conservation policies, however, are often driven by the conception of animals as honorary pets – as individuals – and as a result enter into inevitable conflict with the interests of the species. Badgers, for example, are a protected species. Yet with their only remaining predator – man – out of action, badgers have become more and more diseased. They are now riddled with TB and have begun to spread the disease to cattle. Since they became protected, their numbers have indeed escalated; but the species has suffered a qualitative decline. Because the badger looks attractive, however squalid and dangerous its habits, it has the sympathy of urban people, and enjoys the kind of individual solicitude of the urban pet. Respect for the species, and for the other species which perforce must share the badger's habitat, would be better served by allowing farmers to control the badger population.

By interfering with the balance of nature, conservation often creates more problems than it solves. Raptors and harriers, for example, are preserved, thanks to pressure from the Royal Society for the Protection of Birds. The Langholm study (1992–6) tracked the impact of raptor predation on red grouse numbers on the moor in south-west Scotland near where I write. It showed that the predation had reduced the post-breeding numbers of red grouse by 50 per cent in a single breeding season. Ask any gamekeeper and you will get the same answer. By demanding the preservation of one species, the Royal Society for the Protection of Birds has caused a catastrophic decline in the population of another, the grouse.

Most controversial of wild animals is the fox. Here the issue is not one of conservation. On the contrary, even urban critics would concede that it is in the interests of the fox *as a species* that hunting should continue. For the fox is a pest. As is well known, the fox is a mass murderer of chickens and young game birds. It takes free-range piglets, and also lambs – a fact which is now well attested, in spite of efforts to disprove it during the 1970s and 1980s. As the placards proclaimed on the Countryside March in March 1998: EAT BRITISH LAMB – 50,000 FOXES CAN'T BE WRONG. Without hunting, farmers and gamekeepers would have no option but to kill foxes which threatened their livestock. In some areas, fox populations would be wiped out. Farmers and landowners would no longer have an incentive to preserve foxes for the hunt. Hunting is not merely an exercise in fox control; it is a social event, a celebration of the rural community. For the sake of the hunt, and for the hunt alone, farmers allow horses to gallop over their fields; part of the bargain is that the farmer will provide entertainment in the shape of a fox.

Proof of this argument is afforded by the case of the wild red deer on Exmoor. In areas where hunting with hounds has been stopped, the deer population has fallen. Not only is the deer a pest to farmers, destroying their crops: venison is valuable meat. The National Trust, which banned hunting on its properties in 1997, now sells each deer that is shot for £300 per carcass. On land where the deer shooting is uncontrolled, trophy hunters single out the stags with the best 'heads', with catastrophic effects for the herd. There is little doubt that the herd is better off under the stewardship of the hunt, rather than subject to the uncontrolled greed of the trophy hunter or the anger of the farmer.

If urban critics concede that hunting actually conserves species, then why do they continue to press for a ban? It seems to me that in the case of fox hunting we have a supreme example of the welfare of the species being subordinated to the welfare of the *individual*. The case for banning fox hunting focuses, not on the effect on the species, but on the manner of the individual death. During the build-up to Mike Foster's bill to ban hunting London was placarded with gruesome posters showing hounds killing a fox. There is little doubt, however, that terrible though the death may look, it is instantaneous. When the fox is 'broken up' and eaten by the hounds, it is already dead.

Critics are right to insist that the method of the fox's death be strictly controlled. This is already happening, thanks to the self-regulatory efforts of the Masters of Fox Hounds Association. It is forbidden to 'bolt' a fox which has gone to ground and allow hounds to kill it; foxes which run to ground are killed by humane killer. This accounts for the great majority of fox kills: only a minority are killed in the open by hounds. True, the fox is subjected to the hunt beforehand, and all the stress that this involves; however, it is never wounded, as it would be by a shotgun or a snare or poison. And even if we accept that hunting by hounds is unpleasant, we must also accept that nature is cruel. Nature has no analgesics. Animals die stressful, painful and premature deaths. No one who has heard the screams of a rabbit being killed by a weasel could pretend otherwise.

Urban critics are appalled by the hunt because they persist in perceiving the fox as a pet, like the toy cuddly fox held aloft by Mike Foster in triumph after the first reading of his bill. If we ban hunting on the basis of this kind of sentimental misconception there is a real danger that we will end by doing damage to the fox species, and also to the precarious balance between man and nature which self-regulating practices like hunting help to preserve.

Town and country must come together on these issues. Biodiversity, a healthy and thriving food chain, and a countryside replete with both wild and domestic animals are vital to all of us. The image of our country and of the borderline between urban and rural space has been shaped by animal husbandry, by hunting, and by the distinction between the tame and the wild. Coherent policies are now required, if animals are to continue to play the central role that we require of them. And policies will be coherent only if rural and urban interests are each consulted in a spirit of compromise. It is this spirit which has been so evidently lacking in recent debates.

14. *To Know What We Eat*

Jeff Rooker

On 4 March 1998, Jeff Rooker MP, the Minister for Food, addressed the Town and Country Forum for an hour in the middle of a busy schedule. He had been asked to talk about the issues that he faced on coming to office and what it was like to become a Minister. We are grateful for his permission to publish this edited version of what he said and how he responded to some of the questions.

I am going to talk about what it has been like for me to take office in MAFF (the Ministry of Agriculture, Food and Fisheries). The issues of town and country are affected by many other offices of state, so I am not going to give an official overview. Nor is my experience typical of the new government. I have been, indeed I am still, on an exceptionally steep learning curve. My background is totally urban. I am in my present position because the Prime Minister told me that he wanted someone without a MAFF background to get a grip on this BSE crisis and it needed my attention to detail. So I don't claim any credentials. But perhaps an initial discussion of my experience might help a wider understanding of the problems of farming and food.

I am probably the only minister in the government who as a backbencher initiated a debate on rural deprivation from an urban perspective. It was in 1990. I had a period when I was on the back benches voluntarily so I could go on a select committee. I wanted to do one or two other things as well, including something on rural deprivation, which I could see was not being raised in Parliament. I visited some farms in East Anglia and went to a couple of food factories. But I was criticised quite bluntly. People said: What are you doing? You're from Birmingham – sod off. Such was the attitude until only recently towards urban MPs who took an interest in rural matters.

I had no idea about MAFF and its structure in May 1997. Like everyone else, you are given this great big book, literally about four inches thick, which is a briefing on the Department; and you are told, read this,

Minister, and by the way whilst you are doing so there are some early submissions that require your decision. I suppose my perception like a lot of people's was that the Department was run by farmers for farmers – you know the joke, it was in the *Financial Times*, that MAFF stands for More Aid to Farmers Fast. That is actually quite cruel; but perceptions are important.

When we started we held open, transparent listening sessions with staff and I was struck by the bitterness within the part of MAFF dealing with the food standards, with the other half of MAFF who they felt were giving them all the problems. It was the bitterness of what I call the consumer safety staff against what they perceive to be the farmers' half of the Ministry. The comments were pretty strong. And I thought, blimey this is actually happening within the Department.

I've come to the conclusion after nine months that MAFF is a bit like the way people used to describe the Home Office, in the sense that it deals with such a variety of issues, many not generally appreciated: little ones that are hidden away in corners that come out and nip you in the ankles as it were. It is a bit of a dustbin department which ends up with any issue that people are not sure what to do with that touches food, animal welfare, the land, health.

At any rate, nine months ago I walked up Whitehall on the Tuesday morning. The only possessions in my hand were three old large aerial photographs of my constituency – in black and white. I'd always thought that if I ever became a minister I'd take them and pin them up. That way I'd always see the houses of the people that elected me. When I'm being lectured by civil servants and businessmen about what I should or shouldn't be doing I'd be able to say, 'Hang on a minute, Sunshine, the people in those houses are the ones that sent me here.' About a day later I was walking in the other direction towards Smith Square having looked at my list of responsibilities which I'd agreed with Jack Cunningham as Secretary of State, and I discovered Ergon House.

Ergon House is bang slap on the corner at Horseferry Road by Smith Square. An old building that has been converted. In it are the best part of 250–300 MAFF civil servants who, except for the one floor dealing with personnel, work exclusively on food standards, food safety, chemical surveillance, microbiological contamination, labelling, the tick-tock sheep which we still check out after Chernobyl and so on. Hundreds of people working to protect our food. We've got an emergency centre over there, ready for any great crises that might arise. I had no idea they were there or that Ergon House existed. I hadn't got the slightest idea that an arm of MAFF is doing all this work. I don't have to talk up what they are doing. But at every meeting I give I point out that this work is going on.

Like most people, all I ever knew was that there was BSE, *E-coli*, salmonella and some pretty crass political management at the top that failed adequately to prevent or limit them. Then you realise that there have actually been two ministries. You've got a group of people that consider themselves not part of the farmers' Ministry but, if you like, as working on the consumer side. You could say that Jack Cunningham and I were put in, in part, to take a cleaver to the Department and separate out the food standards safety and consumer side. I am a minister whose job is to put myself out of a job, because my present brief will be entirely taken over by an independent Food Standards Agency, the FSA. I hope this means we will have a better producers' side as well.

Tessa Jowell at Health and I put a group together called the Joint Food Standards and Safety Group. We've got about 250, they've got about 50. It is the embryo of the FSA. The joint group is led by a civil servant called Mr Podger. It was brilliant to discover him working in MAFF as a health official on secondment at senior level and acceptable to both sides. It helped a great deal that we came in with the Manifesto commitment to establish a FSA. This made it a guiding principle and saved us a lot of battles that we might otherwise have had in terms of pushing the policy through. It was accepted from day one in MAFF that it had to happen. If we hadn't had that commitment, I suspect there would just have been a change of ethos, maybe even a change of a name, a mission statement.

The biggest debate we had over the FSA White Paper was not about nutrition. That got all the headlines and there was discussion of it, of course. But the biggest debate was about the other side of the farm gate: veterinary products, pesticides. Should they be in or out of the Agency? Or split? It only took us a couple of hours as ministers to come to a view once we'd had the discussion and the briefings and looked at the options. But it was an interesting debate because it actually brought the two cultures together around the same table. We took the decision, as set out in the White Paper, that we didn't want to create an agency that has the same problems as MAFF, namely that of representing both consumers and producers. So we've left veterinary products and pesticides outside its remit, although we have given the FSA long-stop powers that it can use if it thinks things are not being done by the regulatory authorities to prevent food contamination. That's very important and will operate openly and transparently and not behind closed doors.

This question of openness has been a big issue. Ministers rarely told anyone what they were doing. I had one case, it was an ordinary issue, where we took a decision and wanted to put out a press release. The civil servant said, 'No, Minister, don't do that.' 'Why not?' 'Well, people may start asking you questions about it.' This is the culture we've inherited – don't put out a press release as it may lead people to ask questions.

The issue of communications goes wider than this. At the moment every six months a report is done on BSE. It is a big report, maybe about thirty or forty pages, that goes to the House of Commons library and is an assessment of the previous six months. It is something we inherited, not invented. The one in July 1997 we didn't really count as ours, as it only covered the start of our government. The recent one is the first one that covers a full six months of us. Jack and I had a look and we thought, hang on, this is not something we can skimp. There might be something in here, a sentence, a nuance that concerns our six months. So I went through it from cover to cover. And I picked up one aspect, which I raise as an example. We churn out information and figures *ad nauseam*. Yet it is not generally known that there are 120,000 farms with cattle in this country – that's an approximate figure, don't hold me to the last 5,000 – and about 100,000 without cattle. Of the 120,000 with cattle, two-thirds have never ever had a case of BSE. And most of those who have are the dairy herds involved in milk production. Let me emphasise, of the beef suckler herds 84 per cent have *never* had a case of BSE. But the figures are not presented in this way. In the relevant paragraph all this information was jumbled up and retrievable only with difficulty.

I looked at this and it came home to me why the farmers are so angry. It is because a small minority – one that understood market forces by the way, they knew cheap animal feed when they saw it – a small minority that have had the vast majority of BSE cases. And it gets smaller when you discount farms who have only had one case. Roughly 35,000 farms have had BSE. But 12,000 of those have only had a single case. The real problem is confined to little more than 20,000 out of the 120,000 herds overall. So you can see why there is such anger and bitterness in the industry when everyone else has lost so much.

I had the paragraph in the Report rewritten. Just two sentences changed.

And I said we must bring out this issue because it is important. It helps explain why there is bitterness in the industry. I'm not seeking to blame the small minority – there is an inquiry looking into the past. As a Ministry we have to look at the present and the future. But we have a legacy to deal with and we need to understand why we got this existing situation of anger.

I also said that the short press release should highlight the fact that the Report contains information on epidemiology and incidence. (The incidence is actually tailing off dramatically, which is really good.) They said, 'Well, Minister, if you highlight the fact that two-thirds of farmers have never had a case of BSE people might say it isn't really a health risk.' Such second-guessing of opinion cuts off public discussion. There is an unwillingness to accept that we ought to put things out as they are and share clear information with the public. In the past they have not been used to doing that. Things are changing. We are publishing more information about food than before, including brand names when we do our chemical surveillance, and we've got the Internet.

Also on nuclear issues – where to find all this stuff from the fifties and sixties buried round the country. Parliament has quite clearly been misled, to put it mildly. We want a new culture and some of the civil servants are embracing it.

In government, paperwork chases round Whitehall and flies round ministerial offices. If you sat and read it all it would be a horrendous demand on your time. Yet sometimes you have to look at the small print. A lot of it is filtered out in terms of external pressures. The submissions, the representations from industry and pressure groups. None the less, when producers come in to see us they will say 'We'd like you to come to our laboratory or our factory.' The advice will be 'Minister, probably not a good idea.' 'Why?' 'Because if you go you'll have to go to six others of the same industry.' I thought, why? What's the problem? I can go to one, as an example. I want to go to a cattle abattoir or a sheep abattoir, an animal feed mill – I've never been in one; to an animal drug manufacturer and a centre for veterinary medicines. There is this idea that if you go to one you've got to go to them all as though you are giving your imprimatur to one of them and they'll use it for commercial advantage. The effect of this is to keep ministers at a disadvantage, to keep them ignorant. I have not accepted such advice.

For example, an invitation came to Jack Cunningham to open the vegetarian food fair at the Labour NEC last autumn. The advice scrawled across the top was 'Strongly advise against as it will send the wrong signals with respect to beef'. Jack could not do it and I said I would. I had to explain, 'This is not the Ministry for red meat.' I had to tell this to the Meat and Livestock Commission – the guy nearly fell through the floor. But it was part of trying to explain that we are not trying to push a product. We have got a problem with the industry on beef, it's quite clear, and we want to do what we can to restore the industry; but I'm not a Minister for Meat and it is not illegal to be a vegetarian in this country. I have to remind them – there is an aspect of a client mind-set that we are breaking through.

I went to an organic farm the other week. Farming is not my responsibility but one of our key priorities is to do more for organic farming. Not to subsidise production but to help with conversion. We said we want more aid for organic farming both on research and on conversion. It is minuscule what we do in this country – it is the worst in Europe.

You wouldn't believe the argument and tussle to shift a little bit of a research budget. We have a research budget in MAFF of about £132 million out of our basic budget of £740 million. (You have to forget MAFF when you see the figure of £4.5 billion, because that is all European, CAP and intervention board money.)

The £130 million budget produces 900 papers a year. As a result of our research budget we get three papers in every day. So I said to the chief scientists' group, don't you think we ought to tell a few people about this research? And they said, 'Well, we haven't really got the time to tell people what we are doing because we are dealing with so many papers'! I said I would rather deal with 2.9 papers a day and, with the resources of the other 0.1 per cent, employ a science writer to tell opinion-formers, the industry, MPs and the public what we do with the budget, as no one knows. This has also met with a lot of resistance. I've just issued a note to put together a glossy brochure on aspects of the science work we have done on food safety.

The present organic research budget is very small, roughly half a million. So you would think it was easy to double it. No way. It takes time to make changes even in £130 million. Some of the research may take six months, but some takes three years. Each piece is tightly controlled. We do not have an overall research and development programme. Projects are policy driven. They go out to tender and are not all force-fed through the Central Science Laboratory. We finally identified £14 million for the financial year that's coming in November. Then they told us that the £14 million is crucial. We pointed out that they have allocated the other £116 million. 'Yes,' they say, 'because that was the easy bit to do.' The only real chance we have to influence the budget is in the next financial year and then there is the problem of working within the spending limits of the previous government. We are having to cancel or delay some programmes in order to achieve a shift. You are told, 'Well, Minister, it wasn't done that way, it will take time.' We say, 'Fair enough: you say two years, I'm saying twelve months.'

But the instructions are given. We have problems with the Treasury on some aspects. But there will be a push for organic farming in order to send the right signals. It is a priority. Jack addressed the annual meeting of the Soil Association, the first minister to do so. Yet all this is a very minor part of our operation. It is like turning round a big tanker.

The larger, more important point is that the ethos of the Food Standards Agency will be transparency and openness. The Agency will be in advance of the Freedom of Information Bill. It will be set up, and staffed by civil servants who report not to ministers but to a commission that will be appointed on individual merit, not as representing groups. Advice to ministers will be published automatically. Now that changes the culture straight away, I can tell you.

On the one hand you seem to imply that the Ministry is lumping together things which belong independently, like handling the interests of farmers and consumers even when these can be antagonistic; on the other there seem to be problems which belong together, particularly environmental ones, that are dealt with by separate ministries. Might not now be a time to take an overview in order to see whether we need a new ministerial structure?

We may need a better system for overview. Planning powers need to stay with local authorities. No one wants them with central government, for heaven's sake. But ministries come and go. By and large the structure we've got now is fairly old. Some say there is no role for MAFF. Fishing can go to Trade and Industry and the whole thing could be split between it and Environment. Because of the European Union and the way that the Agricultural Council and the Fisheries Council require senior ministers, there is an EU constraint for those who would seek to divide up the Ministry. Government is also split into a large number of agencies. Some, such as that dealing with pesticides, report to more than one ministry and it seems to be reasonably successful. I think there is a need for a new overview and I think gradually, though it is early days for us, we will look at the machine we've inherited. But it is not right to mess about with it for the sake of it.

There is also confusion because of what does not come to MAFF. We have environmental pollution, as when farmers injure themselves with sheep dips. But when the disposal of the sheep dips might affect the watercourse it is not our concern but that of the DoE. I was up in Cumbria the other week when a check was done on 4,300 farms. Forty tractors were banned immediately. I regard this as a sign that the system is working. But it was done by Health and Safety, not MAFF. Issues relating to what are perceived to be MAFF may in fact be dealt with by Environment or Trade and Industry. Sometimes we can be perceived as dealing with something when we are just the fall guy. The government ought collectively to think about this at a much higher political level.

To make an opposite point, on a smaller scale, consider what has been done with utility regulation. Even though it is much more focused, it is hard to imagine separating out the regulation of producers and protecting the consumers in, for example, gas. It would be a recipe for chaos since regulating the producers is a matter of setting rules that lead to the outcome that you are trying to promote for consumers. Regulators are mediating between the two sides and need to be answerable to both, whereas you are separating them out. Where, then, are the mediating powers?

That's a fair point. But unlike most other ministries we are very circumscribed by our membership of the European Union and the Common Agricultural Policy. Not that I am against Europe now. I campaigned against in 1975, but I wouldn't dream of it now. But we are not free agents. The amount of legislation we are required to implement from Brussels, even in terms of food law, is considerable and that's something we have to learn to live with. We are taking this up now with the establishment of the FSA. We need to give it powers so that it knows what drugs and pesticides are being approved in the first place, and if things are misused and not put right by the regulatory agencies the FSA will have overriding powers. They won't necessarily use them. In the end the only person who will decide the structures will be the Prime Minister.

One of the things you do is handle questions of risk: the risk that the consumers are able to take and what risks farmers are allowed to take. What is the nature of the advice you receive on this from experts and scientists and how have you responded? To put it in populist jargon, are you trying to be a nanny state?

On risk you are absolutely right: there is a real hole here. There is no common structure in the way risks are put to us on different issues. The way we analyse it and the way risks are presented to us isn't satisfactory. We've appointed someone in MAFF as a specialist in risk analysis and risk communication. One of the things the FSA will have to do is communicate risk. For example the tick-tock pigeons from Sellafield. The pigeons when checked had horrendous levels of radiation. But we were told that as nobody is eating them the risk is negligible. There is no risk. A general warning was issued, and we are trying to catch them and bump them off. Somebody took 40 out of 700, by the way, and we don't know what happened to them. But if we thought there were people eating them then we'd have to do something else.

Green-top milk is a good one, beef on the bone, B6 vitamins, TB badgers. These issues are all presented in different ways, I don't know if they could all be presented in the same way. There is a Department of Health chart on how to analyse risk, in terms of how many deaths per million. But what if you don't know? On CJD no one can tell us the incubation period of this new disease. It could take off into an epidemic, or not. On beef on the bone, Jack, myself and Frank Dobson had to take a decision and carry the can for it.

I told the House, when they cut up people's brains to check if they've died of new variant CJD the medical instruments cannot be sterilised and have to be destroyed afterwards. It is that bad. Now when you are in that kind of field, you have to say as a government, giving people an informed choice about beef on the bone doesn't work as we do not know the risks. You can cook away salmonella and *E-coli*. But not CJD. And it's the cooking process that's the problem because it spreads the juices. It is not the meat, the meat's all right; but the marrow juices could be lethal and you don't know if beef products have been cooked on the bone. It is front-line science here. You want to give people enough information to make an informed choice. But if no one has the information the public good may mean you have got to take regulatory action. Because we do not know the incubation period of new variant CJD we have to fix on the precautionary principle and be ultra cautious.

The House of Commons tried for years to get compulsory wearing of seat belts. All the evidence was it would save lives, but we had to have an awful lot of dead bodies before the House got convinced. Asbestos regulations, exactly the same: we had to have dead bodies before we took action. My view is I'd rather take the action, not to be nanny state, but not to wait till we get the dead bodies – it is a fine line to draw but you know it when dead bodies are possible. The press does not help here. A journalist from the *Guardian* wrote something that upset me on green-top milk. She asked, 'Where are the bodies that justify Jeff Rooker's proposed ban on green-top milk?' However, the same journalist wrote a piece about beef on the bone before the debate that I could have read instead of my prepared speech, saying precaution was right because of the uncertainty. The inconsistency is amazing.

Or take vitamin B6. I have a problem in that I deal with food law and not with medicines. We've got a lot of products in this country that are counted as food, not medicines, that we never have occasion to look at. This one started because of a request from the Consumers' Association in 1995. We have the most liberal regime for vitamins in Europe alongside Holland. In France and Germany you can't buy such vitamins. In this country you cannot make a health claim on a product sold as a food. That is illegal under the Food Safety Act. If you make such a claim it has to go through the regulatory process to become a medicine. And if it is a medicine you have to prove that it does what you say it does. That of course takes a long time and is expensive. So instead you have a whole range of food products being sold on a nod and a wink: 'This'll do you good.' And under food laws they never get regulated nor are checked for potential damage or long-term effects. If they were medicine this would be looked at.

The last thing I want to do is tell someone what to eat. But a central role for the FSA is 'protecting public health'. Some say it should be 'protecting and promoting public health'. But the key guiding principle is public health: to give the public the information so as to make an informed choice, from genetic labelling to irradiation of food. This is what we are going to do with the beef labelling scheme in April: sex, method of slaughter – people don't realise but some of the meat sold in the supermarket is ritually slaughtered. And in the Central Science Laboratory in MAFF they are doing real blue sky work. Without being asked they are using seed corn money to see how to check the make-up of supermarket foods, because if you can't check on the contents you cannot check the accuracy of labelling. They are looking at the DNA route for doing this. We've not commissioned this yet but I was impressed that they are looking at what may need to be done in the future to ensure the public knows what it eats.

15. *Confessions of an Urban Vet*
David Coffey

Nature is a wasteful system. It has no purpose: no objective. It just is. Indifferent to the survival of individuals or species, it propels and is propelled by the unpalatable but inviolable biological dictate: adapt or die.

Life on earth depends on the ability of plants to trap energy from the sun by the process of photosynthesis. Animals are dependent on this energy, either eating plants directly or acting as predators. More individuals of each species must be produced than could ever hope to survive to fulfil their potential. Biology personified as nature is a strange, unlikely and perplexing system, with a built-in propensity for struggle, cruelty, waste and tragedy.

Animals are genetically programmed for adaptation to the environment in which their species evolved. They do not, however, fit an environmental niche with precision. Behavioural and physiological mechanisms provide the essential fine-tuning for adaptation. Each individual of each species can adapt to a range of environmental conditions. So long as the animal remains in adaptive harmony its welfare is assured. At the limits of its adaptive competence it encounters a grey area of maladaption. If the situation is not reversed the animal either is forced to exist in conditions which compromise its well-being or it dies.

Human Evolution

When evolution directed proto-humans to adopt bipedalism, their ability to live in deep jungle was jeopardised. The open plains presented a potential environmental niche, ripe for exploitation. However, the sparser vegetation demanded the adoption of a more carnivorous diet. Bipedalism proved to be an inefficient method of moving at speed across open ground. The evolutionary accident which was to lead to the human species would surely, therefore, have proved immediately disastrous had it not been accompanied by an increasing cerebral capacity. With improved problem-solving ability it became possible to capture fleet-footed prey by stealth, social co-operation, the use of traps, tools and language.

Whatever were the precise details of early human evolution, the ability to modify and control the local environment must have been adaptive. The cumulative effect of this endowment over the brief period of human history is, however, more contentious. A serious biological defect in the human species may be summarised thus: our technical ingenuity is not complemented by prophetic wisdom. Hence the environmental consequences of technical innovations have never been predicted.

Science and Technology

Although science and technology are generally admired,[*] there is an emerging realisation that they may be inflicting irreversible damage on the environment;[†] we may be creating an environment to which we are not adapted. The inevitable consequence of maladaption is extinction. Unable to anticipate or compute the adverse effects of science and technology, it is nevertheless to science and technology that we turn for solutions to the problems that they themselves have caused. This is the absurd position in which we find ourselves. Our survival depends upon mobilising our intellect in order to recognise, and control, these inherent dangers.

Unquestioning adulation of science has been instrumental in deceiving the human species into believing that subservience to biological dictates can be circumvented; that human beings are above the law of nature. A further consequence of increased cerebral capacity is a moral concern for the entire species. Anthropocentrism elevates the human species to a position of superiority in which other species and the living environment are subject to its metaphysical musings and utopian aspirations. Anthropocentrism also contains the seed of human maladaption; indeed of our extinction.

The Role of the Veterinary Profession

Members of the veterinary profession, as biologists concerned with adaptive mechanisms, have a vital role in understanding the problems associated with the relationship between an animal and its environment. Human survival depends on understanding the need to live in dynamic harmony with the living world. Clearly, the profession should be making a

---

[*] L. Wolpert, *The Unnatural Nature of Science* (London, 1992).

[†] B. McKibben, *The End of Nature* (Harmondsworth, 1990).

significant contribution to this understanding. Sadly, it has jettisoned its intellectual integrity and social responsibility. It has failed to reveal that scientific reductionism promises only the illusion of progress.

The veterinary profession deals specifically with problems arising in animals which are forced to live in domestic environments to which they are not ideally adapted by evolution.* Veterinary teaching should be based on an understanding of adaptation, ecology and environmentalism. Well-adapted animals are healthy, contented and productive; their well-being is assured. Society perceives the profession as having a moral obligation to concern itself with animal welfare. Indeed it tentatively accepts that responsibility. New graduates, on being admitted to the profession, are required to declare that it will be their 'constant endeavour to ensure the welfare of animals committed to their care'.

Modern veterinary science emerged during the latter half of the eighteenth century.† It was established amidst enthusiasm for scientific investigation and its presumed benefits for humanity. The embryonic profession's perceived purpose was to ensure a functional cavalry, to ameliorate lost production in agricultural animals due to disease and to prolong the useful lives of transport horses. The welfare of animals was then, as it has remained, at best a poorly understood, accidental adjunct. The use of horses in war and for transport has all but disappeared; but the application of veterinary science to agriculture has had detrimental consequences for the environment and has led to profound and unremitting abuse of animals.

My own ambition to become a vet was motivated, at the age of eight, by the naive emotions of a child. I accepted without question the many unrealistic myths which colour our relationship with animals and the living world. My training and biological education, together with an analysis of environmental reality, forced upon me in over thirty years' experience in various branches of the profession, have not clouded my appreciation of animals but have jaundiced my jejune enthusiasm. Far from embracing the human scientific heritage it has set me on a pathway to pessimism.‡

The sanguine climate in which the veterinary profession was established

* D. M. Broom and K. G. Jonson, *Stress and Welfare* (London, 1993).
† E. Cotchin, *The Royal Veterinary College London* (London, 1990).
‡ J. Maddox, *The Doomsday Syndrome* (London, 1972).

must be replaced by one of misgiving, if we take the pessimistic perspective on human evolution and its consequences that I have outlined. Other professions have a limited, but unequivocal, philosophical basis for their activities: lawyers exist to dispense justice, doctors to cure disease and prolong human life, nurses to care for the sick and the dying, architects to design safe, sound and aesthetically pleasing buildings. The veterinary surgeon's purpose, however, is confused. The profession is torn between concern for the welfare of its patients and subservience to the demands of its clients, and therefore of human society. Perhaps because clients pay the bills, animal welfare, adaptive mechanisms and the dangers of reductive science have been ignored.

Subservience to the naive expectations of society is particularly regrettable in a profession which ostensibly bases its teaching on a profound understanding of biology. Concern for the survival of humanity and the welfare of both human beings and other animal species should lead to promulgation of the importance of the adaptive process. It should caution that the dictates of biology cannot be thwarted. Vets, however, remain silent.

Recently, in a topical radio programme, scapegoats were being sought for the fiasco surrounding bovine spongiform encephalopathy (BSE). The item was immediately followed by scientists extolling the virtues, and lightly dismissing the unpredictable consequences, of genetic engineering. The irony of this juxtaposition was presumably lost on the producer, the presenters, the participants and most listeners. The veterinary profession should have condemned the affront to biological reality when it was first proposed to feed animal protein to herbivores – the believed cause of BSE. The profession should now be at the forefront of the campaign to stop the madness of genetic engineering, both in support of the dignity and welfare of the animals which will thereby be misused and in order to modify the dangerously arrogant belief that biology is infinitely manipulable.

There are two courses open to the human species. It can continue to exploit its scientific abilities in order to find temporary solutions to the problems posed by science; or it can devise a system which restricts its activities in accordance with the demands of dynamic environmental harmony. An intellectually perceptive and socially responsible veterinary profession should advocate the latter. Unfortunately it promulgates the former.

Agriculture

In agricultural practice, the veterinary profession has virtually ignored the welfare of farm animals and the rural environment. Agricultural species are perceived simply as units of production. They are denied sentience. Genetically modified by selective breeding to provide increased production, frequently surgically mutilated to alter quality and ensure easier handling, they are subjected to intensive management systems which deny fundamental behavioural and physiological expression. Intensive management propels animals into the grey area of maladaption. Identification and evaluation of this area is difficult and imprecise; nevertheless it is the primary duty of the veterinary profession. An animal may, for example, enter the grey area as a result of severe traumatic injury or acute pathological challenge; or its entry may develop as a consequence of an accumulation of several small environmental inadequacies any one of which, on its own, would be within the animal's adaptive competence. The survival of intensively managed animals, forced into this area, depends on the continuous administration of antibiotics and allied substances. The consequences for the human population of antibiotic resistance and for the environment of contamination with concentrated effluent and chemical pollutants are serious. While the plight of animals forced to live in intensive systems does not offend the sensibilities of those who elevate the human species to some metaphysical pinnacle above and beyond the material world, it should and does affront those who empathise with sentient creatures which are forced to suffer psychological distress, physical discomfort and pain as a consequence of human indifference. Agricultural animals have been betrayed by the veterinary profession.

In the 1930s the ecologist W. C. Allee showed that for any species, in any given situation, there is an optimum group size. He also demonstrated that there are adaptive disadvantages when the group is too small and that similar problems emerge when there is overcrowding.[*] This simple, but elegant, work is totally ignored by designers of intensive management systems. Social animals may variously be kept in isolation or in conditions where the population density is so extremely high that normal social structure and interaction, even normal movement, are impossible. Further, the work of the ethologist Hediger demonstrated the need for individual space, a principle denied to many intensively managed animals.[†] More

[*] W. C. Allee, *The Social Life of Animals* (London, 1938).
[†] H. Hediger, *Wild Animals in Captivity* (London, 1950).

recent ethological investigations have confirmed the commonsense view that play in young animals and enriched environments are essential for normal psychological and physical development, while numerous studies have concluded that mothering is vitally important.* Management systems which ignore behavioural and physiological parameters may condemn animals to maladaption, thereby compromising their welfare.

Conservation

Familiarity with the principles of adaptive dynamism should have led the veterinary profession to express concern at the exponential increase in human population: a continued increase cannot be accommodated ecologically. Increasing human population density has direct relevance for at least one aspect of veterinary involvement.

Some veterinarians have concerned themselves with the conservation of endangered species. There are worthy and ambitious programmes to return animals, bred in captivity, to the wild. Sadly, pessimism even pervades the aspirations of conservation. The great mammals are in terminal decline; they cannot hope to compete with the unremittingly rapacious demands of an increasing human population for land and resources. They are endangered because their environments have diminished in size and character as a result of human activity. Only unrealistic romantics could remain optimistic without the formulation and implementation of stringent policies to restrict the growth of the human population.

Laboratory Animal Science

Laboratory animal science presents some difficult problems for moral philosophy.† Human medicine is essentially anthropocentric and reduction- ist. In direct opposition to biological dictates it concurs with a moral respect for the sanctity of individual humans and the value of their longevity. In

---

* Play in young animals: W. H. Thorpe, *Learning and Instinct in Animals* (London, 1963); enriched environments: B. Meyers, 'Early Experience and Problem-Solving', in H. Moltz (ed.) *The Ontogeny of Vertebrate Behaviour* (New York and London, 1971) and J. Webster, *Animal Welfare* (Oxford, 1994); mothering: H. F. Harlow, 'The Development of Learning in the Rhesus Monkey', *American Scientist* 47 (1959), pp. 459–79.

† R. M. Baird and S. E. Rosenbaum (eds) *Animal Experimentation* (London, 1991); T. Regan, 'Ill-gotten Gains', in G. Langley (ed.) *Animal Experimentation* (London, 1989).

acquiescing with this outlook, and contributing to it in the field of laboratory animal science, the veterinary profession appears to be heedless of the need for the human species to remain in adaptive balance.[*] Incidentally, it condones the subjection of large numbers of animals to severe environmental restriction, discomfort, pain and degradation in medical research laboratories.

The Pet Industry

In the translocation from its rural origins to its preoccupation with urban pets the veterinary profession relinquishes any pretence to social and scientific responsibility. While there is a number of organisations which question the scientific sense and moral right to inflict humiliation and discomfort on animals in order to provide human beings with cheap food, medicine and sporting entertainment, very little public concern is expressed for the degradation to which pet animals are routinely and continuously subjected.

It is not appropriate here to consider the psychological quirks and mental characteristics which lead to the human need for pets. Indeed so important have pets become to the human inhabitants of Western society that they have been promoted to 'companion animals'. This promotion does not, however, protect them from abuse by well-meaning, but intellectually myopic, owners.

Evolution dictates that a successful species live in dynamic harmony with the environment in which it finds itself. The gauge against which the welfare of domestic animals should be judged is the environmental conditions to which their ancestral species is adapted by its evolutionary history. It is true that pet animals are protected from predation, given regular supplies of food and provided with veterinary attention. These advantages must be balanced against the deprivations imposed by the domestic environment.

Dogs are wolves in fancy dress.[†] Wolves live in groups with complex social interaction. Successful hunting demands close social co-operation. Social and sexual behaviour is subject to strict pack discipline. All members of the pack are responsible for the care and protection of the cubs.[‡] In

[*] M. W. Fox, 'What Future for Man on Earth', in R. K. Morris and M. W. Fox (eds) *On the Fifth Day* (Washington, DC, 1978).
[†] D. Coffey, *A Veterinary Surgeon's Guide to Dogs* (London, 1980).
[‡] M. W. Fox, *The Soul of the Wolf* (New York, 1980).

contrast, the pet dog is frequently isolated, forced to suffer varying degrees of genetic mutilation and is condemned to a life of boredom without purpose or social interaction, a situation for which its human substitute pack affords only marginal amelioration. Further, it has become fashionable for devoted owners to inflict on these animals the final abuse of mindless despots – sexual mutilation. With hardly a murmur of dissent from the veterinary profession, pet dogs are routinely spayed and castrated in the mistaken belief that it is in their best interests. Every argument in favour of these abuses is an affront to human intellectual and analytical competence. The ovaries and the testicles produce hormones which are an integral part of the complex endocrine system. They are not optional extras. It is claimed, for example, that the sexual mutilation of bitches prevents uterine disease later in life. It has to be true that if a perfectly normal, healthy, functioning organ is removed it cannot later become diseased. Since many women require hysterectomy later in life, does this justify neutering all 12-year-old girls? Sexual mutilation is promoted by animal welfare societies concerned with the dog because, they claim, it reduces the number of unwanted dogs. So we are, it seems, prepared to subject our pets to the physical danger, psychological deprivation and moral indifference imposed by sexual mutilation in order to improve the welfare of dogs that will never be born.

Castration produces canine eunuchs. The *Concise Oxford Dictionary* defines a eunuch as a slave or, alternatively, as a male lacking effectiveness – some reward for devoted 'companionship'! Sexual mutilation is, in reality, performed for the convenience of owners indifferent to the well-being of their companion, or in an attempt to extend their pet's longevity. The mistaken belief that longevity is increased as a result of sexual mutilation gratifies the emotional needs of the owner. It does not improve the welfare of the dog or its quality of life.

The ancestors of the domestic cat may be succinctly described as lone, territory-loving night hunters.* Their territories need to be large to accommodate predation. It may be postulated that the reduction of a cat's territorial range in suburbia is as great, even greater, than the contraction of individual space experienced by domestic hens in battery cages. Suburban cats are managed intensively. One consequence of intensive management is an increase in aggressive behaviour. The commonest reason for a feline visit

* D. Coffey, *A Veterinary Surgeon's Guide for Cat Owners* (London, 1982).

to the veterinary surgery is an abscess caused by fighting. Further, population density in the suburban cat frequently leads to anxiety states which culminate in bizarre behaviour.

Some breeds of cat are subjected to genetic manipulation to produce fur for which the feline tongue is not designed. These unfortunate creatures cannot groom effectively. If its coat is to be kept in good condition the cat must subject itself to the indignity and discomfort of being groomed or its fur becomes matted. The only solution to matted fur is a general anaesthetic and the electric clipper. Selective breeding has also produced a depletion in mental capacity in some breeds. This has led to greater pliability, reduced aggression – stupidity. Some breeds are no longer truly feline. Their behaviour does, however, more closely reflect their owner's desire for a compliant toy.

Pets are generally considered to be of value in education and in the development of social and moral responsibility in children. In pursuance of these objectives, rabbits and a variety of rodents are kept in social isolation in small cages devoid of interest, fed inadequate diets of manufactured muesli and, following a brief period of enthusiasm, largely ignored. Rabbits, when they become neurotic as a result of such deprivation, are often sexually mutilated in an attempt to make them easier to handle.

A recent quirky enthusiasm for 'house rabbits' results in social isolation and routine sexual mutilation of the animals, in an attempt to increase their pet potential. Wild rabbits have complex social lives which perusal of Richard Adams's classic *Watership Down*, factually based on behavioural studies by R. M. Lockley,* demonstrates.

Inconsistency in attitudes to animal welfare is poignantly illustrated by the caging of budgerigars. These creatures naturally live in huge flocks with complex social behaviour. They evolved to fly. As pets they are frequently, indeed usually, subject to social isolation in absurdly small cages, frequently unable to do more than hop from perch to perch. When agricultural or laboratory animals are subjected to such abuse, armies of indignant demonstrators justifiably take to the streets. The treatment of pet budgerigars is, incomprehensibly and illogically, regarded with benign acquiescence merely because they are loved! The irony of this escapes all but a few observers.

---

* R. M. Lockley, *The Private Life of the Rabbit* (London, 1954).

Hunting with Hounds and Animal Welfare

Animal welfare is a complicated and confounding subject. The confusion is exemplified by the debate on fox hunting. While I have an antipathy towards hunting, careful consideration of the arguments provides less than unequivocal grounds for condemnation. An objective analysis must first separate the welfare of the fox from contemplation of related moral aspects of human behaviour. The fox lives in conditions which provide many features of the environment in which it evolved and to which it is adapted. It is able to explore and exploit its physical and behavioural potential. While predation is an unpleasant and unedifying feature of the natural world it is not an activity devised by human beings. To abhor predation is simply to express an understandable distaste towards aspects of the natural order. Those who oppose hunting on moral grounds argue that it detracts from human dignity and moral integrity. There are blatant elements of anthropocentrism in that proposition. What, one muses, is so special about humanity that it should be obliged to desist from predation? Eating the flesh of farmed domestic animals is controlled, even sanitised, predation! It is claimed by protagonists of hunting, without biological justification, that foxes must be controlled. A natural balance between predator and prey would, with periodic population fluctuations, be achieved without the intervention of human agency. Control is demanded by farmers to protect their intensively managed, but inadequately protected, animals. Much of the opposition to hunting is not based on concern for the welfare of the fox, but on a moral disapproval of those who enjoy the activity. Shooting, it is frequently claimed, is preferable. Were hunting to be banned, however, foxes would be shot by people who enjoy shooting foxes, not by those opposed to hunting with hounds! Listing animal welfare priorities, given the choice between life as a dairy cow, a laboratory mouse, a pet budgerigar, a house rabbit or a wild fox, one would surely incline to the latter with little hesitation. The hunting debate serves to illustrate the difficulties and complexities of an academic contemplation of animal welfare.

Conclusion

Were the veterinary profession to discharge its social responsibilities, it would encourage and undertake a profound multidisciplinary academic study of animal welfare and relate the results to its knowledge of adaptive mechanisms in the interests of all sentient creatures. Currently, in every field in which the veterinary profession functions, it betrays the animals for which it claims social responsibility. It ignores its intellectual foundation which should have led to a profound understanding of adaptive mechanisms and the inviolable dictate of biology: it fails its patients, its clients and society by failing to counsel caution in the exploitation of human technical and scientific ingenuity.

To be fair to the profession, it provides the service society demands and is prepared to pay for. Veterinary services are a business. Professional activity is constrained by the demands of the legal system, by the promotional enthusiasm of the multinational drug and animal feed companies and by the competitive world of commerce. Society demands cheap food, modern medicine, uncontrolled human breeding, longevity and pets. If the human species is to endure for more than a wink of geological time, society must change.

It has been my intention to consider the human predicament from a biological perspective using the veterinary profession to illustrate some of the difficulties. It would, of course, be wonderful to aspire to a world in which human beings live long, disease-free lives in harmony, respect and friendship with all of their fellow sentient beings: a world in which sentient creatures derive only benefit from human technical and scientific ingenuity. Unfortunately, that scenario is not an option. Human survival, whether in rural or urban environments, demands acceptance of the inviolable dictate of biology: adapt or die. The question to ponder is whether the human understanding can ever really accept this.

IV

Development and Settlement

16. *Those Four Million Houses*

John Gummer

M ere head-counting tells us little about the impact of population growth. It is an estimate of the demands upon resources which that population will make that provides the best guide to future need. It takes 120 Bangladeshi children to make the energy demands of one American baby. So too with the other requirements which go with the most affluent of societies. High among these are the expectations of living space.

In general the richer the people, the greater the living area that they are likely to demand. Yet there is considerable variation between cultures. Outstandingly, the Japanese have retained a willingness to put up with very cramped quarters because of the real restrictions which their geography imposes. In continental Europe, the urban requirements of most citizens are significantly less than the expectation of the British. We have traditionally demanded more living space and we continue to do so. It was one of the distinguishing features of the old Parker Morris standards for council housing, unparalleled in other European countries.

Indeed, when the last government sought to tackle the question of under-occupation of supported housing, it was taken for granted that everyone should have a spare bedroom and there was no question of under-occupation unless there was more than one such room. Anyone who has friends living in Paris or Rome will know how rare and how prized such a spare room would be. The expectations of urban owner-occupiers in the great cities of the continent are significantly below those of subsidised tenants in London.

So any consideration of population changes in the UK has to be made against this background of traditionally high demands for space. For this reason, even the relatively small absolute growth which we expect will require more provision in the UK than elsewhere. However, this is hardly important compared with the much greater impact of three other changes, each one of which brings with it the same demand for greater space in addition to the absolute numbers.

The first is the fact of greater longevity. It is not only that more and more people are living longer but that they are living in their own homes longer. Government policy is encouraging this, as recent changes in social service provision seek to provide support so that people can stay at home. Financial considerations have driven this change, and they are particularly effective on the ground, as the local authority struggles to keep within budgets under stress because of the growing numbers of old people. It is very much more cost-effective for them to keep people out of residential accommodation. The tendency is therefore to prolong this period of support even beyond what is objectively the best answer. In any case the house continues to be used by the older person and not released on to the market as would have been the case in earlier years. This means that more units have to be provided to make up the shortfall.

Nor is there any sign that the prolongation of life expectancy will cease. Twenty-five years ago, when I first went to Suffolk and visited old people's homes, they were filled with people in their seventies. Now they tend not to take people in until the late eighties. Every year the average entry date moves on so that we must expect it to be well into the nineties by 2020.

At the other end of the age range is the earlier formation of independent households. The driving force here has been the significant increase in the proportion of young people who go on to university and the change in the backgrounds from which they come. Back in 1979 one in eight of teenagers went on to some form of higher education. By 1997 that had increased to one in three. This growth meant that more and more students came from backgrounds where their parents and close family had not themselves been educated beyond the school-leaving age. This in itself tended to make for a wider generation gap so the likelihood was that a significantly greater number would not remain at home but would seek to live on their own or with others away from the family.

This is a tendency which is seen throughout Europe, but is particularly a feature of the UK scene because of our peculiar university structure. In most continental countries a high proportion of young people go to a local institute of higher education. In Britain they are much more likely to choose a university some way away from home. Indeed it is the normal decision to go to the opposite end of the country in order to make a real break with one's schooldays. So children brought up in Brighton seek places at the University of Durham and those from Newcastle vie for acceptance by Sussex. Scots universities are filled with English students, as are Bangor and Swansea. The changes in the grants arrangements which will make university education more expensive may introduce a marginal change in the pattern; but it will not be more than marginal.

These habits reinforce the tendency of young people to leave home earlier than before. Traditionally most children from C2, D, and E families stayed in the family home until they got married. That pattern is increasingly destroyed as more and more go away to university. These are the very young people for whom the world of university very often makes a much greater contrast with the home scene. They are more likely therefore to stay away when their studies are completed. This contrasts with a very much smaller number of more privileged children who tend to return home, at least for a year or two. Overall, however, young people leave home earlier and stay away thereafter, thereby requiring more accommodation than in the past.

Even more important is the effect of higher rates of family break-up. Even twenty-five years ago, only one in five families experienced divorce. Among younger families the figure is now nearer one in two and the proportion is moving up the age groups, so that it is likely to become the norm. Children caught in these breaks are much more likely to leave home early. Indeed they are often thrown out by new partners who do not wish to be bothered by former family responsibilities. All this is exacerbated by the proportionally greater growth of divorce among the lower socio-economic groups. These were once restrained by the costs of break-up as well as by traditional morality. In a welfare state, where it is easy to slough off responsibilities to the community as a whole, these restraints have been weakened. It remains to be seen if the Child Support Agency will have any effect, but there is as yet no sign of the figures falling.

This greater frequency of divorce has had further direct effects upon the demand for housing. More and more divorces are not followed by remarriage but by sequential partnerships. Once when Mr and Mrs Brown divorced they each remarried and so, although a different couple lived in each unit, their overall housing needs remained the same. Now it is more likely that one or both partners will not remarry but instead will live with someone who recognises that the relationship may well not be permanent. They therefore retain their own accommodation so that where once two homes would be needed, now there will be a requirement for three or even four.

So too is there a change in the amount of room that is expected, even by those who do not form new partnerships. Twenty-five years ago it was much more usual for the mother to have sole custody of the children. Now the courts encourage at least significant visiting rights for the fathers. For this reason both parents need enough room to be able to accommodate the children. The father no longer goes back to the spatial requirements of a bachelor but retains a need for much the same size of home as he once shared with his wife. Indeed, even without the children, it is rarely acceptable to return to the sort of home which sufficed for a young unmarried man. Nothing is as habit-forming as the occupation of space.

A family home is not just a function of having a family. It is the expectation of a man of a certain age. That expectation adds significantly to the housing demands if it is to be satisfied outside marriage.

Altogether these pressures add up to a demand for 4.4 million new homes in England before the year 2006. This is indeed the lowest figure which one can safely present. Even though it was criticised when I first produced it, there are now few who will disagree with the total except to suggest we may need to raise it even further. Nor should that surprise us. No minister will wish to inflate such a figure. I chose the lowest number I could truthfully support.

Yet, having accepted what that figure is, it is important to underline what it is not. The numbers do not imply any continuity in the pattern of settlement. To say that 4.4 million homes are needed does not mean that they will be demanded in the places which have seen growth in the past. This is a point which has recently been well made by Ken Clarke, the former Chancellor of the Exchequer. He complained that the growth figures for Nottinghamshire were taken as implying growth in the areas around Nottingham, not least in his own constituency of Rushcliffe. In fact, he argued, there is no reason to believe that former settlement patterns are immutable. The closure of the Nottingham coalfield has meant that many former mining villages could form the basis of new communities where there is plenty of opportunity for the reuse of land. Similar opportunities exist throughout the nation and we need to be careful that we do not assume that people will automatically revert to the choices they made in the past.

Nor is it sensible to assume that people will all be looking for the same sort of housing as they have sought in the recent past. More than half the new units which are required are for single-person households, yet our house-builders are still fixed in providing the same standard family home which has been their staple since the First World War. At a recent Ideal Home Exhibition, Bellway – one of our most innovative builders – had a superb exhibit in which they traced the development of the typical middle-class home over the past 100 years. It was a trip down memory lane. I saw y grandparents' house, and my aunt's. I recognised the homes of friends whose parents were younger than mine and I saw the best of the homes now being built in my constituency. The changes were indeed remarkable and the growing influence very clear. From linoleum to fitted carpets and from the crystal set to the cable TV, I saw how differently we live now. Yet these houses were so very much the same. They were all designed for the conventional family, for parents and children living together until the new generation leaves to find work or get married. Even these most enlightened of house-builders were meeting needs which are wholly different from those presented by about half the households who will demand new homes. The single person needs a different configuration of accommodation. One or two bedrooms with a single living room, a flat or duplex without a garden will replace the three-bedroomed family house. It is not that there will be no demand for homes with a traditional layout. It is just that studios and lofts, open plan and shell apartments will form an increasingly important segment of the market, to cater for single people.

Their choice of situation will also be different. They will be likely to want to be close to their work and their play. They will want to shop conveniently and yet expect the full range of choice which the supermarkets provide. So they will be more likely to choose a home close to the city centre than one in the suburbs. Even if they have connections which lead them to favour the suburbs, they will still be more likely to seek a central position with easy access to a shopping centre and public transport.

All this argues for a significant change in the pattern of housing demand: different housing types, differently situated, designed for different kinds of household. What was merely a forecast five years ago is now happening. We chose to encourage building in the centre of our towns and cities before we had clear evidence that it would meet a pent-up demand. That is now evident, as homes built in central positions sell easily and quickly. A quick trip round Clerkenwell in London will prove the point at once. This once unfashionable area close to the City has become very popular in the last two years, with every available office and warehouse block being sold for residential conversion. Some of the most unlikely buildings are altered into so-called 'lofts'. It appears that even a semi-basement can be called a 'loft'. So expensive has Clerkenwell become that house-hunters are now looking beyond into even less fashionable areas like Shoreditch and Hoxton. One estate agent waxed philosophical as he told me of the large number of homes for conversion he had sold. 'Here I am selling them to middle-class buyers desperate to move into Hoxton, when my father spent his whole life trying to get out of the place.'

Until very recently the pattern of social improvement was very clear. Hoxton to Woodford and then, if you really had done well, retirement in Southend. Today the young are coming back from Essex into the centre of town. When the first of the urban villages was opened in Docklands, the earliest purchaser brought his family back from Bagshot so that he could cut out the commuting and see more of his children. So too in Birmingham where the enlightened leadership of the planning officer poached from Bath, Len Peach, has meant increasing opportunity to buy town houses in city-centre development. Again many of the new purchasers are bringing their families back from the leafy suburbs so that they can enjoy the opportunities of the city centre and substitute family life for commuting. So it is not only those whose marriages have failed that succumb to the lure of the towns. It is also those who fear that the combination of long hours and commuting will put an impossible strain on relationships which ought to come first. As a result the demand for centrally positioned homes is growing all the time.

Five years ago the house-builders argued forcefully that there was no call for homes except on greenfield sites. They suggested that they would not be able to meet the real needs of the population unless they were able to build new estates of executive homes. It had always been that way and they saw no reason to suggest that it was going to be otherwise. Conservative politicians were faced with a real dilemma. Believers in the free market do not easily seek to frustrate the customers' requirement. Experience has shown how foolish that is. Yet the very existence of a planning system means that the free market does not operate. In any case we are stopping people from building where they most would like. Since 1948, the Town and Country Planning Acts have been specifically designed to ensure that the countryside, the green belt, and other areas of importance or beauty are protected from development. These are of course in need of such protection precisely because they are the very places where people would choose to build if left to their own devices. So the idea that we have a free market in house-building is very wide of the mark.

Nevertheless, year after year successive ministers of both political parties have released open land to satisfy the growing demands for houses. The New Towns represented a massive incursion of development into the countryside. Lord Silkin, then a Labour minister, spoke movingly of the new lives for Londoners which these settlements would provide. The vision of the Garden City, which had inspired so many architects before the war, was being transformed into a more workaday solution to the housing shortage, which had been exacerbated by bombing and wartime neglect. Standards were rising and there was a universal feeling that better housing was the essential key to better health and a better life.

Yet it was not only the New Towns which took up large swathes of land. In city after city, the bomb damage, combined with the inheritance of slum housing, demanded emergency solutions. The only answer seemed to be to build high. The population had already been softened up to the changes that would entail. During the war the army education organisation and magazines like *Good Housekeeping* had sought to convince people who wanted to live in a small terraced house with a little garden that there was a better alternative – a modern flat with every labour-saving device. *Good Housekeeping* was particularly pressing. An insufferably superior young lady was portrayed interviewing a mother about her hopes for a new life after the war. The older woman expresses her desire for a house with a little garden, only to be subjected to a barrage of propaganda. She is alternately cajoled and castigated until she admits, out of sheer fatigue, one imagines, that the clever young lady may indeed be right and she would opt for a flat.

The town planners had indeed got it all sewn up. The *Good Housekeeping* woman at least had a chance to argue her case. Most people just got what they were offered. The hearts of great cities like Liverpool, already laid waste by the bombing, were now to be desolated as the remaining population was moved out to satellite towns. Later the television series *Z Cars* showed the world just how dreary were the huge estates called in the programme 'Newtown' and in reality 'Skelmersdale'. There were 'New-towns' all round Glasgow, without a pub between them. The city fathers were concerned to improve the community through social engineering; they were seeking to impose sobriety upon communities which had not themselves sought that improvement in their mores. The result was that those communities became even less viable. Elsewhere these huge new complexes were served by exiguous public transport and provided with little in the way of amenities.

The spirit which animated the building of these projects seemed universal in post-war Europe. That only came home to people in the United Kingdom when, after the fall of the Berlin Wall, the cameras were able to range far and wide in East Berlin. It could have been any collection of GLC estates. In fact the size and specification in Britain were significantly higher; but the reasoning was the same. The workers deserved hot and cold running water and such other amenities as officials thought proper. Nothing else mattered. There was no attempt to preserve communities or local loyalties, nor to foster relationships, in this barren but hygienic world. The policy was the ultimate in materialism. All that counted was the physical conditions in which people lived.

This was understandable. Many had lost their homes entirely; many more came back from the war to begin a family without a home of their own. Even where the bombing had spared them, a huge number of homes were downright intolerable. In the Medway towns where I was brought up, people lived in Sawyers' Alley and in Manor Street, up stairs and down cellars, in conditions which would be inconceivable to my children today. I remember my father, an Anglican clergyman, visiting a woman dying of consumption in a single room, with water literally running down the walls and a pail lavatory, shared by several other families, just outside the door. It was in no way removed from the situation Dickens described in the previous century. With housing conditions like that, it is not surprising that the local council regarded improved physical conditions so highly.

Yet, now that the Wood Street and Garden Row of my childhood are no more and the tower blocks have taken their place, we have lost much more than the dreadful housing. The connections and the community preserved through two world wars and the Great Depression are no longer there. Instead people have been isolated in their improved conditions and the old intimacy has gone. Perhaps it was bound to happen – at least to some extent – but the fact is that no one did anything to prevent it. There was no attempt to think through the nature of community. Nobody asked the people what they wanted. Nothing was done beyond the provision of new kitchens and bathrooms. The world was filled with people inspired by reach-me-down Corbusiers. They had not heard what he said about high-rise blocks: 'These are certainly not suitable for bringing up a family.' The physical needs were too urgent and too overwhelming to allow for anything other than building as quickly and cheaply as possible. Post-war reconstruction inevitably meant homes without a heart.

Rebuilding on the spot was too difficult and too expensive. It was also not seen as the best alternative. The old towns were not good enough for the people. They deserved something better and the new settlements outside were thought to be just that. This was the time when city living was devalued. Moving out had long been a middle-class phenomenon and now socialist Britain was extending that privilege to the workers. If they couldn't move out, then at least they should have the benefit of entirely new communities built on the ruins of the old. There was no thought of renewal or refurbishment. This was the brave new world. The noise and smell of industry and commerce had to be kept away from where people lived. It was wrong that what the rich had been able to escape the poor had had to endure. The new settlements away from the workplace were designed to separate living from working, since working was, of necessity, a dirty, smelly, noisy business.

So the theories which had built Welwyn and Letchworth Garden Cities and earlier had inspired Bournville and Saltaire, now created Stevenage and Harlow, Great Cornard and Milton Keynes, Runcorn and Thetford. These indeed offered conditions undreamt of by the inhabitants of the crowded cities of pre-war England. Yet they were created with no thought for their impact on the countryside and no consideration of the effect on the old towns, which were left to decline.

This attitude has lain behind the way in which we have used our planning powers until very recently. We have maintained a system of zoning which has kept residential areas separate from industry and commerce. We have assumed that the towns and cities are not the preferred places for new housing. We have released huge areas of countryside for the creation of new estates, both public and private. The results are for all to see. Our cities have declined in population and in vigour. Their centres have been left to the very rich and the very poor or just to the very poor. As old industries died, so the huge spaces they once occupied have died with them. It is this industrial dereliction which has so scarred our cities and even many of our smaller towns. Places as different as Braintree and Liverpool saw their centres destroyed, not by bombing, but by closure. The downward spiral led inevitably to no-go areas, to growing urban crime and ultimately to the riots of the early 1980s.

It was in coming to terms with the fact of urban decay that the last government began to change the attitude to urban living. The change in policy was not premeditated but instead rose naturally out of the work of the Urban Development Corporations and other new instruments of regeneration. They held none of the assumptions which so dominated municipal planning departments. They looked for partners wherever they could get them. The building of the residential units as part of a mixed development seemed a necessary part of regeneration. From Chatham Dockyard to Liverpool's Albert Dock and from Plymouth Sound to Tyneside, these new developers made housing an integral part of their plans. The old notions of zoning were jettisoned and the even older idea of mixed development was espoused.

It was obvious, really. Regeneration meant state-of-the-art factories and commercial premises. It meant making the best of features which had been overlaid or overlooked in the days of decline. Canals and other water features, former warehouses and good industrial buildings – all these lent themselves to residential development. Meeting modern environmental regulations ensured that industry was a good neighbour and the considerations which once led to zoning simply did not apply. Real communities were rising out of the dereliction and there was a sense of excitement when people saw that this was possible.

Indeed the men who led these enterprises were enjoying themselves: Sykes in Sheffield and Pickard in Docklands, Pitcher in Manchester and Eyre in the Birmingham heartlands. They were open to new ideas. They were untrammelled by the post-war orthodoxy. They came out of business and they were free to innovate. Michael Heseltine had seen to that. There were few of the rules and tight specifications which hemmed people in and made imagination a positive encumbrance. Freebooting was encouraged and the unconventional demanded. As a result there were some serious problems; but they were, for the most part, the problems of innovative and determined people.

While all this was happening, politics was changing outside. The success of the regeneration programmes began to overcome the antagonism of local councils to the Urban Development Corporations. They began to think differently and to want to emulate that success. There was a much greater willingness to go for mixed development and public/private partnerships. In the course of that change came a growing acceptance of mixed development. The Department of the Environment was pressing the issue, but many of the schemes were developed quite independently of that pressure. The increasing success of schemes in the centres of cities meant that some house-builders were beginning to catch up with a real change in public sentiment.

Yet the House Builders' Federation continued to press for the release of more land. Greenfield sites have always been the preferred route for them. It is easier and cheaper to develop in that way and the conventional argument is that in-town sites are more difficult to assemble, more expensive to use, and less easy to market. In much the same way there has been strong opposition to the kind of mixed development which in continental countries has contributed so much to cities. Shops, offices and flats in the same building or as part of the same complex bring employment, commerce and living space together. It is one of the ways in which cities have become and remained vibrant centres.

The British antipathy to flats and the particular way in which we have financed development has made all this very difficult in the UK. It was put to me clearly by a senior manager of a major insurance company when I was Secretary of State: 'I'm not investing in mixed development. The occupiers of flats will get hold of the telephone number of my chairman and ring him up if there's a burst pipe!' Major institutions want good covenants and they want as little hassle as possible. To most of them mixed development spells trouble.

Yet mixed development could play an important part in rejuvenating our cities and towns. Three things could make all the difference. Firstly there is now a consensus about rented property. The new government is not going to upset the shorthold tenancy system; letting has therefore become a reasonable long-term option. Secondly we made a change in the law so that housing associations can manage this kind of property and are not confined to their role as the providers of social housing. Thirdly I set in train an examination of how we might bring together the building regulations so that there could be one code applying to the whole of a mixed development and not three or four. This last is still awaited but the other developments have already led to a greater willingness for institutions like Friends Provident to become much more adventurous in these areas.

However, the central issue still remains, even though house-builders have to some extent changed their tune. In a recent forum on greenfield versus recycled sites held at the Royal Agricultural Society, the Deputy Director of the House Builders' Federation was supported by developers when he suggested that greenfield developments were more expensive than those built on already used land. They cited the cost of infrastructure and of the demands by local authorities for all kinds of payments as 'planning gain'. The argument now is not that building on recycled land is impossible, nor that it is expensive or unwanted. It is instead that such building is too difficult and that it will take some time to approach the proportions which the government now wants.

The truth is that the house-builders have begun to see that they will have to find ways of using more recycled land and that it will be increasingly difficult to get the planning permissions necessary to build in the open countryside. What they hope is that this change can be more limited and gradual than is necessary.

If we accept that there is a demand for 4.4 million or more new units we could, of course, simply refuse to allow the demand to be met. The trouble with that answer is that the people who would be hit are those least able to cope with the result, and often the most deserving of a new home. It will not be the richer and more competent members of society, since they can afford to pay the higher prices which such a shortage would inevitably produce. It is also quite clear that no government would see this solution as remotely politically possible. It is one thing to say you won't build any roads – that has a diffuse effect which is pretty hard to pin down. People who see house prices rocket, and who find that they cannot afford the home which once they expected to buy, will take their political revenge.

What is almost politically impossible, too, is to continue to build extensively on open land. That is not true everywhere. There are many villages who do want a little growth in order to safeguard their services and balance the ages of their population: villages like Darsham in Suffolk, where the parish council has long demanded limited growth in order to keep the village alive. Not all development is politically unpopular. Indeed, however many of the new homes we manage to build on once-used land, there will still be many – maybe a million or more – which will need careful siting on greenfield sites.

Developers will certainly smell out the places where such homes will be welcomed, or at least accepted. There is no problem with that. The difficulty comes in the use of brown-field land. Despite the best efforts of Lord Rodgers's committee, institutional searches will not deliver. Local authorities, the NHS and Railtrack, companies like ICI and BG, all have very large holdings of land which has been used for other purposes. They have an important part to play in bringing it forward. Yet in the end it is the imagination, expertise and single-mindedness of developers and builders which will find and assemble the sites we need. It is because I believe in the efficacy of private enterprise that I have heeded the warning of a successful developer: 'Don't give us the option. We'll go for the easy solution, every time. Make it clear that we either use recycled land or we shall not get any development at all. Then we shall find a way.' We need to harness the development industry to deliver what we want.

We needs towns and cities where people can live, work, play and shop. We cannot continue to leave the centres to dereliction and deprivation. Instead we must create the kinds of community which give to cities the vibrant life that once characterised them. We cannot refuse to build the homes our modern lifestyle demands. We may hope to change the mores which make that necessary, but that will take time. What we need is to recognise our good fortune that the two problems which face us provide a mutually satisfactory answer. We have to regenerate our run-down cities and we have to do it now, when we have a real and continuing need for more homes.

It is not just a matter of percentages. We should of course take on the Round Table on Sustainable Development's target, which is that 75 per cent of new units should be built on recycled land. What's more, we have to manage the release so that we don't get the other 25 per cent built disproportionately early! We shall need higher densities; but we shall not need any so-called town-cramming. Traditionalist 1960s planners are wrong in their contention that cramming is inevitable. If we adopt the kinds of density which have led to elegant living in cities like Bath and London, we can achieve our ends: rejuvenated urban centres, an enhanced and protected countryside, and a green belt which is secure so that it can provide the necessary green lung between settlements.

If that seems prescriptive then it is necessarily so. It is universally accepted that a small country with huge competing demands upon its available land must have a planning system. Such a system cannot but be prescriptive. Surely it is better to seek to achieve the kinds of community which history has shown us are the most successful than to choose to build in a way which has manifestly failed. Planning may be a disagreeable necessity, but it is a necessity. Let us use it in a way which saves the countryside for our children and creates towns exciting enough for them to want to live in.

17. The Unofficial Countryside
Colin Ward

The amiable naturalist Richard Mabey wrote a book in 1973 describing his wanderings and discoveries in *The Unofficial Countryside* of suburbia, factory sites, reservoirs, docks and railway tracks, canals, churchyards and allotments, parks and rubbish tips. A quarter of a century later, we have learned to take for granted that many species of plant and insect can no longer be found in agricultural counties doused in pesticides and herbicides and denuded of 130,000 miles of hedgerows. In October 1997 the British Trust for Ornithology reported that a greater variety of bird species were recorded in urban than in rural Britain. The notion that the owners and occupiers of agricultural land are the guardians of flora and fauna has been shown to be an illusion.

There has always been another kind of unofficial country, populated by members of the human species, outside the recognised system of land tenure and land use. By this I don't mean outlaws, emerging from their forest hide-outs to rob the rich and feed the poor, but those cotters and squatters who had managed to survive in the margins and interstices of the landlord and tenant system. Surveys of land ownership from Domesday in the eleventh century, through pipe rolls and subsidy rolls for many centuries, down to the tithe maps of the early Victorian period often failed to notice their minute and marginal holdings, simply because most of these surveys were undertaken to register taxable land or produce. The most devastating blow to the unofficial country was enclosure, when those cottagers who could show no title to their land were simply evicted to seek their future in the densely packed slums of industrial Britain.

But in several parts of the country the Industrial Revolution itself began in these uncharted and unregistered settlements of landless peasants scraping a livelihood in the margins of the economy. The places where they sought survival were often in the 'wastes' between parishes where it was possible to keep a few pigs and chickens while picking up an income from quarrying, mineral extraction or smelting, and later in the enormously labour-intensive work of building the canals and, still later, that of constructing and manning the railways in the valleys below.

In our attempts to read the unofficial landscape, whether on the ground or on the map, we use an old and useful classification of parishes, that of 'open' and 'close' villages. There is, in practice, a continuum between the two, but we associate the 'close' village with a single landowner who, through his agents, stewards, bailiffs or tenants, and his links with or patronage of other institutions like law enforcement and the Church, had effective control of everything that happens.

The 'open' village, on the other hand, is a struggling, unpredictable parish with evidence of owner-built and improvised housing, of mixed occupations and the growth of industry, of religious nonconformity and political radicalism, all of them associated with the dispersal of land ownership. The authors of *The Penguin Guide to the Landscape of England and Wales* have an attractive passage evoking this unofficial environment:

In order to sense the atmosphere of the pre-industrial rural scene it is desirable to leave the beaten track (as far as this is still possible) and seek out those corners of England and Wales where odd vestiges of that vanished era can be glimpsed. Such places are usually quiet and sheltered, devoid of features likely to attract the attention of the compilers of guidebooks, and unremarkable in terms of architecture, scenery or historical and literary associations. For reasons of physical geography, land use, social structure or the pattern of communications, these districts have been to some degree protected from the winds of change, which, although they may have swept, have not in every case swept clean. The traveller may come across them quite unexpectedly, struck by an indefinable change in the scale and quality of the landscape.*

This unofficial countryside could also be found on roadside sites between the metalled road and the hedgerows. Long and narrow cottages by the side of roads are still to be seen, as are those which local legend attributes to the belief that the occupiers of a house erected between sundown and sunrise could not be evicted by the landowner. Folklore of this kind has an astonishingly wide distribution in Britain, in continental Europe and beyond. Barrie Trinder explains that

* Paul Coones and John Patten, *The Penguin Guide to the Landscape of England and Wales* (Harmondsworth, 1986).

Often the lords of manors tacitly encouraged such settlement, particularly if labour was needed in the vicinity. Squatters could not be charged a rent for the use of common land, but they could be fined annually for encroachment. Their cottages were usually set in plots of about an acre, enclosed by a hedged earthen bank in which such useful plants as the damson, the hazel, the holly and the rowan would be planted. Such settlements became the nuclei of large-scale industries in areas like the Black Country, the Forest of Dean and the Potteries. Others remained as service centres, providing goods and such services as well-digging or carting for the surrounding areas.[*]

One such service centre was the hamlet of Headington Quarry, just outside Oxford, one of the few such settlements whose story was gathered from survivors before it disappeared in the usual suburban expansion. The historian Raphael Samuel had been in time to record the memories of old residents before they died and before the anarchic economy and settlement pattern had been expunged from the landscape. He provided a rich mixture of oral recollections and local archives which revealed a community of unofficial residents, some working in the quarries and the small brickworks that provided the building materials for nineteenth-century Oxford, and others servicing its residents.

Most of the cities of Victorian Britain had these service settlements just beyond their fringe, in the same way that Notting Dale provided personal services for Notting Hill and Kensington in London or, as Samuel pointed out, Kensal New Town ('Soapsuds Island') catered for the fashionable districts of Bayswater and Belgravia, as 'chief recipient for the weekly washings of the rich'.[†] This is, of course, a function of the unofficial settlements surrounding many cities of the southern hemisphere today, but Headington Quarry was also favoured as a source for building materials and techniques. It had both stone and clay, and the skills to work them to meet the city's demands. At the same time the quarry's semi-rural situation ensured a range of poaching, rabbit-snaring, pig-rearing and cow-keeping activities. Every family had an allotment garden and used a range of gathering techniques to exchange within the community or to sell to the farmers or the city. The importance of this vast variety of activities was that,

---

[*] Barrie Trinder, *The Making of the Industrial Landscape* (London, 1982; Stroud, 1987).

[†] Raphael Samuel, 'Quarry Roughs: Life and Labour in Headington Quarry, 1860–1920', in Raphael Samuel (ed.) *Village Life and Labour* (London, 1975).

however poor, quarry people stayed alive outside the official system of poor relief.

Settlements like Headington Quarry, with a singular lack of landlords, as Raphael Samuel puts it, 'enjoyed what was virtually an extra-parochial existence, a kind of anarchy, in which the villagers were responsible to nobody but themselves'.* They were joined, early in the nineteenth century, by a series of 'mushroom towns', springing up overnight to serve the needs of the people involved in building and then operating, first the canals and then the railways. By the end of that century another form of unofficial settlement had appeared, known first as 'bungalow towns' and later as the 'plotlands'.

This usefully descriptive word was coined by town planners to describe new rural settlements arising during the prolonged agricultural depression that began in the 1870s with cheap imports of grain and meat, and continued, with a brief hiatus in the First World War, until 1939. There were too few potential purchasers at the auction sales of bankrupt farms, even at throwaway prices. So speculators seized upon the notion of dividing fields into small plots, and selling them in unorthodox ways to city dwellers who, in those days, were frequently only one generation away from rural life. They hoped, on their plots costing between £5 and £50, to start a smallholding or chicken farm, or simply to build a holiday home or country retreat. The word evokes a landscape of a gridiron of grassy tracks, sparsely filled with army huts, old railway coaches, sheds, shanties and chalets, slowly evolving into ordinary suburban development.

Several factors created the plotlands. The most important was the availability of land. To the bankruptcy of the farming industry was added the effect of Lloyd George's doubling of death duties and the slaughter of sons and heirs of rural land in the First World War. Sellers of land were obliged to find a multitude of small purchasers in the absence of a few large ones. Added to this was the spread of the holiday habit and the idea of the 'weekend' away from home, thanks to cheap railway tickets, as well as the romance that became attached to camping and the open air.

In the south-east of England, the plotland landscape was to be found in pockets across the North and South Downs, along the Hampshire plain, and in the Thames Valley at riverside sites like Penton Hook, Marlow Bottom and Purley Park. It was interspersed among the established holiday

* Ibid.

193

resorts on the coasts of East and West Sussex at places like Shoreham Beach, Pett Level, Dungeness and Camber Sands, and most notoriously of all, at Peacehaven. It crept up the east coast, from Sheppey in Kent to Lincolnshire, by way of Canvey Island and Jaywick Sands, and clustered inland all across south Essex.

Nor was the plotland phenomenon confined to the south-east. Every industrial conurbation in Britain once had these escape routes to the country, river or sea. For the West Midlands there were sites along the Severn Valley; for the Liverpool and Manchester conurbations, places in North Wales and the Wirral; for Glasgow, the Ayrshire coast and even the banks of Loch Lomond. Serving the West Yorkshire towns and cities there was the Yorkshire coast and the Humber estuary, and for those of Tyneside and Teesside, the coasts of Northumberland and Durham. It is as though a proportion of the population was obeying an instinct or a natural law in seeking out a place where they could build for themselves.

Any reader familiar with the lives of city dwellers in the former Soviet Union or of its empire – countries like Poland, Hungary, Bulgaria or Czechoslovakia – will be thoroughly familiar with this aspiration for a little patch of land out of town which evolves from an allotment garden to a weekend family dacha and ultimately into the home base to which the parental generation retires. This was a characteristic of the plotland settlements of south-east England in the first forty years of the century. They tended to remain in the hands of the same family and to become the owners' retirement home. What seemed to the outside observer to be inconvenient, substandard and far from shops and services, was for them loaded with memories of happy summer days when the children were small.

The plotlands had other characteristics in common. They were invariably on marginal land. The Essex plotlands were on the heavy clay known to farmers as three-horse land, which was the first to go out of cultivation in the agricultural depression. Others grew up on such vulnerable coastal sites as Jaywick Sands and Canvey Island, or on estuary marshland or riverside meadowland in the Thames Valley, also subject to flooding, or they are to be found on acid heathland or chalky uplands.*

A final common characteristic of plotland sites was their capacity for upgrading over time, unless obstacles were put in the residents' way (as

---

* Dennis Hardy and Colin Ward, *Arcadia for All: The Legacy of a Makeshift Landscape* (London, 1984).

they quite often were by planning authorities, hoping that the plotlands would simply disappear). Extensions, the addition of bathrooms, partial or total rebuilding, the making up of roads and the provision of mains services are all part of the continual improvement process in any old settlement that has not been economically undermined or subjected to the restraint on improvements which we have learned to call planners' blight. The process can be traced in many farmhouses, where the original cottage has become one of the outbuildings, and the subsequent house has become the kitchen, while a four-square front dates from the eighteen or nineteenth century.

But the pre-war literature of planning and conservation reveals the intense horror felt by all privileged people at the desecration they saw, or so they thought, everywhere, not noticing that farmers were becoming bankrupt every week. Howard Marshall, in the compendium *Britain and the Beast*, declared that 'a gimcrack civilisation crawls like a giant slug over the country, leaving a foul trail of slime behind it'.* It is hard not to feel in restrospect that part of this disgust was ordinary misanthropy: the wrong sort of people were getting a place in the sun.

Time changes attitudes, of course, and several plotland sites have been designated as Conservation Areas, in order to retain their 'arcadian' character and preserve them from redevelopment. Anthony King, in his monumental history of the bungalow as a building type, drew the significant conclusion that

A combination of cheap land and transport, prefabricated materials, and the owner's labour and skills had given back, to the ordinary people of the land, the opportunity denied to them for over two hundred years, an opportunity which, at the time, was still available to almost half of the world's non-industrialised population: the freedom for a man to build his own house. It was a freedom that was to be very short-lived.†

It was indeed short-lived, since the powers given to planning authorities by the Town and Country Planning Act of 1947 and its successors effectively brought a halt to plotland development. They also sanctified a series of rural mythologies. The first of these was the concept that the history of rural settlement ceased in 1948. Rural industry was different. The agricultural

---

* Howard Marshall, 'The Rake's Progress', in Clough Williams-Ellis (ed.) *Britain and the Beast* (London, 1938).
† Anthony King, *The Bungalow: A Global History* (London, 1984).

business was exempt from planning control and was subsidised for every kind of environmental change: from filling ditches and destroying hedges to creating ditches and rebuilding hedges; from eliminating woodlands to attempts to recreate them.

In the post-war years, the New Towns programme catered for some of the outward movement from the cities, and was, in fact, far less of an encroachment upon the national stock of agricultural land than the suburban expansion of the 1930s, or that of subsequent decades.* By the 1990s, when most of the cottages and the former local authority houses of rural England have changed hands, only the affluent can afford to live in the countryside. The adult children of local families find that they have no means of living in their own locality, since in south-east England a plot of land costs 65 per cent of the whole cost of building a house. The arrival of the mobile rich does not improve the situation of the rural poor. The newcomers don't use the remaining local shops and can afford to laugh at the county council's efforts to keep the buses on the road, since they rove at will in their Range Rovers. They don't improve the numbers that might make the village school viable, as their children are privately educated. They are certainly active in the village preservation society, since as the late Gerald Wibberley explained years ago, they 'want their particular village to stay as it was when they decided to move there'.†

Gilbert White wrote that in the eighteenth-century village, 'we abound with poor' and he described how they found a livelihood. In the nineteenth-century village, the poor lost their livelihood and migrated in vast numbers to the new industrial towns and the colonial Empire. A century ago politicians were vying with each other in offering solutions to the problems of the deserted village. Today the village is not deserted. Its houses and cottages change hands for incredible sums and there is no room for the poor, nor for the adult children of long-resident local families.

Beyond the village, since farmers have long resolved to dispense with permanent employees, the cottages have been sold off for upgrading with double garages, while all those abandoned barns, cowsheds or granaries earn planning permission for what the local builders call a 'barn job', conversion into a luxury dwelling. Planning permission itself has become a commodity beyond price, since it makes the rich richer while excluding the poor from rural England. Meanwhile in England in 1995 the owners of

---

* Colin Ward, *New Town, Home Town: The Lessons of Experience* (London, 1993).

† In Davidson, Joan and Wibberley, Gerald, *Planning and the Rural Environment* (Oxford, 1977).

544,900 hectares of farmland were being paid under the terms of the European Union's agricultural policy for growing nothing on them.

This situation is too absurd, as well as too unfair, to last long into the next century, yet few people are willing to break the deafening silence about making space for the future unofficial countryside.

One of those who is bold enough to enter this forbidden debate is the urban geographer Peter Hall. In the 1960s he was one of a memorable quartet of authors who launched a squib called 'Non-Plan: An Experiment in Freedom' which urged 'a precise and carefully controlled experiment in non-planning . . . to seize on a few appropriate zones of the country, which are subject to a characteristic range of pressures'.* This proposal was received with a deafening silence, but years later was followed up with the concept of the 'Do It Yourself New Town', which linked the concept with the experience of the pre-war plotlands and with the post-war adventure of the self-built settlements that surround every city of Latin America, Africa or Asia.†

The one part of the English land economy where these hints and suggestions were sympathetically heard was within the New Town development corporations, then still in existence. Both Milton Keynes and Telford agreed, with various degrees of subsequent failure, to provide sites for the proposed alternative settlements.‡

Many years later another propagandist, Simon Fairlie, provided a wholly reasonable series of arguments for very slight changes to the planning machinery which would actually enable local authorities to foster experiments in low-impact rural development, 'some of them carried out at the margins of society, others designed to cater for more conventional people'. He argues, persuasively, that

If permission to build or live in the countryside were to be allocated, not just to those who can afford artificially inflated land prices, but to anyone who could demonstrate a willingness and an ability to contribute to a thriving local economy, then a very different kind of rural society would emerge. Low impact development is a social contract whereby people

* Rayner Banham, Peter Hall, Paul Barker and Cedric Price, 'Non-Plan: An Experiment in Freedom', *New Society*, 20 March 1969.

† Colin Ward, 'The Do It Yourself New Town' (1975) reprinted in Colin Ward, *Talking Houses* (London, 1990).

‡ Dennis Hardy, *From New Towns to Green Politics* (London, 1991).

are given the opportunity to live in the country in return for providing environmental benefits. Planners will recognise this as a form of what they call 'planning gain'. The mechanisms to strike such a bargain are for the most part already written into the English planning system.[*]

Yet another absorbing reflection on the future of the unofficial countryside comes from Joan Thirsk, a veteran agricultural economist. She has examined three phases of alternative agriculture, perceptible in English history. The first occurred after the Black Death, the second between about 1650 and 1750, the third in the later nineteenth century, lasting until 1939. She believes that we are now in a fourth such phase and concludes that,

> judging by the experience of the three previous phases of alternative agriculture, the strong assumption of our age that omniscient governments will lead the way out of economic problems will not, in practice, serve. The solutions are more likely to come from below, from the initiatives of individuals, singly or in groups, groping their way, after many trials and errors, towards fresh undertakings. They will follow their own hunches, ideals, inspirations, and obsessions, and along the way some will even be dismissed as harmless lunatics.[†]

Her historical perspective turns upside down many current assumptions and much of the conventional wisdom. For she hopes that maintaining and increasing village populations could 'relieve the heavy pressure on towns'. Impressed by the cogency of Kropotkin's century-old study of *Fields, Factories and Workshops*,[‡] Dr Thirsk automatically sees the 'diversion of the rural economy, permitting agriculture and industry to coexist in the same communities, and even in the same households' as a way of avoiding 'the painful social disruption which followed later when industrial growth demanded that workers live in towns'.

This handful of dissenting voices is important if we are to reassert the claims of the unofficial country against the misanthropic and unhistorical rhetoric of the defenders of the privileges of the new migratory rural gentry.

[*] Simon Fairlie, *Low Impact Development: Planning and People in a Sustainable Countryside* (Oxford, 1996).

[†] Joan Thirsk, *Alternative Agriculture: A History from the Black Death to the Present Day* (Oxford, 1997).

[‡] Kropotkin, Peter, *Fields, Factories and Workshops*, (London, 1974 (first published 1899)).

18. *Light Pollution*
Libby Purves

'We are all in the gutter, but some of us are looking at the stars.' When Oscar Wilde tossed that immortal scrap into *Lady Windermere's Fan* it was 1891. A century on, the image cannot by any stretch of the imagination be made to work. Any part of Britain sophisticated enough to have gutters will have virtually no view of the stars.

Whether city or suburb – or, increasingly and alas, village – it will be so garishly overlit that even Venus cannot compete with the dull foggy glow it throws into the sky. The nocturnal drunkard's prospect from the urban or suburban gutter these days is of a neon and sodium haze pierced variously by golden McDonald's arches, improbable pink skyscrapers, winking corporate logos, the floodlit dereliction of construction sites and the surly, fearful Rottweiler-lights of nervous householders.

This is called 'light pollution', has – as yet – no firm legal status, and is one of the curses of our age. It would be bad enough for city dwellers to be deprived of the immemorial comfort of the stars, even in their parks, but the plague is not confined to cities. Satellite pictures of Britain taken on clear nights show very few areas which do not glare relentlessly at the sky: look at the image of our land by night and the dark patches lie only over Dartmoor, decreasing areas of Cornwall and Wales, the Yorkshire Moors, bits of Lincolnshire, slivers of East Anglia, the Border Country and the Highlands of Scotland. Over the great part of the kingdom sprawling conurbations, suburbs, motorways, public buildings, bridges and industrial sites clothe themselves in garish lighting. Most of it – even the motorway lighting – is so badly designed that it throws nearly as much light upwards as downwards.

Look wider and the satellite tells us that apart from the Netherlands we are unquestionably the most glaringly overlit country in Europe. England, where some of the greatest and most solemn poets of the world once hymned the stars, now shouts defiance at the night sky: hectically, heartlessly, blotting out the constellations. Against our lights even the brightest moon is a poor anaemic anachronism. As for the delicacy of the Milky Way, it has no chance at all except in a few blessed places. One summer recently I sat in our remote Suffolk farmhouse garden looking up with a Japanese visitor at that swathe of brightness and she told me its Japanese name: *sky river*. In a French schoolchildhood, I learnt to call it the *ceinture de la Vierge*, the Virgin's girdle. There is actual pain in knowing that many British children of today will never give it any name at all, nor see it except on distant holidays.

Perhaps it is not surprising that we have overdone artificial lighting. Long centuries suffered the dim smokiness of oil-lamps and tapers and lanterns that blew out; so light – any light, however inappropriate – has been treated as an unchallengeable blessing. Even the deepest countryside embraces it unthinkingly. There are industrial farms with cold sad lighting along their grim aisles and barns, power stations shining across tracts of wild coast, and new rural housing estates which install bright suburban lighting as a matter of course. Even old villages, where inhabitants for centuries passed quietly through the night with lanterns, often have street lighting imposed on them by fussy councils. Individual householders, conned by the artful paranoia of the anti-crime industry, surround their homes with ultra-bright 'security' lights. The actual security value of these latter atrocities, incidentally, is now accepted by almost everyone but their greedy manufacturers as a piece of nonsense. Even the Home Office has now conceded that ultra-bright domestic exterior lights probably make life easier for burglars: a dark shape can move freely around unseen in the deepened shadows which lie along the edge of their blinding corridors.

This rural plague is new, and to anybody over 35, distinctly alarming. Even twenty years ago it was a commonplace of country life that you did not go down the lane to the pub after dusk without slipping a torch into your pocket: as for outside lighting, few people bothered to switch on the dim iron lantern in the porch unless they positively expected company. It was a velvet, solemn darkness that fell each night: the few interruptions to it brought a sense of wonder. A full moon gave useful light as well as inspiration, a distant lighthouse might loom beyond the cliffs and sweep the fields far inland in eerie arcs, and the church tower carved a black ancient shape against the stars – with perhaps, if it were lit for a winter's evensong, the glimmer of stained glass falling into the churchyard as a gentle blessing.

There are still such villages, but they grow rarer every year and most of them have a view of something overlit. If they are lucky, at least it is only the local church, now floodlit into Disneyland unreality (often with money from some electricity supplier wanting publicity). It may be momentarily striking, but its architectural subtleties will be effaced and its solemn meaning flattened into blandness by free-standing floodlights throwing their light upwards. The floodlights stand free, and have a worse effect for that, because we are too neurotic about stonework to fasten them closer. It is interesting to note that many continental churches and castles are in the hands of organisations less obsessed with the niceties of the fabric and more respectful of the actual beauty of the building: where we habitually put floodlights on the ground, glaring upwards, they put smaller lights on the building itself, to pick out its beauties rather than scream at the sky.

The village may suffer also from a runway of lights, electronically triggered, along the drive of the Big House (where newcomers from the city live, who are in their hearts afraid of the ancient dark). And all along the chi-chi street, lesser security lights will flick fretfully on and off as an innocent cat trots past their sensors. If the village is really unlucky it has some more obtrusive glare on the skyline: the glow of the ever-encroaching city or factory, ensuring that no star can be seen until it is at its zenith. So it is that London blots out most of the stars for fifty miles around it, and tens of millions of homes will never – short of a catastrophic national power cut – lie naked to a real night sky.

Thus, in cities and in the countryside, we have lost something precious without ever deciding to. The stars have been taken from us by default. Not only from us: nocturnal mammals and nesting and roosting birds have their patterns of feeding and resting, courting, migrating and mating all influenced by hours of daylight. Night birds in flight become disoriented in bright artificial light: they collide with brightly lit structures. Insect life, it is suggested, may be equally disastrously affected. Even fish suffer: trout exposed to an excess of light breed early and have weakened progeny.

These things have been pointed out energetically for some years now by the UK Dark Skies campaign, by the British Astronomical Association and by the Council for the Protection of Rural England. Even the last government's rural White Paper mentioned the value of wild unlit landscape. But regulation and law have still not caught up with technology. Light is not regulated as a pollutant, or seen as something needing planning permission. In an excellent paper for the January 1998 *Journal of Planning and Environment Law*, the barrister Penny Jewkes reviews the situation.

Light pollution itself, she points out, is not yet recognised by our law as an evil; the most significant weapons against it – weak as they are to fight it – are planning law and the civil law of nuisance.

The law of nuisance does have a few successes chalked up. Or at least, in the private arena it does; the time has not yet come when overlighting can be deemed a 'public nuisance'. Jewkes cites private cases successfully brought under New Zealand law, which is very close to ours; and one interesting case in Scotland, in which an angling association successfully restricted the right of a tennis club to floodlight its courts (and, by spillage, their river). We could do with more case law: who will be the first to bring a successful civil case in England against next door's glare? Who will face down the sneering suggestion of defence lawyers that they should just get 'thicker curtains', and demand their right as a free citizen to see the night sky? As Jewkes points out, even this would be of no help in protecting the 'unowned' environment or solving the wider problem of what we must learn to call 'skyglow'. For that, planning and public nuisance law is essential.

So why hasn't it been used? Planners can, at least, influence the design and installation of lighting schemes in new developments. But only huge enterprises, like the lighting of a football stadium, are generally counted as new developments. In one case, where a London hotel suddenly floodlit itself, the inspector only considered whether the actual lighting apparatus was detrimental to the look of the building *by day* – not by night. As with the churches and castles, we must try and overcome this exclusive obsession with the ancient or venerable fabric: it also matters how we see it, how it is set both by night and day, and whether our perceptions are being degraded.

The roads are as bad. Cheerless sodium ribbons extend the hand of the town out through the countryside, often with unwarrantable intensity. Yet there are large numbers of modern, downward-directed street and road lights which could considerably cut down this problem, and some councils at least are picking up the idea. The Institution of Lighting Engineers offers valuable advice on designs where cowling and bulbs help to throw nearly all the light downwards, where it is needed, rather than upwards where it is a curse. New roads therefore are better than old ones. But there are 6.5 million road lights in the UK, and they last some thirty years each; councils are not likely to replace them out of astronomical compunction. And the big danger is that during the years that we must wait for the worst ones to go out, other neighbouring lights – not least on these fresh greenfield estates we are balefully promised – will proliferate on the principle of in for a penny, in for a pound. If you can't see the stars anyway because of the main road, why spend thought and money on restricting the obtrusive glare of your new development? What developer will ever dare to tell his buyers to carry a torch in their back pocket, and refrain from installing 'security' lights?

Gloomy to record, a great many approved millennium projects involve lighting of the most garish kind. Large tranches of money lately released into potty schemes will aggravate the plague of skyglow. Floodlighting public structures in chemical-sweetie colours is one of the current vogues of authorities and companies, and also, let us admit, of the kind of 'artist' who is never happier than when blowing several millions of someone else's money. Short-term projects perhaps do not matter so much: but many of them are long-term. Up go the lights on skyscrapers, city centres, bridges, cathedrals, everything. There are, these days, curtsies made to fuel conservation and to doing these things with stored solar energy or whatever; but rarely is it questioned why we need do them at all. Croydon's planned 'Skyline' project will have bright pink and purple buildings, a blaze of laser luridity will shine over Portsmouth harbour, and all over the country churches and castles are coming to be considered incomplete without a set of ugly lamps on gantries pointing up at them, as if they were so many Dame Barbara Cartlands unwilling to be photo-graphed without their personal uplighter to smooth out the wrinkles. Aesthetically this often backfires: take Caernarfon Castle. We moored our boat beneath it for three nights once, and it was twenty times as impressive on the night when the toy-fort lighting failed, and it brooded black and grim, a timeless shape against bright stars over the Seiont river.

Part of the problem is the speed at which this century has changed ordinary lives. We are still close to generations which lived, perforce, with only guttering candles and fragile gas mantles to see them through the long darknesses of our northern winter, and to those generations – whose legacy still lurks in all of us – it would have been ludicrous to regard light, ever, as anything but a blessing. Nor can the Second World War blackouts have helped: when Vera Lynn sang 'When the lights go on again all over the world' it was something devoutly to be wished for. *Lux aeterna*, everlasting heavenly light, has been sung about by yearning generations which suffered far more dark than they liked; it is a wrench to have to admit that now we have far, far, too much of a good thing, that the lights we make are devilish devices which actually block out the heavenly variety, and that it matters very much. Whatever good work is done among planners and lighting engineers who see the problem, unless we have a policy of controlling light as sternly as we have tried to control noise since the Noise Abatement Act, things will only get worse in city and countryside alike. As more and more money sloshes around in corporate bragging-budgets, and in the Lottery system, there will be more and more temptation to spend it on the quickest, showiest, most dramatic of assaults on nature. Of course all the floodlighting will be pretty at first, and a novelty – just as being able to walk down a street at night without a torch was once a novelty – but we will soon grow sick of it. The pinks and purples and virulent greens will blaze on for far too many hours of each night, the factories and leisure centres and roundabouts will splash the landscape and jeer at the grave night sky, and we will be wretched. Wretched without quite knowing why, as the stars vanish and leave us in our swamp of neurotic pagan vainglory.

It is not just the wastefulness that dismays me – though wasteful it is. Nor is it just the effect on the wildlife, although I saw that at close quarters during the long months when the Sizewell B construction site was throwing a hideous glare over this part of Suffolk: the Minsmere reserve had serious concerns for baffled migrant birds and disrupted nesting patterns, and sometimes, walking in the evening near the site's bleak borders, we saw the birds of daytime flying confusedly through the cold night air. Nor is it just the effect on the science of astronomy, which has always depended partly on enthusiastic amateurs at home, and which gained many more aspiring watchers of the sky during the spring 1997 visibility of comet Hale-Bopp on our skyline.

These things are bad enough: but our loss of the night sky matters too at a deeper level: a romantic level, if you like, even a religious one. To say so is in no way elitist. In fact, we sniffy aesthetes of the middle classes have less to grumble at than most, since we can after all afford to nip off to Tuscany or Provence or to take a little yacht out to sea and draw nourishment from Orion and the Pleiades. It is the less lucky, less mobile, less affluent people who suffer most from the theft of this aerial majesty: and I do not think it is an exaggeration to say that the obscuring of the night sky's majesty from the vast majority of the people of Britain has already had a perceptibly negative, depressing, dangerous effect.

For, at the risk of being dismissed as a New Age loony, I say plainly that I believe that in a deep and primitive way these heavenly bodies have always served an essential psychological purpose for human beings. I would be very unhappy indeed to let a child grow up – or an adult live permanently – in circumstances that make it impossible to see the moon and stars overarching the workaday world on a cold, clear night. There are philosophical implications, religious implications, even moral ones. To stand under the stars is to know humility, to glimpse infinity and hence eternity. Impulses to literature, art, religion and science have grown, ever since man's beginnings, from the contemplation of these cold, silent spheres. As the hymn says, 'The spacious firmament on high / With all the blue ethereal sky / And spangled heavens a shining frame / Their great original proclaim.' The more we veil our eyes with neon and sodium, the less open we are to philosophy, to worship, to admitting any possibility of the great original. It makes us poorer.

When I first wrote that, in *The Times*, I fully expected to be jeered at by its more robust readers as a sentimentalist yearning back with feeble religiosity to an empty idyll. Instead I was astonished by the passion and the breadth of the letters I received: the shared sense that indeed a wonder is passing from our lives, and that those who suffer worst from its passing are the poorest, the youngest and the weakest. There was fear in the letters: fear that as the suburbanisation of rural Britain continues, before long the whole nation will glow unhealthily all round the clock and the deep rest and wonder of night be lost to us entirely.

One woman wrote: 'I know it is reversible, unlike many of our other assaults on the environment. I keep telling myself it should therefore matter less. But each of us only lives once, and I am old and rarely travel. When I accept that I may never see the night sky properly again, or teach my grandchild to find the belt of Orion, I feel lost and threatened. I sleep worse. The city has swallowed us all, down to our very dreams.' But she did not live in a city. She lived in what its developers still call a village, in Essex.

From the gutter, we have a duty to look at the stars. Or, at least look *for* them, so we can protest at their faintness or absence. We have to press upon MPs and councillors, industries and neighbours, the simple message that while easy light is a blessing, it is stupid to squander a new blessing in a way that deprives ourselves and our children of a far older one: the dark, the velvet, the jewelled and sacred mantle of the Night.

19. *Edge City*
Paul Barker

Cities are being turned inside out. 'Edge City' has arrived. Around the urban periphery, the retail parks and the shopping malls continue to spring up. In London, the Oxford Street Association wonders whether it should roof the street over and employ private security men, to fend off the competition from malls like Lakeside Thurrock, in the inner armpit of Essex, or Bluewater, in a disused cement quarry in north Kent. Market towns see their old functions sucked out, like the juice from an orange. Campaigners fear for the future of our green and pleasant land.

But before we rush to praise or blame, we must try to understand exactly what is happening. In the late twentieth century, it is as important for us to understand Edge City as it was for Friedrich Engels, in the early nineteenth century, to understand the cotton capital, Manchester. We are talking about a new use of space. Given the importance of the car in all this, we are also talking about a new psychology of time.

Greater understanding will perhaps lead to less bossiness. Unfortunately, planners – both professional and amateur – are very quick to fall into this way of talking, and acting. It is best to remember that other people have preferences of their own, and usually for good reason. These should be respected.

Let me take a parochial example. In a row about tea-time and breakfast-time traffic congestion, I recently saw a letter in a local newspaper from the borough councillor who chaired a transport committee. In trying to overcome this, he announced, 'We will not totally succeed until we can reduce the *selfishness* [my emphasis] of those who drive their children to school.' This is the kind of bossiness I mean. No doubt, in an ideal world, many mothers would prefer to use their time differently. No doubt, too, many mothers might ideally prefer to shop the way people did in the 1950s. But we have to value our time according to the way things are. Many mothers judge that more time is best used taking their children safely to school, however wearisome the drive. This leaves less time for shopping.

The supermarket (for food) or the mall (for just about everything else) beckons. If the malls were a superfluous invention, they would have gone the way of the pogo stick and the hula hoop. Instead, they are with us, not for ever, but for many decades at least.

It is extraordinary to observe how the social geography of cities, across the industrialised world, falls into similar patterns – though at greater or less speed – in spite of widely divergent histories, politics and planning systems. Deep shifts of economics and behaviour are very hard to stop. The malls are the emblem of just such a shift.

Dikes and ditches can be built, of course, to direct the stream of urban change one way or another. But the stream carries on. A recent French study of the way Paris and London have grown, in the past half-century, drew many distinctions between south-east England and the Île de France. The most striking is the way Paris has flowed out into its surroundings with little interruption, whereas London has been surrounded by the Great Dike of the metropolitan green belt. The economic and demographic pressure from London did not vanish. It re-emerged across the green belt, in a ring of small towns and formerly independent cities. These became exurbs: suburbs divided from the core city by a veil of countryside or semi-countryside. In the past thirty years Oxford, for example, has become an exurb of London. Structurally, Oxford is to late twentieth-century London what Hampstead was to mid-century London. The Oxford intelligentsia catch the shuttle bus in to central London, just as their Hampstead predecessors took the Northern tube line. Halfway between London and Oxford, on the edge of High Wycombe, the motorway through the Chilterns is now lined with out-of-town stores, pretending to be brick-built barns.

Many British observers of what is happening in and around cities – and especially in and around London – panic as they look at these dark, Satanic malls. (Meanwhile, the cotton mills of Lancashire – which may or may not be what William Blake originally had in mind – are now the subject of preservation orders.) But cities are, of their nature, ever-changing. Or, if they are not, they are dead. Cities are anarchic. The living city is forever 'in crisis'. That is one way you can tell that it is alive.

Those who find this appalling (and attractive) vigour unacceptable would like to stop change in its tracks. Human nature being what it is, they would also often like to stop it at the point where they themselves benefit most. When they look at the retail-driven growth of Edge City – all those car parks, those glittering domes, those store fronts calling themselves 'Lillywhites of Piccadilly Circus' a few hundred yards away from the M25 orbital road and many miles from Piccadilly – they throw up their hands. The totemic curse-words, 'suburbia' and (deeper horror) 'suburbanites', are uttered.

It is an attitude with a long tradition. Sitting in his house in Clerkenwell, George Cruikshank was horrified by the swift, spec-built creation of the new suburb of Islington (so handy for the City of London along the world's first-ever bypass, the New Road). He drew his celebrated cartoon, *The March of Bricks and Mortar*, which has been used in every anti-suburbia campaign from that day to this. Yet suburbia gives most of the people what they want from a house, most of the time. Market research shows that four-fifths of the English would like to live in the countryside. They would probably like a cottage in an open landscape with a clear view of the sea. But there isn't enough land or sea or cottages to go around. People can, instead, live in a form of semi-countryside. The modern suburb was an English invention. An English architect, C. F. A. Voysey, eventually gave it an architectural form, the semi-detached house. This has been amazingly successful. Not too far away from most semis, there is now a retail park or a mall.

Strange liaisons are entered into by those who are hostile to suburbs in general, and Edge City in particular. The leftish *Guardian* is their citadel. It becomes the task of the rightish *Daily Telegraph* to note that, in the words of the headline on one commentary in early 1998, GREEN BELTS SUIT THE RICH. (Certainly they keep the price of property up.)

In all this, the great English vice of snobbery plays a big part. The attacks on the shamelessly populist design of the shopping malls follow in the footsteps of the earlier onslaughts on 1920s suburban semis or 1930s super-cinemas, on 1950s TV aerials or 1980s satellite dishes. The motto often seems to be: Find out what those people are doing, and tell them to stop it. Yet, a generation later, nostalgia always sets in, and what was despised becomes 'heritage'. You dare not today pull down an art deco Odeon, though you may well decide to convert it from its grey half-life as a bingo hall into a J. D. Weatherspoon real-ale pub. (Or, to put it another way: from working class to middle class.)

London is, and has always been, a city of suburbs. It is as multi-centred as Los Angeles. The point was made, once and for all, in the greatest book about London, Steen Eiler Rasmussen's *London: the Unique City*. London cannot be crammed into the pint-pot of some ideal vision of Florence or Barcelona or Paris. And, in fact, in an un-ideal world, France was the first European country to surround most of its towns with American-style 'strips', offering everything from cheap furniture to cut-price petrol.

Why do the new malls arouse such anger? Why do they produce the fierce desire to force people, somehow, back into the kind of shopping they have abandoned? In a recent discussion group I reported that, when I had visited Poundbury, the Prince of Wales's garden suburb of Dorchester, all the inhabitants I spoke to told me they drove round the Dorchester bypass to Tesco's to do their shopping. 'Couldn't they have gone by bike?' I was asked. I wonder how many family packs of yoghurt, Coke or Persil you can fit into a bicycle pannier.

We ought, by now, to know that the worst mistakes in planning come from trying to force other people to live the way they wouldn't choose to, and often the way we wouldn't want to live ourselves. If you want evidence, make sure you go along next time the London borough of Hackney decides to blow up one of its tower blocks. No one has a 'right' to build a house in the middle of Rutland, and drive to a Leicestershire retail park for all their goods. But, equally, no one has a 'right' to tell them that they should be happy to live with their parents, rather than set up on their own, and do all their shopping at Mr Patel's general store round the corner, just to ease the pressure on rural land and make life pleasanter for those who are already there.

This is not, at bottom, an argument about town versus country. Hardly anyone in the countryside any longer has any functional economic link with the land. Villages are dormitories at best; collections of second homes at worst. (Sometimes they also include telecottages. But the prevalence and importance of long-distance work has been fashionably exaggerated.) The argument is between haves and have-nots. The shopping mall becomes the focus.

Perhaps the trouble is that the malls are stupendously popular. They are as popular as Gaumont, Regal or Odeon cinemas were in the 1930s and 1940s, when the main feature film changed three times a week, and performances were continuous, so you could go any time and all the time. All malls now contain the kind of cinema, the multiplex, which has turned round the once inexorable decline in cinema attendances. The first multiplex in Britain opened in Milton Keynes. Both Milton Keynes and multiplexes are mocked for their suburbanism. (The first general manager of Milton Keynes described it, rightly, as 'a cut-price Arcadia'.) But the suburbs are now often the main source of social innovation. Without suburban hen parties, enjoying the friendly foyers and car parking of multiplexes, *The Full Monty* would never have become the most profitable British film ever made.

Everywhere nowadays the dominant architectural image is suburban. Even in the grandest schemes of urban renewal – for example, London Docklands – most of the housing is suburban in style, and the main place to shop is a new Asda or Safeway superstore. When the architectural history of late twentieth-century Britain is written, Sir Lawrie Barratt will demand as much space as Sir Norman Foster. Malls soon start to become the core of new suburban and exurban settlements. Drive out of Lakeside Thurrock eastwards, and you are very soon in the 'new community' of Chaffont Hundred, where you can choose a house from among Wimpey Tudor, Bovis Vernacular and Barratt Conventional.

All this is as Joel Garreau predicts in *Edge City: Life on the New Frontier*, his pioneering study of the impact of the American mall on city form. In the United States, he observes, the mall attracts not only housing but also offices. The centre of urban power moves further and further from the city centre. The suburbs are where the people are, and the money is. The mall is a magnet for development in the same way that cotton mills or docks once were. In Britain, Gateshead's MetroCentre, Sheffield's Meadowhall and the rest, with their hundreds of thousands of square feet of retail space, were a landmark in the onward march of Edge City. By the time government decided that there should be no more – at least for the time being – change was already irrevocable. Three of the largest malls, Kent's Bluewater, Manchester's Trafford and Bristol's Cribbs Causeway, went ahead after the prohibition.

Edge City flourishes, like a red-flowering horse chestnut or a *leylandii* cypress, whereas many town centres show every sign of being afflicted by an urban version of Dutch elm disease. Britain's first air-conditioned shopping mall opened in north London, at Brent Cross, in the 1970s. (The first in the world had opened in Milwaukee in 1956, one year after the first McDonald's.) But the new malls are of a different order of size. Drive past Sheffield's Meadowhall along the M1, and look down on its green dome in the old wasteland of the lower Don valley. To the 1.2 million square feet of shops in Meadowhall itself, you must add the multi-acre retail park, and the new office parks. This is the Edge City of the home town of *The Full*

Monty. Warner built here an eleven-screen multiplex. And where did Sheffield decide to put its first super-tram line? From the old city centre to Meadowhall.

The first of the new malls was the Gateshead MetroCentre, which opened in 1986. A power station ash dump was waste land until the local developer, Sir John Hall, saw the benefits of its Enterprise Zone tax breaks, and built his mall. And Meadowhall? The mall's brochures tell you that this stretch of South Yorkshire was written up by Sir Walter Scott in the first paragraph of *Ivanhoe*. More to the point, the lower Don valley was the home of the gigantic Hadfield's steel firm. That era of industrial history ended in blood and tears in the first great union battle of the Thatcher years. In 1980, during the British Steel Corporation strike, mass picketing outside Hadfield's East Hecla works led to scores of arrests. Three years later, the last Hadfield's works closed, and the land became derelict. A parable of our time.

A special retail index recently gave the national trading ratings for the main concentrations of shops. The top three, judged by turnover and profitability per square foot, were MetroCentre, Meadowhall and West Midlands's Merry Hill, in that order. Oxford Street was down at No. 11, and Princes Street, Edinburgh, at No. 12. (Special buses took shoppers down from Edinburgh to shop in Gateshead.)

In 1993, when he was Secretary of State for the Environment, John Gummer produced his ordinance ('Planning Policy Guidance Six'), which embodied a strong presumption against giving planning permission for any more. But even this decree states that 'It is not the role of the planning system to restrict competition, preserve existing commercial interests or to prevent innovation.' You have to remember the crumminess of much of what the new malls have supposedly destroyed. If *your* alternative were to shop in Sunderland's depressing high street or in the squalid precinct at Peterlee New Town, you too would go to MetroCentre. Further south, I recommend an afternoon in Dagenham. Four square miles of uninterrupted council housing were built at Dagenham by the London County Council in the 1920s and 1930s – as the biggest public housing estate in the world* – with hardly a shop or a pub. Someone eventually got round to building an off-centre town centre for Dagenham. They called it Lakeside Thurrock. No one, who can get away for the afternoon, shops in

---

* See Willmott, Peter, *The Evolution of an Urban Community: a Study of Dagenham after Forty Years* (London, 1963).

Dagenham. All you can find there are pawnbrokers, Butlin's booking agencies and charity shops selling second-hand wedding dresses. Lakeside undoubtedly gave some Dagenham shops the kiss of death. But what grade of shops were they? If a town centre is good enough, it does not succumb. The shopping heart of Newcastle upon Tyne beats vigorously, in spite of MetroCentre.

One difference from the United States is that in Britain the new malls have generally been built on derelict or low-grade land, rather than on green fields. In America, Joel Garreau says, 'We created vast new urban job centres in places that only thirty years before had been residential suburbs or even corn stubble.' In the orbit of London, you could argue that a town like Newbury – sprouting offices, shops and houses in Berkshire, far beyond the metropolitan green belt – is closest to an American Edge City. The new Newbury was based not on a shopping mall like Lakeside, but on a winning combination of defence contracts and pony paddocks. Garreau says that Edge City developers in America go weak at the knees when they see horses anywhere near a potential site. One of the laws he promulgates is that, after all the market research into the relocation of a company headquarters has been done, the essential outcome is that 'the commute of the chief executive officer always becomes shorter', and there should ideally be horses for his family to play on.

The new malls and their ambient Edge City are, as Garreau says, 'atria reaching for the sun'. The modern atrium, the developer's art form of choice, was invented by the American architect, John Portman, for the first Hyatt Regency hotel. With their glittering office blocks and air-conditioned malls, American Edge Cities 'are still works in progress', Garreau writes. We may all have thought about the future city, he muses, and 'hoped it might look like Paris in the 1920s', but here is the future as it really is, 'wild, raw and alien'. Edge City may be a prime example of what Tom Wolfe called 'the hog-stomping Baroque exuberance of American civilisation', but there is an underlying simplicity to the motivation. Edge City 'moves everything closer to the homes of the middle classes'. It may seem chaotic to the eye of the observer, but this is true of all new city forms.

Edge City is created by the car, the computer and the fax machine as surely as New York or Liverpool were created by ocean-going ships, and Chicago or Manchester by the railway. Many of the ill-effects blamed on the new malls are due to broader social and economic changes. 'Watch the little filling station,' Frank Lloyd Wright said. 'It is the agent of decentralisation.' Every village now proves the truth of this. More and more often, the local petrol station has become the village shop. It is open all hours. It sells milk, newspapers and lottery tickets.

A campaign group, Action for Market Towns, was set up to combat the decline of many country towns. (It is a decline in urban energy, not necessarily in population. Small towns are now the most popular place to live.) The group notes that 'market towns are subject to a multiplicity of pressures', and not just 'the growth of out-of-town shopping'. It points out that 'economic pressures are causing the closure of livestock markets, and other traditional sources of employment, such as dairies, breweries and manufacturing businesses'. In fact, many of the new urban inhabitants of old market towns would now jib at being downwind from a brewery, a cattle market or a factory.

It is wrong to see malls as mere parodies of traditional cities. In *The Death and Life of Great American Cities* – the book that launched a thousand civic trusts – Jane Jacobs said: 'The bedrock attribute of a successful city is that a person must feel personally safe and secure on the street among all these strangers.' Historically, the city with its wall was invented because life was safer here than outside. Enclosed and video-scrutinised, the new malls make people, especially women, feel safer. Shoppers and browsers walk down the arcades of Lakeside or MetroCentre with happy smiles on their faces. They have dressed up to come. There are no panhandlers, no alkies, no sad folk peeing in the street. Women don't need to carry their shoulder bags slung across their chest for fear of snatchers. American malls started the fashion for glass-sided crawler lifts, not because of the view out but because of the view in. Rape is unlikely in a glass elevator. The malls' success, first in America, and now in Britain, is inseparable from the upsurge in women going out to work and the arrival of the family's second car. It has become ever harder to manage life without a car to dash to and from school, job and the one-stop-shop mall.

The malls are not, as their critics allege, all the same. At Lakeside, about 93 per cent of the visitors come by car. But at MetroCentre and Merry Hill, about 20 per cent come by public transport. Marks & Spencer, which knows its business, refused to come to MetroCentre until there was a bus station. Go to Lakeside, and you will find it has an unmistakably east London, even East End, feel. In the Rendezvous restaurant, on the top floor, women break off from lunch to touch up their mulberry lipstick.

The Délice de France *café français* has *pain au chocolat*, but also Cornish pasties and sausage rolls. English Fayre sells pizzas, pasta and garlic bread. At Crofters, 'traditional fare' means shepherd's pie, and egg or beans on toast. At Wok's to Eat, you can have curry sauce with anything. 'Have a nice face,' says a cosmetics ad, stuck on one glass door. A menswear shop called Envy advertises its goods at '50 per cent off'. Even a deadly sin costs you less at Lakeside.

Campaigners weep for dying high street shops. But there are simply too many of them for the present-day demand. They should be allowed to close, and revert to other uses, including housing. Nothing is more depressing than a row of charity shops interspersed with estates agents' 'To Let' signs.

Streets lined with shops selling everyday necessities were a nineteenth-century invention. As working men and clerks grew more prosperous, the front gardens of terrace houses were converted into shops. New national retail chains emerged, like the Home & Colonial Stores (the profits from the groceries went into building Lutyens's Castle Drogo in Devon) or Dewhurst the Butchers (the profits from the New Zealand lamb and Argentine beef went into building the central tower of Liverpool's Anglican cathedral). One of these chains was J. Sainsbury, originally of Drury Lane, but soon of almost every high street in the south-east of England. Unlike many others, Sainsbury's is still with us. The firm adapted.

Before the mid-nineteenth century, shops were only there for specialist services for the well-to-do: hatters, milliners, tailors, wine merchants, booksellers. Everyday goods were bought at markets. Against all predictions, the love of markets has outlived the love of high street shops. Now you go to market again. At one end of the scale there is the car boot sale, which is many people's favourite Sunday morning pastime. At the other end there is the mall, which is only an elaborate indoor market, in direct line of descent from the Victorian arcade.

The malls' other parent is the funfair. They remind me of the old Fun House at Blackpool Pleasure Beach. Coming in from the bus station at MetroCentre, you reach 'Metroland'. You can buy a day ticket for your children. A friendly dragon floats above the entrance. A rollercoaster whooshes overhead. A Ferris wheel turns. The toy train ride clangs its bell without ceasing. The din is all very satisfactory.

Architects' drawings of their urban projects always show little sketches of happy citizens chatting over a glass of wine at a café table under a bright umbrella. This is, they feel, the good life. It reminds us of outings to Urbino or Arezzo. In drizzly reality, you seldom see this in Britain. But you can see it at MetroCentre. In the upper-floor 'Mediterranean Village', you have a choice of restaurants around the village fountain: Greek, Spanish, Italian. In the courtyard of Romano's, the customers share a bottle before lunch is served. Gossip flows. Napkins are unfolded. Umbrellas complete the paradisal picture. The only illumination, however, comes from electric lights, far overhead, in the grey enclosed roof. The sun never shines on Romano's – but then it never rains, either.

The English landscape is an artificial construction, strewn with the dry-stone walling of parliamentary enclosure, the architectural follies of the aristocracy and the reservoirs of the city water boards. I await, with confidence, the first conservation-listed shopping mall.

Bibliography

Action for Market Towns, *Newsletters* (Bury St Edmunds, 1997–8).

Banham, Reyner, Barker, Paul, Hall, Peter and Price, Cedric, 'Non-Plan: An Experiment in Freedom', *New Society* 13 (338), 20 March 1969; reprinted, in part, in Andrew Blowers, Chris Hamnett and Philip Sarre (eds), *The Future of Cities* (London, 1974).

Barker, Paul, 'Non-Plan Revisited: or the Real Way Cities Grow' (Reyner Banham Memorial Lecture, 1998), *Journal of Design History*, forthcoming; 'The Stones of England', in *Towards a New Landscape* (London, 1993).

Engels, Friedrich, *The Condition of the Working-Class in England in 1844*, English edn including Engels's 'Dedication' (London, 1952).

Garreau, Joel, *Edge City: Life on the New Frontier* (New York, 1991).

Hall, Peter, Breheny, M., McQuaid, R. and Hart, D., *The Containment of Urban England* (London, 1973).

Hoskins, W. G., *The Making of the English Landscape*, revised edn with notes by Christopher Taylor (London, 1988).

Institut d'Aménagement et d'Urbanisme de la Région Île de France, *Les Franges franciliennes et le sud-est anglais: étude comparative de sept territoires* (Paris, 1995).

Jackson, Alan A., *Semi-Detached London* (London, 1973).

Jacobs, Jane, *The Death and Life of Great American Cities* (New York, 1961).

Olsen, Donald J., *The Growth of Victorian London* (London, 1976).

Rasmussen, Steen Eiler, *London: the Unique City*, abridged edn (Harmondsworth, 1960).

Sudjic, Deyan, *The 100 Mile City* (London, 1992).

Ward, Colin, *Social Policy: an Anarchist Response* (London, 1997).

Williamson, Elizabeth and Pevsner, Nikolaus, *London Docklands: an Architectural Guide* (Harmondsworth, 1998).

Willmott, Peter, *The Evolution of an Urban Community: a Study of Dagenham after Forty Years* (London, 1963).

20. *Carmageddon**

John Adams

The human scale of settlements is *everywhere* threatened by the growth of car dependence. It is a process in which humanity appears to will the means, but not the ends; opinion polls have established that all around the world most people want cars, but it is far from clear that most people would wish to live in the sort of world that would result if everyone's wish were granted.

Urban congestion is the main target of most transport planners today. Congestion wastes both time and energy and adds to pollution. The favoured solution to this problem is electronic road pricing. It is now becoming possible, with clever technology, to charge motorists for the use of specific roads at particular times of day. If the charges are properly set and if, when collected, they could be directed to improving public transport then, it is argued, everyone would benefit. One of the main advantages claimed for this approach is that it can be aimed accurately; it imposes charges only where they are needed in congested urban areas, not, it is usually added, in rural areas.

This is a diagnosis and prescription that politicians with rural constituencies find attractive. It would be unfair, they complain, to increase the cost of motoring for those who need their cars because there is no public transport alternative. Both this diagnosis and prescription, I shall argue, are myopic. *The cost of car travel in rural areas should be increased substantially*.

What Do We Want?

> My working class constituents . . . want cars, and the freedom they give on weekends and holidays . . . They [the affluent middle classes] want to kick the ladder down behind them. (Anthony Crosland)†

---

* Based on a paper prepared for OECD Conference 'Towards Sustainable Transportation' Vancouver, 26 March 1996

† A. Crosland *A Social Democratic Britain*, Fabian Tract 404 (London, 1970).

Crosland had a strong moral point which translates readily into a political imperative. All around the world most people who do not have cars would like to have them and governments everywhere applaud this aspiration and seek to help people realise it. In Britain both the main political parties have made this support explicit in official statements that remain party policy to this day. The Labour Party, in its environmental policy statement *In Trust for Tomorrow* (1994), proclaimed 'We would like to see more people owning cars.' Since that time the argument has been refined: the government wants more people to own cars but not to use them. The official position is now 'We want to reduce car dependency, not car ownership.'*

This view can even be found in the supposedly scientific and dispassionate work of the Royal Commission on Environmental Pollution. In its 1994 Report on Transport and the Environment it declared

> We have recommended that the increased cost of mobility should be imposed on the use rather than the ownership of cars, in part because we do not consider it equitable to erect high barriers against car ownership.†

Before the last election an editorial in *New Ground* – the journal of the environmentalist wing of Britain's Labour Party – declared that 'it would be electoral suicide to go into an election advocating reduced car ownership.' This view appears to be common ground for almost all politicians everywhere in the world. It might appear that they have had considerable success in meeting their electorates' aspirations; over the last fifty years the world's car population has increased tenfold, to 500 million. However, over the same period the number of people in the world who do not own cars has doubled, to more than 5 billion.‡ The fastest car-ownership growth rates are now being experienced in the world's poorest countries, and it is now official policy in China that every family should own a car.

---

* Transport Minister Gavin Strang, *Daily Telegraph*, 21 February 1998.

† *Transport and the Environment*, Report of the Royal Commission on Transport and the Environment (London, 1994).

‡ Worldwatch Institute, *Worldwatch Database Diskette* (Worldwatch Inst. 1776 Massachusetts Ave., NM, Washington DC 20036, 1995).

Does China Matter?

What would be the result should China, and the rest of the poor world, sustain their growth rates in motorisation, and succeed in their aspirations to catch up with those currently at the top of the ladder? It is possible to begin to answer this question with some simple calculations.

The UN medium projection for the world population in 2025 is 8.5 billion. The United States in 1994 had 201.8 million motor vehicles of all descriptions (774 per 1,000 population). Should the whole world succeed in catching up with the United States, by 2025 there would be 6.6 billion motor vehicles. Parked end-to-end they would stretch 40 million kilometres, and if stationary could be accommodated on a motorway around the equator 1,000 lanes wide. This scenario does not of course represent the global upper limit to the growth of car dependence; the motor vehicle population of the United States is still growing.

What is the relevance of all this to rural transport in Britain? There is now a global context in which the discussion of *all* transport problems must be set. Anthony Crosland's famous ladder metaphor is now being applied to the whole world. The environmental implications of *everyone* reaching the top are potentially catastrophic for *everyone*. Unless those at the top of the ladder can set a sustainable example, they cannot expect those on lower rungs to heed their homilies about the need for restraint. At present we are not setting a sustainable example, and they are not heeding our homilies. Try putting this to your local councillor or Member of Parliament, and you will find that it is a potential catastrophe about which they do not wish to know.

Can Technology Save Us?

Perhaps there is no impending catastrophe. Perhaps science and technology can ride to the rescue. The physical transport of information is now increasingly being replaced by electronic mobility. This, it is argued by information technology enthusiasts, will hugely reduce the need to commute to work, or to travel to shops, conferences or business meetings, and thereby reduce energy consumption, congestion and pollution.

Certainly telecommunications traffic is growing much more rapidly than travel by car or plane. The increases have been greatest for connections over the greatest distances – international traffic is expanding faster than domestic traffic, and intercontinental traffic is expanding fastest of all. As with physical mobility, growth *rates* have been fastest in the poorest countries; yet the absolute differences between rich and poor in levels of use are still growing. In 1994 the average person in the UK spent over an hour on the telephone internationally; the vast majority in the developing countries have never made an international call.

Does electronic mobility reduce physical mobility?

However it might be measured, the growth of electronic mobility has far exceeded growth rates for all forms of physical mobility. This growth has not, however, reduced the amount of physical mobility in the world. Telecommunications may substitute for physical mobility in many instances – including teleconferencing – and it is possible that it may have slowed the rate of growth of physical mobility below what it would otherwise have been. But it is much more likely that it has served as a stimulus to physical mobility for the following reasons.

- The travel industry is one of the most important customers of the telecommunications industry. Advances in telecommunications have enormously reduced the transaction costs of travel and thereby reduced the cost of travel itself. For making reservations, booking hotels, planning meetings, for the quick call to say 'Are you there? Good, I'll come round' – in so many ways telecommunications facilitate physical travel. For all those journeys whose purpose is not exclusively the transfer of information, cheaper electronic travel means cheaper, more convenient, less problematical travel, and hence *more* physical travel.

- Cellular telephones and teleworking have relaxed constraints on where people live and work. And the ability of employers to contact their employees, and the ability of salespersons and customers to contact each other, wherever they are, has freed many workers to spend more time on the road or in the air.

- Teleworking is not only liberating people from the daily commuting journey to work, it is freeing them from the necessity of living within commuting distance of their work, thereby augmenting the already existing pressures that are emptying cities and producing exurban sprawl. Within this sprawl, although there might be a decrease in commuter traffic, all other journeys – to shops, to schools, to doctors, to theme parks, to friends – are longer. According to the *National*

Travel Survey the average person living in a rural area travels 50 per cent further every year than a city dweller.[*]

As the costs of both physical and electronic travel decrease, people acquire a larger number of friends, customers and business associates at ever greater distances from home or office. These relationships are supported and strengthened by the ability to keep in touch inexpensively by phone, fax and e-mail. But most of them, ultimately, will foster a desire to get in touch physically.

A year ago I attended an OECD conference on environmentally sustainable transport in Vancouver. Waiting in Vancouver airport for my plane back to London I got talking to the man sitting next to me who was waiting to fly to Toronto. He was going to play bridge with someone from Toronto, someone from California and someone from Scotland. They had met, and played bridge, on the Internet; and now they wanted a real game. An energy expert at the conference told me that my contribution to sustainable transport, involving a round trip from London, would consume a tonne of aviation fuel.

Be a techno-optimist

Let us not be distracted by arguments about the abilities of science and technology to deal with the problems of energy and pollution associated with the growth of traffic. For the purpose of this essay, let us put them to one side. Let us concede the transport techno-optimist's wildest dreams. Let us imagine the development of cars powered by pollution-free perpetual-motion engines. Let us, in brief, pursue the implications of getting the whole world to the top of Crosland's ladder, cleanly and efficiently.

Trends and Forecasts

Britain is now less than halfway up the ladder. Figure 1 describes the changes since 1952 in the use of the main modes of transport, and the Department of Transport's forecasts to the year 2025. Travel by bicycle has declined by 80 per cent and by bus by 50 per cent. Rail has held fairly constant in terms of passenger kilometres, but far less of the country is now accessible by rail; there has been a shift of traffic from the abandoned

[*] *National Travel Survey 1989/1991*, Department of Transport (London, 1993).

branch lines to the main inter-city lines. Walking has also declined but comparable statistics have not been collected to permit it to be displayed on the graph. Car travel has increased tenfold and air travel thirtyfold.

In brief, the democratic and environmentally benign modes of travel – the 'green' modes accessible to all – are in retreat, and the elitist and environmentally damaging modes are in the ascendant. These trends are still running strong, and are strengthening the motives of those who do not yet own cars to get them. The forecasts indicate what the Department of Transport expects to happen up to the year 2025.*

For air and car travel I have used the high, or 'optimistic', forecasts, because they represent what will happen if the economy grows as fast as the government hopes it will. The air forecasts stop in 2010; I have extrapolated to 2025 at the prevailing growth rates because air traffic forecasters frequently enthuse about the enormous growth potential of their industry – often adducing as evidence

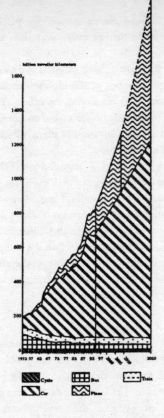

Figure 1: Travel by Britons by cycle, bus, train, car and plane. (Sources: *Transport Statistics Great Britain 1995*, DoT, 1995; *Air Traffic Forecasts for the United Kingdom 1994*, DoT, 1994.)

---

* Late in 1997 the Department of the Environment, Transport and the Regions released a set of new, lower, forecasts for car and road freight traffic. The earlier forecasts have been used in Figure 1 because the new forecasts are accompanied by a number of caveats which indicate that the forecasters do not really believe them. Actual growth is likely to be faster, they think, because:

- the new forecasts disregard the likelihood that 'adaptation of location . . . can be expected to lead to traffic growing elsewhere to make up for some of the growth suppressed . . . in these forecasts';
- 'some growth in longer distance travel has . . . been cut off when it might be expected to continue';
- 'the change [in road freight] modelled in these forecasts is well below the historic trend'; and
- 'no increase in travel has been included specifically to allow for the dispersion effects of providing for additional housing'.

the fact that most people in the world have never flown. The government's bus forecasts, showing a constant level of traffic in the future, are clearly disingenuous; the Department's own research has established that every extra car that joins the nation's car population takes over 300 passenger journeys a year from the bus services. If car use increases as forecast, the decline in bus use will continue. The government provides no forecasts of travel by rail, bicycle or foot. Travel by rail and bicycle have been held constant at the present low levels for the sake of graphic completeness, but are likely to decline if car and air traffic grow as forecast.

Figure 1 offers little hope to those environmentalists who advocate policies to get people out of their cars and back on to public transport; it shows that most journeys now made by car were never on public transport. When people acquired cars their activity patterns were transformed. They began going places previously unreachable by public transport, and travelling at times when public transport did not run. With a time lag, as more people acquired cars, land-use patterns responded. Retailers began locating out of town for the convenience of motorists. Residential developments moved to the suburbs where there was room for garages and off-street parking. Offices moved to out-of-town business parks surrounded by car parks. And hospitals, cinemas, post offices, warehouses all became bigger and fewer in number, and more difficult to reach by foot, bicycle or bus.

Figure 2 shows the way in which Britain's population is dispersing away from the old inner cities into the countryside. Although increasing numbers are moving to the country they are not becoming traditional country dwellers. They remain functionally (sub)urban. Some commute back into town to work, others commute to work in factories, offices, shops and warehouses which have also moved out of town, and some are tied to employers and clients by computer, phone and fax. Those moving out are moving into areas with little or no public transport. They then complain that they have no choice but to use their cars – but, in choosing to move out, they have chosen to have no choice.

It is sometimes argued that if only public transport were improved people would use it instead of their cars. But it used to be better, and cheaper, and more reliable and more pervasive. And even then, when people could afford cars they bought them, and were rarely seen on public transport again. The *total* amount of travel by bus and rail in 1994 is equal to

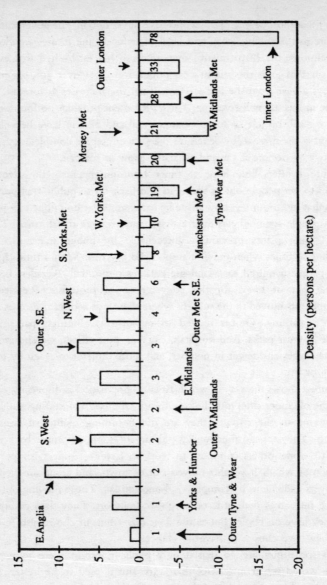

Figure 2: Percentage change 1971–81, by 1991 population density of districts. (Source: *1991 Census*, Government Statistical Service, 1992.)

about five years' *growth* in travel by car. If it were possible, by some political miracle, to divert sufficient car travel to buses and trains to restore public transport usage to its 1952 level, car travel would, according to the forecasts, be back at its present level in less than three years. The longer the trends in Figure 1 continue, the stronger become the pressures that drive them; the more expensive it becomes to maintain existing public transport services, as fixed overheads must be shared among a dwindling number of passengers; and the greater becomes the need to have a car to reach the shops, services and friends that used to be reachable without one.

The longer the trends continue the more the assumption of car dependence becomes built into the planning framework. Surrey for example, one of the most car-dependent parts of Britain, still insists, as a condition for planning approval, that new houses provide off-street parking space for three cars – thereby compelling a spread-out scale of development that discourages walking and cycling. The more dependent a country becomes on the car, the more difficult it becomes for politicians the world over to contemplate pulling up the ladder. And so the world keeps climbing.

In Britain in 1950 the average person travelled about 8 kilometres a day; now it is about 40 kilometres a day, and by 2025 according to the forecasts it will be about 100 kilometres a day. The *number* of trips taken every day is not increasing, and has possibly decreased slightly as the short daily shopping trips to the local high street have been replaced by the once-a-week trip by car to the out-of-town superstore, and as trips to the cinema or theatre have been replaced by television. Thus the *length* of average trip made in Britain now is about five times greater than in 1950.

The amount of *time* that the average person spends in motion has changed very little since 1950. People make their travel decisions within the constraints of time and money budgets. Improvements in transport technology have reduced the cost of travel, and rising real incomes have relaxed the constraint imposed by the money budget, but the number of hours in the day has not changed. The increase in average trip length is accounted for by increased *speed* of travel. Despite congested conditions for motorists, the huge shift from feet and bicycles to cars and planes has approximately quintupled the speed of the average journey.

As we spread ourselves wider, we spread ourselves thinner. If the radius describing our 'daily round' doubles, the area that we effectively inhabit, and the number of people contained within it, quadruple.* We live in a world crowded with strangers – a world in which we have fleeting contact with far more people than we have the possibility of knowing as individuals.

Further, the increases noted above in telecommunications traffic suggest that whatever is happening to the amount of time people are spending physically at home, social life there is being sapped electronically. The now widespread use of the guilt-laden term 'quality time', to distinguish the time during which parents are actually paying attention to their children from the time during which they are merely physically present, is symptomatic of the distracting power of television, computers and telecommunications.

Thus far we have been discussing the changes in the travel behaviour of the average individual. But as many have become much more mobile, many others, those left dependent on dwindling public transport, have become less mobile. Even when they live in close physical proximity to each other the mobile wealthy and the immobile poor live in different worlds. The immobile poor are confined by their lack of mobility in prisons with invisible walls. They are continually tempted and taunted, in ways that prisoners confined to cells with opaque walls are not, by the freedom and conspicuous consumption of the affluent. The wealthy can be seen and heard flying overhead, or driving along motorways through the ghetto, or on television, enjoying privileges that remain tantalisingly out of reach. To the wealthy the poor are often invisible; because of the height and speed at which they travel, the wealthy tend to see the world at a lower level of resolution.

People who live in different worlds are likely to develop different group loyalties. Those who live in the least desirable worlds are prone to rationalise their resentments, and develop ethical codes that favour a redistribution of the world's goods and privileges – by whatever means. And the wealthy, in turn, rationalise their good fortune, and devise means for holding on to it. As science and technology continually improve the physical means of communication, they are at the same time undermining the conditions of shared experience essential for democratic dialogue.

Three Opinion Polls

1. Would you like a car?
The answer to this question, everywhere in the world, is overwhelmingly

---

* Area = πr^2.

YES. In answering, most people probably imagine the world as it now is but with themselves having access to the enlarged range of opportunities that they see present car owners enjoying. It is this opinion poll and the YES replies which are driving transport policy in rich countries and poor countries alike; politicians, technologists and transport planners everywhere are encouraging people to believe that everyone's wish can be granted. This suggests a second opinion poll, which so far as I am aware has never been conducted.

2. Would you like to live in the sort of world you would get if everyone's wish were granted?
For such an opinion poll to yield meaningful answers there would need to be agreement about what such a world would be like. It would probably be grossly polluted, noisy, congested and anxious about the security of its energy supplies. But let us assume, for the sake of our hypothetical poll, that technology will solve these problems. What else might we expect?

- It would be *a polarised world*. Not everyone's wish can be granted. About a third of the world's population will never be old enough or fit enough to drive – they will be too young, too old, too nervous, too short-sighted, too drunk or otherwise disqualified. Their disadvantage will increase as car dependence increases. They will be second-class citizens, dependent for their mobility on the withered remains of public transport or the good will of car owners.
- The world will become *one continuous suburb*. The traditional city, built for people not cars, could not exist. The last unspoilt islands and wilderness areas – which travel writers incite us with a sense of urgency to visit before they are spoiled – will be spoiled. There will be no more secluded beaches – except perhaps a few owned by the very wealthy, protected by barbed wire and armed security guards.
- Geographical communities in which people know their neighbours will be replaced by *aspatial communities of interest*. People with similar tastes, interests and lifestyles will commune on the Internet or meet at conferences and vacation resorts. More high-security enclaves of the wealthy will be developed, but because of the fragmenting force of their inhabitants' mobility, they will not function as true communities

with interests and purposes in common – other than the preservation of their lives and property.

- *Travel opportunities will be destroyed.* The cultural and linguistic diversity in the world – the experience of which provides the motivation for much travel – will be obliterated by the rising tide of tourism. Our sense of place will disappear in a world obsessed with making it easier and cheaper 'to get there'; when we get there we will discover there is no 'there' – it will have been flooded with traffic, or bulldozed to make way for a new road or a fast-food restaurant.

- *Fragile ecosystems will be destroyed.* Wilderness retreats with access to it. The provision of parking and road space for more cars will require paving much more of the world. As the world is criss-crossed with more traffic arteries, the remaining wilderness areas will be chopped up into ever smaller parcels – many too small to support existing populations of rare species.

- *Street life will disappear.* The spread-out scale will defeat pedestrians, and traffic will make cycling too dangerous. There will be no local shops to walk to. Children will become captives of the family chauffeur in a world too full of traffic and alienated strangers for them to be permitted their traditional independence. The 'stranger danger' campaigns now run in primary schools in Britain are inculcating paranoia at a tender age; they are symptomatic of the mistrust that breeds in anonymity.

- *Law enforcement will become Orwellian.* A world full of highly mobile strangers will require ever more ingenious technology to detect and apprehend wrongdoers. The use of CCTV surveillance, DNA fingerprinting, and large computerised police databases will spread. Even small villages are now clamouring for surveillance cameras. As travel becomes easier physically it will become more difficult bureaucratically. The wealthy previously protected by distance from mass invasion by the indigent will resort to restrictive prohibition and force. New barriers will be erected to contain the numbers who will take advantage of the mobility afforded by technology. Road pricing schemes will price off the road those who are on the threshold of being able to afford cars.

- *Geographical communities will be drained* of their social content and left with CCTV and Neighbourhood Watch to guard their possessions. The ease with which one can live one's life in a community of interest will diminish the contact that people have with their geographical neighbours. Concern for the local environment and the welfare of one's geographical neighbours will diminish as people spend more time in cyberspace.

- *Political authority will become more remote.* As technology deluges us in information, it leaves us less time for contemplation and reflection, and forces us to employ ever cruder perceptual filters in order to make sense of it all. It can only increase the numbers of people with whom we have relationships at the cost of diminishing the intimacy and intensity of these relationships.
- *Democracy will disappear.* In the whole of the literature of science fiction devoted to imagining futures in which distance has been defeated, there are to be found no plausible examples of democratic government. Democracies, to function effectively, require common values, and a measure of agreement about societal goals forged out of common experience. If distance is vanquished, the requisite minimum level of consensus and trust will be unattainable; the world will be filled with billions of strangers sharing the same physical space, but living in very different virtual communities of interest.

The answer to opinion poll 2 would be, I suspect, a resounding NO. But it is not a poll that appeals to many politicians, implying as it does the need for a grim, grey, virtuous self-denial in order to save the world. We might, therefore, consider commissioning a third opinion poll.

3. Would you like to live in a cleaner, quieter, healthier, more convivial, sustainable world in which you know your neighbours, it is safe to walk and cycle, and children are allowed to play in the street?
Transport planners alone cannot, of course, create such a world, but they can create conditions which will make it impossible. Almost everywhere in the world governments in concert with the world's principal industrial enterprises are devoting most of the resources available for transport to the two modes of transport – the car and the plane – that are the most environmentally and socially destructive and the least democratic. The planners present priorities – measured by spending on research, development and construction – by actively promoting developments that are relaxing constraints on access and mobility, are fast creating the bleak, dangerous, alienated, selfish, socially polarised, environmenally precarious

world of opinion poll 2. The world of opinion poll 3 lies in the opposite direction. It can only come into existence if we collectively curb our appetite for mobility.

Therefore?

Figure 3 is a demand curve taken from an introductory economics textbook; it shows that as the cost of a good (access) decreases, consumption increases. Over time technological progress has reduced the cost of travel – measured in money, journey time, discomfort and unreliability. If Figure 3 is rotated anticlockwise through 90 degrees it produces a growth trend similar to that in Figure 1.

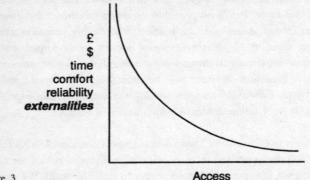

Figure 3

There is now much discussion of 'externalities' – those costs of travel for which the traveller is not directly charged. But the discussion almost invariably focuses on *environmental* externalities – energy consumption, pollution and congestion – for which technological solutions appear possible. But these 'solutions' threaten to increase the *social* externalities discussed above. To reduce these social externalities we must move back up the curve.

The most straightforward way of doing this is to make motorised travel more expensive. The need to reduce dependence on the car is greatest where the growth is fastest – not in the congested inner cities where growth has stopped because they have been full of traffic for some time, but in the suburbs and countryside beyond, to which motorists continue to flee.

Much of the dispersal to the countryside noted in figure 2 can be explained by the fact that urban motorists pay more in *time* per mile travelled than rural motorists. Electronic road pricing, or congestion pricing as it is sometimes called, would make urban car travel more expensive in terms of money. If we move back up the curve *only* in urban areas, we will increase the incentive to move out of town.

Increasing the tax on petrol is one method, currently being pursued by the government, on a modest scale, in the face of protest from rural areas. But traffic is still increasing. The root of the problem, the nettle that the government will not grasp, is car ownership. Its own forecasters are clear; the growth of car ownership – which the government still welcomes – is 'the major contributor to traffic growth.'* When people acquire cars they use them. They also need space to park them, and the urban car park is now full. The transport problems of town and country are inseparably intertwined. A further increase in the nation's car population could only be accommodated by further dispersal of town dwellers into the countryside.

The first priority of an environmentally, socially, politically and morally sustainable transport policy must be the creation of a transport and land-use system in which every citizen has the possibility of leading a full, happy and prosperous life without owning a car.

* *National Traffic Forecasts (Great Britain)* (London, 1997), p. 34.

21. *Railways, Settlement and Access*
David Wiggins and Mayer Hillman

I David Wiggins

A greatly increased proportion of the population of Britain (itself an increasing quantity) is now dispersed into areas that used to be called the countryside. These people have arrived there even as railway access to the towns where many of them want to work has withered away. (Oxford and environs, for instance, in the decade when it was turning itself into a traffic problem, was losing its railway lines to Abingdon, to Wallingford, to Fairford/Witney, to Bedford/Cambridge, to Thame/High Wycombe, to Cheltenham, to Rugby. Even on lines still open, stations such as Kidlington were being shut.) Moreover, a significant further proportion of the population expects to be able to visit the countryside – and not simply once a year for an annual holiday, but frequently. This expectation has come into being even as the plentiful railway access that once extended to national parks and other places of scenic beauty which are threatened by mounting car traffic has been diminished almost to nothing (though not yet nothing).

The time has come to recall some of the history of these things and reconsider some of the myth-eaten assumptions that have eased our passage to a state of affairs that now confronts us with difficult questions, questions that John Adams, in Chapter 20, shows we shall have great difficulty in answering.

In 1963, when the Beeching Report was debated by Parliament, the British mainland railway stood at about four-fifths of its former size. The ravages inflicted upon the railway by the demands of war had been repaired only in part, though the Euston–Manchester electrification was in hand. Road traffic was already beginning to disperse human activities in every direction and obliterate the distinction between town and country. But it was still possible to see the relatively close-knit settlement pattern that the railway had helped, as a system of near-universal access for passengers and freight, to define and reinforce. One still saw the tight clustering of major freight sources and freight destinations about railway spurs, sidings and secondary lines. Looking back at photographs of the early 1960s, one stares in amazement at the stillness and order of street scenes, with the odd motor bus, motor car or goods van, and pavements busy with pedestrians going about their business with the small commercial enterprises of that era.

In 1963, after a period of missed opportunities and prolonged political and managerial uncertainty, the railway was running a working deficit of £81.6 million (including provision for depreciation and amortisation).* The Ministry of Transport's professed hope was that this deficit could be massively reduced by the closure of outlying or less-used parts of the system. (Presumably the most prevalent belief within the Ministry was that the whole future lay with air and motor transportation, though it was not yet the Ministry's business to say so aloud, still less to encourage anyone to speculate what that would be like.) Even in 1963, though, the hopes attached to the closure programme provoked outright disbelief. In the Commons debate, the then leader of the opposition, Harold Wilson, spoke as follows:

> Is [the Minister] satisfied that cutting the railways out will solve British Railways' financial problem?
>
> Over the last ten years, 5,600 miles of track have been closed. That is 19 per cent of the mileage previously in operation. Presumably this 19 per cent – roughly one-fifth of our track mileage – must have been the least remunerative of the lot. Presumably that is why it was first selected for closure. Yet its closure saved only 7 per cent of the working deficit of British Railways in 1960, and this takes no account of the additional cost to the nation of the closures, or the loss of main line traffic caused by the closures of feeder services. Will he explain his calculations?
>
> If the closing of one-fifth of the track mileage makes so little difference to the operating deficit of British Railways, what will the next one-third do? Why should the Minister think that there will be any difference? Or does he agree with the Annual Report of the Central Transport Consultative Committee, which said: 'the negative policy of closing down uneconomic facilities, while contributing a small financial saving, is not the panacea it is sometimes made out to be.' Will he comment on that Report, which I believe has been made to him?†

---

* After payment of interest (including annual payments to shareholders expropriated, payments agreed on the basis of the state of the railway before the war), the overall railway deficit of the British Transport Commission was £133 million.

† *Hansard*, 30 April 1963, col. 915.

The Beeching proposal was to save some £30 million by closing 4,000 to 5,000 miles of passenger line, the supposedly least 'economic'. At the beginning of 1967, when (despite Mr Wilson's words uttered in opposition) the Labour government had completed nearly 85 per cent of the closure programme, the sum that was officially claimed by way of savings was only £17 million. Moreover most of this (if it really was saved) could have been saved without closures. No attempt has ever been officially made or sanctioned to work out how much. It is not hard, however, to do so.

Firstly, we know that in 1963 the average number of people employed per mile of line was 17.5. Compare for that time Netherlands 9, Sweden 4.4. Secondly, consider the East Suffolk Line, forty-five miles long. Gerard Fiennes, an admirer of the forgotten, more positive aspects of the Beeching plan, who became manager of the Eastern Region in 1966, describes in his autobiography how the official costs, which had been represented at a closure hearing as a quarter of a million pounds, were reduced by 'basic railway' operation to £84,000, and how the line then made a profit of £8,000 a year. 'Of such is the crass folly of parts of the Beeching Plan,' he noted.[*] Let us round £84,000 per annum up to £90,000 per annum. Let us forget not just the fact that Fiennes made a profit but the fact that passengers pay fares. (If more than a basic railway is needed, let these fares pay for the difference.) Then we can say that in the 1960s it would have cost less than £2,000 a mile a year (including depreciation, amortisation and interest on capital costs of adaptation) to run a basic railway (with equipment that passed muster then and would still pass muster nowadays if the alternative were to have nothing). Thus it would have cost less than £10 million a year (to be offset by direct and indirect revenue) to run the most uneconomic 5,000 miles of the network. This was a very small fraction of the 1963 loss.[†]

Another thing that was noticed by critics of the Ministry's policy (both in 1963 and later) was that every reduction in the accessibility and

[*] *I Tried to Run a Railway*, London, 1967.

[†] There is a third fix on the same point. Fiennes wrote an article in *The Times* (Business News, 24 August 1968) about a new labour agreement:

'Let us begin with the general point that the agreement deals with what is to happen on the main lines. One must ignore what the Board's own public relations stress; namely that the salvation of railways lies in chopping off rural branches. It does not. Of the reduction of the staff of the railways between 1955 and 1968 by over 245,000 men, not more than 25,000 or so came from the closure of nearly 6,000 miles of route. The arithmetic in broad terms has been: 40% less railway; more than 40% less staff; but only 4% of these staff were saved by the 40% railway cut.'

connectivity of the system was going to put at risk all putative mainline traffic either starting or ending at a point that was to be severed from the system. This hazard of withdrawals had been recognised even by Beeching. But, as the populace began from the 1960s onwards to disperse itself from tighter urban and suburban concentrations deeper and deeper into the countryside (often in one-car families), it became more and more evident how serious a mistake it was for the railway to cut itself off from many millions of putative passengers. (Not only, but not least, putative passengers trapped by the motor congestion that was destined to result from the demographic changes already described.) This is a point to which I shall return.

If the 1963 working deficit was £81.6 million, then how is one to compare this cost to the public with what the railway costs now? Constant changes to the system accounting make strict comparison difficult. But one obvious counterpart to the 1963 working deficit is the P.S.O. grant to the British Railways Board for 1993, namely £1,155 million, added to British Rail's 1993 operating loss for 1993, namely £164 million, amounting to a total of £1,319 million. (Capital expenditure was a further £1,384.) Multiplying the 1963 working deficit figure by 10 or 11 (in accordance with the GDP deflator indices) to allow for price inflation, one may say that in 1963 the railway deficit on a much larger system was costing the taxpayer the equivalent at 1993 prices of something between £816 million and £897 million. It need not have cost so much. But, however wastefully it was run, this was much more connected railway for much less money in real terms than we had in 1993.

And in 1998? In 1998, after the franchising of railway services and the privatisation of Railtrack, it is said that the annual cost to the government will be more than *twice* times £1,319 million – though this will reflect the Treasury's expectation that the government will not need to fund capital investment in the railway from the Public Sector Borrowing Requirement.

These are large commitments, absolutely unthinkable (even at 1963 prices) in 1963. Moreover, even at the time of writing, Railtrack, which owns the railways' track and fixed installations and charges the franchise companies for their use, has announced plans to invest on the network £17 billion of the money that it will derive from the railway franchise companies (who derive their money from HMG and from passengers). The money will be invested over ten years on a network which is nearly 5,000 miles smaller than in 1963 and can no longer make any claim to be the dense medium-speed network it once was, of near universal accessibility for passengers and freight.* (Most bus replacements for withdrawn railway links have failed as miserably as it was predicted they would; and they have not failed through ill-will or incompetence. See Part II (p. 246). One of the several things that first prompted Fiennes's East Anglian experiment is that local people proved on the ground that it was physically impossible for any bus to drive fast enough to make replacing connections.)

Railtrack's announcement comes (let it further be noted) within less than a week of transport and environment ministers' entreaties to the travelling public to make less use of the car and more use of public transport – entreaties coming not without the usual promises of sticks and carrots.

All these things, like most of the other consequences of all the policies that went along with the Beeching Report, were clearly predicted by numerous critics, as were most of the difficulties that now prevent so many people in so many places from making less use of the motor vehicle.†

Once upon a time, well within living memory, most people arranged their choice of place of dwelling, their place of work, their choice of shopping or other facilities, even their choice of recreation or weekend activities, along a good line of communication perceived as permanently available by foot, bus or train. The practical problem of access (access which is a need; contrast mobility, which is not as such a need, except in so far as it is a sole method of access) was solved almost effortlessly as a sort of simultaneous equation. That is no longer the norm. Understanding of this change and its consequences (the new concentration and centralisation of all sorts of facilities that were previously, perforce, much more numerous; the impossibility without a car of many sorts of life) is not new. There has even been time for this understanding to spread from long-standing critics

---

* It is profoundly to be hoped that none of this Railtrack money will be diverted into making the journey from Paris to London by Channel Tunnel half an hour shorter. If there was any rationale at all for the new arrangements, then one of the things worth sticking to is Railtrack's duty to plough back into the railway network and its services the money it is paid by HMG for these services. The transport access problem is not a problem of national prestige.

† Among these critics, the present writer went so far as to seek and to secure an interview (11 a.m., 14 December 1965, MOT, Southwark) with Mrs Castle's economic adviser, C. D. Foster, to exhort the Ministry of Transport not to permit the breaking up of the formation of the Great Central Main Line, which was being closed under Mrs Castle's ministership. The Great Central Line was the only railway in the north engineered to a European loading gauge – something that is very badly needed now. These representations were heard, but they made no difference. It must have seemed certain to Mrs Castle and her advisers that no Channel Tunnel would ever be built. But the future was more open than they thought. On these matters, see Roger Calvert, The Future of Britain's Railways (London, 1965), Chapter 6.

of stated official policy, which held for a long time that car ownership '*ought to increase*', to the Departments of Environment and Transport themselves. For a remarkable transitional moment, compare *Transport Policy, a Consultative Document* (London, 1976), Vol. 1, Section 13.3 which says car ownership 'ought to increase', with Section 3.5 of the same document, which reads as follows:

> At the same time as mobility has been reduced for those without a car, its advantages have increased. For as car ownership spreads, schools become larger, hospitals are regionalised, out-of-town shopping centres multiply and the Council Offices are situated further away; meanwhile, the local shop and post office have disappeared. Mobility becomes ever more necessary: but command over it for the minority grows less. This is perhaps the most important problem which emerges from this review of the Transport scene.

The trouble with this way of putting the point is that it is understated. Labour ministers will find a more vivid and informative statement in the words of a real live practitioner of road transport, Sir Daniel Pettit, addressing fellow professionals (in the year before the consultation paper just quoted) at the Mercedes Benz conference in Eastbourne, 18–20 June 1975:

> Responding to the freedom and the new opportunities that road transport has given it, industry has moved steadily away from locations near the railheads, ports or inland waterways and has evolved a new, more dispersed approach to Land Use than was evident in the 19th Century with its emphasis on consolidation in metropolis and conurbation. Much new light industry is situated either on industrial estates on the outskirts of established towns, or in new towns. Warehouses in which goods are prepared for final delivery are often located in rural or semi-rural areas where land prices are lowest and supplies of labour are still reasonably consistent and of quality. Research into this area consistently underlines and reflects the irrefutable hold which road transport now has secured over the channels of supply, illustrated by the Mercedes Blue Book and the FTA handbook and studies in my own organisation and the ever increasing and well justified need for road infrastructure as a pre-requisite for growth . . . There can be little doubt

that growth will continue and, while it will extend the pleasures of increased affluence to more sections of the population, it will also make more pressing the problems that affluence brings, and highlight the less attractive aspects of the road transport industry as it responds to the increasing demands made on it.

We must give a great deal more thought and determination to developing the concept of the dispersed society, one which in both its appeal to individual liberty and mobility and its use of land is more attuned to the motor car and the lorry responding to individual needs than the concentration and conurbation developments of the 19th Century dependent on and conditioned by the railways, providing for the pattern of supply in commodity terms to the population en masse.

That is what we are up against. Having done – or permitted its public servants to do – almost everything possible to hasten this state of affairs, society now refuses to acquiesce in it.

What is to be done? No one thing. If we are in a hole, we can stop digging. Let us halt the road-building programme in its tracks, then; let us pay the cancellation charges for abandoned road projects as if they were a bargain. Let us be less deterministic or fatalistic about future traffic volumes; and, even if there is no political intention to make the cost of motor transport reflect its external costs, let us strive to promote or enhance or preserve all the alternatives to motor transport. Before anyone says that any of these alternatives is too expensive, let us make sure that such alternatives are modest, durable and not overpriced. (They do not need brand new equipment: they need the committed intelligent use of existing equipment. A railway carriage built without gadgetry used to last fifty years.) Let us remember the old adage that facilities create traffic; and let the *collective import* be considered of all decisions that will combine to prevent doing without a car from being even an option within the lives of an open-ended assemblage of persons. Finally, let us remember that the future is not yet fixed. It partly depends on what we think now and do now.

What else? And what about the railway? Well, let the railway Regulator and the Transport or Environment ministers forget any lingering commitments they feel to prestige projects and, in their place, let them encourage Railtrack to spend a sizeable portion of its £17 billion, not on upgrading main lines to ever higher speeds (which reduces their capacity), but on the restoration of the real accessibility and connectivity of the railways. Let all these human agents behave as if, under the new thinking already referred to above, society is seriously determined to give the alternatives to air and motor transportation a real future (not simply to direct its public servants to find ways for us to escape residual obligations to these alternatives, in the manner of all previous decades since the Second World War). Let the complicated legal arrangements covering the estate activities of Railtrack and other proprietors of former railway lands be modified in order to encourage industrial redevelopment to be conceived and projected in tandem with the exploration of future markets for railway freight opportunities. But above all, this time, let everyone think a little harder, more discursively, and without enslavement to the doctrines of transport economists or other professionals who have brought us, by their studied refusal to acknowledge the existence of questions that their expertise does not embrace, to the present pass.

As our contributions to this effort, Mayer Hillman and I offer something on two of these several levels. On one level, I shall try to show the special implications that the locational insights already mentioned have for the operation of railways put into deficit by competitors that are unlikely either to disappear or to become less socially destructive. Then Hillman will examine the myth, so eagerly propagated by the advocates of railway contraction, that railway closures were devoid of serious social consequences. Together let us hope these efforts can amount to one whole drop in an ocean.

I begin with a passage from the nineteenth-century railway engineer, A. W. Wellington, author of *The Economic Theory of the Location of Railways*:

Taking the entire population of a country . . . and conceiving it to be made up of a great number of units, either of single individuals, or of groups of 10, or 100 . . . it is plain that each one of these units has potential traffic relations with every other unit. The components of each unit visit those of the other socially; they buy and sell from each other; they visit each other in the hope of buying and selling; they produce more (this is an invariable law) for the especial purpose of supplying the necessities of others with whom they have or finally secure traffic relations. Until such traffic facilities exist, these relations are inchoate, or merely potential. As the facilities are extended, they become actual . . . We may regard each person as the traffic [source], and while it will be by no means literally true that he will have actual traffic relations with all those for whom the facilities exist, but only with every tenth, hundredth, or millionth person, according to his character and occupation, yet practically the result is the same. [Each person's] aggregate contribution to railway traffic will vary in close accordance with the total population connected with him by traffic facilities, and his payments to any particular line will be in direct proportion to that fraction of the total of the whole population connected with him by traffic facilities which is reached by him over that particular line.*

On this basis and on the basis of experience, Wellington propounded the following law: the traffic on a transport mode is proportional to the square of the population best served by that mode. Wellington sought to back up this generalisation not only by a mass of statistical data but also by a mathematical argument founded in the fact that the number of directed linkages on a network of *n* points is $n \times (n-1)$ and the fact that for larger and larger *n*, $n \times (n-1)$ approaches closer and closer to *n-squared*.

One good way to think about Wellington's point is this. Actual traffic between two points on a network under conditions *t* is some *t*-governed proportion, *L*, of the potential traffic between these points. But as extra points are added to a network, the potential contribution to total traffic of each new point must be larger than that of the previously added point (provided of course the new points are not *so* distant or *so* awkwardly placed that no other point will want to communicate with them, etc.). If the total potential traffic on a network of *n* points is some function of *n*, call it *P(n)*, then the larger *n* is, the closer *P(n)* may be thought of as coming to being proportional to *n-squared* and the closer actual traffic *T(n)* may be thought of as coming to being the proportion *L* of something that is proportional to *n-squared*. The traffic on a system of equally weighted points varies exponentially with the number of points, all things considered.†

The next thought we may take from Wellington is this: the *cost* of putting each additional point on to the network and maintaining it there is a constant, not proportional to the increased size of the system. Or it is proportional (*ceteris paribus*) only to mileage.

The conclusion Wellington drew was that, even though the traffic on

---

* *The Economic Theory of the Location of Railways* (New York and London, 1887).

† Wellington also allowed for distance, in an argument that anticipates the gravity models of modern geographers. It can be shown, on the condition stated, and expressing traffic in revenue received, why an exponential law should hold.

feeder and branch lines is 'usually thin', it remains 'universally true that they are far more profitable than appears on the face of their returns separately considered' (para. 983). For the traffic they contribute 'may be handled over the main line at no appreciable cost by simply filling up trains, and the branch is then enormously profitable ... the prosperity of the system increasing in something like the square of the population' (para. 982), 'even though branches are rarely profitable when considered in themselves and apart from the main line'.

Wellington was writing at a time of expansion, not contraction. But that makes no difference. The point can be shown in particular instances where there has been a detailed study.* But there is a more general thought that his work may suggest about systems in deficit. Larger ones may make a smaller deficit than smaller ones make.

Order the separable (separately closeable or openable) parts of a railway system from more remunerative (on direct costs and receipts) to less remunerative. There will be many ways of doing this. Choose an ordering which, at each point on the horizontal axis of the graph depicted in Figure 1, defines a connected railway system. Then every point n on the horizontal axis of the graph (which is purely notional, and illustrative simply of one logical possibility under later twentieth-century conditions) represents both a size of system in miles and also (relative to the ordering) a definitive railway system. Then on the vertical axis we place £ to register ton and passenger miles (translated into gross revenue T) and working expenses, C. Costs increase constantly with addition of nodes and increase of mileage (or not quite constantly, given economies of scale). But potential traffic units P, of which, on Wellington's theory, actual traffic units are some proportion, L, determined no doubt by historic and demographic conditions, increase more than constantly.

The graph depicts a connected railway system, in deficit, but benefiting from the network traffic generation effect. What it illustrates is the possibility that, for all system sizes n where the slope of C at $C(n)$ is flatter than the slope of T at $T(n)$, reduction in the size of network can result in net aggravation of the deficit. *A fortiori*, reduction in the size of network can diminish the number of traffic units carried per £ of subsidy.

---

* E.g. the Exeter–Barnstaple line, where S. Williams, P. White and P. Heels showed (*Modern Railways*, 1967) that contributory revenue exceeded costs. Contributory revenue is revenue on the rest of the network for whose existence as revenue the branch's being open to traffic to or from the rest of the system is causally responsible.

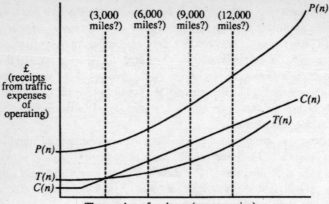

Figure 1

If we are not to repeat the errors of recent history we have first to understand them. Consider then Table 1, of results for the era of closures (the largest sequence of years for which satisfactory statistics exist on a single basis). It illustrates the possibility just mentioned.

Table 1

Year	Total deficit £m	Working deficit £m	Route miles	Route miles for passengers	Ton miles (millions)	Passenger miles (millions)	Units traffic carried (000M)	Traffic units per 1963£
1962	n.a.	108.7	17,471	12,915	14,993	19,728	35.83	n.a.
1963	133.9	81.6	16,982	12,631	15,398	19,230	35.77	267.1
1964	120.9	67.5	15,991	11,670	16,052	19,874	35.92	304.8
1965	132.4	73.1	14,920	10,884	15,429	18,713	34.14	273.4
1966	134.7	71.6	13,721	10,165	14,790	18,453	33.25	272.5
1967	153.0	90.4	13,172	9,882	13,609	18,089	31.70	237.2
1968	147.4	83.5	12,447	9,471	14,693	17,835	32.50	259.5

Notes: The deficit for 1962 is not available on the same basis as for 1963 following. For the last column the deficits were first converted to 1963 prices.

It is remarkable that the best year here, by almost every indicator, is 1964 – after some modernisation of the railway, but before many of Beeching's closures. Note too that the period 1962–8 was one of great expansion of demand for transport. Total passenger miles by all modes together rose from 173,000 million to 236,000 million. The total ton-miles offered for carriage by all modes rose from 64.6 thousand million to 79.5 thousand million. Yet in Britain the railway lost traffic. Not even the opening of the Euston–Manchester electrification in April 1966 sufficed for the railway to hold on to its existing passenger and ton-mileage. Scarcely another railway administration in Europe failed to increase its absolute passenger and ton-mileage during this period, even though car ownership was increasing in those countries no less rapidly than it was in Great Britain. There is something here to be explained.

In the Beeching Report it was claimed:

One third of the route mileage carries only 1% of the total passenger miles. Similarly, one third of the mileage carries only 1% of the freight ton miles of British Railways . . . The proportion of British Railways' total passenger and freight revenue corresponding with this proportion of total traffic movement is £4.5M, while the cost of providing this route is some £20M.

But now let us ask: how was it that closures of lines amounting to one-third of the system, applied at a time when newly modernised parts of the railway were making large quantities of new traffic and when population was increasing and more freight and passenger traffic was on offer to all modes, were followed by the loss of much more than 1 per cent of the traffic? How was it that the closure of that part of the one-third which happened between 1964 and 1968 was followed in practice, and in spite of new traffic from modernisation,* by a reduction in traffic of *nearly 10 per cent* and a reduction of passenger traffic of over 10 per cent?

Nobody who backed the closures policy can duck this question. Wellington's answer is before us. Let Railtrack study it, and let the Ministers of Transport and Environment. For the longer term, let political

* Examples: Birmingham–Lichfield traffic trebled; Leeds–Barnsley traffic increased 221 per cent.

scientists and philosophers pause for a moment from more abstract or spectatorial labours and consider what it will take for elected politicians and permanent civil servants to transcend the failures of the last forty years. Over the last forty years, we have moved through a sequence of steps by which each *coming* stage of transport and land use has held out the *prospect* of being something better than the stage it would replace; yet, when it has come, it has so often been seen as worse in its actuality than its pre-predecessor or its *pre-pre-predecessor* was. If we are to have practical wisdom, self-conscious positive efforts will be needed to render the relation *appears better than* transitive in the domain of states of transport and land use that society plans at each stage to bring about at the next. In this connection first see, and then generalise, E. J. Mishan, 'A Note on the Interpretation of the Benefits of Private Transport' (1967).*

II Mayer Hillman

The Beeching Report of 1963, *The Reshaping of British Railways*, recommended that British Rail initiate a major programme of rail closures on the ground that much of the network at the time was 'uneconomical'. In the sixteen years following its publication, successive ministers of transport approved the withdrawal of passenger services on 265 lines, altogether accounting for about 4,000 route miles, that is not far short of a third of the network existing at the time of the Report.

It is quite remarkable that, during this period, neither policy-makers within central government nor those within British Rail had considered it necessary to understand, let alone monitor, the nature and extent of the impact of rail closures on the lives of people in the affected areas and on the social structures and economies of the areas. Clearly, the consequences of a few closures should have been assessed before the programme of outstanding ones was continued. Evidence revealed in this way would also have aided the process of determining a rational national strategy on the rail network. It was solely the narrow financial costs of maintaining rural services set against the revenue derived from rail fares covering travel on the branch line alone, and not on the rest of the network, which were weighed in the balance in drawing up the list of closures. Nor was

* E. J. Mishan, 'A Note on the Interpretation of the Benefits of Private Transport', *Journal of Transport Economics and Policy*, 1 (1967), pp. 184–8.

consideration given to other effects that the closures may have had on local communities. It is possible that the idea of doing so had not even occurred to the policy-makers.

In 1979, however, Peter Parker, then Chairman of British Rail, commissioned such a study, which I undertook, in collaboration with Anne Whalley.* Its primary aim was to determine the 'social consequences of the closure of rail passenger services in rural areas'. To this end, the study sought to answer questions about the use of the lines before the closures, public attitudes to them, the adequacy of the process leading to decisions on closures, the adaptations made by different groups in the community to the loss of local rail services, and about the quality of the buses replacing these services. Ten case studies, broadly representative of the different characteristics of rural lines, were chosen from a list of forty-seven lines closed after 1968.

The findings of the surveys undertaken as part of the study showed that there was considerable public disaffection with all ten closures. Half of the respondents said that they had been very upset at the time of closure, and only a very small proportion – almost exclusively car owners – expressed little or no concern. Though feelings had abated somewhat over time, one in three still felt 'very upset' in spite of the fact that, in some cases, it was nine or ten years since the services had been withdrawn.

Regret about the closures was not the sentiment of a small minority: no less than half the local population had previously travelled on their branch lines in the year or so before closure. A few had used the line daily for getting to work or to school, some used them more than once or twice a week to go shopping, to make social visits or to get to leisure destinations. Many used them, albeit less frequently, for journeys for medical purposes and for holidays.

Marked differences were found when comparing patterns of travel before and after the closures. Nearly three in four of the former rail users reduced or stopped making some of their journeys, with the effect of limiting travel to about two in three of the destinations they had previously reached by rail. At one extreme, under three in ten former rail users reported no change in behaviour apart from the obligatory change of travel method. At the other, almost one in twelve reported a total curtailment of their previous rail-based activity, no longer visiting any of the places formerly reached by rail and not going anywhere else instead.

* Hillman, M., and Whalley, A., *The Social Consequences of Rail Closures* (London, 1980).

Although travel by train after closure was still possible for journeys on the regional or national network, much less use was made of this network: before closure, the great majority had used it to varying extents whilst, after closure, only a minority did so – travelling to the railhead by bus or car. As a consequence, British Rail lost patronage on the main network. In fact, only one in three of those who used to make longer-distance journeys by rail (beyond the end of the branch lines) at least a few times a year, had continued to do so. Evidence from the study indicated that the added inconvenience of journeys involving interchange from one form of transport to another at the nearest railhead, particularly when combined with the general disadvantages of bus travel, strongly contributed to this decline.

The attractions of the former rail services compared with the replacement bus services were reflected in the fact that, whereas previously nearly half the respondents had used the bus services immediately after closure, this proportion had fallen on average to only one in three by the time of our surveys, typically only a few years later. More people had transferred at least some of their former rail journeys to car rather than to the replacement bus service.

The reasons for this relatively low use of buses were revealed on examining the characteristics of the rail services before closure and replacement services after. In most of the ten areas, the bus services were fewer in number than were the rail services and did not run as late in the evenings, and journeys took longer. The buses were less advantageous in other respects too: mention was made by respondents of the absence of toilets needed on lengthy trips, proneness to travel sickness on the often winding roads, and difficulties in taking children in pushchairs or in carrying bulky luggage. In only one respect were the buses considered better. They were easier to reach, as the stops were often closer to people's homes than were the stations. However, this did not compensate for the loss of time, because buses were much slower than trains and jeopardised connections.

A further way of revealing how well the alternative buses met the travel needs of former rail users was sought by asking those who had not used the replacement buses why they had not done so. The reasons given largely mirrored the problems cited by those who did use them, although the cost of fares and the problems of connections and interchange were more often mentioned. They also included aspects of bus travel about which modifications to improve the service were not feasible on cost grounds and therefore highly unlikely to be made – for instance, increasing its frequency in spite of the low patronage.

The inadequacy of the replacement bus services could be inferred too from the fact that, whilst before closure the train was clearly a preferable form of travel to the car for some of the journeys made by people living in car-owning households, this was far less so in situations where the bus was the alternative form. A higher rate of increase in household car ownership in the affected areas was also recorded.

The report on the study concluded that it was difficult to see how further branch lines could be closed without requiring local communities from which the services were to be withdrawn to suffer a serious reduction in the quality of their public transport and that this would inevitably lead to a significant curtailment of the activity and opportunities of their populations. On the rough assumptions that the services whose loss had caused the least hardship and inconvenience had already been withdrawn, we argued that it would logically become progressively more difficult to effect further closures without generating adverse consequences on a greater scale than those identified in the ten areas examined and that for these reasons the remaining rural services should be retained if at all possible.

In anticipation of any suggestion that such a judgement would not necessarily hold if a better standard of replacement bus service were provided, the report highlighted the fact that the differences between rail and bus travel were so marked – both in terms of objective evidence on use and in terms of the judgements of respondents – that it would be an illusion to believe that even much-improved bus services could adequately replace or compensate for the loss of a rail service. So influential was the report that British Rail's programme of further closures was abruptly curtailed shortly after its publication.

Postscript

With the benefit of hindsight, covering another eighteen years since the study was undertaken, what further evidence is available to strengthen or weaken that decision? Several issues can be mentioned. The first and most important is certainly that relating to the implications of climate change for patterns of travel. Like wilful children obliged to listen to unwelcome truths, so reluctant politicians and public alike are having to learn that the only moral and internationally realistic political response to evidence on climate change is a *dramatic* curtailment of our own use of fossil fuels, especially in those energy-consuming sectors such as car and air travel (which are clearly less essential than, for example, winter heating). Medium-speed railway travel and its combination, given the necessary rolling stock, with cycle use, represents an ideal means of catering for long-distance travel with relatively low use of fossil fuels.

The second issue relates to the wider consequences of the withdrawal of rail services which, by their nature, do not reveal themselves in the short term, particularly ones affecting the age and social profile of the population in the areas affected by closures. Although no comprehensive study of these aspects has been made, it is apparent that the inadequacy of the bus services laid on to provide for the daily travel of those without cars has contributed to the continuing erosion of the relative self-sufficiency of many rural communities, especially as more and more day-to-day local facilities for education, shopping, recreation and work have been lost at the same time. Young people have been encouraged or obliged to move out to seek employment and, given the paucity of work opportunities in villages and surrounding areas, they have not returned.

The third related issue is that people in car-owning households – increasingly in multi-car-owning ones and therefore in far less need of public transport – have been attracted to move from congested and noisy cities to these areas of rural tranquillity or to acquire second homes in them. Almost by definition, the lack of public transport services hardly matters to them. Indeed, it could be observed that there is an inverse correlation between public transport access and house prices in the country. In the process, prices have been pushed beyond the reach of the indigenous population. Young first-time buyers have been denied the choice of whether or not to continue living in the areas in which they were born, further accelerating their move to towns and conurbations. As if to add insult to injury, many of the more affluent newcomers have adopted a pattern of long-distance commuting which tends, twice daily, to degrade the quality of the environment of those living along the extended routes they take.

There is a final issue which appears to have received insufficient attention. Beautiful countryside is damaged by the effects of the motor traffic that its very appeal generates. Many existing rural rail lines can provide tourists with more comfortable and less intrusive or damaging access.

So far the closure of railway lines has seemed an almost irreversible process, and especially so for long rail routes. Informed decisions are clearly called for in determining the future of those that are not heavily utilised. It cannot simply be left to market forces led by the narrow economic logic of 'value for money' or the myopic forms of accounting criticised in the first part of this chapter. There would appear to be a strong case for a comprehensive review of these under-utilised assets, taking account of the wider indirect issues as well as the more direct ones that formed the main focus of the PSI study. The justification for retention and, wherever possible, restoration of closed lines would be strengthened as the result of changing perceptions not only of the function of the lines in maintaining more socially balanced and economically viable rural communities, but also of the role of railways in catering for longer-distance travel without the present environmental cost.

Bibliography

British Railways Board, *The Reshaping of British Railways* (London, 1963).

Calvert, R. G., *The Future of Britain's Railways* (London, 1965).

Crosland, A., Fabian Lecture, Fabian Society, London, 1970.

Department of Transport, *Transport Policy: A Consultation Document* (London, 1976).

Department of Transport, *Transport Policy*, Cmnd 6836 (London, 1977).

Fiennes, G., *I Tried to Run a Railway* (London, 1967).

Fiennes, G., in *The Times* (Business News) 24 August 1968.

Hillman, M. and Whalley, A., *The Social Consequences of Rail Closures* (London, 1980).

Mishan, E. J., 'A Note on the Interpretation of the Benefits of Private Transport', *Journal of Transport Economics & Policy* 1 (1967), pp. 184–8.

Pettit, D., 'The Role of the Truck'. Paper presented to the Mercedes Benz Conference, Eastbourne, 18–20 June 1975.

Wellington, A. W., *The Economic Theory of the Location of Railways* (New York and London, 1887).

V

Urban Futures

22. Greening the Cities
Liz Greenhalgh

How can we improve the quality of urban life? This question, which so many city and town dwellers have hardly dared to ask for fear of the silence that followed, is now, at last, being posed by those who have the power to make some difference. Indeed, the decision-makers have become preoccupied with the question since the publication of a now famous government paper – *Household Growth: Where Shall We Live?** – which foresaw large numbers of people wanting to move out of cities. This shift is naturally encouraged by developers, who prefer greenfield sites, since it is easier to build on them and easier to sell the product.

It is clear that if things are left as they are there will be a continuing exodus to the countryside. The force propelling the move, however, is not simply the perceived attractions of rural life but also the experienced inadequacies of cities: their infrastructure, facilities and environment. Even if suburban countryside leaves much to be desired, people seem to prefer the hope it offers to the unease of living in a city and watching its life break down. Dangerous parks, poor schools, closed libraries, hopeless transport, high pollution – a two-income couple who decide to have children are naturally motivated to leave this for a larger house and more space, over which they have more direct control. Policy-makers have now realised that this 'push' factor needs to be remedied if we are to stem the movement to exurbia and the countryside, and the accompanying demand for new houses.

Until now, the appeal of suburbia has been misunderstood as an aesthetic appeal – the attraction of a green and pleasant environment with all that that means by way of associated ideas. Hence arose the attempt to reproduce suburban aesthetics in cities: the policy of 'Greening the City', which became a stated target of government policy towards the end of the last Conservative administration.

---

* *Household Growth: Where Shall We Live?* Paper presented to Parliament by the Secretary of State for the Environment, November 1996 (London, 1996).

Greening was not so much a pre-emptive strike as a pre-emptive image, an attempt to fill the intellectual and political void with a positive icon of the city. It did indeed draw attention to the need to improve urban quality and design, and as such gave these issues the profile they deserve. But the call for greening of cities was less a policy than an exercise in cosmetics. 'Greening' hijacked all environmental schemes and made it look as though it were enough merely to spruce up the visual appearance of urban areas. Moreover, an improved appearance is taken to be a green appearance. The policy was to disguise the city as countryside, which it is not, instead of finding beauty and vitality in the thing that it is. We are locked into a simplistic binary opposition of green and brown, where the objective of government policy is to turn brown into green, without basing this policy on substantial analysis of British cities. Instead of a serious approach, building on the best of urban life and aiming to improve safety and security, to manage cities effectively and to use housing demand to drive urban regeneration, we are offered a new colour scheme.

There are urgent questions before us concerning the quality of urban life: how do we reduce pollution, control crime, make good schools, health centres and libraries, create a fertile mix of parks and open spaces? But these have been turned around in government thinking so as to concern only the quality of the built environment, its design, appearance and aesthetics. For it is far easier to change the appearance of a place than to change the reality. But it is the reality that disturbs the people who have to live in it. Public investment in the 'greening' of cities has been substantial. The answer to all environmental questions concerning derelict land, poor industrial estates, new business parks and transport routes is to introduce a green element: to plant up the verges and reception areas around offices; to screen the motorways; to create wildlife habitats and to plant many thousands of trees. It is almost impossible to calculate the number of bushes and trees that are planted every year or how many of them actually survive to become established. (There is a hidden story to tell of how people destroy trees because of fears about views being blocked, foundations undermined, gardens being overshadowed, and so on.)

The appeal of a green environment has always been strong; but the policy of greening the city has watered down a much more radical approach than that traditionally associated with parks and gardens. It includes food production in cities, green buildings (with roof gardens, green cladding for temperature control, water collection and filtration), urban forests and waste-water recycling schemes. It involves rethinking the form of the city, in terms of an underlying green structure of rivers, green open space, walkways and cycling links, with habitat corridors rather than roads as the principal linkages. This more substantive ecological approach represents a fundamental challenge to the way we think about the future of cities.

The first part of this essay looks at the terms and language of the soft environmental programme and the way the ecologists have changed our taste in green spaces, so that the formal landscapes of Victorian parks are replaced by natural habitats. The second part discusses implications for the way we think about cities in future. Finally I attempt to bring environmental questions together with political and social issues.

The Uses of Greening

The idea of folding nature into the city expresses the frequently commented ambivalence within English culture towards cities and city life. This ambivalence is reflected within the political parties. The confusion about how to address urban and rural interests is not just apparent among the Labour and Conservative political elites. It is present in all our ways of envisaging environmental questions. Here values, ideas, views and opinions conflict and compete. Environmental issues in Britain range very widely: organic foods, recycling, countryside access, endangered species, road protests, consumer choices and now, defending countryside pursuits. After the turmoil in recent years over BSE, food production, out-of-town development and the future of the green belt; after the simultaneous demands both to protect the freedom of rural people (to eat beef on the bone, to drink unpasteurised milk, to go hunting) and to restrict the freedom of others (e.g. to roam), it is not surprising that the major political parties find it very difficult to articulate a consistent view of the future of city, country and the relationship between them. The attempt to present the issues in traditional party terms, as a clash between urban values and the threatened shires, looks increasingly implausible. Nor is it plausible to see the relation between country and city as a zero-sum game, in which one side wins and the other loses. Despite the hasty attempts by politicians to find favour by repositioning themselves, environmental interests seem to have left the political parties behind. Far from leading debates about the country and the city, the politicians are struggling to keep up with them.

Finding the Words

Part of the difficulty in finding clear ideological expression stems from the ambiguity of the language in which environmentalism is expressed. The meanings of 'environmental' (ecological concerns) and 'environment' (our surroundings) slip imperceptibly into each other. This elision prompts people to assimilate the natural environment to a beautiful and nurturing haven (the world of green), and the built environment to an ugly sphere of pollution (the world of brown).

The very vagueness of the term 'sustainability' is both an advantage and a curse. It is a young and open word, giving unity to an otherwise messy global debate. It is also a debased piece of jargon. Although vague, the idea of sustainability has nevertheless made its mark. It represents a shift in thinking which has to be reflected (however tokenistically) in every aspect of government urban policies. And we should not regret this. Sustainability marks out a space for consideration of environmental issues; on the other hand it does not advance our principal need, which is to introduce the social dimension into the totality of urban policy.

Government Greening

A Greening Unit was set up in the old Department of the Environment to keep tabs on greening initiatives and on the already developed work of the Groundwork Foundation and the Groundwork Trusts as well as the National Urban Forestry Unit. There are dozens of other governmental and voluntary groups delivering environmental projects. These organisations have been working in the fringes of towns and cities, reclaiming derelict land, for many years; more recently they have become part of the flotilla of agencies engaged in greening the cities.

Such agencies are a response to the widely held view that the countryside should be given aesthetic expression in cities. The most interesting recent manifestation of this view has been the establishment of 'community forests'. Just like the Victorian urban park, the community forest is a man-made environmental feature designed to emulate natural qualities of 'open space'; it is a new version of the 'green lungs' – a metaphor that exerts a powerful hold over the imagination, as we contrast the stifling air of the city with the freely flowing breezes of the countryside. But the motive behind this policy was less sanitary than aesthetic. 'Greening' was intended to improve and soften the aesthetic appearance of cities and to answer to the sense that the countryside represents, as environmental journalists claim, a primary value for Western society and will therefore always be the place to aspire to live.*

Green Taste

Modern aesthetics, and the environmental movement, demand that 'open space' should not be the manicured artifice of landscaped lawns, imitation Japanese pagodas and municipal beds, but wildlife habitats where real nature can flourish. The Countryside Commission, the Forestry Commission, the National Urban Forestry Unit, English Nature, and the Woodland Trust are all developing community forests as part of a plan to make forests as common in the twenty-first-century city as parks were in the cities of Victorian Britain. As the wildlife trusts announce: most people don't realise that they live within three miles of a community forest, whereas in fact 24 million people in England are said to live within three miles of such a forest. The replacement of the urban park by the urban forest shows how our expectations have changed. There are thousands of schemes for wildflower meadows, wood-pile habitats, ecological gardens and tree plantations, along with wider environmental messages about protecting wildlife and biodiversity, which encourage stewardship rather than domination over nature. But they have also killed off the old aesthetics of municipal horticulture, with its temporary bedding displays, its intense flashes of colour and its chemically reared and artificially bred hybrids which can hardly survive a season. However much you may criticise their cosy, kitschy homeliness, those old municipal gardens were also urban and public places, owned, admired and cherished by the residents, and making a genuinely urban contribution to the life of the city. By contrast, contemporary approaches to greening are in many ways antithetical to the idea of the city as a place for public life.

Greening is Regeneration

The government has explored greening as a way of enhancing the image of cities, their quality of life and, importantly, the confidence of those who live and generate business there. A green environment confirms a post-industrial city status. Greening is therefore linked to an economic strategy,

---

* See David Nicholson-Lord, *The Greening of the Cities* (London, 1987), p. 211.

which suggests that a pleasant suburban environment is one to which business will gravitate. Hence, greening is part of urban regeneration. It is part of the new city image.

Inward investment is central to every city's economic development strategy (particularly in the light of the apparent ease with which companies can move their operations around Europe and beyond). An attractive green environment is one of the 'soft' factors that could make a difference. From this perspective 'greening' is part of a cultural appeal (in the widest sense) which says, 'This looks like a good place to invest.' Green means not only clean, but also high-tech research and development, forward-looking science and office-landscaped parks. Brown means run-down, backward-looking industries and polluted sites. By association of ideas, nature becomes a symbol of our triumph over nature.

The Future of Cities

Wrapped up in the greening agenda, however, is a much more radical concept put forward by those who see future settlement patterns as made up of homes and gardens in a continuous suburbia. For example, the journalist David Nicholson-Lord, in his book *The Greening of the Cities*, puts forward a vision of low-density towns with small populations interspersed with wild areas, along with agricultural land and gardens. It is a vision that sees cities as burnt-out vestiges stranded between, 'a resurgent localism and an advancing globalism'.* From this perspective, past land-use categories are archaic and restrictive. Areas of inner city should be cleared and turned into a new 'urban countryside' and countryside areas could be opened to form new settlements with low-rise houses individually designed to catch the sun and recycle water, with space for environmental activities such as recycling and small-scale food growing. For many serious ecologists, the environmental future is suburban.

In looking back to the industrial-era Garden City ideal, this vision inadvertently meshes with much more recent analysis of the post-industrial city-regions, in which the model of the compact city insulated by green-belt land is superseded by a model of a more dispersed city-region with many centres, and a mix of housing, agricultural, industrial, research and development and recreational land uses. The accepted view of the densely populated and compact European city is being challenged by a new city-

---

* David Nicholson-Lord, *The Greening of the Cities* (London, 1987), p. 212.

regionalism. Functions of work, living, shopping and socialising are disaggregated and allocated to different kinds of urban centre across a wider city-region. These ideas are being given serious consideration in places like the Netherlands, where the distinction between agribusiness and new service industries is becoming harder to align with any distinction between country and city locations.

By contrast the concept of the 'urban village' has been proposed in order to emphasise the distinctive character of urban centres. London and other cities, Sheffield for example, are often described as a series of urban villages. The phrase has become a clarion call for a coalition of planners and architects who wish to express a new form of urbanism and an optimistic view of the urban future. The notion of the urban village is one of the few models we have for discussing high-density development. It proposes that we should remake the city as a series of villages and reject the anonymous and nihilistic projects of large-scale urban planning – projects which make no real room for people and their needs. The urban village concept counters the idea of a dispersed, suburban solution to future urban development and retains the value of high-density and mixed use. But is it really necessary to return to past rural settlement forms in order to acquire hope for the future of cities? The Greenwich millennium village on the site of the millennium Dome, to be planned by Ralph Erskine, will be a high-profile model of a new urban settlement. Plans to date show that it will combine advanced ecological design in house-building surrounded by natural environments, with elements of an old town street pattern to create possibilities for social contact. It combines serious ecological design with older European principles of urban form, drawn in particular from Alvar Aalto's 'organically' formed modernism.

Cities by Default?

The recent decision by government to contain as much new housing as possible within cities does not reflect any new confidence that cities will meet the needs and aspirations of people, or that new housing fits into a larger vision of a transformed urban life. Instead, it seems that the overriding determination is to protect the countryside. Again this betrays a lack of faith in urbanisation. To compensate the urban population for the grief of living in cities a number of nature substitutes will be created – many of them with Lottery funds. Community forests are only the start. Soon 'millennium greens', an initiative led by the Countryside Commission, will take shape; so will urban wetlands, a series of canal restorations and the substantial programme for rehabilitating derelict land run by the Groundwork Foundation, under their Lottery programme 'Changing Places'. Sustrans is laying a national network of cycle paths and a number of environmental interpretation centres are being built in order to manage the urban use of countryside areas. The belief that cities can only benefit from 'greening' runs deep.

The urban environmental programme (made up of all these separate initiatives) is of course very welcome, and in many ways the processes of community involvement and practice in delivering schemes on the ground are well ahead of traditional planning procedures, and help to shape more desirable neighbourhoods. Yet they do not engage with any coherent view of the urban future. Can it really be argued that if nature were more obviously part of urban life people would not wish to escape the city? It must be a fantasy to believe that if cities were greener, the countryside could be left alone: protected, unchanged and unchanging.

Furthermore, it is not clear where the greening project ends. Despite the energy, commitment and Lottery money, most campaigners argue that there is still far to go. Where is the end point? The implicit aim of nature conservation is, it seems, an urban wildlife habitat at every street corner and 'woods on your doorstep' (the name of the Woodland Trust's £13 million project). There is an implicit vision that becomes clearer when all these environmental projects are put together: urban areas become *de facto* conservation sites for urban wildlife. Can this really be the future for cities and for urban life? Is this really what people want for their cities?

Changing the Quality of Urban Life

Tony Travers, a specialist in local government at the London School of Economics and commentator on London, puts forward a rather pessimistic view in his prognosis that it is unlikely that the real factors that make up the quality of urban life will be improved in the medium term. There is, therefore, no alternative to the continuing drift of people into the countryside.* The discussion of urban quality must now consider these more difficult questions. Environmental improvement is important, but it can never assuage the fundamental anxieties over schools, hospitals and public transport, over crime and the management of cities. People move to the countryside in order to escape the dysfunction of the towns. Their fears

* Tony Travers, 'Quality Control', *Society Guardian*, 11 March 1998.

and aspirations need to be properly understood, rather than truncated into a desire that cities should look like suburbs, while being nothing of the kind. In this context, environmental programmes may seem gestural, almost desperate. Yet 'greening' at times seems like the only game in town.

On the other hand, Michael Breheny has suggested that green suburban environments are in fact successful in attracting residents.* We need a better understanding of what greening represents – health, privacy, and nature. The current problems of some 1960s and 1970s housing estates, inspired by or adapted from Le Corbusier's 'towers in the park', are not just down to the towers. The parks don't help either. On very many estates residents and estate managers are equally hostile to those wastes of sterile, trampled grass that separate, position and frame the tower blocks and isolate buildings from each other and from estate facilities. The original vision of space, light and surrounding green hardly survives the first downpour or gale. And the swathes of roughly mown grass extend the time it takes to walk to everyday amenities and further isolate people from the symbols and habits of social life.

Who could oppose tree-planting? Most people would agree that it is an unqualified good. Yet trees are constantly ripped out, chopped down or vandalised, often because environmental schemes have not taken full account of how people wish to use the places where the trees are planted. Trees planted on traditional informal football areas, which obstruct the view of the lake, or which obscure vulnerable entrance ways can quickly be destroyed by people who see them as a nuisance or a threat. Similarly, large private gardens on estates (again judged to be an unqualified good) can be too much for tenants to maintain. Abandoned, they quickly become an eyesore. Poor parks and unmanaged playing fields become a source of fear and misery for residents living nearby. There are many such examples of urban greening that detract rather than add to the quality of the environment.

Green Planning

Of course, greening embodies a number of very positive aspirations. Energetic environmental projects can involve people directly with projects in their localities and preserve local habitats. Thus, while large-scale habitats are disappearing from countryside areas, wildlife is being reintroduced in

.* Michael Breheny, unpublished paper delivered to the Town and Country Planning Association, 1997.

the towns. Such schemes have in positive ways often usurped the more formal and distanced traditional planning processes. The new environmental project officers, parks rangers, urban foresters and tree wardens make up an intermediary profession dedicated to the management of the urban environment.

Yet in Britain the processes of urban development remain fundamentally divided among professional disciplines. The duality between architect and landscape architect reflects a distinction between 'hard' buildings and 'soft' (usually green) landscapes. But where are the professions that build city places that are neither buildings nor open space, but whole neighbourhoods? The making of other urban spaces – squares, walking routes, canalsides – has been left, for better or worse, to the public artist. What do planners or city-builders want to achieve? The future for city life will depend upon much more than getting the right balance between green and brown.

In 1991 a 'Green Strategy' was written by the landscape specialist Tom Turner for the London Planning Advisory Committee. This envisaged layers of networks for pedestrians, cyclists and wildlife. Parkways or greenways imply a network of urban circulation routes that are not built for the car. Turner rejects the idea that space in cities is divided between green and brown and suggests extending the colour chart to comprehend the many varieties of urban space. He comes close to making more social arguments for different types of space, and reiterates the great American urban designer Kevin Lynch's view, that there are pitifully few types of green spaces in cities and that much more attention should be given to creating a variety of park, garden or playground places with multiple uses. Once stated, it is obvious that the public use of space is more important than whether the space is green or not. This was a starting point in 1994 for the Comedia/Demos study of urban parks, *Park Life*.

Environmental Projects and Social Renewal

The history of public parks is inseparable from the history of the development of modern cities. It is a history of the social life of cities. Urban parks were considered as social places. The eighteenth-century commercial pleasure gardens, such as Vauxhall Gardens – lit up for evening music, dancing and eating – perhaps found a later hidden echo in the pleasure grounds of post-war British seaside resorts and ultimately in theme parks. But it was the nineteenth-century Victorian municipal city park, rooted in a nonconformist culture of moral improvement, that defined a model of the urban public park that has endured throughout most of this century. A great number of urban parks that now exist were established by municipalities in response to the growth of the industrial cities from the 1840s. They encapsulated many of the social concerns of Victorian politics, particularly in engineering the infrastructure for public health, and the social life of the Victorian town.

The People's Parks

However partial and flawed, the idea of the public park or public walk was a recognition of an urban public. People's parks were created in an attempt to provide alternatives to activities which were socially disapproved; they were also intended to improve public health and were in some instances provided as concessions in return for the enclosure of common land. Above all, public parks were an expression of a growing sense of the urban public as a body politic. As cities grew in size and population, public parks were built as places that symbolised civic culture and aspiration.

Victorian parks were lavishly designed, much like the major engineering projects of the time. The landscape construction often provided serious technical challenges requiring new expertise and knowledge. They were showcases for plant species collected during the management of the Empire, and for monuments symbolising the Empire's grandeur and power. Above all, however, they were sites for social display. Park design created criss-crossing walks that allowed people, often family groups, to pass each other several times. They were places where city residents could see themselves – a kind of mirror before which society composed itself and made up its face. The public park was a metaphor for the Victorian idea of a civilised society.*

The Crisis of Public Parks

Park Life showed that, as the organisation and dynamics of cities and the patterns of people's lives had changed, so had the role and use of urban parks. A century and a half after the public parks movement began, it was clear that many urban parks were in poor shape. They no longer served a captive population living and working to a common regimented timetable

* Hilary Taylor, *Age and Order: the Public Park as a Metaphor for Civilised Society*, Park Life working paper no. 10 (London, 1995).

and crowding into the park in their many thousands on public holidays. Instead they were part of an array of attractions for an increasingly mobile public. Parks are no longer the single obsession of an emerging civic structure, but are just one amongst the many responsibilities of the modern municipality.

Most importantly, the *Park Life* research showed the social value of good parks, and the largely unrecognised benefits they confer on city localities. It is the social rather than the ecological values of these green spaces that was highlighted. These social values still reflect the nature of the park as a place of social display. They remain open public places which strangers share. They are common ground where competing groups have to find ways of coexisting. Parks are valued as places of freedom where playing, resting, running and sitting in public are all normal. Public parks can add to the mix of moods and pace of a city. For example, in the intense urban environment of the centre of Camberwell, it was noted that many people crossing Camberwell Green slowed their walking pace as they entered the Green. Taking children to the park is the most common reason for a park visit. Parks are everyday places and also one of the social places of childhood. It is precisely because parks are social places and not just wildlife habitats that they need good management. A good public park works because it is a social place, not just a green one.

The social geographer Jackie Burgess and her colleagues have shown how strong are the memories we retain of childhood play in natural green places, and how these represent some of the most powerful recollections of childhood.[*] Yet many programmes for the greening of cities do not make the freedom of children to use wildlife spaces an explicit priority. Whilst the benefits of environmental education are stressed, the value of open green spaces as places for play mostly takes second place.

The startling lack of consideration of environments for children is made clear in research by Wendy Titman on the state of most school grounds.[†] This is important, not just because children can spend long hours in bleak tarmac-coated yards or on the windswept plains of school fields, but because they understand very clearly what is conveyed by the poor

---

[*] Jacqueline Burgess, Carolyn Harrison and Melanie Limb, 'People, Parks and the Urban Green: A Study of Popular Meanings and Values of Open Spaces in the City', *Urban Studies* 25 (1988), pp. 455–73.

[†] Wendy Titman, 'Special Places, Special People: the Hidden Curriculum of School Grounds', in *Learning Through Landscapes* (Surrey, 1994).

treatment of urban environments. Titman describes how children read the signs and symbols – the semiotics – of an environment, so as to understand the identity of the places where they are, and thereby to acquire a sense of their own identity as belonging there. Children are subjected to wider cultural and educational appeals to respect wildlife and protect endangered species. But these appeals conflict directly with the messages of neglect, vandalism and mistreatment apparent in the adult world that surrounds them.

As Colin Ward argued in *The Child in the City*,* understanding the place of children is not about turning cities into risk-free places full of plastic primary-coloured play equipment; it is about acknowledging that children are part of urban societies and should be able to see themselves reflected there. This goes beyond an occasional corralling of children to carry out tree-planting in the vain hope that if they plant trees they will also look after them. We must understand urban environments as places that shape children's identity and their sense of the way the greater society works. As Ken Worpole has shown, children's play helps to form basic sensibilities, such as the qualities of trust, fairness, justice and loyalty that make civil society and life in cities work.†

To allow children greater freedom to roam we must make better and safer public places, not necessarily green spaces. We must increase the numbers of people *managing* public space – park rangers, concierges, conductors on public transport. This in turn will increase the use of public spaces and further enhance their safety. Only when childen can grow up in cities can their parents happily reside there. If we do not manage public space so that children are an organic part of it, the flight from the cities will inevitably continue. And the people who flee will be the ones with families, with a commitment to the future, and with the sense of responsibility that comes from the effort to bring up children – in other words, the very people of which the city stands most in need.

This is not to say that ecological and social thinking must always conflict: on the contrary. The regeneration work currently being carried out around Deptford Creek in south-east London, takes advantage of the creek itself and its unique ecological value in order to revitalise the social amenities. Archaeological significance, relevance to local history and the opportunity

* Colin Ward, *The Child in the City* (London, 1990).
† Ken Worpole, *Nothing to Fear? Trust and Respect in Urban Communities*, working paper no. 2, Comedia, in association with Demos (London, 1997).

that the creek presents as a dangerous recreational amenity (it has very rapid tidal flows) make for an urban regeneration in which nature is not only an integral part but something more real and exciting than a veneer of green.

To give primary value either to the aesthetics and visual appeal of urban environments or to the ecological worth of plants and trees is to lose sight of how people use, understand, value or fear urban living. The introduction of elements of the natural environment into cities has been perhaps the strongest symbol we have of an optimistic view of an urban future and a sense of balance between the country and the city. Yet real improvements to the quality of urban life depend upon far more than cosmetic changes. Most of all they depend upon respect for the town, as an environment made by people for the uses of people.

Several local authorities are now directly confronting questions about the future of urban living and how to retain and attract what used to be called 'middle-class' residents. Studies are now being commissioned of people's aspirations and of the factors which push them out of cities. The answer to inner-city deprivation, it is increasingly recognised, is not to build more and more social housing, but to build middle-income housing, so as to attract people who will make demands on city managers and fight for better health care, policing and schools. This is surely the best way to ensure that urbanisation in the twenty-first century will finally move beyond the soft environmental agenda, and concern itself with reviving the town as it is and should be, rather than decorating the town as it shouldn't be with baubles of distracting greenery.

Bibliography

Cranz, Galen, *The Politics of Park Design: A History of Urban Parks in America* (Cambridge, MA and London, 1982).

Lefebrve, Henri, *The Production of Space*, trans. Donald Nicholson-Smith (Oxford and Cambridge, 1991).

Lynch, Kevin, *City Sense and City Design: The Writings and Projects of Kevin Lynch*, ed. T. Bannerjee and M. Southworth (Cambridge, MA and London, 1990).

Vidler, Anthony, *The Architectural Uncanny: Essays in the Modern Unhomely* (Cambridge, MA and London, 1992).

Ward, Colin, *The Child in the City* (London, 1990).

23. *The Life in New Towns*
Tim Mars

'The last days of my childhood were also the last days of the village,' writes Laurie Lee in *Cider with Rosie*, his autobiographical evocation of growing up in the Gloucestershire countryside. He goes on:

I belonged to that generation which saw, by chance, the end of a thousand years' life.

The change came late to our Cotswold valley, didn't really show itself till the late 1920s; I was 12 by then, but during that handful of years I witnessed the whole thing happen.

Myself, my family, my generation, were born in a world of silence; a world of . . . villages like ships in the empty landscapes and the long walking distances between them; of white narrow roads, rutted by hooves and cartwheels, innocent of oil or petrol, down which people passed rarely, and almost never for pleasure, and the horse was the fastest thing moving . . .

Then . . . the brass-lamped motor-car came coughing up the road, followed by the clamorous charabanc; the solid-tyred bus climbed the dusty hills and more people came and went . . . Then scarlet motor-bikes, the size of five-barred gates, began to appear in the village, on which our youths roared like rockets up the two-minute hills, then spent weeks making repairs and adjustments.

Soon the village would break, dissolve, and scatter . . . It had a few years left, the last of its thousand, and they passed almost without our knowing. They passed quickly, painlessly, in motor-bike jaunts, in the shadows of the new picture-palace, in quick trips to Gloucester (once a foreign city) to gape at the jazzy shops.

Time squared itself, and the village shrank, and distances crept nearer. The sun and moon, which once rose from our hill, rose from London now in the east . . . The horses had died; few people kept pigs any more but spent their spare time buried in engines. The flutes and cornets, the gramophones with horns, the wind harps were thrown away – now wireless aerials searched the electric sky for the music of the Savoy Orpheans.*

Around the time Lee was ruing the impact of the internal combustion engine, radio and the cinema on the village of Slad, on the other side of the Atlantic the American architect Frank Lloyd Wright was excited by the potential of these technologies:

> In the 1920s Wright saw that the motor car and electricity would loosen cities, enabling them to spread out into the countryside. Here was an opportunity to use new technology to take people back to the land, for them to reclaim their native birthright.
>
> For him the basic living unit was to be the homestead, with factories, schools and stores scattered across a fundamentally agricultural landscape. The new technologies would emancipate Americans from ties with the city: each citizen would have 'all forms of production, distribution, self-improvement, enjoyment within the radius of, say, 10 to 20 miles of his own home'.†

Wright called this vision of a disurbanised – or 'rurbanised' – future Broadacres City. It was not to be an individualistic free-for-all, however, but planned and controlled aesthetically. What of course has come about, in the US and to a lesser extent in Britain, has been mostly unplanned and uncontrolled, more suburban than rurban, more Brookside than Broadacres. But Wright had correctly anticipated the way new technologies would revolutionise the relationship between town and country, blurring the distinction between the two.

If the nineteenth century was characterised by a tidal wave of people flooding into the cities, in the twentieth century the tide has been going out – first into the suburbs and then, when the green belt and other postwar planning measures put a limit on the natural outward expansion of cities, leapfrogging into the countryside beyond. And it's not over yet. Planned or unplanned, promoted or discouraged, people continue to quit the centre for the suburb, the suburb for the countryside.

* Laurie Lee, *Cider with Rosie* (London, 1959); paperback edn (1990), pp. 187–9.
† Michael Breheny, 'Centrists, Decentrists and Compromisers: Views on the Future of Urban Form', in Mike Jenks, Elizabeth Burton and Katie Williams (eds), *The Compact City: A Sustainable Urban Form?* (London, 1996), p. 17.

Ours may be the century of the suburb, but suburbia remains something we're deeply ambivalent about – ashamed of, even. We admire formal architectural set-piece cities, we adore quintessential villages that look as though they grew organically out of the landscape. We would be happier if the world was made up exclusively of cities like Jane Jacobs's 1950s New York* – bustling, urban, vital – and villages like Laurie Lee's Slad 'where life moved as slowly as honey from a spoon and was as sweet and delicious'.† Sadly, prosaically, our century's contribution has been mostly the stuff in between.

In the century of the suburb, however, the intelligentsia have for the most part been elsewhere, conducting a passionate affair with the city and all things urban – from Georgian London to Renaissance Rome, from the towers of San Giminiano to the skyscrapers of New York. Even Victorian cities, excoriated as 'ulcers on the very face of our beautiful island' by Garden City propagandist Ebenezer Howard,‡ have been re-evaluated, and rejection has been replaced by respect. This reverence for the urban past has gone hand in hand with a raft of schemes for new cities or the comprehensive rebuilding of existing ones.

So, while Wright wanted to plan for the car and the countryside, most architects and planners were dreaming of monorails and megastructures. The Italian futurist architect Antonio Sant'Elia set the ball rolling in 1914 with his seductive drawings of 'Città Nuova' – vast, stepped skyscrapers straddling multi-level transportation corridors. In the same year (1935) that Wright published *Broadacres City: a New Community Plan*, Le Corbusier proposed *La Ville radieuse* – a city of gigantic tower blocks standing in acres of parkland.

Since the war, suburbanisation and counter-urbanisation have continued apace, but there has been no let-up in urbanist schemes. The 1960s produced Archigram's plug-in city, while in 1971 the *Architectural Review* proposed 'Civilia', an ingenious collage of photographs of exemplary modern buildings crammed together to form a high-density monorail-served city. But perhaps the high point of urbanist fantasy came in 1973 with Dantzig and Saaty's 'compact city' – a two-mile-wide, eight-level tapering cylinder housing a quarter of a million people in climate-controlled comfort – a scheme which makes even Le Corbusier's radiant city seem a trifle suburban.

* Jane Jacobs, *The Death and Life of Great American Cities* (New York, 1961).
† Blurb to the 1990 edition of *Cider with Rosie*.
‡ Quoted in Jenks et al. *The Compact City*, p. 16.

Less grandiose and certainly less well known than any of these was Pooleyville. In the late 1950s Fred Pooley, Buckinghamshire's county architect, dreamed of building a new town between Newport Pagnell and Bletchley. He produced a speculative scheme for a city (instantly dubbed 'Pooleyville') which was modernist, impeccably urban and straight out of Sant'Elia – stepped 'cluster blocks' interconnected by a figure-of-eight monorail.

Nothing came of this scheme. But in 1967, partly thanks to Pooley's energetic lobbying, a much enlarged site – incorporating Bletchley, Stony Stratford and Wolverton, and engulfing eleven villages – was designated for the biggest and most ambitious of the post-war new towns: Milton Keynes. It was also to be the site of a pitched battle between urban and suburban tendencies and a salutary lesson on the limitations of romantic urbanism.

As conceived by its master planners, Llewelyn-Davies Weeks Forestier-Walker and Bor, MK was to be the antithesis of Pooleyville: low density, low rise, premised on high levels of car ownership – a suburban realm loosely tied together by a fishnet of roads thrown almost casually across the landscape.

If Pooley was the officious uncle, the real father of Milton Keynes was Melvin Webber, American sociologist and 'urban society' consultant to the original planning team. Based on his observation of greater Los Angeles, Webber had developed an analysis of late twentieth-century urbanism that eschewed the concept and imagery associated with the word 'city' altogether. He coined the phrase 'non-place urban realm' to describe a region loosely bound together by cars and telephones rather than defined by space and place on the traditional urban model.* Mobility and communications, he argued, had replaced propinquity and conversation.

If Broadacres City was rural, the non-place urban realm was defiantly, endlessly, relentlessly, unapologetically suburban. And under Webber's guidance, Milton Keynes was to be Little-Los-Angeles-in-Bucks. Pooleyville gave way to Webbertown, urban fantasy made way for suburban reality.

Or so it seemed. But the team charged with implementing the master plan had other ideas:

Derek Walker, its first chief architect and planner, promptly set out to

* Melvin Webber, 'The Urban Place and Non-Place Urban Realm', in L. Wingo (ed.) *Cities and Space* (Baltimore, Maryland, 1963).

build a scaled-down version of the sort of city – urban, visual, monumental – that Webber had shown to be both obsolete and irrelevant . . . Bequeathed a Los Angeles-inspired plan, Walker and his team of Europhile urbanists turned their backs on California and looked to . . . the leafy squares of London, the axial boulevards of Paris, the canals, pedestrian squares and alleys of Venice, Milan's Galleria, the crescents of Bath, the quadrangles of Oxford and Cambridge. Respectable cities, unimpeachably urban places.*

The message was rammed home at every turn: straight streets, terraced housing, gridiron layouts, squares, crescents – urban imagery was plundered from just about everywhere, even if the architectural language was uncompromisingly modern: flat roofs, horizontal bands of windows, steel cladding – no retro-urban here!

The urban aspirations of Walker's team are most apparent in the centre, where the street naming is a bewildering palimpsest of prehistoric Britain, Haussmann's Paris, medieval cities and modern Manhattan. The three principal streets running east–west – broad straight dual carriageways lined with London plane trees – are called 'boulevards' and named Avebury, Silbury and (aligned on the sunrise) Midsummer. The principal cross streets which run at right angles – also broad straight dual carriageways lined with London plane trees – are, however, *not* boulevards but 'gates' (Witan Gate, Saxon Gate and Secklow Gate)† evoking the city walls which never enclosed this bit of Buckinghamshire, but suggestive of cities like Gloucester where the Roman walls are gone but the street names (Northgate, Eastgate, etc.) remain.

As if this wasn't a rich enough stew of urban and historical references, the gridiron of subsidiary cross streets is numbered (North Fourteenth Street, Upper Second Street, Lower Ninth Street, South Seventh Street, etc.) in a way that conflates Manhattan street numbering (West 14th Street, East 57th Street, etc.) and districts (Lower East Side, Upper West Side). Unlike the suburban sprawl of Los Angeles, the skyscrapers of New York are a widely admired twentieth-century image of urbanity. Given the chance, no doubt the designers of central Milton Keynes would have loved to adorn it with tall towers, but high-rise buildings are the product of

* Tim Mars, 'Little Los Angeles in Bucks', *Architects' Journal*, 15 April 1992, pp. 22–6.
† The 'witan' or 'witenagemot' was the assembly of wise men which advised the king in Anglo-Saxon times.

demand or subsidy, high rental yields and acute land shortage – none of which pertained to a field in deepest Buckinghamshire in the 1970s. But nor did they obtain in New York in the 1870s, so there's hope yet – and who, in the 1970s, would have predicted office skyscrapers on the Isle of Dogs? So central Milton Keynes is 'skyscraper savvy' with a gridiron plan like the one which worked so well for New York and some Manhattan flavouring for good measure.

But despite these strenuous efforts, central Milton Keynes as built – a jumble of buildings of all shapes, sizes and styles, each girdled by its own car park – still feels more like an out-of-town retail and business park (albeit one with an unusually orthogonal road system) than a city centre. Even at its core, Milton Keynes remains stubbornly suburban – still more Webbertown then Walkerpolis.

Of which Derek Walker seems all too well aware. His book on the architecture and planning of Milton Keynes positively creaks with urbanist anxiety. Lavishly illustrated with photographs of Georgian London, Renaissance Rome, Haussmann's Paris, contemporary Manhattan – Los Angeles doesn't get a look-in – the very first chapter asks 'Will Milton Keynes feel urban?' After acres of sophistry around the definition of the word 'urban', Walker finally admits: 'If we look to our experience of existing cities as our only criterion of "urbanity" then we will in some ways be disappointed in MK.' But he ends triumphantly by asserting: 'If, instead, we think of the city in terms of performance, we can see that MK compares well, or can compare well, with the compound image which is our vision of the cities of the past; our view of urbanity.'* But does 'performance' have anything at all to do with 'image' or 'urbanity' in the first place?

Webber didn't think so and nor did Milton Keynes's residents. In 1979 Milton Keynes Development Corporation, beset with urbanist anxieties about the 'failure' of MK, commissioned the School for Advanced Urban Studies to interview residents to see what *they* thought. The results were wholly unexpected. Residents generally did not consider MK a 'city', but this was regarded as a *good* thing. Rather, they conceived it as 'a series of villages with bypasses clustered around "the city" (Central Milton Keynes)'; nevertheless they 'use the whole area very extensively'.† Not for the residents compound images of urbanity, visions of cities of the past, but

---

* Derek Walker, *The Architecture and Planning of Milton Keynes* (London, 1982), p. 17.

† Jeff Bishop, *Milton Keynes – the Best of Both Worlds?*, Occasional Paper 24, School for Advanced Urban Studies, Bristol (1986), pp. 100–4.

performance; and in their view, MK performed pretty well, not as a city but as an urban realm: 'It was clear that the very elements which we had set out to study because it was felt that they had gone wrong were precisely those which the residents felt had gone right – and also felt strongly should be retained.'*

Similarly, residents conceived of MK as 'somewhere only a little better than usual; a normal landscape dotted with villages which have managed to appear without spoiling the countryside, complete with bypasses'.† This was particularly galling in that the residential areas in MK were deliberately not called 'villages' or even 'neighbourhoods' but 'grid squares' – a neutral, technical term for parcels of land carved up by the grid roads.

Not Rome, Paris, Bloomsbury or Bath, then, but a landscape of bypassed villages. In this the residents were surprisingly astute. For while Derek Walker cites the urbanist's bible, Kevin Lynch's *The Image of the City*,‡ as one of his inspirations, Lynch later came to resent what he considered the dangerous simplification of the ideas set out in that book – and in particular the obsession with a single image of good development: the dense, urban city. His last book ends with an alternative model which has uncanny echoes of MK:

Imagine an urban countryside, a highly varied but humanised landscape. It is neither urban nor rural in the old sense, since house, workplaces and places of assembly are set among trees, farms, and streams. Within that extensive countryside, there is a network of small, intensive urban centres. This countryside is as functionally intricate and interdependent as any contemporary city.

A major grid of public transport, within a broad right-of-way, covers the entire region. It is distorted to accommodate natural features, to avoid the wild lands on the one hand and to serve the centres on the other. Yet it is regular and continuous. This grid, like the centres, the wilderness, and certain symbolic sites, is permanently located. Within it run the major conduits which carry people, goods, messages, wastes and energy.§

The only false note here – the triumph of hope over experience, perhaps –

* Ibid., p. 100.
† Ibid., p. 147.
‡ Kevin Lynch, *The Image of the City* (Boston, MA, 1960).
§ Kevin Lynch, *A Theory of Good City Form* (Cambridge, MA, 1981).

is the idea of an urban countryside tied together by *public* transport. (In the case of Milton Keynes, no fewer than forty-six public transport systems were trawled through when the original plan was drawn up. All manner of gee-whiz high-tech transit technologies were evaluated before it was concluded that the best bet remained the bus. Not *quite* in the same league as a monorail, image-wise. Not really what Pooley had in mind.)

Broadacres City is premised on the car. It's the car and the phone that brought about the non-place urban realm of southern California. The urban countryside that many of us inhabit today is inconceivable without the car, increasingly in symbiosis with the intercity train. The process which started in the last years of the nineteenth century with the extension of the Metropolitan Line into Hertfordshire and Buckinghamshire and the concomitant development of new suburban settlements there, has continued apace in the years since the Second World War, spreading ever further from the major conurbations, with the car journey to the intercity station increasingly superseding the walk to the Underground station.

The tentacles of this post-war intercity 'metroland' now stretch across large parts of England – as can be seen by the increasing size of the car parks around well-connected stations and the glittering sea of cars parked there from morning to night.

MK, too, is part of this new metroland – another blow to its aspirations. For if cities are urban, cities are also self-contained: they have boundaries beyond which is the country (or so urbanists like to think). Early on the development corporation, set up to build a self-contained, self-sufficient community, had had to come to terms with the not altogether surprising fact that people were commuting *in* to Milton Keynes to take the jobs it had created, while people living in the houses it had built were commuting *out* to jobs elsewhere – a process accelerated by the opening of Milton Keynes Central station with its good intercity links to London and Birmingham. Furthermore:

studies of search patterns amongst private purchasers showed that people generally surveyed a large swathe of the country north of London within which MK was merely another option. Add to this the fact that most MK houses were not advertised as being in MK but in Linford or Heelands (etc) [and it confirms] a 'village focused' perception of MK as a whole.*

* Bishop, *Milton Keynes*, pp. 146–7.

274

Thus the grid square 'villages' of Heelands and Linford within the designated area are, from the point of view of the car-borne commuter, interchangeable with the villages of Haversham and Leckhampstead just outside – differing only in distance to station and motorway junction. In other words, Milton Keynes is part of a much larger urban realm pulled between the twin poles of London and Birmingham. Game, set and match to Melvin Webber.

Since Frank Lloyd Wright saw the way the tide of history was flowing, the centrifugal forces driving urbanisation outwards have intensified. The motor car may have lost its brass lamps but it has gained speed, reliability and the flexibility to carry or tow almost anything. And, for good or ill, it has also become infinitely more affordable to own and run. The telephone has spawned the fax and, married to the personal computer, brought e-mail and the Internet into being. Television aerials and satellite dishes now search the electric sky, while the gramophone has gained a new lease of life as the compact disc player. Refrigerators and freezers, washing machines and tumble driers have further loosened ties with the town and its facilities.

None of these technologies and the transformations they have brought about are the prerequisite of the country, but neither are they exclusive to the town. Of themselves they are neutral, but they erode the advantages of living in town.

In Laurie Lee's childhood, the citizens of Gloucester enjoyed a range of opportunities for work and leisure, shopping and education incomparably greater than the villagers of Slad or the townsfolk of Stroud. Today the reverse is the case: the denizens of Gloucester live circumscribed lives compared with Slad's affluent mobile new settlers – or anyone else living in the urban countryside around Stroud.

The Slad valley is one of five which radiate from Stroud. Together these valleys form a highly varied but humanised landscape, neither urban nor rural in the old sense, with open commons on the hilltops, houses hugging the slopes, and mills and industrial buildings scattered along the valley floors. This particular pattern of urbanisation is the product of the woollen industry in the seventeenth and eighteenth centuries, when the area was the richest in the country outside London and Bristol.

Within this extensive countryside there is a network of small, intensive urban centres, among them Nailsworth, Stonehouse and Stroud. Stroud today is encircled by three superstores and a DIY warehouse. The town which once boasted two picture palaces today has no cinema, but there's a multiplex seven miles away on the outskirts of Gloucester. Gloucester's shops are today more shabby than jazzy, but a new regional shopping centre, Cribbs Causeway, has recently opened twenty-five miles away on the outskirts of Bristol.

This countryside is as functionally intricate and interdependent as any contemporary city. While the railway line between Gloucester and Swindon provides a theoretical backbone, the car is what ties it all together. Factories, offices, schools and stores are scattered across a landscape which is, however, no longer fundamentally agricultural. Within a radius of ten to twenty miles – a distance which takes in Gloucester, Cheltenham and Cirencester – there are many forms of production, distribution, self-improvement, enjoyment. A little further away are Swindon, Bristol and Bath.

At the very point when the sort of urban countryside represented by the Stroud valleys or Milton Keynes – and there are many other examples which could be chosen – would seem to have triumphed, however, there has come a new urban backlash. To the social and aesthetic case for urbanism has been added the new post-Rio moral imperative of 'sustainability'. And from a sustainable perspective, the dispersed, low-density, car-dependent urban realm is anathema while the high-density, public-transport-friendly city is looked to for salvation. 'Cities are good for us,' proclaims Harley Sherlock,[*] and the Council for the Protection of Rural England (and just about everyone else) agrees:

> Cities are the most environmentally sustainable way of housing people and providing factories, offices, shops, leisure facilities and many of the other things society wants. Cities can absorb development better than the countryside. They use · less resources, save land, reduce car dependence and can improve the local environment.[†]

And not just cities, but *compact* cities – only this time it's not some gigantic power-station cooling tower sitting in open countryside but the intensification of existing cities. New development, it is argued, should be concentrated in existing cities and densities raised.

If sustainability is the new religion, then planners are its priests and the

[*] Harley Sherlock, *Cities Are Good For Us* (London, 1991).
[†] Tony Burton and Lilli Matson, 'Urban Footprints: Making Best Use of Urban Land and Resources – a Rural Perspective', in Jenks et al., *The Compact City*, p. 299.

compact city the new Jerusalem. It sounds plausible and seductive – the latest and sexiest model from the school of romantic urbanism. But it is a chimera – a fact that won't stop us expending vast amounts of time, effort and money in a vain attempt to bring it about.

In environmental terms cities – even compact ones – are hardly benign. As the Council for the Protection of Rural England itself acknowledges:

> Cities place an enormous burden on the countryside. They consume land, demand water and construction aggregates, produce waste and provide a focus for commuters.[*]

So the argument would appear to run: cities are environmentally extremely damaging but the alternatives are even worse.

But, heeding Michael Breheny's warning of 'the probable impossibility of halting urban decentralisation, whether it is regarded as desirable or not',[†] are the alternatives really so bad? Certainly cities would seem to score over urban countryside in terms of reducing the use of the car and maximising the use of public transport. But even here, as Michael Breheny has demonstrated, the gains are relatively trivial. Breheny has modelled the total transport energy consumption of Great Britain in 1991, and then simulated the equivalent energy consumption if *no* urban decentralisation had occurred in the thirty years since 1961. The result is an energy saving per week nationally of 2.5 per cent. As Breheny observes: 'This is hardly the scale of saving politicians are expecting when asking the planning system to take the lead in confronting the sustainability problem.'[‡]

The argument for high densities and urban compaction is even harder to sustain in other areas. Low-density developments allow more space for trees which, as well as providing valuable habitat, 'embody' carbon and clean and purify the air. Greater space and larger gardens mean more opportunity for people to grow their own food, make use of rainwater (via waterbutts, etc.), and compost kitchen and garden wastes – which is vital if we are to reduce the methane generated by landfill sites. There is also much greater scope for burning wood to provide heat and hot water.

But the environmental balance tilts dramatically in favour of an urban

---

[*] Burton and Matson, 'Urban Footprints', p. 298.

[†] Breheny, 'Centrists, Decentrists', p. 30.

[‡] Michael Breheny, 'Compact Cities and Transport Energy Consumption', *Transactions of the Institute of British Geographers* 20 (1) (1995), pp. 81–101.

countryside pattern of development if we contemplate building one from scratch. It then becomes possible to conceive a layout which starts with the convenience of pedestrians and cyclists before providing for motorised modes. Adequate space would enable reed-bed sewage treatment and other benign aquatic technologies to be implemented. All buildings could be constructed to the highest insulation standards and so oriented and designed as to be almost entirely heated by the sun. The maximum use of timber-frame construction – only possible in relatively low-rise applications – would enable such a settlement to 'store' large quantities of carbon. And the list goes on.

But while the compact sustainable city, surrounded by 'a beautiful and living countryside', is the flavour of the moment, new settlements are profoundly unfashionable – even as we contemplate projections of unprecedented rates of household formation over the next few years. Yet in the 1960s, in response to far more modest projections, *three* new towns were designated: Northampton, Peterborough and Milton Keynes.

For all its undoubted success and many virtues, Milton Keynes is a thirty-year-old and in some respects obsolete solution to the challenge of twentieth-century urbanism. We live in a changed world with very different priorities. Perhaps not too far into the next century we might once again take up that challenge – and build a *better* Milton Keynes.

24. *Planning and the Citizen*
Sophie Jeffreys

My knowledge of planning and development has not been gained from an attempt either to develop or to prevent development in my back yard, but from my experience as researcher for a society devoted to preserving the architecture of Bath: the Bath Preservation Trust. Members of the Bath Preservation Trust and those who look to it to represent the city's interests understand this. 'Preservation' for them does not mean shoring up the past for the sake of it, but rather making good use of inherited resources. From an enlightened and conscientious vice-chairman, Peter Woodward, I learned that 'preservation' is not a retrograde activity, but one as much concerned with the future as with the past.

I also learned from my experience of Bath that the planning process in Britain suffers from a democratic deficit which gives developers the advantage.

Moreover, institutions like the Royal Institute of British Architects (RIBA) have been able to impose planning conceptions and building types which have no popular mandate, which can ignore local concerns and which may have nothing to recommend them except the easy profits they bring to those who design them.

There can be no better place to meditate on the nature of planning and development than Bath. The Georgian city was developed in roughly seventy years, beginning in 1730. John Wood the elder conceived what we should now call an 'urban plan'. After his death in 1754 his son continued to design in the same spirit, as did other skilled local architects such as Thomas Baldwin and John Pinch. The elder Wood's original conception included showpieces: a Forum, a Circus, promenades, assembly rooms, squares and churches that were connected by terraced streets providing accommodation for visitors, artisans and tradesmen. Amenities such as schools, the hospital and the prison were treated with equal care and located centrally. The plan was truly urban, and included no 'green space' within the city. There were neither turfed squares nor city parks. Today people admire the tall plane trees in the centre of the Circus that cast their shadow on the grassy cushion beneath them. Originally, however, the centre was cobbled and Wood envisaged an equestrian monument of George II as the centrepiece. Bath, as Wood conceived it, was built on the premiss that human beings are urban in their nature and content to dwell in purely architectural surroundings. The truth of this was borne out by the increasing popularity of Bath, not just as a resort, but very soon as a permanent residential city.

It is often said that the architecture of a town must be 'human' if people are to be happy in it. Georgian Bath amply illustrates what this means. The city is moulded to the shape of the land: the string course that links a row of terraced houses travels parallel to the hillside, creating a line that declines through the levels in a graceful curve. Many of the streets that cross the hillside horizontally are themselves sculpted as crescents on a natural curve, like the ledges of animal tracks that hug a steep incline in the countryside. Some crescents snake from one hill to another, becoming convex and concave by turns. Buildings that follow natural contours, or that are related to some central feature such as a river, a square or a church, have a commodious effect, bringing people *into* the centre. Modern new towns tend to be centrifugal, throwing people ever further from the centre and from each other. In Bath architecture is a centripetal force, preventing the town from spilling over into the surrounding countryside.

Terraces such as those in Bath, which people now find so attractive, would be architecturally impossible were each resident determined to have a garden on four sides of his home or a garage adjacent to it. They would be equally impossible if every façade differed in width or height. In a city, though perhaps not in the suburbs, residents value the overall architectural effect of an area as much as the specifications of their own particular houses. The popularity of attic flats in Bath – obscured behind high parapets, without a balcony, a rooftop garden or walk-through garage – seems to prove the point. Only a love of urbanity and the city itself can explain why people are happy to settle in a garret. Paris offers further proof of this. The master plan suggested by Wood and his successors and insisted upon by the town corporation of the day, shows that nature and the city are not opposed, but, when properly related, mutually reinforcing. The city grows from the land and embellishes its natural contours, giving it the specificity and character of a human dwelling place. The result has been saluted ever since as a triumph of academic town planning.

The creation of parks and the greening of squares became popular later in eighteenth-century Bath, but the original conception was retained until recent times. The style happily accommodated the Kennet and Avon canal and the Great Western Railway. Two fine railway stations were raised. Where the railway runs through Sydney Gardens, a popular open space, the line occasionally tunnels below the lawns, so as not to destroy people's enjoyment of the park. It snakes along the valley with the same rhythm as the Georgian terraces, and is raised and bordered by carefully moulded stone walls which harmonise with the built environment. The route is still used by the modern intercity trains. The important point is that nobody today regards the railway and its architecture as either intruding on or spoiling the urban harmony. On the contrary, it is a welcome modernisation.

It was only during the second half of this century that architects and city planners abandoned the habit of harmonious innovation. Instead of terraces with the occasional showpieces there arose isolated buildings in the monolithic vernacular of modernism. As a result the Bath Preservation Trust acquired its role in opposition to the city planners and their appointed architects and architectural advisers. In a dramatic twenty years, from the late 1950s to the early 1980s, the city was radically altered. 'The Sack of Bath', as it became known, involved bulldozing scores of Georgian and Victorian terraces (regarded as architecturally insignificant) in order to accommodate the flat footprint of massive new blocks, each greedy for surrounding space.* 'In few places,' wrote Adam Fergusson, 'has the notion of "urban renewal" been applied with such destructive vigour or with such callous disregard for the finer subtleties of urban charm.'† All at once the neighbourliness of houses, shops and offices in a street was banished and the potential for mixed use obliterated.

Snowhill Flats, the first skyscraper in a convenient and desirable area, obscured the aesthetic effect of the whole hillside, and was so out of keeping with the rest of Bath that no one wanted to live either in it or near it. The architectural knights leading the Sack were (or became) figureheads of the Royal Fine Art Commission (RFAC) and the RIBA. The council employed Sir Hugh Casson as consultant architect. One of his proposals for

---

* *The Sack of Bath* by Adam Fergusson (1973). Fergusson also reported the story on numerous occasions in his column in *The Times*. His columns caused a public outcry and helped to halt the destruction.
† Ibid.

Bath was described even by the RFAC itself as heavy and monolithic. The council followed a conservation report written by Sir Colin Buchanan,[*] a member of the RFAC, who was also intent on building a new road network around the city and a tunnel beneath it – a scheme outlined in his earlier transport study.[†] Buchanan's conservation study endorsed both his own transport proposals and the city's development plan for modernisation. Sir Frederick Gibberd (RFAC), architect of London Airport's terminal buildings, built the Bath Technical College and Owen Luder (now Sir Owen and twice President of the RIBA, 1981–3 and 1995–7) cut his teeth in Bath, designing the much-hated Southgate shopping complex, itself now due for demolition.

By 1973 enough of Bath was threatened to cause local societies, including the Bath Preservation Trust, to mobilise citizens against the developers. The difficulties facing the activists were numerous. One activist described the problem thus:

The preservers had to make their own time, usually in the evenings or at weekends when they would prefer to be with their families, acquiring what facts and figures and plans they could get hold of, often finding that action was too late, too difficult, or too expensive; they had to raise the money for it themselves, organise petitions, and pay for legal and architectural expenses out of their own pockets.

The first and most significant victory, following a public inquiry instigated by the Trust, was the saving of Kingsmead Square. The square was due for demolition. It is adjacent to the Theatre Royal and is a delightful place to congregate before a performance, quite apart from the architectural importance of its buildings.[‡] After this victory, the Bath Preservation Trust began to use its financial resources to purchase threatened properties and to restore them to use. Today it gives grants to private owners to help them restore their own properties.

Since the Sack, local residents' societies, amenity groups, the guardians of open spaces and parks, the Bath Preservation Trust and the Bath Society

---

[*] *Bath – A Study in Conservation* (London, 1968).

[†] *Bath – A Planning and Transport Study* (London, 1965).

[‡] The main house built by Thomas Rosewell in 1736, after a design by John Strahan, has an elaborate, baroque façade, unique in Bath, more like some of the buildings in Bristol that were designed after Dutch and Flemish precedents.

have kept vigil over the planning process. Such institutions are necessary, for the reason that the planning system favours the developer rather than the citizens, who are regarded more as inconveniences than as the rightful judges of what is done to their environment. I feel this every time I want to read a planning application notice – the text is so small that you practically have to step up the applicant's path to read it* – something which easily embarrassed English people are reluctant to do.

The planning notice is a small but vivid reminder of the democratic deficit in the planning process. Planning remains a dialogue between applicant, planners and councillors in which the citizen is hardly represented. The process concentrates on assessing new schemes and, where possible, progressing them through the system for approval. Councillors have a narrow democratic mandate and must respect party political affiliations. Very few people trouble to vote in local elections: hence, even though a councillor must acquire the necessary 30 per cent of votes to be successful, he or she may have the support of only 17 per cent of the electorate. Without any architectural training it is also difficult for councillors to visualise how the architect's drawing (complete with attractive long-term landscape proposals) will appear once constructed.

Planners advising the councillors and recommending approvals have no democratic mandate at all. Hence, the system need not take into account the views of other interest groups. Furthermore, the parties involved may be susceptible to corruption (with the kind of devastating effect to be observed in the once beautiful Newcastle). Most important of all there is no provision for appeals against *approvals*, but only for appeals against *refusals*. Hence the legal balance always favours the developer. There can be just twenty-one days before the application comes before councillors. To prevent an approval being granted, opposition must be highly motivated, highly organised and highly efficient. In the absence of organised residents and preservation societies, the developer is likely to win.

In the last twenty years legislation has helped to bring about a change in attitude among planners and local government. In particular, Conservation Areas have been enabled by law. The Department of the Environment also

---

* In the case of agricultural development, notices are printed on a red background and therefore impossible to read without close scrutiny. This is especially significant in view of the fact that planning restrictions for agricultural buildings are in any case very lenient, easily abused and of far greater environmental significance than people have so far recognised (see chapter 8 in this book by George Monbiot).

issues 'Planning Policy Guidance' notes (PPGs) which stipulate the type of building that is acceptable in historic and sensitive areas. The legislation has eased the onus on interest groups to keep vigil, and a repeat of the 1960s and 1970s is now highly unlikely.

In the case of Bath, the authorities have also shown greater willingness to co-operate voluntarily with interest groups. The council now employs an expert team of advisers dubbed 'Built Heritage', who conscientiously investigate the majority of development proposals in the city and listen to representations made by neighbours and local groups. Built Heritage advise planners and speak to councillors at monthly planning and development control meetings. The hopes of the campaigners are vested in the care that this department takes over its work and its ability to influence the decision-makers.

During this decade think-tanks and policy-makers have applied them-selves to the matter of urban development. Proposals have been made to widen the franchise, obliging councils to work in partnership with interest groups;* the principle of networking has also to some extent been encouraged at government level. Nevertheless, local authorities are not obliged by law to adopt a more democratic working method and many prefer the simplicity and directness of the old-style dictatorship.

The voluntary change in approach from the Bath planners has required, in response, a change of attitude among interest groups. The Not In My Back Yard (NIMBY) phenomenon was an instinctive and necessary reaction to the 1960s and 1970s and to the democratic deficit that I have just described. This now will not survive for long when every town needs to adapt to new uses, new employment patterns and new domestic arrangements. Defending a vanished utopia will sooner kill than give life to an historic city. The very thing that makes Bath so attractive – its organic relation to the landscape and to its residents – requires that it should adapt, both socially and economically. But it also requires a radical change in attitude for a preservation society to move from a role of opposition to one of co-operation.

The Trust has responded to the challenge in a positive spirit. It has issued a document explaining its philosophy towards preservation, in the opening paragraph of which Peter Woodward writes: 'Our policy is to try to balance the aspirations of scholarly conservationists against the needs of

* See e.g., Comedia and Demos, *The Richness of Cities* – a series of working papers forming a study of urban policy (October 1997–May 1998).

ordinary householders and the activities of a lively, interesting, beautiful but work-a-day city.' If the Trust is able to live up to this policy and uphold the interest of Bath's residents it will serve the city well.

The popular base of a preservation society should be as wide as possible, the only qualification for membership being the enjoyment of the town and its amenities. Moreover, if it has charitable status conferred on it, the Chairman is under a legal obligation to ensure that none of the trustees gains personally rather than generally from its activities. Since a preservation society claims to speak for a city it is bound to be in touch with its members and to invite their views. In all these respects a preservation society, properly conducted, may be a more reliable exercise in civic democracy than much local government on the British model. Furthermore, a society can call on the range of expertise and knowledge its members can contribute to it and this may well surpass the competence of anything that is available to the official town planners. One member might be a retired architectural historian, another an aspiring engineer, another a teacher, another a doctor, another a lawyer and so on through the professions. Some members will be able to write in local newspapers, an architect member might draft alternative schemes, so enabling the society to make viable architectural recommendations. A society will also have its 'doers', members prepared to clear the cemetery of brambles, plant the square's flowerbeds or spend half a day at their word processors producing newsletters or organising events. The wider the membership, the closer the trustees will be to the city's everyday users.

Moreover, a society with a broad membership guided by clear principles has a great advantage over local government, the cohesion of which is at present inhibited by its departmental constitution. Separate departments regulate planning, the environment, transport, etc. Each department pays great attention to its own special concern, but may not be guided by an overall conception of the city and its future. A transport department has the task of propelling people through the city, while planners are supposed to help them reside there. The efforts of planners to ensure that a street face is not marred by brazen, illuminated fascias or vast advertisement hoardings might be completely ruined by an elaborate traffic control system consisting of shiny bollards, glowing chevrons, a flashing amber light and a giant illuminated signpost, authorised, with good intention, by the transport department and not subject to normal planning regulation.

The different objectives held by local authority departments generate problems which do not trouble a preservation society. Its members are also the users of the city, whether as habitual commuters or habitual pedestrians, who must inevitably consider and hope to balance the various problems of movement and dwelling. If the society has enthusiastic members, they may set an example of civil association, and show how the city should best be lived in. At best a popular preservation society might provide just the type of life-giving network which a city needs. The society could become not just an interest group but an experiment in citizenship.

One trustee of the Bath Preservation Trust, Timothy Cantell, was always ready to remind other members that matters of concern to the Trust should be widely discussed with the public. The Southgate shopping centre (the 1970s complex mentioned earlier) is now likely to be demolished and replaced. Timothy Cantell has therefore organised public open days and consultations with the developer and architect.

It turned out that one of Timothy's early experiences of the role preservation societies can play was gained when he went, as a member of the Civic Trust, to lecture to a gathering of the High Wycombe Society. One day he noticed that the author of two books on my desk was Roger Scruton.* He was prompted to enquire whether I had ever known or heard of Jack Scruton, Roger's father, and the founder of an early and successful preservation society – the High Wycombe Society. Timothy recalled its formation and early campaigning years under Jack Scruton. Against all the odds, leading the fight against a town council dominated by developers, Jack managed to save the Rye at Wycombe from the plan to drive a dual carriageway across it. He stood from dawn to dusk collecting signatures. He knocked on doors asking for support and money to fight the case through the courts; when he found himself without sufficient funds he returned to the streets to ask for more. When not on the beat, he was at his desk, poring over plans and drawing up alternatives to show that the destruction of the Rye could be avoided.

The mobilisation of citizen power in High Wycombe was successful. Standing before a joint parliamentary committee, opposed by QCs hired with ratepayers' money, and with nothing but his convictions to arm him for the fight, Jack uttered words that spoke for everyone: office clerks, mothers, schoolchildren, teenagers, pensioners, servicemen, dog-walkers,

* *The Aesthetics of Architecture* (London, 1979) and *The Classical Vernacular* (Manchester, 1994).

bird-watchers, sunbathers and footballers. In demotic English he evoked nature, aesthetics, memories and inheritance, and so captured the ears of the committee appointed to hear him, that the town council's case collapsed.* The example of good citizenship was heartening to me. I never met Jack (who posthumously became my father-in-law), but his example shows that the spirit behind preservation is not selfish nimbyism but an active concern for the future.

The last decade has, on the whole been a good one for Bath. A new shopping mall in the heart of the city itself – Shire's Yard – set behind the restored façades of Milsom Street, is extremely popular, with boutiques, sandwich shops, key-cutters and cafés. New residential streets, with private residential courtyards, are both attractive and popular.† A 1960s ground-scraper that ran from Theatre Royal to Kingsmead Square has been replaced by a neo-classical building that so closely replicates the Georgian vernacular that it is difficult to believe it is only ten years old.‡

As I write, a proposal has been made to convert the riverside area of Walcot Yard into a modern artisan residential area, with workshops and local stores among the houses. Now Walcot Yard *is* Bath's back yard and it will be instructive to see how the various interest groups will respond. Already the rumour about the redevelopment of Walcot has shaken those who remember the Sack and who fear that only the developer will score. But now that the relationship between architects and developers, planners and interest groups is no longer automatically confrontational, the proposal may be regarded as an opportunity rather than a threat. The architect is a local man with an instinct for environmental cohesion.§ He proposes to build an artisan residential area to attract freelancers working from home.

Freelancing is not easy. Files and fax machines take over the front room and the family takes refuge upstairs. For the industrious freelancer the resulting domestic disorder can easily get out of hand. Hence the self-employed worker may look for office or workshop accommodation in the

---

* The speech addressing the Joint Parliamentary Committee during the hearing held on 1–3 June 1965 is published in a memorial booklet to Jack Scruton, *A Pioneer in Conservation* (1991) published by the High Wycombe Society. The Society also holds a full transcript of the proceedings. The petition against the road was signed by 11,068 people, more than 10,000 being people in the borough; the whole document when presented was more than five inches thick.

† Carriage Court (1996) designed by David Burley with restoration and construction by Emery Bros. Both are Bath firms.

‡ Seven Dials (1990) developed by Future Heritage and designed by Aran Evans Associates and Tectus. All are Bath firms.

§ Edward Nash, Edward Nash Architects of Bath.

commercial environment. In 1977 the city architect, in an effort to justify the grotesque proposals for redevelopment that were then in vogue, said: 'If you want to keep Georgian artisans' houses, then you will have to find Georgian artisans to live in them.' In the 1990s there are many artisans and many developments (whether new or conversions) designed to accommodate them. The houses proposed for Walcot will include a workshop or office. Stores and cafés are also envisaged; a scheme has been suggested to provide incentives to limit car use; and a warehouse is proposed to accommodate the needs of existing tenants. The architecture is original in appearance and a new departure for classical Bath, something which may upset purists. Since the site is next to the river, houses are planned with overhangs, with prominent eaves and gables to contain the studio room. Unusual materials for Bath – such as long-boat coloured timber for decoration – have been proposed, again challenging purists. Nevertheless, such materials are not necessarily inappropriate for a new development on such a site.

I mention this proposal since it represents a special challenge for the planning authorities and for interest groups. At best, it is a chance for the authority to demonstrate its support for the new 'mixed-use' planning philosophy and for interest groups to show the developers and the authorities that consultation and discussion can serve everybody's interest and result in a scheme acceptable to all. At worst, the authorities will prevent an innovative mix of uses for some technical reason (e.g. violation of the minimum parking provision) and interest groups will whip-up a 'Not In Bath's Back Yard' campaign, eliciting the old intransigence from planners and developers, who will use their inbuilt power to prevail.

A co-operative approach is not always possible. A new development, on a green field behind Bath's longest terrace, has obliterated a delightful recreation area used by many people and which was a haven for birds and wildlife.[*] The application was approved in spite of strong local opposition. Little effort was made to encourage the developers to offer anything other than a standard suburb from their catalogue. Forty identical, or nearly identical homes with no relation to one another or to the town have been raised in a matter of months. No amenity centres or shops are included in the plan, which is designed as much around the family motor car as around

---

[*] Lansdown Heights estate developed by Crest Homes. Houses have been built according to two standard house designs from its national catalogue; the types are referred to as 'Richmond' or 'Belgravia'.

the family. Interest groups (preservation societies and residents' associations, nature societies, etc.) did everything in their power to persuade the local authority to invite alternatives, and in a democratic system they would have been more successful. They commissioned an architect/builder to draw up an alternative scheme with the same number of houses and for a comparable cost, with parking and access more carefully considered. Signatures to a petition as long as the field itself lent their support. All to no avail.

One great opportunity now lies before Bath's residents and local authority – the construction of a new Bath Spa to celebrate the millennium, a building by which twentieth-century architecture will be remembered. It is a £13.5 million project, of which nearly £7 million has been awarded by the Millennium Commission and the rest will be raised from local sources, including a local authority contribution. For the first time since the creation of the Assembly Rooms by the elder Wood, a 'people's building' will be raised in Bath. Knowing the consequences of the Sack, when London architects tried their hand at designing Bath, many people would have liked to see the commission go to a local firm (there are plenty of them) and for this project to be a source of co-operation between the local authority and the community. This could have been initiated by an open competition with all the entries exhibited and the public invited to vote.

This is not the approach the Bath Spa Project has taken.* Although there was a competition, it was between four architectural firms, selected from approximately 140 responses to EU-wide advertising. The three co-ordinators of the Bath Spa Project and an adviser from the RIBA made the short list and judged the final selection. The short list included one firm from Bath and another from Bristol. The winner, however, was the London firm of Nicholas Grimshaw and Partners.† This was announced in April 1997. The short-listed firms were not asked to present drawings, only to describe a concept for the Spa; and the judging committee visited all the firms to evaluate their working practices in order to gain a perception of their likely efficiency and project-management skills. It was Grimshaw's office that impressed them the most. Since the result was announced,

* The Bath Spa Project refers to a working team of three people seconded from the city centre managers' department of Bath and North East Somerset Council in association with the Bath Spa Trust which was formed in 1977 and devoted to providing a public spa facility in Bath.

† Grimshaw has built a couple of buildings in the area before: the Herman Miller Factory (1976), a factory in the 1970s shoebox style on the outskirts of Bath and the company's distribution centre on the outskirts of Chippenham (1981–2) that appears like a giant electric-blue container.

however, no drawings have been publicly presented and no plans submitted.

What if the citizens don't like the scheme? Will it or the architect be changed? Already archaeological preparations have begun and in June of this year the demolition of a 1920s classical building will clear the site; shortly afterwards building will begin. But where are the plans? According to the Bath Spa Project newsletter the architect's concept is to create 'a symphony of water, glass and stone, utilizing natural thermal resources'; the building will be, 'one of the most energy efficient buildings in the UK'. Fine, but what will it look like?

The Bath Spa Project can justify this apparent delay in requiring and presenting drawings since the RIBA has suggested phases for the presentation of such projects. These require first a 'concept' and then an 'outline' before the final presentation of the 'scheme' and the ensuing detailed plans. But we should remember that the RIBA is the protective and promotional body of British architects and not an institution devoted to safeguarding the built environment. It is an interest group representing one side to the negotiations, which ought not to determine the way in which negotiations are conducted.

The Millennium Commission's application procedure left the Bath Spa Project only six months to present its application. Preparing the application was both lengthy and expensive, so it was imperative that the application presented should be approved. It is not surprising that the Project was lured to an establishment architectural practice likely to be familiar to the Commission, rather than to a lesser-known local firm. The majority of local people desperately want a spa and are delighted that the application achieved its funding objectives; but the pleasure they will take in the Spa would surely be greater had they been involved in choosing a design, especially if the winner had been a familiar local figure.

With funding secure and the millennium deadline just eighteen months away, it is vital that there are no delays in starting the project. Already the project has slipped by a couple of months, so that aspects of the site-clearing and demolition stage are being merged. Consultation with local bodies has begun in earnest, lest objections be raised to the plans. By the time the plans appear there will have been lengthy discussions with the local authority's planning control department, with preservation societies, interest groups, access groups, landowners and the London cultural bodies such as the RFAC and English Heritage. The ordinary citizen and any interest group that has outstanding concerns will then have one month to assess the plans and to form a response in writing before the deadline. Anyone interested will have to visit the planning office and read through weighty documents that are likely to be stored in five or more box files. If someone else is looking at the plans in the one lunch hour you can spare, then your opportunity may be missed.

When the statutory consultation period is completed (after twenty-one days, although it is often extended over two or more months if there are many external representations) the application will be sent to the Secretary of State for the Environment for approval, since the local authority cannot decide on an application submitted by itself. In many ways, the Secretary of State is not in a position to make an independent judgement either, since millennium projects are *de facto* projects of the state. Furthermore, the Minister may never have visited Bath except for a political campaigning event and his officials may, like proconsular officials, have never visited the city at all. In this case some kind of referendum – which will test the opinion of people who are most likely to be affected by the project, namely the local residents – is surely obligatory, there being no other independent forum of judgement.

The case typifies the history of town planning in this country, whereby establishments representing minority interests (the architectural modernists being a good example) have been able to dictate large-scale transformations for which they have no popular mandate.

I hope that the story of development in Bath during the twentieth century will have a happy ending, with which the majority of citizens will be pleased. For this to happen the gap between city authority and citizen must continue to narrow. Planning must be oriented as much towards the citizens as towards the developers and architects. Development should be guided by a civic idea – with all the variety of uses that implies – comparable to the one that prevailed when modern Bath was conceived and constructed. It will then be down to the citizens to demonstrate how the city can be used so as to maintain it for future generations.

25. *Education and Environment*
Francis Gilbert

Jean Jacques Rousseau is the most influential educational theorist of modern times. His writings mark a sea-change in attitudes, both in his belief that education was vital in order to reform society and in his notion that there should be a radically different form of education modelled on the order of nature as he saw it.

Rousseau elaborated upon John Locke's theories of education in *Emile* (1762), which described the ideal education of the eponymous hero. Rousseau held that the child should undergo three phases of education: sensation, memory and understanding. The key idea of the book was the possibility of preserving the original perfect nature of the child by means of the careful control of his education and environment. The first phase, 'sensation', should concern us the most because it is the phase in which nature is the real educative force. Rousseau believed that the child should enjoy unrestricted play in natural surroundings from the ages of 2–12 years. Learning from books was not important: instead, the child had to have as many sensory encounters as possible.

Industrial reformer Robert Owen managed to amalgamate good common sense with the theories of Rousseau when setting up his school for working-class children in New Lanarkshire, Scotland, in 1816. Owen put great emphasis on the teaching of natural history: one of his ten educational principles was that every child must enjoy regular rural excursions. As well as natural history, Owen's pupils learned the three Rs, geography, history and even group dancing. Owen shared a belief with the ancient Greeks, that music, physical training and learning were inextricably intertwined.

In our own century, John Dewey (1859–1952) has been Rousseau's most formidable champion. *Imagine walking along a country lane and being confronted by a ditch. How do you cross it?* John Dewey believed that 'real' learning only took place when the mind dealt with 'real' problems such as that one. In Dewey's classrooms, the values of co-operation and experimentation were stressed above all else. In Gary, Indiana, from 1908 to 1915, the whole structure of the school was redesigned as a 'meaningful space': classrooms were replaced by an auditorium, playground, shops and laboratories. Moreover, the school was open for eight hours a day, six days a week.

Many environmentalists regard Patrick Geddes (1854–1933) as the father of modern environmental education. According to Wheeler: 'He argued that a child brought into contact with the profound realities of his environment would not only be more likely to learn better, but also develop a creative attitude towards the surroundings.'* Geddes's special emphasis on improving urban environments through education may have been new, but his philosophy undoubtedly owes a great debt to Rousseau in its insistence that a child's unmediated experience of his environment is educative.

Post-war developments in Western education could be seen as a delayed reaction to the lessons of Nazi Germany, where an ill-digested mix of Darwinism and racism dehumanised the regime. Horror at the Holocaust became universal horror at indoctrination of any form. Hence Dewey's libertarian ideas gained ascendancy, particularly in England. When, in the 1960s, the grammar and secondary modern schools were abolished and replaced by the comprehensives, it was partly under the influence of the 'child-centred' approach to learning.

In 1967 the Plowden Report, *Children and their Primary Schools* advocated many of Dewey's ideas about child-centred learning as well as making the link between poverty and illiteracy. Concern over the environment, and the pre-war move towards child-centred education arrived together in the classroom.

The Plowden Report had a huge influence upon the environment of education: for the first time in Britain the environment which a child experienced at school and home was perceived to be as important as his teacher. 'Evidence shows how closely associated are social circumstances and academic achievement. The most vital factor in a child's home is the attitude to school.'†

Unfortunately, there was an implicit defeatism in the emphasis upon the link between a child's poor social environment and his poor academic achievement. Moreover, Plowden's insistence that the teacher was no more

---

* 'The Genesis of Environment Education', in Wheeler and Martin, *Insights into Environmental Education* (Edinburgh, 1975).

† Department of Education and Science, *Children and their Primary Schools*, (London, 1967), p. 48.

than a facilitator who should awaken the child's mind to the world around him led to literacy and numeracy not being 'taught' in any explicit sense. In the 1970s, many state schools expected their children to discover these crucial tools for themselves.

The Conservative government tried to counter the effects of the chaotic curriculum that resulted from this, with the introduction of the National Curriculum in autumn 1989. Its reaction to the vagaries of Plowden was to impose a curriculum which was overburdened with content. Teachers were expected to teach too much irrelevant detail and had very little time to teach the three Rs.

By the time I joined the teaching profession in the late 1980s there was a fatal blurring of values. I was trained by progressive educationists to deliver a hopelessly confused curriculum which was later junked in Ron Dearing's review of the National Curriculum in 1994. When I was observed teaching a particularly rowdy inner-city class of adolescents by a local authority inspector, I was informed that their behaviour would improve if I provided them with more group work. This child-centred remedy, which I'm sure Dewey and Plowden would have endorsed, proved to be disastrous: there was no way that these streetwise pupils were going to read *Romeo and Juliet* of their own accord. As I became more experienced I would use group work to vary my lessons, but it never formed the backbone of my teaching technique.

In much the same way that a Shakespeare play does need to be explained by the expert, environmental education must be a 'taught' subject. Pupils cannot be expected to discover nature by themselves. The head of Parents of Young Gamblers claims that many young children would much rather be standing in front of a fruit machine than walking through the woods. The pedagogue needs to use every trick of the trade to awaken young people's minds to the natural world. The countryside, city farms and parks are not commodities which are marketed and advertised to young people. If Rousseau's Emile were alive today, he would probably prefer watching the television to roaming free in the fields, since the mass media go out of their way to appeal to children. The countryside makes no such effort.

The 1992 Earth Summit in Rio de Janeiro aimed to improve the way the global population is educated about the environment. *Agenda 21*, the major publication from the Summit, set out the commitments agreed to by the heads of state or government who attended. This committed them to the worldwide implementation of 'sustainable development' to halt the environmental damage caused by the human population. Educating young people was seen as vital to the achievement of this aim. Principle 21 stated: 'the creativity, ideals and courage of the youth of the world should be mobilised in order to achieve sustainable development and ensure a better future for all'. The local authorities may have people employed to promote *Agenda 21* issues within communities; but how successful are they in raising awareness about the environment? It is impossible to measure, but anecdotal evidence suggests that not many teachers know about *Local Agenda 21* (LA 21), and even fewer pupils.

Currently, knowledge about the environment is predominantly delivered in the science and geography curricula, with smatterings in design and technology and physical education. Much education about animals, habitats, the food chain and people's effect on the environment may be swept aside by the government's decision to relax the National Curriculum requirements at primary level (January 1998) in order to concentrate on literacy and numeracy. In secondary schools all children have to learn about the drawbacks of technology, the greenhouse effect and the hormonal control of plant growth within the science curriculum and sustainable development, stewardship and conservation within the geography curriculum. In PE, pupils must perform at least one outdoor and adventurous activity either on or off site.

But Nick Jones, the Education Officer at the Council for Environmental Education, believes that even if environmental education is sometimes of a very high quality, in some schools it is merely a 'bolt-on extra in the curriculum and patchily provided in many schools'. This seems particularly true of secondary schools, where most pupils are taught about the environment in different subject areas and may have difficulty in connecting the issues.

An integrated approach may not be easy to achieve, however. A 1995 report by the National Foundation for Educational Research stated that there is not usually a budget within schools to support environmental education. The Report went on to note that this is a special difficulty since the most effective forms of environmental education seem to be those involving hands-on experience and expensive out-of-school visits.

But there is a wider problem, which Peter Martin, Head of Department at the Education Section of the World Wide Fund for Nature, identifies: 'Environmental education should be part and parcel of the whole way we educate a child.* He believes the approach of LA 21 and the National Curriculum to be too prescriptive and too narrow; it presupposes that there is a distinct body of knowledge that should be imparted to the child, whereas the care of the environment requires the inculcation of an attitude of vigilance and thoughtfulness, running through all things.

This stance is in direct conflict with current policy. The *Excellence in Schools* White Paper, which the Education Secretary David Blunkett published in 1997, has definite similarities to the nineteenth-century monitorial approach to education. Where Dr Andrew Bell would use a reward and punishment system in order to motivate his pupils to learn the three Rs, the government is applying a similar philosophy to schools, by emphasising the three Rs, by naming and shaming under-performing schools and by praising high-achieving schools. Turning students into literate, numerate workers seems to be the ultimate goal.

Robert Owen's observation of the Lancaster/Bell system could almost be applied to Blunkett's approach: it is not enough to teach pupils to be good employees. They must become rational and useful members of society too. But the language of Owen's philosophy is not to be found in *Excellence in Schools*. The emphasis is not on making everybody 'good, wise and happy' but on producing pupils who can 'read and write fluently, handle numbers confidently and concentrate'.

In Britain, various political factions are striving for the environment to be placed at the centre of the curriculum. In his book *Teaching Green* teacher Damian Randle writes: 'what we want amounts to quite a lot: a curriculum based on green values'. Randle argues strongly for all of us to 'co-operate with and care for the earth' and for education to enable pupils to 'take part in a spiritual transformation'.†

When I asked some pupils at an inner-city comprehensive in London for their views on environmental education, their answers showed that they wanted their teachers to change attitudes and not only inform them. They all agreed that they had learned some important information on global warming, pollution of the land, sea and air, and the destruction of wildlife in their science and geography lessons, but some complained that other pupils were not being taught to have the right attitude to the environment. Donna Hammond, 14, said: 'The pupils don't care about the environment. They haven't been taught enough about it.'

---

* F. Gilbert's interview with Peter Martin, 22 January 1998.
† Damian Randle, *Teaching Green – A Parent's Guide to Education for Life on Earth* (Wales, 1989), p. 54.

A fundamental rethinking of the philosophy behind the National Curriculum is needed. Educationalists must address some very fundamental questions. Why are we alive at all? Is there any purpose to life? Why is learning important beyond getting a job? I believe that love of learning should be the philosophical *raison d'être* of the curriculum.

The best kind of environmental education does achieve this. As a teacher I have accompanied groups of inner-city children to a rural study centre in Wales. The teacher who ran the centre insisted upon the highest standards of behaviour from the children and only allowed them to explore the countryside under his guidance. In the course of one simple country walk, he taught them more about biology, geography, history, natural history and literature than they had learned in a term at school.

A good 'environmental education' would send pupils regularly to rural study centres such as these. It would also take pupils on 'guided walks' through the important city and town centres, where the local history and geography would be explained to the children.

First and foremost, an environmental education should arouse a child's curiosity about the diversity of the world around him. Ignorance breeds vandalism, whereas curiosity breeds care. Young people often take revenge for their ignorance – revenge against the adults who have betrayed them by giving them no access to the adult world. During my time as a teacher, I have seen too many adolescents suffer, boys in particular, because of their inability to articulate their emotions, to understand or take an interest in the motivations of other people, or to adapt to their constantly changing living and learning environments. Their most common response is to try to establish control of their immediate environment by intimidating other people in a few, narrowly prescribed ways: graffiti, and verbal and physical abuse. As long as other people are frightened of them, they enjoy the illusion that they have some power. They fail to see that true power arises from the ability to understand the world, not destroy it.

Rousseau's idea that a child is innately curious and observant is not borne out by experience. Pupils have to be in possession of a definite body of scientific, geographical and literary knowledge before they can begin to marvel at the world around them and thereafter build on what they know.

Lessons should arouse the child's curiosity, prompt solutions, and then provide answers which should in turn prompt more questions. Although this approach has many similarities to Dewey's, it is crucially different in one respect: the majority of the lesson would not be devoted to letting children work out hypotheses and little time would be devoted to allowing children to test their hypotheses in experiments. The fundamental presupposition would be that the teacher knows a great deal more than the pupil and indeed that there is something objective to be known. Until the child has a conception of knowledge as something objective, independent of himself, to be gained from the one who really knows, he is not motivated to learn, and all his 'experiments' are pointless. Hence learning must be a kind of dialectical process, with the teacher giving the framework, and the child gradually climbing it. The pupil must be guided, helped to observe, given a sense of what is worth observing, preserving, consuming, recycling and reusing.

Too often urban children have a negative image of their living environment, encouraged by 'dirty realist' crime shows on TV or even in the textbooks which they read in school. I have yet to read a class textbook which wholeheartedly celebrates the modern city. On the other hand we cannot insist that writers offer positive paeans to the modern city when there is often so little to praise. Some of our top writers and directors need to be involved in an explicitly didactic project which aims to produce films, books and multimedia exhibits in order to provide young people with a more balanced perspective. This doesn't mean that they would ignore the more negative aspects of the modern city; but the project would use the etymology of the word 'city' as its guiding principle: the classical concept of the *civis*, the citizen – the well-informed, empowered and responsible member of a civilised community – would be central.

It is time that the media developed much closer links with our schools. Schools are far too reluctant to embrace the outside world while the media, television in particular, see teachers as an easy target to mock in their children's programmes.

When I was teaching in Tower Hamlets my pupils were only a tube-train ride away from some of the most amazing art galleries, theatres, parks, churches, cathedrals, buildings and castles in the world. Because of their own lack of money and the school's impoverished resources none of my tutor group had even stepped inside a theatre until a private benefactor paid for them to go to see *An Inspector Calls*.

Teenage gangs roam the streets searching for action. The problem is not confined to the inner city; some of the worst gang violence I have seen has happened in the suburbs. How are we to deal with this catastrophe? Surely, this is an area where councils could learn from Rousseau and Dewey. Their ideas might be counterproductive in the classroom setting, but they should be taken on board when designing urban spaces: play areas, well-lit and carefully monitored parks, safe roads, youth clubs, schools which are open in the evenings and city farms would give children opportunities to explore their environment in ways other than the teenage gang. They would provide children with rites of passage and forms of membership which are essentially law-abiding, responsible and looking to the future. I have seen the difference made by after-school football teams and other types of club in both socially deprived and affluent areas. The aggression that many teenage boys seem to suffer from finds a civilised outlet on the football pitch. They are also learning important socialising skills by being part of a team.

However, there is a wider problem here: the consumerist mentality, which the majority of children acquire, has a detrimental effect on the environment. The simple problem of pupils dropping litter is endemic in most schools. Many of our children become avid consumers from a very early age: they either dream of owning, or already are in possession of, many consumable goods. Part of a school's function must be to show children that there is more to life than accumulating material possessions. My experience as a teacher has led me to believe that many children are the consumerist equivalent of alcoholics: their craving for material wealth could be described as an addiction. In every school I have taught in, children's obsession with wearing the 'coolest' and most expensive trainers, or owning the latest computer game, borders on the pathological. Many children's whole sense of personal worth is bound up with the possessions they own and consume. The problem of children taking drugs is a logical extension of this mentality; initially, they seem to take drugs because it's seen to be the 'cool' thing to do; thereafter, they become addicted.

Ultimately, children must learn that being a consumer is not the prime reason for living. A key element in the Alcoholics Anonymous programme is that the addict must believe in some 'higher power' – God, an authority stronger than himself – in order to recover from his addiction. The influence of Rousseau and Dewey has led to children not believing in any authority other than themselves in the classroom setting, and the increasing secularisation of our state schools has meant that many children have no concept of religious authority within the wider community. Most children love assemblies where they learn about sacred texts and sing traditional harmonies. When I was teaching in Tower Hamlets I attended an assembly where the Deputy Head explained the story of the Tower of Babel to a rapt audience of adolescents, the majority of whom were Muslims. It was very moving to see the power that the rhythms and cadences of the King James Bible had over the children and observe the respect that they gained for the text.

None of the state schools I have taught in have encouraged their students to sing or dance together regularly. This is unfortunate, because as Plato and Robert Owen saw, singing and dancing in harmony go to the root of the educative process. They are socialising and civilising processes which children love and their omission from school life means that pupils do not learn to interact with their environment and colleagues in a creative and harmonious fashion.

Obviously, we should not force children to take part in worship against their will. But a spokesman for the Muslim community once said to me that he would much prefer his children to be brought up in a Christian school than a secular one, since that way they would at least acquire an understanding of what religious faith means.

Too many children are deprived of any religious points of reference. The values which the Gospels espouse form the moral, legal, historical and spiritual foundations of our civic society and yet we hardly ever allow children to experience a 'religious environment'. We leave them to flounder in a world where self-interest and self-gratification seem to be the only creeds. The logical conclusions of these creeds is a form of moral nihilism – a belief that nothing has any importance beyond the individual self. I have definitely seen a moral nihilism exhibited in many pupils' behaviour. With issues such as caring for the environment, many pupils shrug their shoulders and ask why they should do anything if it is not of any benefit to themselves.

One of the great debates we should be having as the millennium – originally a Christian construct – approaches is on the place that religion should have in a child's education. At the moment, the environmentalists are lone voices in their insistence that children must be given reasons, other than purely material ones, for taking the long-term perspective.

Schools in inner-city areas can no longer count on a religious community as their social context. But they can do more to involve parents in the educative process, and give to it some of the wholeness and direction that comes from a shared religious faith. At present schools lie inert and unused for two-thirds of the day. Were parents to gather there for meetings, clubs, continuing education or entertainment, schools would lose some of their alien quality, and become living parts of the community in which they stand. Moreover, parents would begin to take more interest in the quality of the school environment.

However, in 1996, local authorities in England claimed that years of 'appalling neglect' had led to a dramatic deterioration in school buildings. They estimated that it would cost £3.2 billion simply to keep existing buildings in use. The survey found that more than 600 primary schools still had outside toilets and that 765,000 pupils were being taught in temporary classrooms. Nearly 2,000 primary schools lacked facilities regarded as essential under the National Curriculum. Although David Blunkett, the Education Secretary, has mobilised substantial funds to deal with these problems, it will take some time before they are solved.

These figures do not surprise me. The majority of my classrooms were temporary prefabricated huts. These rooms are often badly heated in the winter and poorly ventilated in the summer. When a cohort of thirty children squeeze into a flimsy prefab, the oppressively low ceilings and the lack of windows create a claustrophobic and noisy atmosphere even with the most docile classes.

Levels of achievement are profoundly affected by the architecture of the classroom. I taught one tutor group in two different classrooms over the course of two years. The first classroom was airy and spacious with good ventilation and heating. I had no behavioural problems and most pupils performed well. Their second classroom was a prefab. The students hated it. They were cramped, the acoustics of the room were so poor that quiet talking was deafening, and the heating often failed. I had to deal with many more disciplinary problems and the work of the students suffered greatly.

Although a limited amount of leasing of school buildings to the local community out of school hours already happens, schools could be much more proactive in this regard; it is a particularly good way of raising revenue. In our desire to return to 'traditional' teaching methods, we shouldn't reject Rousseau and his followers entirely. There were aspects of Dewey's Gary Plan which were eminently sensible: making a school the focus of a community by drawing in adult learners, shops and workshops could be the way forward both in terms of raising revenue, promoting lifelong learning and improving the school environment and by giving parents a day-to-day relationship with the school.

Mr Blunkett could yet learn some hard-headed lessons from John Dewey, even if Dewey did not believe in hard-headed lessons.

Bibliography

Bowen, James, *A History of Western Education*, 3 vols (London, 1971–81). This exhaustive account is refreshingly free from ideological dogma. Bowen's discussion of the educational theories of the empiricist philosophers, Bacon and Locke, is particularly noteworthy.

Council for Environmental Education, *Our World, Our Responsibility* (London, 1996). This is a superb folder of practical ideas and suggestions for teachers to improve the environmental education provided in both secondary and primary schools.

Council for Environmental Education, *Annual Report 1997* (London, 1998), illustrates the fine work which the Council is doing in drawing together various environmental and educational organisations.

Esso Schoolwatch, *Learning Through Landscapes* (Winchester, 1997). A resource for teachers and pupils which contains an informative account of the history of the built environment of schools.

Hayes, Dennis, (ed.) *Debating Education. Issues for the New Millennium?* (Canterbury, 1996). Dewey-based progressivism survives! One chapter argues that environmental education damages our children's desire to explore and experiment because they will be indoctrinated to preserve and conserve.

Higham, Anita, 'Morning, Noon – and Night', *Guardian*, 24 June 1997.

Lawson, John and Silver, Harold, *A Social History of Education in England* (London, 1973). Contains some fascinating insights into the conditions of Victorian schools and the social forces which moulded them.

Millar, Stuart, 'School's Urgent Need for Repairs', *Guardian*, 3 July 1997.

National Foundation for Educational Research, *The Cross-curricular Themes in Primary and Secondary Schools*, (London 1995). Some important research into the environmental education provided in schools at the time.

Randle, Damian, *Teaching Green*, (The Green Press, Wales, 1989). An interesting, if controversial, book which argues powerfully for much smaller schools which are more community based and ecologically minded.

SCAA, *Teaching Environmental Matter through the National Curriculum*, (London, June 1996). Do not be put off by the horribly official name;

this is an excellent little document for teachers and the interested reader which contains a wealth of good information on how to integrate environmental issues into all curriculum areas.

Stewart, W. A. C., *Progressives and Radicals in English Education, 1750–1970*, (London, 1973). Explores the impact which Rousseau had upon progressive educational thinkers. It contains a particularly good section on Robert Owen.

26. *In the Midst of Life*
Ken Worpole

There is nothing quite like a public funeral to turn a city inside out. Crowds gather on the pavements, chatter and then fall silent. Cars and buses are reduced to a crawl or even stilled for a moment, and the principal mourners, awkward, and unaccustomed to the plush seats of sleek black limousines, their pale faces indistinct in the inner gloom, find themselves unexpectedly the objects of pity and concern. Familiar streets take on a new relationship to each other, as their separate identities merge into a continuous route or processional. Quietness descends on the city, leaving distant sirens and traffic as a slightly disturbing background.

Big, show-stopping, funerals are rare today, but when they happen we see the city in one of those rare moments of illumination, as a place solid and substantial, rich with human meaning and memory. It is likely that the funeral of Diana, Princess of Wales, changed the topography of London for ever. The public impact of that extraordinary event quickly led to proposals to close the Mall and gave added impetus to the campaign to make more of London's principal streets and squares accessible and welcoming to those on foot. The walkable, yet still monumental, city had returned to the public consciousness. There is a renewed demand for a sense of the epic and the historic that is part of any city's appeal, but which seems to have disappeared or been occluded by the noise and fumes of endless traffic, and the relentless pace and frenetic imagery of an unceasing consumer economy. The recent attempt to restore the two-minute silence on Armistice Day suggests another attempt to arrest the decline of public memory.

The last journeys of illustrious corpses of one kind or another are great urban occasions. The 1995 funeral of Ronnie Kray followed a long tradition of East End funerals, bringing thousands of people out of their houses, as in the crowd scenes of some great pageant. Such processionals thread together the separate elements of the familiar street scenes of the past – pubs, street markets, tenement blocks, chapels and churches – and put them back into familiar patterns again, reassembling the jigsaw of post-war social history. On such occasions, the city takes on the intensity of newsreel film. It is also an invaluable fictional device, as we know from James Joyce's protean novel of Dublin life, *Ulysses*, which opens on the day of Paddy Dignam's funeral, the starting point of Leopold Bloom's morning perambulations and thoughts of mortality, or from Malcolm Lowry's great novel, *Under the Volcano*, which takes place over twenty-four hours in Mexico City on the Day of the Dead. A funeral restores all the unities of time and place within the classical aesthetic tradition.

Such public rituals of mourning are becoming rarer; the impulses more attenuated. In the course of writing a book about contemporary British provincial social life, some years ago, I interviewed a High Anglican priest in Middlesbrough. When I asked him what aspects of the old industrial city and its cultural life had changed most, he immediately replied, 'We don't have any large funerals any more.'* Today, many of the most prominent citizens are buried quietly and discreetly, without causing a ripple of disruption to the daily life of the town and its busy streets. It is as though people now disappear unnoticed, with hardly a trace left behind on the civic memory or public consciousness.

The Privatisation of Grief

There are many reasons which may account for this rapid decline of the public funeral. There is the cost: what people once saved for funerals they may now choose to spend on holidays, subscribing to the 'live now, think about dying later' principle. As affluence increases, paradoxically, people appear to pay less attention to saving for a 'proper' funeral; yet this was once the greatest shame of poverty: the prospect of a pauper's funeral. The fear of being buried at the early morning 'nine o'clock drop' was widely spoken about by many elderly people until quite recently. Hannah Arendt noted that the greatest honour a Roman slave could wish for was to be buried in a marked grave. As life gets materially better, the grandiloquence and pomp of our manner of leaving it seems to have become less important.

There is also the increased individualisation and privatisation of family life, with the extended family no longer as influential with respect to such ritualistic or ceremonial decisions as before. Cremation now accounts for

---

* Ken Worpole, *Towns for People* (Buckingham, 1993). This conversation was very important in alerting me to the role that public ritual plays in sustaining civic identity.

nearly 70 per cent of all funerals, and the technical finality of cremation, with the disposal of the ashes a secondary and separate event, somehow no longer seems to warrant a great processional. Modern cremation ceremonies often take on the character of industrialised processes rather than spiritual occasions. The popularity of cremation is usually attributed to a modern taste for cleanliness and hygiene, and the anthropologist Mary Douglas has noted how cremation gained popularity at the same time as the vacuum cleaner and the water closet, an efficient, unambiguous and clinical form of waste disposal as opposed to gradual organic decomposition.* Yet we do not properly know to what extent the choice of cremation is made for financial reasons. It is certainly cheaper, and involves none of the long-term endowment costs that may be incurred for the upkeep of grave and headstone or monument. Interestingly, people appear more reluctant to have the remains of children who have died cremated, as if a life cut prematurely short should somehow be commemorated in the more substantial form of a proper grave and memorial.†

Yet one of the most obvious reasons for the disappearance of the public funeral is simply that there is no longer any room left in many city centre churchyards and cemeteries to bury people any more. Britain's cities are filling up below ground at the same time as they slowly empty out above, as those who can decant to the quieter residential suburbs or to more rural settings. As a result, burial becomes, literally, a distant prospect. A modern funeral often involves a ceremony in a local church or chapel followed by a high-speed motor cavalcade, headlights blazing, through the suburbs and out of the city, to some bleak, featureless cemetery far beyond the ring road. A study of the current availability of burial space in London carried out in 1996 revealed that three boroughs – the City of London, Islington and Westminster – had no facilities for burial, and Camden, Hammersmith & Fulham, Lambeth, Lewisham, Harrow and Hillingdon had burial space remaining for no more than five more years.‡ Local burial, if not a legal human right, ought where possible to be regarded as a natural right, given the symbolic significance that cultures of all kinds, and at all times, have attributed to burial sites, grave markers and tombs, as sites of ancestor worship and respect for the dead.

* Mary Douglas, *Purity and Danger: an Analysis of Concepts of Pollution and Taboo*, London, 1978.

† This and many other invaluable insights into contemporary attitudes towards death and disposal comes from *Reusing Old Graves: a Report on Popular British Attitudes*, by David Douglas and Alastair Shaw, (London, 1995).

‡ LPAC (London Planning Advisory Committee), *A Study of London's Burial Space Needs* (London, 1997).

The Broken Pediment

This indeed is the principal theme of this essay: that the link between the living and the dead is now broken, particularly in cities, and perhaps for the first time in human history we are in danger of creating a culture lived in the continuous present, with the past eradicated or denied in modern urban architecture and planning, and the future, similarly, rendered off-limits by the reaction against all forms of teleological or utopian idealism. Only environmentalism seems now capable of holding past, present and future in any kind of relationship or set of related and mutually influential understandings.

Yet to insist on the importance of local burial is to insist on the necessary meaning of the city as a site of historical consciousness. For to be buried in or close to the place where one has mostly lived is also a way of 'coming home', and of satisfactory human 'closure', or a fitting end to a cycle. The grave is always a place of mystery and intense emotion – reminding one of Bachelard's dry comment that there is always more in a closed box than in one that is open – and this sense of mystery should be part of our daily lives, whether we are religious or not. Even atheists, such as myself, cannot remain indifferent to the conundrum of death and our own ultimate extinction. Local burial means that friends and loved ones are more likely to carry on visiting the grave (this is borne out statistically in the Douglas and Shaw study),[*] and so the cemetery remains an integral part of the symbolic urban public realm. Interestingly, the right to 'local, accessible' interment sites is now one of the central tenets of both the *Dead Citizen's Charter* and the *Charter for the Bereaved*, themselves evidence of a renewed concern with restoring meaning to bodily disposal.[†]

The failure to attend to creating burial space in towns and cities, and the neglect or shoddy maintenance of existing cemeteries are clearly leading to a serious diminution of the symbolic realm within many urban cultures.[‡] 'Pas de cimitière, pas de cité!', the cry of the Parisian crowds demonstrating against Baron Haussmann's proposal to dig up and relocate the city's principal cemeteries in the nineteenth century, was prophetic in understanding how crucial is the link between the burial site and the psycho-

---

[*] Douglas and Shaw, *Reusing Old Graves*.

[†] National Funerals College, *The Dead Citizen's Charter* (National Funerals College, Stamford, 1996). See also Institute of Burial & Cremation Administration, *The Charter for the Bereaved* (IBCA, London, 1996).

[‡] Ken Worpole, *The Cemetery in the City* (Comedia in association with the Gulbenkian Foundation, London, 1997).

geography of any locality or human settlement. A more recent example of the strength of this connection can be seen in Boston, North America, where in 1928 the Quabbin Valley was flooded to create a reservoir for the city, and in which not only were the churches and schools of four towns taken down and moved before the flooding, but the cemeteries were moved too.*

Yet today we choose to allow existing and overcrowded cemeteries to grow wild and lie neglected, while making no arrangements to create new burial places or gardens of remembrance within the city domain. The neglected cemetery is now a symbolic space of another kind, often of self-hatred and rejection, as Tony Harrison's poem, *V*, attests, with its linking of the vandalising of the graves in Beeston Hill Cemetery in Leeds, where his parents are buried, to the destruction of community which arose out of the pit closures and the ravages of high unemployment.†

The concern with finding additional space and the question of the reuse of graves is now a pressing issue for those who value the symbolic and emotional life of cities. There have also been other alarms. In 1988 there was a public outcry when it was reported that Westminster City Council had sold three of its cemeteries to a property agent for 15p. Concern was especially acute among those who had relatives buried in these cemeteries, but the bigger issue of how to fund and manage cemeteries no longer available for new burials (and therefore no longer 'economic') has remained.

This problem affects many other cities too. In 1994 a property developer and owner of Bristol's 45-acre Anros Vale cemetery, with many Grade II listed monuments and buildings, announced that the cemetery would be developed to provide a site for 400 new houses. While the city council opposed the plan it was unable to explain how it was going to pay for the upkeep of the site. The developer remains convinced that in the end economic realism will triumph. At present there is a stalemate, with on one side a developer with money to spend but no planning permission, on the other hand a council in alliance with amenity groups with highly laudable aims and objectives but with no money to support them. How we finance the maintenance and management of these vital sites is a real issue. No longer financially profitable because they are full up, or only available for the burial of family members who already own a plot, they have lost their

---

* Anne Whiston Spirn, *The Granite Garden: Urban Nature and Human Design* (New York, 1984).
† Tony Harrison, *V* (Newcastle upon Tyne, 1985).

'market' rationale, and as such move into the realm of public goods which need to be provided for their amenity and civic value. This means funding them out of some form of taxation, yet modern political attitudes to public expenditure currently forgo such notions.

The Sleeping World

A city is defined by its cemetery as much as it is by any other of its historical artefacts. There are few more melancholy, ghostly and historically reverberant settings than the Jewish Cemetery in Prague, with its overcrowded, tessellated jumble of gravestones, or of Père Lachaise in Paris, a rather more ordered city of the dead, with the Mur des Fédérés and the adjacent monuments to the many victims of the concentration camps, in which expressionism at last found a wholly appropriate theme and setting. In contrast one is reassured by the ordered tranquillity of Copenhagen's Assistens Kirkegård, for example, where a monument erected to the great Danish physicist Niels Bohr stands close to the rough-hewn stone marking the grave of American jazz musician Ben Webster – itself surrounded by the graves of other jazz musicians – a happy propinquity of two great revolutionaries of twentieth-century culture. Søren Kierkegaard is also buried here: the fact that his surname literally translates as churchyard adds piquancy to our knowledge of this gloomy Protestant's austere philosophy. This beautiful Copenhagen cemetery is anything but funereal; during the summer months it is a popular place for sunbathing and picnics.

One thinks also of the social gazetteer evinced in Glasgow's hilltop Necropolis, or in London's Highgate Cemetery. These great plangent reminders of human mortality add a depth and a necessary corrective to our enervated urban emotions. Likewise with their palette of evergreens, weathered stone, broken or crumbling statuary, dark and dank under-growth and teeming wildlife, these places represent the antithesis of the newer public spaces fashioned in anodised alloys, artificial York stone, and other modern compound materials now favoured by the consulting engineers or borough architects.

The urban cemetery is a reminder, then, not just of another world, but of a different topography, not so much the country in the city, *rus in urbe*, but a vegetative, entropic, timeless world, that is beyond human or bureaucratic control. The cemetery evokes a sleeping world, a horizontal world, a world of permanent darkness and rest. As the philosopher Yi-Fu Tuan has noted, 'In deep sleep man continues to be influenced by his environment, but loses his world; he is a body occupying space. Awake and upright, he regains his world."* The contrast between the horizontal world of the cemetery and the footloose, upright, hurrying bustle of the streets around it is always affecting. Similarly, at night, the cemetery evokes quite other emotions and sensibilities, *entre chien et loup*, between dog and wolf, as the French say.

It is also a place where it is proper and appropriate that things decay, and time takes its toll on the material world. Cemeteries provide micro-climates all of their own amidst the overheated summer streets, where the dark undergrowth and overhanging bushes and trees can reduce the temperature by as much as 10–15 degrees from that in the streets immediately surrounding them. Such extraordinary and sudden changes in topography and setting provide an emotional sanctuary as well as a physical sanctuary, and it is the possibility of such unexpected and changeable places that gives any town or city its richness and depth.

At another level the local cemetery is not simply a book of the dead but an encyclopaedia of social history. The inscriptions on the headstones remind us of the brief life spans of so many children in earlier times, or the premature deaths of women in childbirth, as well as of those who worked in certain trades, and of just how precarious life has been for so many. Structuralists may tell us that most epitaphs are simply forms of rhetoric or conventional tropes that formalise human emotion, and yet it is difficult to read such poignant or heart-rending public declarations of grief and loss without being moved or affected. Over the years I have wandered through chapel cemeteries in the tin-mining areas of Cornwall, stopped to examine beautifully carved headstones in the churches of East Anglian fishing towns, as well as those in cemeteries in the East End of London, or in South Wales mining communities, and it is the churchyard or cemetery that often speaks the history of a place more eloquently than the topography or architecture.

The Rise of the Urban Cemetery

There are historical reasons for the symbolic power of these places. Burial sites have always possessed immense religious and mythical significance, from prehistoric barrows and cairns through to modern war cemeteries. They represent a powerful link to generations of others gone before, and forms of ancestor worship are common to all cultures. While in Egypt,

* Yi-Fu Tuan, *Space and Place: The Perspective of Experience* (London, 1977).

China and Mexico, for example, family visits to graves may still involve picnics and even parties in and around the grave sites, the grave visit in most European cultures is very much a sombre, private and introspective affair.

In very early times, burial grounds were usually established outside the city walls or away from the village or the town, but with the rise of Christianity, burial within, or immediately adjacent to the church became the more common practice. It was the early Christian practice of burial in the catacombs – because of the belief in the final resurrection – that marked a different attitude towards bodily disposal to that of pagan Rome. As a result most town or city churches provided the places for burial and the focus for this relationship with the dead. The churchyard was not always a place of terror or piety. As the social historian Philippe Ariès noted,

> The [medieval] cemetery, together with the church, was the centre of social life. It took the place of the forum. During the Middle Ages and until well into the seventeenth century, it corresponded as much to the idea of a public square as it did to the notion, now become exclusive, of a space reserved for the dead . . .
>
> The cemetery served as a forum, public square, and mall, where all members of the parish could stroll, socialise, and assemble. Here they conducted their spiritual and temporal business, played their games, and carried on their love affairs.*

The churchyard was also a place of asylum, a sanctuary where the normal rules and laws (and even taxes) were suspended. These residual attributes still shape our attitudes to these green groves and silent places.

A New Kind of Cemetery

With the rapidly increasing populations of cities in the nineteenth century, largely as a result of industrialisation, not only did the churchyards begin to run out of space, but different religious beliefs, coupled with commercial interests, combined to create a new kind of urban cemetery, the very large landscaped Victorian cemetery, in which most of the land remained unconsecrated and therefore could be used to bury people of all varieties of religious belief – and even non-belief. The inspiration and model for many

---

* Philippe Ariès, *The Hour of Our Death* (London, 1981), p. 62.

of these – in spirit if not landscaping tradition – was Père Lachaise in Paris, a secular, even revolutionary model of the burial ground as a 'garden of equality', devoid of Christian symbolism and watched over by a statue representing Sleep. It is these large Victorian cemeteries which are now the subject of so much concern.

The best of them were expensively designed and landscaped, and often occupied sites with impressive hilltop views (Glasgow, Bradford, Bath, among many others). They took their dominant visual and design languages from that of the landscaped park or garden, a comforting setting which allied human death to the processes of the natural or 'vegetable' world of growth, decay and renewal. Indeed some were designed and laid out simultaneously and adjacent to public parks, such as Phillips Park in Manchester. From the beginning they were designed as places to visit and stroll in, not just for those with relatives buried in them. At the opening of Cathay's Cemetery in Cardiff in 1859, the *Cardiff Times* predicted that it 'would form the principal walk of the inhabitants of Cardiff'.*

The design of many Victorian cemeteries was influenced by John Claudius Loudon's book, *On the Laying Out, Planting, and Managing of Cemeteries* (1843), which emphasised formal planning and the extensive use of evergreens. He felt that cemetery design and planting should combine a simple patterned layout, to make it easy to locate graves, with a darker palette of trees such as conifers, cedars of Lebanon and laurels. Terraces and promenades were an essential element in the planning. Indeed, Loudon anticipated that, when full, cemeteries would become new types of urban gardens, a source of moral instruction and public remembrance.† Yet he could not have predicted that the structural idiosyncrasies of market economics – and there are few places where its writ does not now run – would have produced a culture that would find it almost impossible to maintain these places, or justify expenditure on their upkeep in the name of some greater civic good. In other cemeteries, those parts as yet unused for burials were often bedded with flowers. Their designers regarded them very much as places of promenading and relaxation – not the forbidding, wild and eerie places many of them have subsequently become. The architecture, of the buildings, monuments and statuary, was frequently of a very high quality. The University of York Cemetery Research Group

* Cathay's Cemetery Heritage Trail, City of Cardiff, 1994.

† I owe this insight to a research paper outline kindly provided by Dr Doris Francis of the University of North London.

recently found, in their detailed survey of sixteen local authority cemeteries of more than eighty years old, that 'All the cemeteries had at least one building of architectural merit, with the majority having two or three.'*

Abolishing Death

The neglect of established cemeteries, and the subsequent provision of newer burial sites away from the city, is not simply a matter of inappropriate planning. Our urban emotions are also diminished. Pretending to abolish death by locating its sites and rituals far away from the business and bustle of everyday life is not new. In one of his poignant entries from *The Journal Written at Night*, the Polish writer Gustaw Herling-Grudzinski tells the story of Filippo Maria Visconti, the Duke of Milan, who lived from 1392 to 1447, and who was obsessed with avoiding death by whatever means, so much so that anybody mortally ill was sent out of the walled city, there was to be no mention of death in the Duke's presence, all ravens, crows and other 'funereal' birds were exterminated, and all withered or dying trees had to be uprooted and replaced with healthy ones.† He died, facing the wall, in silence. While death, like the sun, may not be looked at directly for too long, as La Rochefoucauld remarked, we are reduced by pretending that it doesn't exist, or by averting our gaze completely.

This situation cannot be allowed to continue, for without places of burial within the city purlieu, our urban and historical consciousness is diminished. A secular society also needs forms of ritual and a symbolic architecture and geography. There are signs of hope. The City of London Cemetery, for example, now has annual open days. Although it is a secular cemetery, there are areas for Muslim burials, Jewish burials, and burials of those of other religious faiths. It is currently completing a new reception building which families can hire for receptions, before or after funerals. This kind of modern thinking about the cemetery as a public facility is not crass at all; it is sympathetic and responsive. The people who manage this cemetery are absolutely committed to the spiritual and public role which the cemetery can provide in the modern city, and which can only add to the richness of urban living.

* Dunk, Julie and Rigg, Julie, *The Management of Old Cemetery Land: Now and The Future*, Crayford, Kent, 1994, p. 38.

† Gustaw Herling-Grudzinski, *Volcano and Miracle: A Selection of Fiction and Non-fiction from The Journal Written at Night* (New York, 1996).

In the end, though, the cemetery is a reminder of our temporal, fallible, finite bodies. Many people choose to live in cities because they value the life of the mind, and cities are great crucibles or engines of thought and creativity, as well as being monuments themselves to generations who have gone before. It is, however, salutary to remember that we have bodies too, which will one day fail us, extinguishing the vital spark of consciousness. I personally do not find this depressing, since I value memory and the permanence of ideas and human thought as a collective endeavour as much as material existence. Without the presence of the cemetery in the midst of our busy lives to remind us of these mortal things, the experience of the city remains ungrounded, and therefore incomplete.

Bibliography

Ariès, Philippe, *The Hour of Our Death* (London, 1981).

Bachelard, Gaston, *The Poetics of Space*, (Boston, MA, 1994).

Brooks, Chris et al., *Mortal Remains: The History and Present State of the Victorian and Edwardian Cemetery*, (Exeter, 1989).

Etlin, Richard A., *The Architecture of Death*, (Cambridge, MA), 1984).

Greenhalgh, Liz and Worpole, Ken, *Park Life: Urban Parks & Social Renewal*, (London, 1995).

Schama, Simon, *Landscape & Memory*, (London and New York, 1995).

Sennett, Richard, *Flesh & Stone: The Body and the City in Western Civilisation* (London, 1994).

Tuan, Yi-Fu, *Space and Place: the Perspective of Experience*, (London, 1977).

Worpole, Ken, *The Cemetery in the City*, (London, 1997).

VI

Conclusions

27. *Conserving the Past*

Roger Scruton

Since the beginning of the Industrial Revolution, the relation between town and country has been an object, in Britain, of pressing social and political concern. Witnessing the flight of the rural population to the expanding cities during the 1830s, William Cobbett forecast the imminent demise of the countryside. A decade or so later Disraeli forecast, on the same grounds, the imminent demise of the town. Like all such forecasts, Cobbett's and Disraeli's proved to be premature. Nevertheless, with the battle over the Corn Laws, with the uprooting of the rural workforce, and with the emergence of a politically mobilised working class, the relation between town and country began to epitomise the social divisions of Victorian Britain.

Subsequent history served only to emphasise the uneasy nature of the relation. World wars showed the inability of our agriculture to cater for emergencies, and encouraged the interventionist policies which many people blame for the ruin of our traditional landscape. The flight to the towns has been replaced by a flight away from them, while new forms of subsidised agribusiness have transformed the economy and appearance of the countryside, and now pose unprecedented threats to wildlife. The loss of the railways and the rise of the motor car have had a seismic effect on the environment, on settlement patterns, on shopping, on the landscape and townscape and on social and economic life. And on every side there are bodies – from the National Trust to the Council for the Protection of Rural England, from Nature Conservancy to the Countryside Commission, from the Wildlife Network to the Civic Trust – which work for wiser, more humane or more sustainable development, and for a division between town and country that will preserve the integrity and spontaneity of both.

Nothing is more surprising about the urbanisation of Britain than the educated reluctance to believe in it. At the very moment when economic and social life shifted decisively to the towns, the countryside became the focus of artistic and literary meditation. Dickens, perhaps, was an exception; but Dickens portrayed the city as something monstrous, wondrous, phantasmagorical, a place of alienation and abnormality. Other writers and artists gave their energies almost entirely to rural and pastoral themes, taking up the artistic agenda of the *Lyrical Ballads* and Sir Walter Scott: the Brontës, Hardy, Trollope and George Eliot in prose; Morris and Tennyson in verse; Turner and the Pre-Raphaelites in painting. Ruskin, the great theoretician of Victorian England, devoted himself to the study and portrayal of nature, and saw art and architecture as continuous with botany. Under his influence the Gothic, which took the rural church as its paradigm, became the favoured style for city architecture. With Gilbert White's *Natural History of Selborne* (1788), there sprang into being a new literary genre: documentary writing devoted entirely to nature, the landscape and rural life. This soon became, with Richard Jefferies and W. H. Hudson, the most popular form of non-fiction among the reading public – a position that it has retained to this day.

By the time of Housman's *Shropshire Lad* (1896) the pastoral theme had acquired a decidedly nostalgic character: but it remained, nevertheless, the central preoccupation of art, literature and music right up to our times. Vaughan Williams's setting of Housman's verses (*On Wenlock Edge*) comes with the same tone of voice as the poet, and this composer, who died in my lifetime, gave us, in his Fifth Symphony, the finest rendering of English pastoral that music has received. Vaughan Williams began his career by collecting folksongs, at the very moment when people were ceasing to remember them, and went on to edit and complete the Anglican hymnal – a musical and poetic record which is in both senses thoroughly pastoral, and the epitome of our national culture. Rural evocations dominate Elgar, Bax, Finzi and Bridge, and are there still in Tippett and Britten, much transmuted indeed, but transmuted in such a way that young composers today can still inherit them.

Everywhere in the recent literary and artistic life of our country we find the same phenomenon. Despite the experience of total war – and also because of it – the countryside has remained the primary focus of artistic attention. Paul Nash, who made his reputation as an official war artist, afterwards devoted himself to recreating the English landscape – and succeeded too. From Collins and the Nashes to David Inshaw, from Henry Moore to Glyn Williams, the human figure has been either placed in or replaced by a pastoral context which is both recognisably English and imbued with a valedictory sadness. The debate over culture began with Cecil Sharp's attempt to revive folksong and dance, was taken up by Leavis in the context of an agonised protest against the urban machine, and pursued by Eliot, first in literary criticism, and then in *Four Quartets*, in which a rediscovered English pastoral is elevated to a quasi-religious ideal. When the debate was politicised by Raymond Williams, it was partly in protest at the pastoral idea, but partly with a sneaking regard for it, and a desire to detach it from its aristocratic protectors and reclaim it for the people. And in his fiction Williams returned to the pastoral context, with decriptions of a border country where the rural idyll is inextricably mingled with nostalgia for the vanishing decencies of working-class life.

Meanwhile, from *The Country Diary of an Edwardian Lady* to *Cider with Rosie*, from *The Archers* to the TV *Pride and Prejudice*, the rural ideal continues to occupy a seemingly immovable place in the national culture, feeding illusions, soothing troubled hearts, and – let it be said – often preventing us from seeing things as they now are or debating them creatively. The fact is that if we try to preserve things beyond the point where they regenerate themselves, then we preserve them merely as 'heritage' – parts of the ubiquitous kitsch of the consumer society, valuable only as spectacle, and only for those who have no lasting commitment to the people and places they visit.*

The pastoral legend can no longer be retold; not even as a tale of class war and rural frustration will it bear the remotest relation to the landscape we encounter. Nor do the market town and the cathedral city bear much relation to the life that fills our conurbations. At the same time, people hunger for the past, are distressed beyond measure by spoliation, by the destruction of monuments, and by the 'insensitive' gutting of historic towns. For all of us, therefore, has arisen the question: what should we conserve, why and how? It is fair to say that the most rigorous of our planning laws are those devoted to conservation, and that there is no more common response to the accelerating changes brought about by modern methods of production, modern lifestyles and modern forms of physical and social mobility, than to 'protect' what is 'threatened' – whether it be the landscape, the townscape, the history or the way of life of a particular part of Old England.

This reaction is not to be despised: it is part of living properly that one

---

* See Robert Grant's contribution to this volume (Chapter 3).

should love one's surroundings; and it is part of love to resist unprecedented change. That said, however, it is clear that we cannot base our policy towards the past on mere resistance. We need a philosophy of conservation, one that will make the distinction between policies that conserve the life of a nation, and those which merely pickle what is dead. After all, no conservation makes sense if it is directed *only* to the past. It is for the sake of future generations that we do these things.

Nevertheless, our love of the countryside is inseparable from its historical character. Ancestral patterns of ownership and labour speak to us from our landscape – patterns which have been wiped away from the industrialised prairies of East Anglia, as they have been wiped away from the collective farms of Russia, Hungary and the Czech Republic. We lament the vandalising of our countryside not only for the loss of vegetation and wildlife, but also for the destruction of a human monument – a monument built over centuries by people who imprinted their life in the soil. The need that modern people feel for the countryside is not a need for fresh air and vegetation only; it is a need for another and older experience of *time* – not the time of the modern conurbation where things constantly accelerate and the pace is set by busy strangers, but the time of the earth, in which people work at unchanging tasks and the pace is set by the seasons.

Conservation is also about history and its meaning. And we should distinguish two conceptions of history – the static and the dynamic. According to the static conception, history means the past, and we conserve the past as a book in which to read about things that have vanished. The test of the book is its accuracy, and once deemed to be part of our history, objects, landscapes and houses must be conserved as they were, with their authentic surroundings and details, as lessons for the restless visitor. This is the concept of history that is found in the American 'heritage' trails and historic landmarks: meticulously preserved ephemera of brick and timber, standing on concrete between hostile towers of glass.

According to the dynamic conception, history is an aspect of the present, a living thing, influencing our projects and also changing under their influence. The past is not a book to be read, but a book to be written in. We learn from it, but only by discovering how to accommodate our actions and lifestyles to its page. It is valuable to us because it contains people, without whose striving and suffering we ourselves would not exist. These people produced the physical contours of our country; but they also produced its institutions and its laws, and fought to preserve them. On any understanding of the web of social obligation, we owe them a duty of remembrance. We do not merely study the past: we *inherit* it, from people to whom we are bound by natural piety. Inheritance brings with it not only the rights of ownership, but the duties of trusteeship. Things fought for and died for should not be idly squandered. For they are the property of others, who are not yet born.

The desire to conserve things should be seen in this second context, as part of a dynamic relation across generations. People grieve at the destruction of what is dear to them, because it damages the pattern of trusteeship, cutting them off from those who went before, and obscuring the obligation to those who come after. The wastelands of exurbia – such as those which spread from Detroit for fifty miles in every direction – are places where past and future generations have been disregarded, places where the voices of the dead and the unborn are no longer heard. They are places of vociferous impermanence, where present generations live without belonging – where there *is* no belonging, since belonging is a relationship in *history*, a relationship which binds both present and absent generations, and which depends upon the perception of a place as home.

This dynamic relation across generations is also what we mean, or ought to mean, by dwelling. At their best, our conserving instincts are attempts to preserve a common dwelling place – the place where *we* are located (however loosely this 'we' is defined). The concept of locality illustrates the deep connection in the human psyche between space and time. A locality is marked as ours through the time scale of the 'we'. By bearing the imprint of former generations a corner of the earth pleads for permanence. And in becoming permanent, it becomes a place, a somewhere. True landmarks identify places by testifying to time. Places in the countryside are subsumed by that older, quieter, diurnal time that still moves and breathes in the human psyche. They are spoiled when this old experience of time can no longer be retrieved from them. They cease then to be themselves, cease to be country places, and become part of the ubiquitous nowhere.

Britain is a patchwork of haunted places, in which the eyes of the dead keep constant vigil, and to which the natives return in search of home. This experience forms the background as much to the novels of Lawrence as to those of Hardy, and is the root cause of the contemporary disquiet at the ruination of old and peaceful things. It is not that we wanted these things to remain unchanged; it is rather that we wanted them to move through time as we do, adjusting, compromising, bearing always a weight of memory, and facing the future from a character-forming past.

It is in terms of this dynamic conception of history that we should understand the disquiet that is expressed at the prospect that millions of new houses might be built in the countryside. Heidegger, not given to lucid utterance, nevertheless touched on the deep truth about architecture when he wrote that building and dwelling are the same idea. How you build is how you dwell. What disturbs people in those suburbs dropped from nowhere is not the environmental damage but the sense of these buildings as *apart from* the landscape, shelters for nomads who are not dwelling but passing through. Forms, materials and orientation all contradict the surrounding order. The houses hide in clusters from the seasons and from the rhythm of life; night never truly falls on them and the day never truly dawns.* The roads that lead to them join them not to fields or woods or pathways but to suburbs and supermarkets, and the spaces between them contain no places of work or worship, no shop or clubs, no precincts which are neither yours nor mine but *ours*.

People value the countryside precisely for the 'we'-feeling, the sense of a common destiny, common inheritance and a continuity that is greater than a lifetime. That is what we mean, or ought to mean, by dwelling; it is what traditional building instinctively expressed and perpetuated; and it is what the architect Leon Krier has attempted to recreate, in the context of a modernised rural economy, at Poundbury.

But if we ask ourselves *why* traditional building conveys a sense of dwelling, we return again to the really troubling question. The old stone barn and farmhouse were not merely shelters: they were places of social and economic life, which expressed a commitment to settling and remaining. This commitment extends in an open-ended way over generations. The buildings fit into their surroundings because they are the outward form of an activity which shaped and was shaped by the landscape. When we praise their 'natural' appearance, it is because we notice that the force which formed them also formed the 'nature' by which they are surrounded.

In such a context the ugly is the intrusive, the provisional, the temporary – the prefabricated structure which stands in the fields like a visiting insect. The commuter suburbs violate the landscape partly because they violate the sense of rural time. Even if they remain there for ever, people feel, it will be

---

* See Libby Purves's contribution to this volume (Chapter 18).

with a stagnant impermanence. The fault does not lie in the life that they contain. It lies in a carelessness towards the rural context. They occupy both space and time, while defying the contours and the history of their setting. Hence they will be dilapidated without ever becoming weathered.

We should not think that these conservationist feelings are new. They have existed since the beginning of the Industrial Revolution, and were never more in evidence than during the nineteenth century, as we see from Pugin, Ruskin and Morris. But the focus of attention has shifted during the present century, and public opinion has shifted with it. After the upheaval of the First World War the nineteenth-century migration from country to town was reversed, and the bungalows sprang up in the 'beauty spots'. It was then that the first serious efforts at conserving the countryside began.

Undeniably the most impressive of these has been the National Trust, established in order to buy up sections of coastline and retain them in their 'unspoiled' condition. The idea was greeted with enthusiasm, and the Trust has become the most successful and the wealthiest of our national charities, with a large popular following, and vast holdings in land and property. It very quickly became apparent, however, that scenes of natural beauty were disappearing not only through thoughtless development, but also because those who had formerly maintained them could no longer afford to do so. Death duties and taxation were driving the landed gentry from their estates. The mansions were falling to ruin and the parks were being turned to the plough. The Trust responded by extending its mission; it began to buy up the great estates and their houses, and to open these too to the public. The public also greeted this move with enthusiasm, able now not merely to wander in the soporific glades that had been the exclusive haunt of aristocracy, but also to peer into rooms where grandeur had set foot and where history had been forged across polished tables.

The popularity of the Trust does not stem merely from the fact that it is doing what it can to preserve the landscape and to open it to visitors. It stems also from the offered information about the past, from an experience of history, and from the peculiar historical catharsis that comes when feelings of class are evoked in a context where no one need bow down to them.

But notice what happens to the country house when the Trust takes over. Although the family, impoverished by death duties, may be allowed to go on living in a wing of the building, it does so as a humiliated vassal in its former domains, unable to renew or expand the economic life which once radiated from its seat of power. The National Trust takes on the house as a liability, rather than a going concern – for what makes a country house 'go' is precisely that it is lived in and loved by its owners. The Trust proceeds to maintain lavishly and imprudently as a mausoleum what had maintained itself and many beneficiaries prudently and modestly as a house. An army of experts is moved in, to dissect and catalogue the sad remnants of a life that will never again inhabit these rooms – for gifts to the Trust are exempt from tax only when inalienable. The unselfconscious muddle of a family household gives way to an 'authentic' interior, conducted by a fashionable Chelsea decorator. But it is not concocted *for* anyone: he does not paper over the traces of one life in order to prepare it for another, but to extinguish life for ever. His task is to create not a home, but a museum.

The cupboards, chests and writing tables, the carpets and tapestries, the landscapes and family portraits, all of which were once the source of the liveliest domestic pleasure, have ceased to be the familiar companions of a daily routine. They are no longer the home which gives industry its purpose. Detached from their customary uses, placed stark and immobile in their now tasteful arrangement, they seem embarrassed and uncertain, as though stripped for a medical inspection. For the first time their minor character, their 'second best-ness', is made apparent. Gone is every circumstance that made them meaningful – the scuffle of dogs and children, the kitchen smells, the clamour of visitors, the homecoming from work and the busy routines of ownership. These objects have fallen out of domestic and economic life, into a void from which they can never be retrieved.

People visit, not from morbid curiosity, but from an insatiable desire for history, in an increasingly dehistoricised world. But what they find is only history in its static form: a collection of 'facts about the past' set in their 'authentic' ambience. The National Trust extends over land and buildings the remit of Madame Tussaud's.

And there are serious consequences of this, not only for our conception of history, but for the local community in which the house is set. The country house was a source of constant expenditure and employment. It provided an endlessly renewable pattern of redistribution, whereby wealth acquired in the city would be invested in the villages. It provided life, interest, loyalty and spectacle. With the arrival of the National Trust all that ceases – and it ceases *for ever*. For a year or more, as at Canons Ashby and Kingston Lacey, the house is closed, while the experts make their ghoulish inventory and the decorators take charge of work that can no longer be entrusted to the 'ignorant' village painter. Huge sums are squandered in the act of taxidermy, performed by firms brought from the city and at no benefit to the local economy, before the house is reopened in its urbanised and sanitised form. A few locals will again find employment there, but in work that no longer has, for them, the charm of historical loyalty or the satisfaction of a domestic tie. Their jobs no longer pass from father to son or mother to daughter, nor do they have those intricate social valencies which join them to all else that happens in the village.

But there is another, and yet more disruptive, result of the transfer to the National Trust. The Trust's holdings are controlled from afar, by people who have no social or economic interest in the people most affected by them, and whose agenda and outlook have no natural relation to the place where their decisions will be felt. An important illustration of this arose recently, when the National Trust, under pressure from the urban tourists who constitute its principal membership, commissioned a report on stag-hunting from Professor Bateson, a Cambridge ethologist. The report came to the astonishing conclusion that hunted deer suffer abnormal levels of stress; the Trust therefore concluded that the stag-hounds should be banned from its land, with the result that vital tracts of Exmoor and the Quantocks can no longer be hunted.

The Bateson report has been much criticised. But even if it were entirely sound, and established its conclusions with whatever rigour science could supply to them, the decision to act on it without consultation with neighbours, and without considering all the human and economic interests which are part of the equation, constitutes a dereliction of duty of a kind that no resident landowner could easily afford. It is a decision that is possible only for the absentee landlord, with an agenda that renders him largely indifferent to, because unaffected by, the local human cost of what he does.

The first result of the Trust's ban on stag-hunting was entirely predictable. Local farmers, deprived of the sport that is the nub of their existence, began to shoot the deer – ostensibly because they no longer had any reason to conserve them, and therefore no means to offset the cost of the deer's predations, but in reality as much from anger and resentment at the unneighbourly treatment of which they saw themselves to be victims. The effect on the Exmoor deer population may be catastrophic; so may the effect on the human population. Even if only a minority is involved in stag-hunting, it is a significant minority both economically and socially. The followers of stag-hounds are the backbone of Exmoor life: the farmers, shepherds, merchants, farriers, vets and stock-breeders without whom the region would be nothing more than space, to be colonised from the suburbs by people with no deep-down economic interest in maintaining the landscape.

The National Trust was established with the laudable aim of conserving what is loved, and making it accessible to the public. But within decades we find that it is actively conserving only the *façade* of what is loved, while importing into the countryside a suburban ethos which is at best indifferent, at worst hostile, to traditional country pursuits – pursuits which enable the countryside to renew itself from its own human resources. The more this process occurs, the more the landscape is voided of its spontaneous life, and the more the economy of the countryside becomes a subsidised economy, maintained by institutions like the Trust and the environmental agencies, set up in order to polish the fabric of a tomb.

Our efforts to conserve the traditional landscape will be no better than those of the National Trust if we do not thereby encourage people to dwell in the land, and dwell there fruitfully. Conservation must take place within a comprehensive view of settlement, in which the new uses of the countryside are attached to new ways of living in it, and in which the old ways of living are protected from needless decay. The policy of subsidising the farmers has been adopted by successive governments partly with this end in view. But, as Graham Harvey has vividly argued,* the policy has had the opposite result. By subsidising production, rather than residence and lifestyle, the policy has merely raised the price of land. Big business has bought out the small producer, cleared the land of its labour force, and turned over the farmhouses to the telecommuters. The environmental costs are familiar; the social costs less so. The countryside is now largely operated from elsewhere: the decisions which most nearly affect it are taken on the boards of nationwide agribusinesses, or nationwide bodies like the National Trust. But the countryside will continue to wear its genial and ancestral face only if this face is remade by those who live in it – and remade through the process of their own reproduction.

The appearance of our countryside will not be determined, in the long run, by laws forbidding change: the best such laws can do is to mummify the skin of rural life, while the inner organism decays. The character of the

---

* *The Killing of the Countryside* (London, 1998).

landscape will depend upon the nature and quality of rural activities, and upon the consciousness of those engaged in them. It is not only economic activities that are important: leisure, culture and community are every bit as significant in motivating people to shape the land as a place of dwelling.

Eloquent things have been written concerning the threat to our countryside from urban sprawl, from roads, from the decline of the railways, from the equally lamentable decline in village churches and village schools, and from the changing patterns of employment and leisure. But deeper than all these threats, and the ultimate cause of them, is the steady increase in the randomness of social life – the steady loss of order, attachment and stillness. This 'social entropy' is the root cause of our 'post-modern' condition. Urban life too has exploded, and in opposing entropy we are not fighting for the countryside only, but for the civilisation that we have inherited, and which is the enduring source of our values and our peace. The second law of thermodynamics – that entropy increases overall – applies here, too, in the realm that we humans have carved out from the cosmos and made our own. But local reductions in entropy can be achieved, at a cost. The question is: what cost, and is it sustainable?

This is the point at which despairing conservationists are apt to quote Burke's famous remark: all that is needed for evil to triumph is for good men to do nothing. But suppose evil triumphs in any case? We should, perhaps, be a little more careful than Burke ever was, to look for the ways and the means to hold on to our inheritance. The Czechs, who have been more successful in this than the rest of us, and against far heavier odds, have a name for these ways and means: *drobná prace* – the small change of work. We should devote our time and our thought, not just to impeding things, but to founding and nurturing things – small-scale things like clubs and societies, in which the individual example can impact upon others and awaken them to the need to live in more social and more rooted ways. Rural life is surprisingly rich in these things, even today. My local village of Crudwell, with less than a thousand inhabitants, has thirty or more clubs and societies, dedicated to singing and dancing, among many other interests. These clubs shape the language and consciousness of their members and provide an image of social peace. Through them people acquire the imaginative and collective knowledge of each other which is the central strand in a culture. And they form a continuous motive not just to live in Crudwell, but to *dwell* there, to treat the village as a home, and to adapt it to modern social and economic conditions.

The example illustrates an important truth: in conservation the effective measures come always from below. The tendency to look to politics and legislation for the solution to our anxiety is also a sign of anxiety – a sign that we have renounced the effort to live by our beliefs. Even if the fabric of modern society is torn, we can still repair it – not so that it looks the same, but so that it holds together. But the work of repair is long, patient and piecemeal, and it is up to each of us to take up the thread.

28. *Securing the Future*
Anthony Barnett

Many of the contributions to this book begin with personal reflections; from the way the beauty of a familiar valley has been preserved by Swiss micro-democracy to a visit to an aristocratic British family displaying the decayed stigmata of its privilege. Such stories illustrate how different relationships of city and rural life are potentially open to being shared. They also communicate a sense of how such relationships may be closed, ruined or wilfully destroyed.

In twentieth-century England the cult of the countryside became a special kind of closure, one that weakened the vitality of that which it proclaimed to celebrate. There were many warnings – what is new is that they are now undeniable. Even the British aristocracy, the historic pioneers and beneficiaries of landed capitalism, are threatened by an agribusiness often driven by pension funds that are no longer run by cousins in the City. They are hardly victims but they none the less suffer, as landscapes and stately homes alike enter the market-places of superstore crops and consumer demand for heritage. Conservatives – or, at least, some of them – are finding it necessary to rethink the divide.

This is a welcome opportunity, not least for those hitherto condemned to be the outcasts in the argument. For example, John Berger, who wrote an extraordinary trilogy of novels in defiance of the 'modern' judgement that condemns peasant life and experience to irrelevance.* More directly in terms of British development, Raymond Williams showed in 1973 that country and city are indissolubly linked and that we must not 'limit ourselves to their contrast but must go on to see their interrelations and through these the real shape of the underlying crisis'. An analysis he

---

* John Berger, *Into Their Labours* (New York, 1990), the trilogy of *Pig Earth, Once in Europa, Lilac and Flag* (1979–87). Also his pioneering essay on how animals accompanied humankind at the centre of our economic and social life until the nineteenth century, and the way zoos and stuffed toys are symbols of the severance of this relationship; 'Why Look at Animals', in *About Looking* (London, 1980).

developed to make his call against the 'linked processes of high land costs, high interest bearing capitalization, high-input cash-crop production'.*

Today, as the mental framework that pinched apart town and country relations in Britain loosens, such meditations need no longer be written as warnings from afar. A debate has begun that promises to reconsider the nature of our country from, literally, the ground up; from drug-dependent inner cities to wealthy prairie farms hooked upon a different variety of chemicals – as people are asking what kind of country we live in. It is now possible to shift aside a once overwhelming mental inheritance, to reconsider town and country as related parts of a single field of human residence, recreation, production and reproduction.

It is easy to show that this complex unity is the necessary starting point for any discussion of policy. Crude examples of the links are obvious enough. If country residents want to stop flight from the towns they must demand good inner-city schools. If town people want safe food, they must subsidise conversion to more sustainable farming. Such remarks, however, are these days suspiciously easy to agree with. Like much 'third-way' politics, they threaten to overdo the on-the-one-hand-*and*-on-the-other, so that a slack consensus follows. Instead a far-reaching change in mentality is called for: one that abandons the English attitude of seeking lachrymose consolation in an idealised past, one that embraces development to contest currently existing modernity with an alternative modernity.

To achieve this we need to govern ourselves differently. This is not *all* that is involved, of course, yet even this begins with the need to rethink who we are, so that we can refuse henceforth to allow ourselves to be belittled by the bleak image of the city that was promulgated in late imperial England in the name of the country.

My personal recollection is of a different kind: the first ideological dispute I had with one of my children. I was reading a bedtime Beatrix Potter book – *The Tale of Johnny Town-Mouse*. The story is familiar. Timmy Willie, a country mouse who lives happily in a farm, falls asleep by mistake in a large hamper of vegetables that is taken to town. There, frightened and bewildered, he is befriended by the dashing, waistcoated Johnny, enjoys a table of urban delicacies but, surrounded by the noises and dangers of town life, not to speak of cats, falls ill. 'I am a little disappointed, we have endeavoured to entertain you,' Johnny tells him. But Timmy is pleased to

* Raymond Williams, *Country and the City* (London, 1975), p. 356 and his 1984 essay 'Between Town and Country' reprinted in Raymond Williams, *Resources of Hope* (London, 1989), p. 237.

escape back to familiar rural ways. Then, when the town family go on holiday and Johnny's food chain diminishes, he in turn arrives at the farm to sample rural life. 'I am sure you will never want to live in town again,' Timmy tells Johnny, when he welcomes him. But Johnny finds the pastoral existence repugnant and escapes back to the metropolis in the next available hamper, complaining that the countryside is 'too quiet'.

Potter draws her moral at the end. Each will find the place best suited to them and, she concludes, 'For my part I prefer to live in the country.' After which, I added quietly that for my part I was a Johnny Town-Mouse and preferred the town.

'You *don't*!'

'I do.'

'You *can't*.'

'But I live in Covent Garden.'

Unknown to either of us at the time we were taking part in an argument which goes back in this precise literary form 2,000 years to Horace's accomplished satire of 30 BC *The Town Mouse and the Country Mouse.** Horace's country mouse is as decisive as Potter's:

I have no use for this kind of life. Goodbye!

Thus debate over town and country has a notable history. The celebration of pastoral ways long predates the eighteenth century. May it long continue! I say this even while I raise *my* glass to urban life and proximity. For one cannot be a cityman without the country, and could no more wish to abolish the contrast between town and rural life as define away the difference between the sexes. Nor, in preferring the country, does Beatrix Potter fail to record the passion of the town. More than that, she also recognises their dependence, of each on the other, as the hamper goes backward and forward between them.

Soon after Potter wrote her version of town and country mice in 1918, however, a distinctly national twist was given to the rural. A significantly more malevolent pastoralism was endorsed, one that refused any legitimacy of preference. Instead, the towns and cities where most of us live were declared a no man's land. A monopoly over the definition of England was

---

* I am grateful to David Wiggins for the reference, Horace's *Satires*, Book 2, 6; see also Horace's *Epistles* Book 1, 14, 'To the foreman on my farm: You can have the city, I'll take the country'.

announced: 'England,' Prime Minister Stanley Baldwin told the Royal Society of St George in 1924, 'is the country, and the country is England.'

> The sounds of England, the tinkle of the hammer on the anvil in the country smithy, the corncrake on a dewy morning, the sound of the scythe against the whetstone, and the sight of a plough team coming over the brow of a hill, the sight that has been seen in England since England was a land, and may be seen in England long after the Empire has perished and every works in England has ceased to function, for centuries the one eternal sight of England. The wild anemones in the woods in April, the last load at night of hay being drawn down a lane as the twilight comes on . . . and above all, the most subtle, most penetrating and most moving, the smell of wood smoke coming up in an Autumn evening . . .

The influence of this attitude has lasted to our own time. Its effects have been pernicious. It casts the towns into an abyss. It also exposes the countryside that it seems to laud to destruction. For the Prime Minister's cultivated attitude is a form of fatalism. When Baldwin looks forward he hopes that England will be recalled in the same way that 'we still speak of Roman strength'. This is not to praise a way of life but to bury it.

First, the view. It is a country seen from afar. Baldwin himself does not scythe or draw the hay, he does not cut the wood nor clean the fireplace, he does not shop in the village nor expect his listeners to either. This is England peopled, in so far as it is inhabited at all, by silent figures in the middle distance. Second, the voice. Who speaks to us about the country in this way? One who told the boys of Harrow School the same year,

> When the call came to me to form a Government, one of my first thoughts was that it should be a Government of which Harrow should not be ashamed. I remembered how in previous Governments there had been four, or, perhaps, five Harrovians, and I determined to have six.

This is hardly the voice of the cornfield. It is someone who says in 1925, 'the duty of the British citizen today is – "Know Your Empire"'.* Its accent is without local inflexion or dialect. School and Oxbridge college

---

* All quotations from Stanley Baldwin, *On England* (London, 1926), pp. 6–7, 267 and 218. The book went through five impressions in the year of the General Strike.

matter more than birthplace in determining its character and manners. It is a voice trained to influence a global empire and despise regional democracy.

Not that Stanley Baldwin created such an attitude; he gave expression to an already gathered feeling when he defined England as 'the country'. In 1924 the belief had at least three sources: structural, immediate and, naturally, tradition. The overarching structure was Empire and its being the best in the world. Unlike the other British nationalities, for the English this was and remains a singular experience – they are British overseas and English at home, these being two sides of a single coin. As I have tried to argue elsewhere, from the viewpoint of the world's largest dominion England's own native cities were 'negated between the ocean swell and the rolling countryside'.* During service abroad, when the English thought of home it was the village that came to mind, and the safety of the rural. The vantage point of this perspective was not where most English lived, not even the world's largest city and grandest capital of the time. It was extra-territorial. Only from the outside could the urban be so completely overlooked. 'The country,' Raymond Williams observed, 'was now a place to retire to' – above all, we can add, from service overseas.†

The immediate context was the trauma of four years of indescribable slaughter. The depth of its injustice was confirmed by making the 'masses', in their row upon row of poor housing, a scapegoat; confirming their sacrifice by excluding them from the definition of the nation. A 'civilisation' – this is Baldwin again – that, 'seemed to our fathers secure and permanent . . . rotted and cracked during the agony of The Great War'.‡ The village green, at least, seemed to represent a worthy permanence. Paul Fussell has shown in his powerful and convincing study how 'recourse to pastoral is an English mode of both fully gauging the calamities of the Great War and imaginatively protecting oneself against them'.§ The negative consequences can be felt in T. S. Eliot's vision of London as an 'unreal city', part of 'The Waste Land' – all that it can be if England is the country.

If military holocaust intensified the imperial overview, both fed from a tradition that had prepared the twentieth-century English mind for the denigration of its urban life. This was the history of rural clearances and

---

* 'The English Question', in *This Time: Our Constitutional Revolution*, (London, 1997), pp. 282–306.
† Williams, *Country and the City*, p. 282.
‡ In his conclusion to 'Truth and Politics', Williams, p. 92.
§ Paul Fussell, *The Great War and Modern Memory* (Oxford, 1975), p. 235.

consolidation of fields that suppressed the peasantry: a process that made the landscape available for the 'view' that Baldwin conjures up. John Barrell has described how in eighteenth-century English painting, peasant life came to be represented in a 'natural' role that censored out 'the dark side of the landscape'. Barrell effectively demonstrates the process at work in the later paintings of Gainsborough. In them, rural poverty is dignified yet diminished by being sentimentalised, as the peasants are reduced to the passivity of animals.* A recent exhibition brought the truth of this home to me with a shock. The Royal Academy had a show of paintings from English regional collections, 'Art Treasures of England'. One was a Courbet. It shows a landscape dominated by the rocks of Ornans that he has made familiar. Across the centre, a large pool of water is approached by two cattle, while just left of centre there are four small figures, three in fine clothes and a peasant girl. The painting is called, *Young Ladies of the Village giving Alms to a Cow Girl*. A late Gainsborough in an adjoining room echoed many of the same features. The sun is setting over water. In place of Courbet's cliffs, there are two stands of Gainsborough's familiar trees. On the left, cattle can be made out in their shadow. Catching the full light of the setting sun at the painting's centre there is also a small group. This time the cow girl is at its centre. She holds a baby and has a small boy at her skirt. Behind them, the largest element in the painting is a small cottage with smoke rising from its chimney and a family group outside – it can be seen that it is home to at least ten people. With sheep in the far distance it is clear this is inhabited land, far more so than the pastures at Ornans. Gainsborough's painting could easily be called, 'Rural poverty and overcrowding'. Baldwin might have titled it 'The smell of woodsmoke in an autumn evening'. Instead, the record of dense human investment is completely denied: it is called, *Wooded Landscape with Cattle by a Pool*. Unlike the Courbet, the human inhabitants have been pressed out of any claim upon the view, even though it is they who tend the cattle and dam the stream.

Were the inhabitants of the painting to speak to us – were they to say, 'Arh, this be England, this be' – consternation would follow. What Harrovians, etc. may describe, the resident natives cannot claim. 'England is the country, the country is England' is not a neutral observation, or even a celebration; it is a description that actively excludes the toiling, drinking,

---

* John Barrell, *The Dark Side of the Landscape: the Rural Poor in English Painting, 1730–1840* (Cambridge, 1980).

arguing inhabitants, their conflicts and contests, from the definition of the nation. Country *as well as* town people are its victims, as its claim replicates the celebration of Empire in which local peoples are no more than so much colour.

The dehumanising love of country encapsulated by Baldwin's phrase was swiftly institutionalised in the Council for the Protection of Rural England. It speaks *of* England. But, interestingly, despite the enormous popularity of its sentiments, it does not speak *for* the English. It has no ethnic content. How could it when most English live in towns? This highly English movement did not look forward to the future. Born in the year of the General Strike and in the shadow of the great Wembley Empire Exhibition, the CPRE was a Trappist movement dedicated to cultivating one's garden and not disturbing the neighbours. Its one-sided endorsement of country spread a plague of negativity through urban life while it expropriated rural voices through its paternalism.

The long influence of this closed cast of mind was demonstrated by a letter sent to *The Times* by a later Prime Minister and other political leaders, published on 9 February 1996:

Sir, In 1926, at the inception of the Council for the Protection of Rural England's appeal for public support, our forebears, Stanley Baldwin, Ramsay MacDonald and David Lloyd George, pledged their support for the English countryside in a letter to *The Times*. In the year of the CPRE's seventieth anniversary, we are pleased to make that commitment again.

During the next few months we shall differ on so many problems of public importance that we gladly take the opportunity of showing that on one subject we speak with a united voice – namely, in advocating the protection of our countryside in its rich personality and character.

We do this in the full confidence that necessary development can and should be directed with thoughtful and scrupulous attention to the charm of our countryside. Much of its beauty is the direct result of man's activities in the past; and in these days when the objectives of planning and land management and the appreciation of landscape are more widely shared than ever before, we ought to be able to make necessary changes in ways that avoid injuring our precious heritage.

We are, Sir, your obedient servants, John Major, Tony Blair, Paddy Ashdown

This is a gem. Forebears! So much has naturalism gone to our leaders' heads that they refer to their predecessors as their ancestors. Charms are frail, but where does it leave the apparently charmless towns, if leaders agree only on the need to protect the rich personality of the countryside? Presumably, the withered personality of British cities can be left to blow in the wind. Even in the countryside, instead of development being embraced as a positive opportunity for which our leaders take some responsibility, it is viewed as an external 'necessity' to be managed so as to avoid injuring 'our precious heritage'. Their approach treats the countryside as a finished image that should not be damaged, not a living inheritance with plenty of room for improvement.

The good news is that this ridiculous letter probably marks the end of the attitude it seeks to continue. One of its characteristics is a maudlin tone of regret — shoulder to shoulder our leaders stand to ensure that there should be *no more* injury to our precious heritage. Professor Cullingworth wrote to *The Times* three days later, to point out that the first letter by Baldwin et al. seventy years before had been promptly followed by the building of 2 million houses, 'with little regard to their surroundings'. We have been warned. The tone of lament functions as permission for developers. Oppose a thoughtless commercial scheme and all our leaders will agree that it is regrettable, as they wash their hands in their crocodile tears. This is how permission is more easily granted.

It is important to seek to understand the way this works. One of the puzzling aspects of twentieth-century Britain is how a society with such a strongly felt love of place, an exceptionally lively and combative cultural inheritance, and an experienced and wealthy ruling class, allowed both town and country to be so badly developed. While the 1945 Labour government's Town and Country Planning Acts slowed down a process that dates from the 1920s, there is no sense that 'we' — the English, Scottish, Welsh, Irish or British — have developed our country at all. It was done to us, apparently. In a swingeing response to the Countryside Alliance, Adam Nicolson observed that

> What the British relish . . . is the sense of loss which our actual indifference to nature engenders. The way we experience our love of nature is as a form of regret, a retrospective treasuring of what can no longer be had . . . It is this retrospective frame of mind, I think, against

which we should be protesting and marching [so that] our relationship to nature is more than just a kind of grieving over what we have lost.[*]

Perhaps the feeling of loss does not mask actual indifference and the regret is sincere. But Nicolson is justified in identifying the grieving as actively contributing to the damage. Just as the countryside is an artefact, however unintended, so the feelings about it are also constructed from the totality of social experience. Loss is not simply observed, it is also – one can see it in our leaders' letter – anticipated. It is not just past losses that are regretted; so too is the future. We advance – this is the English upper-class attitude – towards decline. (Hence the unstated aristocratic attitude that 'one' had better cash in while one can.)

Overall loss could not but be anticipated through the arc from 1918 to today, especially if, following Baldwin's instruction (not to speak of Churchill's), one does know one's Empire. Even as Lutyens's New Delhi arose in all its staggering scale in the 1920s it was foreseen as a monument to the eventual loss of India. Just as from 1982 to 1997 the loss of Hong Kong was anticipated by those who cared about it – and the heir to the throne cared enough to shed a tear in public when it happened. For all its triteness and potentially fatal enchantment with low-quality fashion and glib populism, one impulse behind New Labour's passion for modernisation is a welcome effort to break from such regret. Something that is easier to do now that we have been relieved of overseas possessions.

For it was an imperial vista that cast a countryside emptied of people as a metaphor for England. Its role was to mark the wider loss, and provide consolation for it. Until this attitude is discarded as the dominant or defining one, internal renewal will not occur.

Some readers may recoil at the suggestion that there was an underlying linkage between loss of Empire and the desolation unleashed on the native towns – and landscapes. It may seem an exaggerated, heavy-handed claim. Was Empire so important that it affected the way policy-makers acted at home? No, it was not the Empire – it was the loss that was the affliction. Earlier in this book David Wiggins and Mayer Hillman recount how the small fibres of a magnificent railway network were scraped off the main routes, which then, not surprisingly, withered. The process was initiated by the Conservatives and carried through by Labour. Both the Macmillan and

[*] In a masterly polemic, *Sunday Telegraph Magazine*, 22 March 1998.

the Wilson governments were deeply concerned to prevent 'our' withdrawal from east of Suez, both sought to preserve what they could of Britain's world influence and the role of sterling. To achieve this, they cut back where necessary. The same attitude was then applied to the railways: 'cut what you can to save what you can'. It was impossible to consider long-term investment in the Empire. It was not impossible to have seen the railways as an asset that could be used to advantage to develop the country around its fabulous network. Such public confidence was lacking. Instead, the pervasive pessimism that flowed from British leaders' attitude to that which they cared most about – their world role – infected their approach to what were belittled as 'home affairs'.

Ironically, although today's Countryside Alliance draws on and seeks to perpetuate the familiar Baldwinite themes, by giving them explicit expression it may contribute to their undoing. Its rallies can be compared to the great trade union mobilisations of the early 1970s. They too sought to preserve a special status and way of life, and to protect an inherited immunity from regular government. With hindsight we can see that the marchers who streamed into London at the time – on a far greater scale than the countryside ones and with equal attention to order and discipline – were marking the end of their exceptionalism.

So too, it could prove with the countryside rallies, thanks to the manner in which they now insist that theirs is a way of life and not just a pretty picture. People are re-entering the landscape. Gainsborough's peasants cannot finally talk back, for they are long gone. But rural inhabitants have started to speak up. True, the central motive of the rallies was to preserve fox-hunting. But around this demand a wider set of arguments for rural life was displayed. By justifying hunting because of the employment it creates, the rallies drew attention to the need for more rural employment, more and smaller farms, more jobs in the villages. In short, for the kind of development that demands a dialogue with town dwellers.

This applies to hunting also. What often seems the right to roam of the powerful (although many turn out on foot) will not survive unless landowners swiftly negotiate the right to roam of ramblers.* If they want

---

* Personally, I oppose setting animals on other animals and I am sure that ways to hunt can be devised without having hounds tear apart their victim. Hunters will eventually be persuaded of this. But it is ridiculous to criminalise such a pastime. It is already farcical enough that many of our police understandably enjoy a joint when they relax, while the Home Secretary insists on the illegality of such activity. Reciprocity of toleration is called for generally.

their strange behaviour tolerated, toleration will have to be two-way. For where the leaders of the Alliance failed was in their attempt to take England back to divide and rule. Few in the cities were taken in by talk of 'the urban jackboot'. We know that we love the countryside and farmers drench it in poison. More clearly still, we can see that the countryside is just as man-made as the towns – indeed today East Anglia is even more so. This recognition will eventually be accepted by country dwellers. It will become their starting point for a much needed appreciation of the cities – the first site of citizenship and nationality, including their nationality. If the countryside thinks it can intimidate the towns, it will be a spectacular loser.

One reason why such an attitude is unlikely is the arrival on a considerable scale of a new class of people. Their livelihoods are mainly urban but their primary and most loved homes are rural. They do not keep farm animals or draw a significant income from their country place. But they will probably tend some fruit trees. We can call them England's orchard bourgeoisie. They live across the divide, identify with both sides and, despite their country life, would be bereft, not to speak of being impoverished, if they had to leave their city-centred occupations and access to town culture. This new class, which is well represented in the media, can help ensure that the various occupants of country and city alike can enjoy their different rhythms and respect each other's. Then we can finally see off Baldwin.

A significant shift in national identity will accompany such a reworking of the divide, for the character of a society is in important ways defined by its urban–rural relationships. The shift will reinforce the end of Powellism and the embrace of a multicultural identity. A political culture that appropriated the landscape, mocked rural labour and scorned the towns, has lost its commanding authority. It is possible, now, for it to be replaced with one that expresses the common interest of urban and rural dwellers in the preservation of difference.

The term 'preservation of difference' may seem a paradox. For difference is something that is lived and spontaneous, the result of freedom, whilst preservation is the activity of planning, guardianship and unfreedom. How, then, can we undertake preservation with the energy and spirit of difference instead of resignation and curatorial conservatism? It should not be that difficult. Because people are different and will go on being so.

Which brings us to the question of government. We need a new politics of open planning rather than central planning. Regulation needs to take a form that understands the need for variety, that adopts a Jane Jacobs philosophy of mixed development in both country and town, that encourages spontaneous growth and change within an acceptable ecological framework. The famed 'flexibility' of British government fails to provide this, not least thanks to the closed, upper middle-class mentality that believes power is only safe in its hands. Instead, what is needed is more government, if of a different kind. Doubtless country people will recoil. One can be confident that the countryside marchers to a man and woman oppose 'another tier of government'. This is odd, as the single tier of power we suffer at the moment has done so much damage. The English pride themselves on their commitment to place. Then they allow themselves to be governed from afar. Instead, we could do with government whose principle is 'nearness' – the Danish term for subsidiarity. This is probably the only way that we can secure the future.

An example will have to stand in for the larger argument. In 1991 the EU Farm Commissioner Ray MacSharry sought to reform the CAP. He proposed to direct support away from agribusiness towards small, resident farmers, a policy which would help to end the subsidy of social and ecological destruction. Britain's then Agricultural Minister, John Gummer, declared the government's attitude to the proposals: 'We hate them.' Because the UK has a disproportionate number of large farmers 'we' would 'lose' revenues. He effectively vetoed the reform.*

This is not a party political argument. Overall, British farming revenue would have 'lost' more than it would have gained in relation to the EU budget, as viewed from Westminster. The present system ensures that what is good for big farmers is perceived as being good for Britain. But if English regions had been represented in Brussels like their European counterparts, then a Tory region might well have seen that it would have benefited from the MacSharry reforms both directly and through the lessening of internal distortions. It could have lobbied and spoken for an alternative national interest, and even mobilised its own MPs – such regional blocks being a more effective form of influence than adversarial opposition. Then the Minister might have changed his tune.

The fact that a new government may finally adopt a long overdue approach to the CAP does not alter the need for a new politics of town and country, with accountable power located in the regions where the strategic

* This account is drawn from Graham Harvey's *The Killing of the Countryside*, (London, 1997), pp. 98, 158.

relationship of the rural and urban is tangible to all concerned – as well as more power in the parish or local community. Regional direction is critical because it unites actually related towns and country and is thus the best framework to mobilise the commitment of urban voters to balanced and enjoyable change. If this book's contributors are right to criticize arbitrary fiats, ignorant of local ways, that threaten the social ecology of an area, then policy needs to be decentralised as much as possible. The best way to achieve this is through constitutional democratic structures: to ensure that those who take decisions live alongside, and are answerable to, those who live with the decisions.

I have suggested that the aimless, uneven and often destructive urban and rural developments that have marked the UK through most of the twentieth century have been permitted by a culture of loss and regret. This culture is intrinsic to the lopsided identification of the nation with 'the country'. By identifying itself with the past, it deserts the present. By celebrating a view, it abandons humanity. The destruction that this attitude allows will continue until resistance *to* development is replaced by responsibility *for* it. Until, that is, English political leaders can claim with pride, 'I encouraged these roads, I signed a cheque for these railways, I permitted these housing estates, I assisted these community projects, I agreed to this farm building, because people have decided that they are good.' Such leaders will need to be regional as well as national ones. Best of all, as in Switzerland, such decisions will rest upon direct, popular consent.

England's national identity is being consciously reformed at present. Hopefully the outcome will be a commitment to its cities, towns and their suburbs as the prime source of English society. But they should not be identified in turn as 'the nation' in opposition to the countryside. A vapid anti-Baldwin attitude can already be heard in city-slicker talk of 'Cool Britannia'. It says 'England is the city.' Far from replacing the old terms, such a posture simply reproduces them in reverse: a callow market democracy is no improvement on shallow rural deference. Attractive change demands high-quality, accountable regional government of both rural and urban relations, empowered by direct democracy – such as referendums, citizen juries and deliberative assemblies.

Any such regional decentralisation will be opposed: by MPs who feel they will be undermined, by a Treasury that desires financial control, by agribusiness and developers who are happier in the Westminster lobby, by large landowners who believe they have a line to the top, by local government that does not wish to be overawed (and anyway has a useful intimacy with small developers) and by the metropolitan media. I rest the case.

The countryside is in urban hands already, as it has been since the city generated its trade and capital. Either country and town will be revived by a more honest regional Englishness that identifies with both city and country, or neither will be successfully renewed at all.

Bibliography

The following books are recommended, either for their relevance to the specific topics discussed by our authors, or for their general bearing on the town and country debate. This bibliography has been compiled by David Hayes and Roger Scruton, with suggestions from other writers in this book (identified after each entry).

Ackland, Valentine, *Country Conditions* (London, 1936), an interesting survey of rural life as it was lived in an agriculturally depressed neighbourhood, by a communist activist and enthusiastic supporter of Stalin's collective farms, who was also a poet, author of *The Country Standard*'s nutrition-minded cookery column, and partner of the writer Sylvia Townsend Warner. (Patrick Wright)

Allanson, Paul and Whitby, Martin (eds) *The Rural Economy and the British Countryside* (Earthscan Publications, 1990), gives the orthodox economics of the countryside: read the jargon and understand the problems of orthodox policy-making and perception. (Robin Page)

d'Ancona, Matthew, *The Ties that Bind Us* (Social Market Foundation, London, 1996), a revealing essay on Swindon and the nature of community and civic consciousness in a British town.

Aslet, Clive, *Anyone for England? A Search for British Identity* (London, 1997), a personal enquiry by the editor of *Country Life*, which proceeds from a 'sense of confusion' about national identity. 'Failure to protect the countryside during the 1980s is emblematic of the crisis about Englishness.' Food, fashion, monarchy, the sea and England as a garden are all discussed.

Baker, Alan R. H. and Biger, Gideon (eds) *Ideology and Landscape in Historical Perspective* (Cambridge, 1992), essays which analyse how landscapes bear the imprint of religious and political ideologies, and how ideas of authority and order are expressed in different locations.

TOWN AND COUNTRY

Barnett, Anthony, *Iron Britannia* (London, 1982), considers the consequences of 'Falklands Pastoralism' – i.e. the romantic attitude towards bleak
rural settlements linked to sea and sky, identified as real communities in
contrast to the supposedly unreal communities of industrialised Britain.

Barrell, John, *The Dark Side of the Landscape: the Rural Poor in English
Painting 1730–1840* (Cambridge, 1980), a well-argued overview of the
exclusion of labourers from the portrait of the English countryside, which
draws on both literary and visual sources.

Barrell, John and Bull, John (eds) *The Penguin Book of English Pastoral Verse*
(London, 1974), an anthology from the Elizabethan to the late Victorian
period, demonstrating the range and persistence of the genre in English
poetry, with emphasis on 'the relationships between the conventions of
pastoral and the actuality of rural life'. Includes some examples of 'anti-
pastoral'.

Binmore, Ken, *Game Theory and the Social Contract*, 2 vols (Cambridge,
MA, 1994), a lucid introduction to the dilemmas of rational choice in a
social context. Explores the 'Prisoner's Dilemma' (including the special case
of 'the tragedy of the commons'), and counters the more simplistic kinds of
scaremongering which ignore the social norms and formal rules that
emerge spontaneously among rational players in complex games. (Tony
Curzon Price)

Bishop, Jeff, *Milton Keynes – the Best of Both Worlds?*, Occasional Paper 24,
School for Advanced Urban Studies (Bristol, 1986), is much wider in scope
than the title suggests. Based on interviews with residents, Bishop's
conclusion is that Milton Keynes is a success because of the failure of the
planners to implement the plan. (Tim Mars)

Blythe, Ronald, *Akenfield, Portrait of an English Village* (London, 1969), an
oral history of an East Anglian coastal village.

Blythe, Ronald, *From the Headlands* (London, 1982), essays which show that
there is still intelligence and resilience in the rural English voice. (Patrick
Wright)

Buchanan, Sir Colin, *Traffic in Towns* (Harmondsworth, 1963), the most
influential report on transport in Britain since the war. Thought progressive
at the time, but woefully underestimated the consquences of an uncon-
strained increase in car numbers. (John Adams et al.)

Carson, Rachel, *Silent Spring* (London, 1963), the book which first alerted the public to the destruction of wildlife by our unscrupulous attack on the animal kingdom.

Champion, Tony and Watkins, Charles (eds) *People in the Countryside: Studies of Social Change in Rural Britain* (London, 1991), a series of geographers' essays on changes in work, transport and housing in rural areas, and their effects on people's lives, with several local case studies.

Clark, Stephen R. L., *The Moral Status of Animals* (Oxford, 1984), an attempt to justify liberal attitudes to animals from premisses of moral philosophy. (David Coffey)

Cobbett, William, *Rural Rides*, collected edn (London, 1830), a penetrating account, by the radical pamphleteer, farmer and MP, of his rides through the English countryside, which seemed to be dying from the loss of its labour force.

Cosgrove, Denis and Daniels, Stephen (eds) *The Iconography of Landscape: Essays on the Symbolic Representation, Design and Use of Past Environments* (Cambridge, 1983), studies the associations between place and meaning in art, literature, politics and cartography: woodland in Georgian England, the poetry of John Clare, Landseer and the Highland myth, Canadian art, images of the American West, etc.

Davies, Nick, *Dark Heart* (London, 1997), a moving account of inner-city life in 1990s Britain, describing the 'hidden country of the poor'.

Disraeli, Benjamin, *Sybil* (1845), the famous novel in which Disraeli portrays the life of the industrial towns, and the unhappy condition of England, divided into the 'two nations' of rich and poor.

Everett, Nigel, *The Tory View of Landscape* (New Haven, 1994), a review of vital debates about the 'improvement' of the English landscape from the mid nineteenth-century. Both older, 'Tory' conceptions (natural, organic) and newer, 'Whig' ideas (mechanical, commercial) express far-reaching attitudes to English society and politics. The argument is lucidly explored through the work of Wordsworth, Southey, Repton, Turner, Austen, Burke, David Willetts and many lesser figures.

Fishman, Robert, *Urban Utopias in the Twentieth Century* (New York, 1977), the Ideal City conceived by Ebenezer Howard, Frank Lloyd Wright and Le

Corbusier, understood as a 'unity of architectural form and social content', rooted in utopian visions which are still relevant. The 'anti-planning' strategies of Jane Jacobs and Richard Sennett reflect a 'loss of confidence in the reality of a common good or purpose which can become the basis of city life'.

Fromm, Erich, *Fear of Freedom* (New York, 1969), a remarkable work of social psychology that analyses the contemporary fear of self-dependency and self-realisation. An examination of the 'authoritarian personality', exemplified in Calvin, Luther, Hitler and others, and a unique attempt to explain the urban middle-class acceptance of big brother. (Julian Rose)

Fry, R. G., *Rights, Killing and Suffering* (Oxford, 1983), a balanced approach to the problem of animal welfare, in connection with vegetarianism and meat-eating. Rejects the arguments of Peter Singer (q.v.) in relation to the welfare of animals. (David Coffey)

Fuller, Peter, *Theoria* (London, 1988), a powerful neo-Ruskinian discourse on the moral dimension of art, with a vindication of twentieth-century English landscape painting and an insistence on the continuing validity of an art related to nature. (David Matthews)

Garreau, Joel, *Edge City* (New York, 1991), examines the new exurban developments in the United States that are increasingly evident in Europe. (Paul Hirst et al.)

Girouard, Mark, *Cities and People* (New Haven and London, 1985), a social and architectural history of the city from Constantinople to Los Angeles — and after. Wide-ranging scholarship and enthusiasm combined with a superb range of illustrations. (Tim Mars)

Goering, Peter, Norberg-Hodge, Helena and Page, David, *From the Ground Up – Re-thinking Industrial Agriculture* (London, 1993), exposes the false economics of modern agriculture, and highlights the social and environmental disasters left in its wake. (Robin Page)

Goldsmith, Sir James, *The Trap* (London, 1993), a devastating exposé of the political and economic thinking that generated the CAP. Clear, simple and irrebuttable; hence ridiculed by the agricultural and political establishments. (Robin Page)

Goodwin, P. (ed.) *Car Dependence* (London, 1995) demonstrates that there are considerable possibilities for reducing dependence on the car. Goodwin is an adviser to the Secretary of State for the Environment, Transport and the Regions. (John Adams)

Hall, Peter, *Cities of Tomorrow: An Intellectual History of Urban Planning and Design in the Twentieth Century* (Oxford, 1988), a comprehensive and sharp-witted guide to a century of urban ideologies and their results. (Colin Ward)

Hamer, M., *Wheels within Wheels: a Study of the Road Lobby* (London, 1987), a thorough examination of the influence of the road lobby on post-war British transport policy. (John Adams)

Hardin, Garrett, 'The Tragedy of the Commons', in G. Hardin and J. Baden (eds), *Managing the Commons* (San Francisco, 1977), first published in the 1960s, this ground-breaking article points to the inevitable mismanagement of common assets, when no legally enforceable policy of conservation has been adopted with regard to them.

Harvey, Graham, *The Killing of the Countryside* (London, 1997), a passionate diagnosis of the transformation of the farmed landscape into 'an industrial site set in a rural location'. The massive use of pesticides has made the living tapestry a 'shroud'. A new rural order is needed, and 'with the healing of the land will come our healing as a nation'.

Hennell, Thomas, *Change in the Farm* (Cambridge, 1934), a closely observed evocation of the craft-based agricultural world that was dying in the 1930s, by one of the English countryside's most underrated artists.

Hewison, Robert, *The Heritage Industry: Britain in a Climate of Decline* (London, 1987), a forceful critique of the tendency to institutionalise and celebrate a bogus 'honey and aspic' past, which obscures real history and inhibits creative imagination. The National Trust, Arts Council and proliferating museums are not solutions but parts of the problem.

Hoggart, Richard, *Townscape with Figures: Farnham – Portrait of an English Town* (London, 1994), a discursive, sympathetically observant description of a west Surrey 'servicing town', which also suggests its 'representative significance' within English society in the late twentieth century. The 'typical, unique, humdrum and strange' in the life of Cobbett's birthplace are recorded with a delicate awareness of the resonances of the everyday.

Hoskins, W. G., *The Making of the English Landscape*, revised edn, with notes by Christopher Taylor (London, 1988), the classic study of how the English landscape has been created, from earliest times, by the hand of man, showing that very little is 'natural'. Deep scholarship and loving detail. The notes to the revised edition consider what has happened to and what has been learned about the landscape since the book first appeared. (Paul Barker)

Hudson, W. H., *A Shepherd's Life* (London, 1910), a powerful description, by an American-born writer, of life on the Wiltshire Downs as it was lived by both humans and animals at the turn of the century.

Hunter, Michael (ed.) *Preserving the Past: the Rise of Heritage in Modern Britain* (Stroud, 1996), an exhaustive composite history of the heritage movement and its methods and aims. Contains a chapter on 'Nationalising the Country House' by Peter Mandler. Rounded off by a most useful bibliographical essay. (Robert Grant)

Jacobs, Jane, *The Death and Life of Great American Cities* (New York, 1961), the classic account of the city as a community product, with its own defence mechanisms and a spontaneous ability to change and adapt. Contains an important attack on suburbanisation and the 'disaggregation of functions' brought about by modern planning. The book which launched a thousand civic trusts and community action groups.

Jefferies, Richard, *The Life of the Fields*, (London, 1884), an account by one of the great observers of the natural world of our countryside and its wildlife as they were a century ago and as many think they could still be today.

Jenks, Mike, Burton, Elizabeth and Williams, Kate (eds) *The Compact City: a Sustainable Urban Form?* (London, 1996), in which a wide and diverse range of contributors argue for and against the sustainability – and feasibility – of the compact city. Demonstrates that the issues are by no means cut and dried. (Tim Mars)

Kropotkin, Peter, *Fields, Factories and Workshops* (London, 1974), first published in 1899 this remarkable book anticipates the dispersal of industry and the potentialities of a 'horticultural' approach to food production in an economy combining brain work and manual work. This updated edition stresses its continuing relevance. (Colin Ward)

Lawson, John and Silver, Harold, *A Social History of Education in England*

(London, 1973), contains some fascinating insights into the conditions of Victorian schools and the social forces which moulded them. (Francis Gilbert)

Lee, Laurie, *Cider with Rosie* (London, 1959), the famous and nostalgic account of childhood in a Cotswold village before the advent of motor transport. Loved by all readers, and by none more than those who travel in their cars to see the place that cars have ruined.

Lowenthal, David, *The Heritage Crusade and the Spoils of History* (London, 1996), an interesting, lively and extraordinarily wide-ranging survey of the idea of heritage and the movements associated with it. Good chapters on the distinction between history and heritage. Only problem: almost anything can be made to count as heritage. (Robert Grant)

Mandler, Peter, *The Fall and Rise of the Stately Home* (New Haven, 1997), an excellent, copiously documented history showing *inter alia* how popular appreciation of aristocratic heritage has grown as aristocratic political power has declined. (Robert Grant)

Marsh, Jan, *Back to the Land: the Pastoral Impulse in Victorian England from 1880 to 1914* (London, 1982), an account of the first modern rejection of the 'march of bricks and mortar', and of popular pastoralism from Ruskin and Morris to the Garden City.

Massingham, H. J., *A Mirror of England* (London, 1998), a valuable anthology of writings by this profound and astute observer of the disappearing countryside. Massingham (1888–1952) was a guild socialist, but also a countryman at heart, who brought a wide historical knowledge to bear on the declining craft economy of his day, and left an inimitable portrait of the once settled ways of English rural life. See also his autobiography, *Remembrance* (London, 1942). (Julian Rose et al.)

Meller, Helen, *Towns, Plans and Society in Modern Britain* (Cambridge, 1997), a clear, well-referenced survey of the development of ideas about town planning, with emphasis on the cultural framework shaping the planning movement in the context of political change from the Victorian era. The work of early reformers (Patrick Geddes, Ebenezer Howard, Octavia Hill) brought a crucial 'quality of imagination' to the subject, a visionary dimension which post-industrial, socially diverse modern cities still require.

Mellers, Wilfrid, *Vaughan Williams and the Vision of Albion* (London, 1989), a classic study by our best living writer on music, which sees Vaughan Williams as a 'double man', with a complex relation to both town and country, and so perhaps as the representative English composer of this century. (David Matthews)

Midgley, Mary, *Animals and Why They Matter* (Harmondsworth, 1983), a philosophical rejection of the exploitation of animals by humans, and a defence of an integrated ecological approach to other species. (David Coffey)

Mingay, G. E., *A Social History of the English Countryside* (London, 1990), emphasises the role of conflict, social diversity and war in influencing rural life, and highlights 'the reality of material deprivation and unremitting toil that lay beneath the most enchanting of hamlets'.

Montefiore, Rt. Revd Hugh (ed.) on behalf of the Independent Commission on Transport, *Changing Directions* (London, 1978), a relatively early attempt to take an overall view of transport in connection with social issues and the environment. (David Wiggins)

Moore, Victor, *A Practical Approach to Planning Law*, 6th edn (London, 1997), a useful manual for all those who wish to take an active interest in their environment, and to do something to protect it. (Sophie Jeffreys)

Muir, Richard, *Reading the Landscape* (London, 1981), a detailed historical geography of rural England which examines the unity of landscape as an assemblage of natural and social elements. Practical guidance for students and travellers is a primary concern.

Mumford, Lewis, *The Highway and the City* (London, 1964), was ahead of its time in seeing the consequences of motor transport: 'As long as motorcars were few in number, he who had one was kind ... the popularity of this method of escape has ruined the promise it once held forth'. (John Adams)

Newby, Howard, *Green and Pleasant Land? Social Change in Rural England* (London, 1986), a pioneering work of rural sociology which establishes the need to study the actual conditions of life in the countryside – landownership, working experience, the farming economy, population movement. In criticising 'fashionable nostalgia' the author seeks 'a more rational discussion about how social change in rural England should be achieved and to which ends it should be directed'.

Newby, Howard, *The Countryside in Question* (London, 1988), an overview (connected to a TV series) of the changing uses of the rural landscape – agribusiness, tourism, the new face of village life – and their implications for public policy. Advocates a shift from food production to 'appropriate development', in which farming, housing, services and recreation are managed in balance.

Oakeshott, Michael, *On History and Other Essays* (Oxford, 1983), the classic philosophical account of history as ideally disinterested. History is simply 'what the evidence obliges us to believe', and cannot properly be used to minister to our emotional needs. (Robert Grant)

Packard, Vance, *A Nation of Strangers* (New York, 1972) argues (as against M. Webber, e.g.), that the motor car is the great solvent of community, and establishes no new community in the place of those that it dissolves. (John Adams et al.)

Pawley, Martin, *The Private Future* (London, 1973), a dystopian view of an individual, atomised, privatised and narcotised future, written after the experience of living in California and well before the advent of the technological discoveries – mobile phones, Internet, personal computer, Ecstasy – which have accelerated the process. (Tim Mars)

Paxton, Robert O., *French Peasant Fascism: Henri Dorgères's Greenshirts and the Crises of French Agriculture, 1929–1939* (Oxford, 1997), traces the French farming community's tradition of direct action back to the 1930s, when Henri Dorgères rallied a movement of vigilantes to oppose rural decline perceived as the attendant of national degeneration. (Patrick Wright)

Rackham, Oliver, *The History of the Countryside* (London, 1986), a stimulating revisionist account which is fast becoming a classic. Rackham takes the conventional wisdom about, e.g., Britain's primeval forest and brilliantly demolishes it, using evidence ranging from Anglo-Saxon charters to tree-rings. (Jane Ridley et al.)

Randle, Damien, *Teaching Green* (1989), an interesting, if controversial, book which argues powerfully for much smaller schools which are more community based and ecologically minded. (Francis Gilbert)

Rapport, Nigel, *Diverse World-views in an English Village* (Edinburgh, 1993), an anthropologist's study of the ambiguities of a rural Cumbrian settlement. The landscape is perceived as community, idyll and site of biography, and the interaction of local people is analysed in this context.

Rees, Ioan Bowen, *Government by Community* (London, 1971), a systematic comparison of local government in Britain and Switzerland which has aged all too well: full of insightful details about the way institutions pattern outcomes. (Tony Curzon Price)

Renfrew, Colin, *Archaeology and Language* (London, 1987), defends the view that the Indo-European languages are the voices of agriculture, and form part of the archaeological data for the history of the countryside, as it emerged from the primeval territory of the hunter-gatherer. (Hugh Brody)

Ricardo, David, *On the Principles of Economics and Taxation* (London, 1817), draws the distinction between 'reproducible' and 'non-reproducible' goods. Ricardo's Principles apply only to the former, since cost, value and price are in this case identical. When we apply the logic of choice to goods that are non-reproducible we are often hiding narrow interest behind a spurious objectivity. (Tony Curzon Price)

Ricq, Charles, *Étude de cas et perspectives d'avenir pour une coopération transfrontalière dans les régions de Montagne*, technical report, Centre d'observation européen des régions (Geneva, 1990), a detailed study of the comparative politics of Champéry (Switzerland), Les Houches (France) and Saint Rhemy (Italy). (Tony Curzon Price)

Ridley, Jane, *Fox Hunting, a History* (London, 1990), an elegant and erudite survey of a field sport, and its impact on the social structure, natural ecology and visual order of the English landscape.

Robertson Scott, J. W., *England's Green and Pleasant Land* (London, 1925), disillusioning articles on rural poverty by the founding editor of *The Countryman*, which show something of what was lost when the Aga sagas took over. (Patrick Wright)

Ruskin, John, *Modern Painters*, 5 vols. (London, 1843–60), especially Vol. 4, an unsurpassed account of the meaning of landscape, and the psychic interpretation of earth, vegetation and sky.

Sahlins, Marshall, 'The Original Affluent Society', in his *Stone Age Economics* (London, 1974), one of the first anthropologists to see the specificity and genius of hunter-gatherer societies. (Hugh Brody)

Samuel, Raphael, *Theatres of Memory* (London, 1996), a massive survey of the development and extent of heritage – especially of urban and industrial heritage – as a component of popular experience and the national culture.

Schama, Simon, *Landscape and Memory* (London, 1995), a highly engaging study of the relation between man and the landscape, showing how our perception of the landscape has throughout history permeated art, culture and imagination. (David Matthews et al.)

Schumacher, Fritz, *Small is Beautiful* (London, 1973), seminal work and acknowledged catalyst in the debate over 'sustainability'. Spells out the case for human-scale technology, people-centred economics and environmentally responsible farming. It remains a powerful defence of scale and balance within and between country and town. Hailed as the book that would change the world. (Julian Rose et al.)

Scruton, Roger, *The Classical Vernacular: Architectural Principles in an Age of Nihilism* (Manchester, 1994), a defence of the classical vernacular tradition as a solution to problems of urbanisation, and a devastating critique of modernist building types. (Sophie Jeffreys)

Scruton, Roger, *Animal Rights and Wrongs*, 2nd edn (London, 1998), a philosophical examination of the moral questions surrounding our relation to the animal kingdom, and an attempt to give a systematic answer to, and rejection of, the movement for 'animal rights'. (Jane Ridley et al.)

Sen, Armartya, 'Rational Fools: a Critique of the Behavioural Foundations of Economic Theory', *Philosophy and Public Affairs* (1977), Sen argues that the pursuit of narrowly selfish aims is self-defeating, and that mostly humans are not rationally foolish. (Tony Curzon Price)

Sennett, Richard, *Flesh and Stone: the Body and the City in Western Civilisation* (London, 1994), an engrossing and panoramic meditation of the history of the city that combines anthropology, the history of medicine and the histories of cities themselves. Full of startling insights and vivid evocations of urban life. (Tim Mars)

Shepheard, Paul, *The Cultural Wilderness or What is Landscape?* (Cambridge MA, 1997), a bold attempt to examine landscape through a series of 'cuts', different scales of vision from the global to the very local. (Paul Hirst)

Shoard, Marion, *The Theft of the Countryside* (London, 1981), an influential
and trenchant critique of the despoliation of the rural environment by
modern agricultural methods. The core elements of English landscape –
including hedgerows, woods, coverts and wetlands – are vulnerable to a
system fuelled by subsidies which values output over ecological diversity.
Advocates a new planning framework. As can be seen from Graham
Harvey (q.v.), this unanswerable protest made no difference whatsoever to
anything.

Singer, Peter, *Animal Liberation* (London, 1976), an extreme approach to
animal welfare which defends the 'rights' of animals, while rejecting or
ignoring biological reality. (David Coffey)

Sorkin, Michael, *Variations on a Theme Park: the New American City and the
End of Public Space* (New York, 1992), a brilliant collection of essays that
dissects the problems of American urbanism and exurbanism. A major
theme is the replacement of public spaces and streets by private complexes
and malls. (Paul Hirst)

Stewart, W. A. C., *Progressives and Radicals in English Education, 1750–1970*
(London, 1973), explores the impact of Rousseau on progressive educa-
tional thinkers, and contains a particularly good section on Robert Owen.
(Francis Gilbert)

Thomas, Sir Keith, *Man and the Natural World* (London, 1983), a
groundbreaking historical treatment of man's relation to his environment in
the early modern period, which has mapped territory that few historians
had visited before. The confident anthropocentrism of the Tudor era gave
way to the desire to preserve wilderness, and the questioning of human
ascendancy over nature. (Jane Ridley et al.)

Thompson, Paul, *Living the Fishing* (London, 1983), a comparative study of
Scottish fishing villages under the impact of modern development – which
shows that those where families encouraged independence in their children
and integrated women into their local economy adapted far better as
communities than the more ordered and conservative settlements.

Van der Post, Sir Laurens, *The Heart of the Hunter* (Harmondsworth, 1961),
flights of nostalgic fancy, Jungian digressions, and a confusion between fact
and fiction are mixed with an account of the relation between hunters and

settlers which profoundly illuminates the history and social psychology of both hunting and agriculture, and therefore helps to explain the history and nature of the countryside. (Hugh Brody)

Ward, Colin, *Freedom to Go: After the Motor Age* (London, 1991), points out that the more mobile a society becomes, the larger the scale of its problems, and the more remote the possibility of human-scale, co-operative solutions. (John Adams)

Watkin, David, *The English Vision: the Picturesque in Architecture, Landscape and Garden Design* (London, 1982), a study of the 'major English contribution to European aesthetics' in a variety of fields: architecture, garden design, painting, the cult of the ruin. The author suggests that the picturesque embodies 'beautiful myths' which are rooted in the native climate and 'the relative internal security of the island nation'.

Webber, M., 'Order in Diversity: Community without Propinquity', in L. Wingo (ed.), *Cities and Space: the Future of Urban Land* (Baltimore, MD, 1963), an influential essay in praise of freeways, which will free us to live in 'communities of interest', liberated from burdensome relationships with incompatible neighbours. (John Adams)

White, Gilbert, *The Natural History of Selborne*, (1788, re-issued 1837), collected from the much loved jottings of the Revd Gilbert White (1720–93), founding father of English nature writing. The Selborne Society, founded in his memory in 1885, is devoted to the care of wildlife.

Whitelegg, J., *Critical Mass: Transport, Environment and Society in the Twenty-first Century* (London, 1997), examines the relationship between land use and speed of travel, and shows why high-speed trains reduce the accessibility of rail travel for most people. (John Adams)

Wiener, Martin J., *English Culture and the Decline of the Industrial Spirit, 1850–1980* (Harmondsworth, 1985), an influential argument about the cultural barriers to economic progress within English elites. The relevant complex of ideas and sentiments includes the allure of gentrification for industrialists, and the desire of intellectuals to 'save traditional English life from unwelcome change'.

Williams, Bernard, 'Must a Concern for the Environment be Centred on Human Interests', in *Making Sense of Humanity* (Cambridge, 1995), a note of caution against economists' ways of measuring environmental benefits and costs. (David Wiggins et al.)

Williams, Raymond, *The Country and the City* (London, 1972), explores from a New Left perspective the image of country life, as presented in the largely middle-class literature devoted to its celebration.

Williams-Ellis, Sir Clough (ed.) *Britain and the Beast* (London, 1937), a campaigning preservationist volume, with contributions from J. M. Keynes, E. M. Forster, C. E. M. Joad, H. J. Massingham, Patrick Abercrombie and many others. The book reveals a pervasive fear of encroachment on rural areas by ribbon development, roads, military installations, etc. But it also demonstrates that, in the 1930s at least, it was possible to be both a rural preservationist and an advocate of planning and modernist architecture. (Patrick Wright)

Wright, Patrick, *The Village that Died for England: the Strange Story of Tyneham* (London, 1996), the wartime evacuation of a Dorset village, and subsequent campaigns to reclaim it, are the core of a panoptic analysis of post-war England. The author digs out a range of personal histories (political idealists, organic farmers, conservationists) connected to one tiny corner of the country, and examines how passionate local debates become part of a national discourse of decline and loss.

Notes on Contributors

John Adams is Professor of Geography at University College London. He was a member of the original board of directors of Friends of the Earth in the early 1970s and has been involved in the transport debate ever since. His 1981 book *Transport Planning: Vision and Practice* explored the influence of competing 'visions of progress'. He has returned to this theme in his most recent book, *Risk*. He has published widely on planning, transport and risk management both in specialist journals and the national press.

Paul Barker is a writer and broadcaster, and a senior fellow of the Institute of Community Studies. He is the former editor of *New Society*. His books include *Arts in Society*, *The Other Britain*, and *Living as Equals*. He writes a weekly column in the *New Statesman*, looking at town, country and suburbia.

Anthony Barnett has written widely on British and international affairs, especially on Cambodia and Vietnam, and on sculpture, in particular on Henry Moore. He was founding director of Charter 88, the influential campaign for constitutional reform in Britain. His books include *Iron Britannia* and *Soviet Freedom* and he has just published *This Time*, which concerns the prospects for British democracy in the era of the European Union. He is a Senior Research Fellow at Birkbeck College.

Hugh Brody began his work as an anthropologist with a study of isolated communities in the west of Ireland, and then continued in the Canadian Arctic, subarctic and North Pacific Coast. His books and films have explored specific cultures and their reaction to cultural and economic change. He was for several years a member of the Canadian government's Northern Science Research Group, and consequently played a leading role in projects initiated by Canadian Aboriginal people's organisations. His books include *Inishkillane: Change and Decline in the West of Ireland*, *The People's Land* and *Living Arctic*. His films include *On Indian Land*, *Hunters* *and Bombers*, and *A Washing of Tears*. He is an honorary associate of the Scott Polar Research Institute, University of Cambridge, and Associate of the School for Comparative Literature at the University of Toronto.

David Coffey qualified from the Royal Veterinary College in 1962 and has held a variety of professional posts including six years in the central veterinary laboratory at MAFF, as Research Officer responsible for animal welfare. He was a member of the working party which produced 'Animals and Ethics', in 1980, and has been principal of his own private practice since 1975. Twenty years ago he founded the Centre for the Study of Animal Welfare in order to encourage multidisciplinary academic study of the subject; the Centre is affiliated to the US Humane Society. David Coffey has contributed to academic, popular and veterinary journals and is the author of eight books on animals and their welfare.

Tony Curzon Price, who grew up on the Franco-Swiss border, is an academic economist and consultant, based at ELSE, the Centre for Economic Learning and Social Evolution at University College London, where he co-ordinates private sector work. He teaches at Imperial College and at the Ecole Polytechnique Fédérale de Lausanne. His academic work is principally involved in applying the economic theory of institutional design, while his consultancy work for both private and public bodies concerns environmental policy design, energy policy, utility regulation and strategic competition. He lives in London, and also on the Internet, where he is to be found at http://www.curzon.com.

Francis Gilbert taught English, drama and English as a second language in a mixed comprehensive in Tower Hamlets for two and a half years. He then taught in another much larger comprehensive in Redbridge, where he was an English teacher and deputy Head of the Sixth Form. After three years he was promoted to Special Needs Co-ordinator within a big English department in a comprehensive in Waltham Forest – a post which he held for two years. He is currently working as a supply teacher and a freelance journalist.

Robert Grant is Reader in English Literature at the University of Glasgow, former Fellow of Trinity Hall, Cambridge, and currently Visiting Research Scholar at the Social Philosophy and Policy Center, Bowling Green State University, Ohio. He is the author of *Oakeshott*, and of many essays, articles and reviews in literary and philosophical journals and collections, including *Shakespeare Studies, Inquiry,* and two *Philosophy* supplementary volumes. He is a frequent contributor to *The Times Literary Supplement.*

Liz Greenhalgh is a senior associate with Comedia, a small independent cultural and urban planning group. She has co-directed a number of major research programmes in Britain on changes in the public realm, in town and city centres, urban parks and public libraries. She is currently working with four British cities on a research programme entitled 'The Richness of Cities', which will lead to the publication of a report bringing together debates about the urban future.

The Rt. Hon. John Gummer, MP was Secretary of State for the Environment from 1993 until 1997, and a cabinet minister under both Margaret Thatcher and John Major. He is well known for his efforts, both in and out of office, on behalf of wildlife and the environment, and played a key role in the Convention on Climate Change meetings in Berlin and Geneva. As well as sitting on numerous international bodies, John Gummer was included in the United Kingdom's delegation to the Special Session of the UN General Assembly, the Earth Summit + 5, which took place in Tokyo last year. He continues to campaign for new and sustainable approaches to the environment, which will be attractive both to government and business.

David Hayes is a teacher of politics and author of textbooks on human rights and terrorism. His writing has appeared in the *New Statesman, PN Review* and *The Absolute Game.* He has explored the borderlands between England and Scotland on foot over several years.

Mayer Hillman is Senior Fellow Emeritus of the Policy Studies Institute – Britain's leading independent research organisation in the fields of economic and social policy – where he was engaged from 1970 to 1991 as the head of the Institute's Environment and Quality of Life research programme. He has carried out a considerable body of research on transport issues, ranging from the roles of walking and cycling and the significance of accessibility as opposed to motorised mobility to the impact of road closures on rural communities, and the effect of cars on the quality of children's lives. He has written or co-authored over thirty books on the subjects of his research.

Paul Hirst is Professor of Social Theory at Birkbeck College, University of

London, and Academic Director of the London Consortium Graduate Programme in Humanities and Cultural Studies. He also teaches in the Graduate School at the Architectural Association School of Architecture. He is Chair of the executive of Charter 88, the British movement for constitutional reform, and a member of the editorial board of *Political Quarterly*. Among his books are: *Revising Industrial Decline*, with Jonathan Zeitlin, *After Thatcher, Representative Democracy and its Limits, Associative Democracy, Globalisation in Question*, with Grahame Thompson, and *From Statism to Pluralism*.

Sophie Jeffreys is an architectural historian, who pursued a career in editing and publishing before becoming Research Officer at the Bath Preservation Trust. She is married to Roger Scruton, with whom she lives in the country near Malmesbury, and has made a study of the life and works of William Beckford, while serving as curator of the Beckford Tower in Bath.

Ian McEwan is a novelist, whose works are also familiar from films. His latest novel – *Amsterdam* – appeared this year. He is an enthusiastic rambler, for whom the countryside remains a constant source of solace and inspiration.

Tim Mars is a writer and consultant on urban affairs. Formerly Head of Policy at the Civic Trust, he has also edited Shelter's magazine *Roof*, and worked for housing associations in Liverpool and Cardiff. As a long-time observer and sometime resident, he has written and broadcast extensively on the mysteries of Milton Keynes.

David Matthews is a composer whose many orchestral, chamber and vocal works include four symphonies and seven string quartets. His music is widely performed and broadcast, and a number of his works have been recorded on CD. He is currently Composer-in-Association with the Britten Sinfonia. He is the author of a study of Michael Tippett, and has written widely on twentieth-century music.

George Monbiot has been named by the *Evening Standard* as one of the twenty-five most influential people in Britain, and by the *Independent on Sunday* as one of the forty international prophets of the twenty-first century. He is the author of the investigative travel books *Poisoned Arrows*, *Amazon Watershed* – which won the Sir Peter Kent Award – and *No Man's Land*. All three were accompanied by a series on Radio 4, and *Amazon Watershed* by a TV documentary. He is *persona non grata* in seven countries and has a life sentence *in absentia* in Indonesia. In Britain he started the campaign against mahogany imports, joined the direct action movement against road-building and founded the Land is Ours campaign. He writes a column for the *Guardian*. In May 1997 he was appointed Visiting Professor at the University of East London. From 1993 to 1995 he was a visiting fellow of Green College, Oxford. In 1995 he won a United Nations Global 500 Award for outstanding environmental achievement. He has also won the Lloyds National Screenwriting Prize for his screenplay *The Norwegian* and a Sony Award for radio production.

Anthony O'Hear is Professor of Philosophy at the University of Bradford, and Honorary Director of the Royal Institute of Philosophy. He served on the School Curriculum and Assessment Authority (1993–7) and the Teacher Training Agency (1994–7). He is the author of many books and articles on philosophy, most recently *Beyond Evolution*.

Robin Page regards himself as one of the last English peasants, and as such a member of an endangered species. He lives on the farm where he was born. He was thrown out of teacher training college, having found himself out of sympathy with the educational theories that prevailed there, and in 1969 was sacked from the Civil Service for breaking the Official Secrets Acts. He now writes a fortnightly column in the *Daily Telegraph* and contributes to *Heritage* magazine. He presents BBC TV's *One Man and His Dog* and Anglia's *A Place in the Country*. He saved his deposit as candidate for the Referendum Party in the 1997 general election. His many books include *The Fox and the Orchid* and *Dust in a Dark Continent*, recording his travels in Africa.

Libby Purves is a presenter for Radio 4 and has been making documentaries since 1976. She is currently presenter of *Midweek* and *The Learning Curve*. She is the author of four novels, including *Home Leave* and *More Lives Than One*. Together with her husband, Paul Heiney, she has had eight years of experience in running a small-scale organic farm in Suffolk. She writes regularly in *The Times*.

Hugh Raven is Convenor of the Green Global Task Force, the advisory group to the Foreign Secretary and Environment Minister on international environmental policy. From 1990 to 1995 he was co-ordinator of the Sustainable Agriculture, Food and Environment (SAFE) alliance. He is Chair of SERA, the Labour Party's environmental affiliate, and the

Lochaber Fisheries Trust, a freshwater conservation charity in the West Highlands. He is also a trustee of the Soil Association and of the RSPB, as well as a member of the Agricultural Reform Group, pressing for reform of the CAP, and of the Fisheries Reform Group, with similar goals.

Jane Ridley teaches history at Buckingham University. She lives in the middle of London and also in the depths of the Scottish Border country. Her publications include *Fox Hunting, a History* and *The Young Disraeli*. She is currently writing a biography of Sir Edwin Lutyens, the architect.

Jeff Rooker, MP is a minister in the Department of Agriculture with special responsibility for food.

Sir Julian Rose trained at RADA during the late 1960s and thereafter pursued a career in experimental theatre and education, co-founding the Institute of Creative Development in Antwerp, Belgium (1976). After family bereavements he returned to England and began to manage the family estate as an organic farming enterprise. He has played a leading role in promoting organic farming and is co-founder and Chairman of the Association of Unpasteurised Milk Producers and Consumers and Chair of the Association of Rural Businesses in Oxfordshire. He has served on the BBC Rural and Agricultural Affairs Advisory Committee and UK Register of Organic Food Standards, as adviser to the Centre for Food Policy, Thames Valley University. He is a director of the Dartington Trust and author of numerous articles on socio-environmental issues.

Roger Scruton is a philosopher, critic and novelist who has held academic positions in Cambridge, London and Boston. He now works as a freelance writer and consultant in Wiltshire, where, together with his wife, Sophie Jeffreys, he runs a small farm devoted to a variety of cottage industries, including horses, musical analysis, wildflowers, sheep, literature, carp and government relations. He is the author of over twenty books, the most recent being *The Aesthetics of Music*. His opera *The Minister* was performed earlier this year in Oxford.

Colin Ward is the author of many books on popular and unofficial uses of the environment, from *The Child in the City* to *Freedom to Go: After the Motor Age*. With Dennis Hardy he wrote the history of the plotlands, *Arcadia for All: The Legacy of a Makeshift Landscape*, and with David Crouch the history of *The Allotment: its Landscape and Culture*. In 1996 he was a visiting centennial professor at the London School of Economics, where his lectures were published as *Social Policy: An Anarchist Response*.

David Wiggins was an assistant principal concerned with colonial development and welfare in the Finance Department of the Colonial Office. In 1959, he spent the best part of a year in the United States, whose then increasing dependence on the automobile (like other features of North American life being commented upon at the time by Jane Jacobs, Alan Altschuler and Rachel Carson) he came to see as an unsuitable model for the British Isles or Europe. In 1960 he was elected Fellow and Tutor in Philosophy at New College, Oxford. After holding positions at Bedford College, London, University College, Oxford and Birkbeck College, London, he returned to New College in 1993 as Wykeham Professor of Logic. His chief publications are *Sameness and Substance* and *Needs, Values, Truth*. He was Chairman (1977–9) of the Transport Users' Consultative Committee for the South East and member (1977–9) of the Central Transport Users' Consultative Committee. He was a member of the Independent Commission on Transport, chaired by Bishop Hugh Montefiore, 1972–3. He contributed to Peter Hall and David Bannister (eds) *Transport and Public Policy*.

Ken Worpole is the author of many books and studies of contemporary urban issues. Apart from continuing to work with both Comedia and Demos, two independent research organisations, he is also writing a book on twentieth-century urban architecture and landscape design, including parks and cemeteries.

Patrick Wright is an independent writer and broadcaster. His first book, *On Living in an Old Country*, was concerned with the rise of heritage as a theme in post-war British life. Since then he has written two books which use small stretches of territory as prisms through which to view the English twentieth century: *A Journey through Ruins*, which was set on Dalston Lane in East London, and *The Village that Died for England*, which was concerned with the Dorset coast around Tyneham – a classic stretch of Hardy country converted into a tank gunnery range.

Index

Index

Index